At the Frontlines of Development

Reflections from the World Bank

At the Frontlines of Development

Development

Reflections from the World Bank

Edited by
Indermit S. Gill and Todd Pugatch

THE WORLD BANK
Washington, D.C.

ISBN-13: 978-8-213-60418-5
ISBN-10: 0-8213-6041-8
e-ISBN: 0-8213-6042-6

Library of Congress Cataloging-in-Publication Data has been applied for.

Contents

Tables, Figures, and Boxes

Boxes

Foreword

YOU HOLD IN YOUR HANDS A DIFFERENT KIND OF WORLD BANK DOCUMENT. THIS collection of essays by former World Bank country directors recounts their experiences, both as managers of the World Bank's portfolio in global economic hotspots of the 1990s as well as throughout their careers in development. The essays detail how China and India lifted hundreds of millions out of poverty, while the Russian Federation collapsed; how Bosnia and Herzegovina and Mozambique remade their war-ravaged economies; and how Argentina, Thailand, and Turkey fell into financial crisis, among other stories of development in the 1990s. But those stories have been told before by the World Bank and by others, and it is not the stories themselves that make this volume remarkable. What is remarkable about this collection is that the stories are told in the first person by those who were there to witness them. In a departure from many accounts that the World Bank has published about the same events, these former country directors offer their candid assessments of what succeeded, what failed, and what lessons emerged.

The country directors do not always agree on the policies and aid modalities that best promote development, and their diverse viewpoints reflect the diversity of opinions within the World Bank itself. But they are all agreed on the central importance of economic growth in the development process: those countries that grow rapidly and share the benefits of economic growth widely are most successful at reducing poverty, promoting educational achievements, and eradicating disease. Stimulating and sustaining economic growth is, therefore, the focal point of their perspectives.

This book is part of a larger effort undertaken by the World Bank in 2003–05 to understand the development experience of the 1990s—an extraordinarily eventful decade. Each of the project's three volumes serves a different purpose. The first volume of the project, *Economic Growth in the 1990s: Lessons from a Decade of Reform*, provides comprehensive *analysis* of the decade's development experience. The second volume, *Development Challenges in the 1990s: Leading Policymakers Speak from Experience*, offers insights on the *practical concerns* faced by policymakers. The third and present volume, *At the Frontlines of Development: Reflections from the World Bank*, considers the *operational implications* of the decade for the World Bank as an institution. From an operational standpoint, this book serves an internal mentoring function for current and future World Bank country directors, as well as providing external audiences with a glimpse of the human face behind World Bank operations.

The World Bank's Poverty Reduction and Economic Management (PREM) Network and Operations Policy and Country Services departments combined to supervise this project, which is based on a proposal by Indermit Gill. Indermit Gill and Todd Pugatch of the PREM Network edited the essays, with the assistance of Alfred Friendly. Basil Kavalsky and Roberto Zagha provided substantive inputs and advice from the beginning to publication. Contributors were chosen on the basis of both their management capability and their position as country director of a particularly compelling country or region during the 1990s. Additionally, the contributors no longer serve as country directors of the countries that they have written about, providing them the time and space to reflect properly on their experiences.

The position of country director is a relatively new one at the World Bank, the result of the major internal reorganizations of 1987 and 1996. Many of the former country directors represented here were the first to be based in their country of responsibility during their tenure. As a second generation of field-based country directors takes their place, now is an appropriate time to reflect on the results of this new approach after a lively decade. Like the 1990s itself, the essays that follow are sometimes painful, sometimes uplifting, but always thought provoking.

<table>
<tr><td>Gobind Nankani
Former Vice President and
Head of Network
Poverty Reduction and
Economic Management Network;
now Vice President, Africa Region</td><td>Jim Adams
Vice President and Head of Network
Operations Policy and Country Services</td></tr>
</table>

Washington, D.C.
March 2005

Acknowledgments

THE EDITORS WISH TO THANK THE MANY PEOPLE WHO WERE INSTRUMENTAL IN bringing this project to fruition. First and foremost, Gobind Nankani was this endeavor's greatest friend, providing vital support at every stage. The book would not have been possible without his insights on its format at the inception and his sensible stewardship throughout the process—not to mention the many hours he spent on his own essay for the volume. Danny Leipziger supported the project through its publication after succeeding Gobind Nankani as vice president of the Bank's Poverty Reduction and Economic Management Network. Roberto Zagha provided tremendous support from the beginning to publication, recognizing from the outset that this venture was an integral part of the exercise aimed at understanding the development lessons of the 1990s. Jim Adams and Basil Kavalsky helped us with access to the community of country directors, their own insights, encouraging words, and much more. Alfred Friendly contributed with extensive editorial support and good humor. Ricardo Hausmann and Andrew Steer interpreted early drafts of the essays succinctly and engagingly during a forum with the contributors held on April 29, 2004 at the World Bank, which Hilary Bowker moderated with grace and humor, and for which Muriel Darlington handled logistical arrangements efficiently and cheerfully. Stephen McGroarty, Mark Ingebretsen, and Nancy Lammers of the Office of the Publisher brought the manuscript to press with great humor and patience. The editors also owe a huge debt of gratitude to the thirteen contributors for their conversations with us, their interventions at the April 2004 forum and, most importantly, their essays: by putting on paper what might otherwise have remained thought or anecdote, they have allowed others instant access to—as Andrew Steer put it—more than three hundred years of development experience.

Finally, the production of this volume was made possible by the generous support of the World Bank Learning Board and the World Bank Group Archives. As part of the ongoing effort to capture the knowledge of the institution, the Archives operate an Oral History program (available at www.worldbank.org/archives) to which this volume will contribute.

Abbreviations and Acronyms

AAA	Analytical and advisory activities
ADB	Asian Development Bank
BOAL	Basic organization of associated labor
CAS	Country Assistance Strategy
CDF	Comprehensive Development Framework
CDP	Country Development Partnership
CFA	Coopération Financière en Afrique
CICC	China International Capital Corporation
CLO	Chief learning officer
CMU	Country Management Unit
DPS	Development Policy Staff
EDI	Economic Development Institute
EMP	Emerging Markets Partnership
ERDL	Economic reform and development loan
EU	European Union
FARC	Fuerzas Armadas Revolucionarios de Colombia
FSU	Former Soviet Union
G-7	Group of Seven (Canada, France, Germany, Italy, Japan, United Kingdom, and United States)
GCC	Gulf Cooperation Council
GDP	Gross domestic product
GNP	Gross national product
HIPC	Heavily Indebted Poor Countries (initiative)
IBRD	International Bank of Reconstruction and Development
IDA	International Development Association
IDB	Inter-American Development Bank
IFC	International Finance Corporation

IFI	International financial institution
IMF	International Monetary Fund
NBC	National Bank of Commerce
NGO	Nongovernmental organization
OECD	Organisation for Economic Co-operation and Development
OED	Operations Evaluation Department
OPCS	Operations Policy and Country Services
PAMI	Programa de Atención Médica Integral
PER	Public expenditure review
PFM	Public Financial Management (program)
PMU	Project Management Unit
PPRD	Policy Planning and Review Department
PREM	Poverty Reduction and Economic Management
PRI	Partido Revolucionario Institucional
PROST	Pension Reform Options Simulation Toolkit
PRSP	Poverty Reduction Strategy Paper
RDB	Regional development bank
RS	Republika Srpska
SAL	Structural adjustment loan
SAS	State Assistance Strategy
SEM	State Economic Memorandum
SEWA	Self-Employed Women's Association
SMEs	Small and medium enterprises
SOE	State-owned enterprise
SSAL	Special structural adjustment loan
TA	Technical assistance
TAS	Tanzania Assistance Strategy
TBL	Tanzania Breweries Limited
TESEV	Turkiye Ekonomik ve Sosyal Etudler Vakfi
T&V	Training and visits
TVEs	Township and village enterprises
UN	United Nations
UNAIDS	United Nations Programme on AIDS
UNDP	United Nations Development Programme
VAT	Value added tax
WDR	*World Development Report*
WTO	World Trade Organization
ZCCM	Zambia Consolidated Copper Mines Ltd.

INTRODUCTION

1 Policies, Politics, and Principles
Three Hundred Years of World Bank Experience

Indermit S. Gill and Todd Pugatch

WHY DO SOME DEVELOPING COUNTRIES GROW THEIR WAY OUT OF POVERTY, WHILE others remain poor? Yukon Huang, a graduate student at Princeton University in the late 1960s, posed the question to his thesis adviser, Sir W. Arthur Lewis, a Nobel Laureate in economics and a pathbreaking thinker on development. Lewis gave a simple response: countries that have been led by good policies or "Great Men"[1] grow and thrive, while others do not. That so few have thrived demonstrates either that good policies and Great Men are rare or that development cannot be so simply formulized.

Huang went on to explore Lewis's hypothesis as World Bank country director for the Russian Federation and the former Soviet Union and for China. He and his country director colleagues, who are responsible for managing the World Bank's programs around the world, serve at the frontlines of development, where the international community attempts to strengthen the elements—good policies, Great Men, or otherwise—of successful development. This collection of essays by 13 former World Bank country directors documents their extensive firsthand experience in facing the daily challenge of helping countries raise living standards. The reflections constitute both an insider's history and a critical analysis of the Bank's efforts to work with governments to promote economic growth and reduce poverty. Their stories describe the nexus between development knowledge, policies, and outcomes as it unfolded around the world in the 1990s. They chart how the decade's remarkable consensus on policy reform ceded to a more nuanced perspective in which sound economic principles can be adhered to through diverse policy and institutional paths. For those who have joined the international development community—at the World Bank or elsewhere—the reflections recorded in this volume contain insights that should influence how they do their work.

What Does a Country Director Do?

Each of the contributors to this volume served as a country director in the World Bank during the 1990s. Country directors play a pivotal part in the institution's interface with client governments. For their country or countries of responsibility, their duties include managing the Bank's lending portfolio, providing policy advice, and guiding Bank-government relations. Though the Bank's Board of Executive Directors must ultimately approve all lending operations, country directors exercise broad latitude in directing the Bank's program at the country level. The nature of those activities varies greatly, from countries such as Mozambique and Zambia, where Bank resources make up an important share of the government budget, to countries with large economies such as Brazil and China, where the Bank's share in government budgets is small. But regardless of the Bank's economic weight in a particular country, it is almost invariably active in directing lending support, producing country-specific policy reports, bringing the lessons of international experience to the attention of policymakers and others, and contributing to the national policy dialogue and decisionmaking. Orchestrating these responsibilities requires a blend of technical, managerial, and diplomatic skills, and successful country directors earn reputations as savvy, smart, and sensitive people.

This volume is the third of a trilogy on the development lessons of the 1990s[2] that was undertaken by the World Bank during 2003–05; the other two volumes are a compilation of lectures delivered by leading policymakers (*Development Challenges in the 1990s: Leading Policymakers Speak from Experience* [Besely and Zagha 2005]) and a technical report that addresses the main policy issues confronting developing nations during the decade (*Economic Growth in the 1990s: Learning from a Decade of Reform* [World Bank 2005]). The contributors to this volume met several selection criteria. First, they served as country directors for a country or set of countries during the 1990s. Second, they have long and varied experience, usually numbering in the decades, in the development field—together they have logged more than 350 years of service at the World Bank. Finally, their peers hold them in high regard: the contributing country directors in this volume are seen by staff members to have "street credibility." Their stories will interest and even inspire those who have not had the privilege of knowing them.

The position of country director is a relatively new one in the World Bank, the result of the 1987 and 1996 internal reorganizations. Many of those represented here were the first to be based in their country of responsibility during their tenure. They came to the job of country director with prior notions about development, many of which survive, yet they also have been shaped by the events they describe. They wrote first-person reflections on their experiences as country directors, interspersing accounts of economic and political history with illuminating personal anecdotes from their careers. The countries about which they write are not intended as representative samples, but they do provide a diverse perspective across all regions and income levels in the developing world. The country directors themselves are similarly diverse, hailing from both industrial and developing countries on four continents (see table 1.1).

Writing their thoughts in essay format serves several purposes. First, it is an evaluation of the World Bank's ongoing effort to decentralize and get closer to clients; hence, it is an important, albeit informal, self-evaluation. Second, it serves to promote

TABLE 1.1

All Over the Map: The Diverse Background and Experience of World Bank Country Directors

Country director	Country of origin	Country or countries of responsibility
Basil Kavalsky	South Africa	Armenia, Belarus, Georgia, Moldova, Ukraine, Estonia, Latvia, Lithuania, Poland
Phyllis Pomerantz	United States	Mozambique, Zambia
Gobind Nankani	Ghana	Brazil
Edwin Lim	Philippines	China, India, Nigeria
Shahid Javed Burki	Pakistan	China, Latin America
Yukon Huang	United States	Russian Federation, former Soviet Union, China
Olivier Lafourcade	France	West Africa, Mexico
Christiaan Poortman	Netherlands	Balkan states[a]
Ajay Chhibber	India	Turkey
Inder Sud	India	Middle East[b]
James Adams	United States	Tanzania, Uganda
Myrna Alexander	Canada	Argentina
Jayasankar Shivakumar	India	Thailand

a. Bosnia and Herzegovina, Kosovo, the former Yugoslav Republic of Macedonia, and Serbia and Montenegro.
b. Bahrain, the Arab Republic of Egypt, Jordan, Lebanon, Kuwait, Oman, Qatar, Saudi Arabia, Syria, the United Arab Emirates, and the Republic of Yemen.

institutional memory, ensuring that some of the Bank's wisest officials pass their knowledge on to a new generation of country directors and their staffs. And finally, it may help those who do not know the World Bank well to understand that its work is done by thinking, caring, fallible, and reflective people.

Freed from the technocratic language of typical economic reports, the contributors to this book have taken advantage of the opportunity to write candidly about their experiences. They are forthright in recollecting events and honest in conceding mistakes, a refreshing departure from most institutional accounts of the same events. Yet their reflections, even when harshly self-critical, should not be read as either catharsis or a mea culpa. Instead, the essays should be read as the thoughts and opinions of individuals loyal to their institution and dedicated to making it better.

Three themes emerge most strongly from these reflections: policies, politics, and principles. Country directors are constantly engaged in research, discussions, and formulation of *policies*, and they offer their own analysis of what policies matter for development. But policy is not made in a vacuum: the realities of *politics* inevitably intrude in the process. Because many of the country directors came to their jobs as self-described political neophytes, their forays into politics often provide the most interesting material in the essays. Immersed in muddy political waters, they also came to recognize the importance of operating *principles* to guide their actions, enhance their effectiveness, and promote the integrity of their institution. This introductory chapter discusses some of these policies, politics, and principles—more to sample than to summarize the varied perspectives offered on those themes and, most of all, to motivate readers to explore the essays for themselves.

Policies

Most of the country directors in this collection were trained as economists, so it is no surprise that they often focus on matters of economic policy. The policy issues that they tackle are wide-ranging and too numerous to mention here, but three are noteworthy because they arose frequently in the tumultuous 1990s: macroeconomic stability, privatization, and capital account and trade liberalization.

Macroeconomics Matters

The need for development with a human face hit home most forcefully in the 1990s as the media depicted poverty in the aftermath of the decade's financial crises. Though the dates and places changed—Mexico, 1994; Thailand and its neighbors, 1997; Russia, 1998; Brazil, 1999; Turkey, 2001; Argentina, 2001—the question remained the same: could the crisis have been prevented?

In the case of Argentina, one former country director thinks that more solid analytical work might have pointed out the mounting macroeconomic imbalances before it was too late. Shahid Javed Burki recounts how, in his role as vice president for Latin America and the Caribbean, he told Bank President Lew Preston in 1994 that Argentina should remove itself from its exchange rate anchor in favor of a crawling peg. But Burki had no rigorous evidence to support his position, and Preston remained unconvinced.

Perhaps the Bank could not have averted crisis in Argentina (or in any other country, for that matter) even if Burki could have drawn from a larger pool of research. The political realities that stymied crisis prevention in Argentina suggest limits to the World Bank's ability to take bold action on macroeconomic issues. Other country directors seem to agree: Myrna Alexander picks up Argentina's story several years later, when, in early 1998, macroeconomic imbalances were sufficiently apparent to lead her team to prepare for a crisis that they felt largely powerless to prevent. Jayasankar Shivakumar describes an even worse situation in Thailand, where, when the baht was devalued in 1997 and "all hell broke loose," the Bank was woefully unprepared, having done little analytical work on the country in the preceding years.

Yet in spite of the crisis lapses, some positive lessons emerge. For some country directors, the silver lining of crisis is the golden opportunity it provides for reform. Reflecting on the 1994–95 crisis in Mexico, Olivier Lafourcade notes the positive incentives that crisis generates for governments to undertake tough reforms, and Ajay Chhibber writes of the 2001 Turkey crisis, "Only a crisis could create the conditions for strengthening the state institutions necessary to subject the market to effectively regulated development." Alexander, likening the Bank's steady contributions to structural reform in Argentina to the fable of the tortoise and the hare, concludes, "I firmly believe that our contribution to development in Argentina will outlive the current crisis."

The prevalence of economic crises in the 1990s also serves as the most compelling evidence that, in the words of Basil Kavalsky, "Perhaps the closest we can get to a necessary condition [for development] is macroeconomic stability." Seconding this sentiment, many others suggest the primacy of macroeconomic issues to the Bank's mission, even if the Bank does not wield the most influence in this area of public policy.

Privatization versus Private Sector Development

The collapse of socialism and the fiscal drain of large-scale state enterprises on many developing countries led to a wave of privatization in the 1990s. Although textbook models predicted unambiguously positive effects on revenues and efficiency, the country directors who witnessed privatization up close saw a more complex reality. All agree that ownership transfer of state enterprises to the private sector is, in general, the right policy. But their experiences also highlight the risks involved when privatization efforts become too much, too fast, or too controversial. And they highlight the danger of confounding private sector development with privatization; in particular, the former can take place even when the latter is stymied.

Kavalsky and Christiaan Poortman, former country directors for various Eastern European nations, describe the need for a sound institutional foundation to ensure successful privatization, an oft-repeated lesson of the region's experience. Yet they also describe an additional, often overlooked downside to rapid privatization in transition countries: the risk that privatization can distract policymakers from the broader task of private sector development. As efforts focused on privatizing the largest enterprises, the need to create an enabling environment for small and medium enterprises was pushed aside, with negative consequences for the cultivation of entrepreneurship and employment creation.

Phyllis Pomerantz, former country director for Mozambique and Zambia, writes that controversies surrounding privatization can be more than just unpleasant speed bumps on the road to growth. The heated climate of privatization that she witnessed in Africa—exemplified by the cashew sector in Mozambique, which "became one of the poster children for the antiglobalization movement," in her words—probably diminished long term prospects for other reforms favorable to private sector development and growth. For Pomerantz, "the lesson is clear: in the haste to make progress—regardless of external pressures—governments and their aid partners should not short-circuit a full and transparent discussion of objectives and effects of reforms. Perhaps privatization would have been slower and more selective, but it would have taken place on surer footing."

Market Liberalization

In the remarkable policy consensus of the 1990s, the zeal to privatize state enterprises was matched perhaps only by the zeal to liberalize markets for goods, capital, and

labor. Reasonable economists can disagree on the optimal policies for market liberalization, and the contributors to this volume are no exception. But there appears to
be a tenuous consensus emerging that, because liberalization can have negative consequences, it must be undertaken with prudence and due regard for country context.

Returning to the theme of crisis, Alexander and Chhibber, respectively, cite
Argentina's and Turkey's ready access to foreign capital as a contributor to the macroeconomic imbalances that eventually tipped over into crisis. After citing deceptively
modest fiscal deficits as a major contributor to Argentina's accumulating debt burden, Alexander writes, "Whether because of the general exuberance of the markets
during the early 1990s or because of an underestimation of what level of fiscal performance was sustainable, the market continued to finance Argentina's deficit for a
very long time." Similarly, Chhibber notes that "Turkey's access to private capital
helped finance the profligate and populist policies of that decade." Though neither
advocates capital controls as a solution, they both recognize that miscalculations by
private markets can be destabilizing.

The case for trade liberalization is not as clear-cut as the textbooks would have it,
either. Kavalsky observes that many beneficiaries of liberalized trade are large developing countries that first built up an industrial base behind decades of protection.
"This is not the case for smaller countries," he writes; "indeed, the success stories
among small open economies are few and far between—for every Mauritius there
are two or three Malawis." As with capital flows, the implication is not that trade liberalization is bad, but that attention to the potential downsides in the particular
country context is paramount.

Contrast the mixed record of wholesale liberalization with the liberalization
experience of China, the most successful developing country of the past quarter century. In that time, China has moved in the direction of far greater market liberalization, yet it has done so in a very idiosyncratic manner, as Huang and Edwin Lim
describe in their essays. Price liberalization was only partial at the outset, with the
establishment of a two-track pricing system in agriculture that generated incentives
to increase productivity without unduly disrupting production patterns or community life. Trade liberalization began modestly, with a regime of special economic
zones and limits on foreign direct investment, so as not to abruptly overturn the state
enterprise system on which most Chinese workers relied for employment. Membership in the World Trade Organization did not come until much later. And even private property rights—often thought the sine qua non of economic growth—did not
arrive until very recently, as the Chinese economic system nonetheless generated
effective incentives in the absence of formal property ownership. The lesson is not to
emulate China's liberalization policies, but to adapt its approach—a prudent form of
liberalization, specific to the country's institutional realities and sensitive to its risks.

Politics

The foregoing discussion of policies hints at the difficulty of determining an optimal
course of action, even when economic theory provides a seemingly straightforward

blueprint. Yet in addition to this uncertainty about the *optimal* policy to pursue is the often more important question of the *practical* policy to pursue, because policymaking does not occur in an optimal world. Policymakers inevitably practice the art of the possible, and the country director must be attuned to those political realities to be effective. The successful country director, therefore, must play the role of ship captain as much as economist, setting a strategic direction for the intended policy support program and steering it through the often treacherous waters in which policy is made. As Poortman recalls, "My training in economics revealed its limitations when the solutions most often available were not second best, but fifth or sixth best."

Questions of political economy run strongly through each essay. The numerous anecdotes about facing political realities range from the horrifying (Poortman meeting in a Bosnian city hall with a mayor, fearing assassination, crouched in the corner of the room), to the comical (Lim describing the Bank's relationship with Indian policymakers as an "arranged marriage"), to the sublime (Kavalsky recalling a dinner in 1979 in which a Romanian official, waiting until the music reached sufficient volume, leaned over and told him how appreciative he was of Bank efforts, because "*nous sommes tres isolés ici* [we are very isolated here]"). Many express disappointment at the Bank's difficulty in making allowances for politics in its economic calculus. Kavalsky writes, "Perhaps the most important gap in the Bank's work is that our frequent naiveté about political economy leads to a failure to factor political realities systematically into the economic equation." Pomerantz agrees: "From where I sit, the lessons are not about whether the policy was good or bad. The lessons are really about the need for thorough understanding of the political environment in which reform takes place."

Yet in spite of the frustration, there is also a keen sense that, over time, the country directors learned the political ropes. They pepper their essays with insights on managing political challenges, with three strategies emerging most sharply: selectivity, ownership, and country specificity.

Selectivity

Economics is the study of the allocation of scarce resources among multiple ends; putting economics into practice, country directors must allocate a scarce amount of monetary and staff resources among a multitude of uses, such as lending, research, and advocacy for reform. Charting a strategy for making those choices is a crucial role for any country director. The proliferation of items on the 1990s policy reform agenda reinforced for many country directors the need to exercise *selectivity* in their country strategies. As reform initiatives multiplied in many developing countries, policies seemed to become less and less well implemented and effective. As a result, both policymakers and Bank officials now believe that it is more important to focus on a handful of the most important areas of reform than to try tackling many simultaneously. Selectivity, then, helps to shape a *policy* program, but it is a *political* strategy insofar as it defines a limited, practical set of concerns that the Bank and the country can effectively pursue together.

Gobind Nankani describes the drive for selectivity during his five-year stint as country director in Brazil, explaining how he attempted to blend the country team's research, the input from Brazilian policymakers, and an understanding of the World Bank's overall strategic direction to systematically determine several "strategic thrusts" for his country support program. Facing competing demands from Bank headquarters, Brazilian officials, and civil society, he says that a clear strategy "was crucial in helping us to stay focused on the broader issues that had to be central to our work." It also allowed the team to emphasize long-term development goals, going beyond the typical three- to four-year horizon of a Bank Country Assistance Strategy. "We did not always succeed: sometimes the pressure was too difficult to deflect," he recalls. "But we were able, I estimate, to spend 80 percent of our effort on the most important 20 percent of the issues."

Lafourcade advocates a similar approach: "To be selective, [you need] to know what to select from," he writes, relying on solid analytical work before mapping a strategy. Selectivity also must reflect a partnership between the Bank and the country; Lafourcade's second prerequisite for effective selectivity is to ensure "that what you select is also what the country wishes to select."

Artfully applied, selectivity delivers results. Although many China observers claim that gradualism in policy reform has been its key to success, Huang argues the contrary, drawing a sharp distinction between gradualism and selectivity. "For anyone who has witnessed the speed of China's development over the past two decades, *gradual* is not an adjective that comes to mind," he writes. "The process under way in China has neither been slow nor gradual, but rather it has been selective and in many respects rapid . . . . Since 1978, the Chinese government has had an uncanny ability to identify what needed to be done next—and to keep at it until success was achieved."

At a more parochial level, rigorous selectivity helps to improve the Bank's own portfolio performance and development effectiveness. Chhibber attributes a rise in the average size of Bank projects to a relentless drive to be selective in supporting Turkey's development efforts:

> The average International Bank for Reconstruction and Development loan size increased from US$95 million in fiscal years 1994–97 to US$440 million in fiscal years 1998–2002. As a result, the Bank could offer Turkey meaningful support in the areas selected. Also, our support could be used more strategically for policy change and institutional improvements with the use of programmatic policy lending. The Bank became a significant adviser to the government in several key areas—energy, telecommunications, agriculture, and education—but chose not to lend for health care and transportation because of insufficient ownership of necessary reforms in those areas.

Ownership

The proliferation of policy reform issues in the 1990s led to a greater use of conditionality in the policy lending of international financial institutions (IFIs). Countries increasingly had to meet a predetermined set of policy goals to qualify for aid and loan disbursement. The practice led to charges that the development institutions were unjustly imposing their will on borrower countries. The IFIs first countered that any prudent lender seeks assurance that its borrowers will take steps that increase their ability to pay back debts. In recent years, though, IFIs have expressed some doubts that conditionality is always an effective tool. Likewise, though only one country director represented here—Inder Sud—condemns the use of conditionality outright, many country directors suggest that conditionality is unlikely to be successful where a government is not genuinely committed to the policy conditions it is expected to meet. It is much more effective, they say, for a government committed to reform to take *ownership* of its program, leaving the Bank to play a supporting role.

Country ownership benefits both the country and the World Bank. Contrasting the success of the Bank's China portfolio—where, Burki says, a finance minister remarked that he felt the Bank's country team worked for him as much as for the Bank—with that of early 1990s Brazil, where there was less buy-in of the Bank's program, Burki concludes that "the health of the Bank-financed portfolio depended to a considerable extent on the commitment and ownership of the borrower of the policies that were embedded in the various projects."

Sud, who worked in East Asia before serving as country director in the Middle East, writes, "The East Asians were reforming their economies not under the Damocles sword of International Monetary Fund (IMF)–World Bank conditionality, but because they believed in the changes. What was impressive was that, while they sought Bank advice liberally, they were the ones who decided what to implement." James Adams tells the inspiring story of Tanzania, where a strong effort by the Bank and other development agencies to transfer ownership and to build government capacity merged with an energetic new political administration to spur a wave of policy reform. He credits ownership and capacity building with transforming a former pariah of the donor community into a star performer in growth and poverty reduction in the Africa region.

Fostering effective country ownership implies a shift in how the Bank has traditionally engaged with clients. Shivakumar writes, "Many of the Bank's existing instruments are compared to a hammer that makes every problem look like a nail." Instead, he calls for a more ownership-based model of Bank engagement, which is based on a sense of partnership, flexibility, and borrower commitment. He says the Country Development Partnership, a new framework for Bank assistance that grew out of his experience in the Thailand crisis, is a major step in this direction. Similarly, the Bank's Poverty Reduction Strategy Paper (PRSP) process is an attempt to promote greater ownership by low-income countries.

Yet the country directors also understand that *ownership*, though a catchy buzzword, is difficult to put in practice. Not all governments are equally committed to the transparency, evenhandedness, and strategic vision required for development. "In general, the Bank has been most effective when it can work with a government committed to the objectives of growth and poverty reduction, with a substantial level of capacity to implement programs and policies needed to achieve those objectives,"

Kavalsky writes. "The problem is how to tell beforehand whether the commitment is genuine." Although some cases of commitment or noncommitment are clear, Kavalsky finds that the "most difficult problem for the Bank is how to operate effectively in the gray middle—that is, the large group of countries between the committed, competent states and the failed states." With no clear guidelines, striking a balance between ownership and conditionality will likely remain a political dilemma for country directors for some time to come.

Most efforts to promote ownership focus on buy-in by the government, but Chhibber highlights civil society's crucial role, a frequently overlooked component of ownership. With so much focus on the government's commitment and capacity to supply reform, Chhibber says that country directors do not pay enough attention to the demand side for reform, as expressed by a committed populace: "Without organized civic institutions, there is no mechanism for channeling citizen demands into a relentless pressure on the system for change. Some difficult reforms need precisely such constant pressure."

Country Specificity

The Bank's increasingly ambitious policy reform agenda and use of conditionality in the 1990s led to many critiques from both nongovernmental organizations and the borrower countries themselves of the Washington Consensus model of development.[3] Critics charged that the IFIs promoted a cookie-cutter, one-size-fits-all approach that did not take into account the unique geographical, political, or social realities of each country, thereby leading to a political backlash against IFI-supported policies in many developing countries. The uneven economic success of the developing world in the 1990s—and the mounting evidence that successful countries such as China, India, and the East Asian tigers followed idiosyncratic approaches that often did not match the IFIs' advice—lent credence to those critiques.

The country directors in this volume generally offer an analogous, though perhaps more nuanced, critique of the dangers of a one-size-fits-all approach. For some, hindsight revealed that failed approaches did not take sufficient account of country context. For example, Shivakumar writes of Thailand that "the reform program was, unfortunately, driven mainly by solutions imported from abroad—solutions that did not take into account the local situation, particularly social and cultural factors and Thai business practices." The country directors' criticism of standard approaches to policy issues such as privatization and market liberalization, their comments about the nexus between policymaking and politics, and their advocacy of a more selective, ownership-based model of Bank engagement suggest that these ideas are all elements of a broader framework that is based on unique, country-specific approaches to borrower countries. The essays need not even explicitly mention the term *country specificity* to reinforce this view; their accounts of country circumstances and approaches are sufficiently varied to endorse it implicitly.

This endorsement of country specificity does not equal a call to abandon the principles of the Washington Consensus, however. In fact, Adams credits Tanzania's embrace of a Washington Consensus–inspired policy package with putting the country on sound macroeconomic footing and expresses "fear that undue criticism of the Washington Consensus, even by well-intentioned and well-informed economists, provides cover for developing countries to stray from the macroeconomic fundamentals essential for growth." Yet Adams also makes clear that Tanzania adopted its reforms at a sequence and pace suited to its particular circumstances. Even Sud, who staunchly defends the Washington Consensus, agrees that "economic reform is not a mere science .... The art of reform is just as important. One has to adapt to local conditions."

The alarming frequency with which orthodox reform programs have failed to deliver results has led development economists to focus increasingly on institutions as the key explanation for policy success or failure. Where institutional capacity is sufficient and policies are implemented well, countries succeed, but otherwise they will not; institutional variation forms the foundation of country specificity in this view. Because institutions differ greatly by country, policymakers are told they must carefully consider the nature of the institutions when charting their course. The country directors generally agree: for instance, Lim talks of matching the right policy with the right institution, and Poortman talks of the primacy of institutional constraints in the pace of postconflict recovery in the Balkan states.

The country directors also warn against being too aggressive in using international expertise to circumvent local institutional weaknesses. Though both Pomerantz and Poortman cite project implementation units—specially designed teams of international development experts—as leading to short-term successes in their countries of responsibility, they also cite their long-term downside. Pomerantz writes, "But in our rush to get things done, we do not, in practice, always take the route that will lead to institutional strengthening because we know it will be longer and harder. Importing foreign technical assistance and creating project implementation units are classic examples of opting for the easy way." Indeed, institutional strengthening has emerged as a key concern for country directors.

Yet there is also a sense that the emphasis on institutions has gone a bit too far, without a thorough understanding of the true extent to which institutions influence economic outcomes. Surely corrupt institutions are no benefit to development, but, as Huang notes, China has flourished despite levels of corruption that would be considered problematic in countries that have not achieved as much growth. Kavalsky remarks, "Since good macro and structural policies have not proved sufficient conditions for growth and poverty reduction, the development community has turned to institutions as the missing variable .... This is very close to a tautology." Institutions have become akin to the residual term in growth regressions—the unexplained portion of development that is thought to be known but is not fully understood. There is a consensus on the tremendously important role that institutions play in development but less certainty on how to define, measure, or influence them.

But if institutions remain a nebulous concept and their weight hard to quantify with precision, the Bank's aggressive efforts in recent years to decentralize—locating its country teams in field offices within, or close to, borrower countries—have made a tangible step toward greater country specificity. Lafourcade cites "the permanent connection to the real problems and concerns of the country, with direct communication with the authorities of the country" among the advantages of decentralization. "Being in the country, one is much more sensitized and sensitive to its realities," he says. "In Mexico, I had the feeling of being much more part of the scenery, available to people for a phone call, a visit, a lunch." Kavalsky agrees: "There was no comparison in terms of job satisfaction and effectiveness [in decentralized versus headquarters-based country teams]. In the field, the accountabilities seemed so much clearer, and the feedback loop was so much shorter." At its most successful, decentralization will allow the Bank to be more timely in its actions, correcting the impression, attributed by Shivakumar to a Thai journalist, that "IMF makes wrong decisions on a timely basis and the Bank makes right decisions when it is too late."

With regard to country specificity, as with the political challenges faced by country directors more generally, success may, indeed, depend not only on finding the right policies and the right institutions, but also on acting at the right time. As Lim puts it, "The requirement for effective country management is not unlike the advice Bob Hope had for effective comedians: timing is everything." Critics will surely enjoy the notion of the country director as comedian. But the analogy is apt: these country directors have made the important, though perhaps belated, recognition that, when it comes to politics, they, too, perform on a stage.

Principles

For the country director, policies and politics clearly matter. But even country directors with a good understanding of both may find themselves hurtling along without a strong set of guardrails to guide day-to-day action. Here the essential role of *principles* enters the equation: successful Bank operations require a sound operating philosophy. Pomerantz puts it eloquently: "We in the Bank need to base our assessments less on the quality (according to us) of the product and more on the quality of the process . . . . But it is difficult for us because our expertise—plus, for many of us, our intellectual interests—lies much more in the *what*, as opposed to the *how*."

Though typical Bank reports may seldom acknowledge the point, the essays in this volume demonstrate that the *how* matters. As the country directors give rare glimpses into their meetings with heads of state, finance ministers, and other important officials, they make abundantly clear that, after the reports are completed and the loan documents signed, ultimately it is whether the handshake between Bank and client is warm or cold that determines the long-term success of the partnership.

Knowledge

The first key operating principle identified by country directors is knowledge or, more precisely, country-specific knowledge rooted in rigorous analysis of the economic and political environments. The importance of rigorous analysis to the formulation of good policy is obvious, but several country directors also explain how sound knowledge forms the basis for the other strategies that they advocate. Nankani gives several examples of how the quality analytical work conducted by his staff, often in collaboration with country experts, helped to define the selective areas of focus underlying the Brazil country program. He views such analysis as an investment in delivering quality lending, where applicable, and as a contribution to policy debates, rather than just a service that the client consumes. Burki provides the negative example of the lack of solid analytical work on Argentina's exchange rate regime, but he also offers the positive example of China. In promoting government commitment and ownership in the Bank's China program, he says they "helped by firmly anchoring the lending in analytical work." And Lafourcade says that the "necessary sensitivity" molding country-specific approaches "comes from (a) knowing the country and (b) learning."

The country directors also offer ideas on how the Bank can improve its knowledge operations. Nankani emphasizes the need for country directors to make the knowledge program more strategic, both in determining priority areas of focus and disseminating analytical work among the various stakeholders of proposed reforms. Burki calls for greater efforts to acquire *thick* knowledge—the type of multidimensional knowledge that comes from lengthy country experience and consideration of the political, social, and economic contexts. Both also refer to the opportunities to take better advantage of the Bank's global reach to connect the dots between global, regional, and local research.

Trust

"Without trust," Pomerantz writes, "it is hard for others to hear what you have to say, let alone adopt your advice. Without trust, open and frank dialogue, which leads to mutual influence, is impossible." Numerous contributors to this volume make clear that a trusting relationship between the Bank and its clients goes well beyond merely generating feelings of respect and friendship, often making a real difference in getting the most from Bank assistance. Adams equates country ownership with "trust[ing] the client enough to allow the client to commit mistakes," an essential element, in his view, of Tanzania's success. Where trust erodes—Pomerantz cites the Zambian government's frustration with what it perceived as changing conditions and evaluation criteria—it becomes more difficult for the Bank to find support for its recommended policies. Yet building trust pays dividends. Nankani recalls how trust made a difference in his interactions with Brazilian Finance Minister Pedro Malan: while their interaction following the Mexican peso crisis in 1994 consisted only of a brief phone call, after the Russian crisis broke four years later Malan and Nankani were both trying to contact each other and a lengthier dialogue ensued—a result of the relationship that had developed in the intervening years.

Nankani also notes pointedly that "trust is not without cost." Both he and Lafourcade caution against the risk of trust sliding into complacency, in which each side fears disagreeing with or pointing out mistakes by the other. For Nankani, a truly trusting relationship surmounts this risk: "This does not mean that such situations [disagreements] do not often involve frustrations on both sides. It does mean that the relationship overcomes them."

Burki gives the most dramatic example of building trust and how risky it can be. Burki went to China shortly after the Tiananmen Square incident in 1989, when most foreign governments were pulling out, and he fought hard for the Bank to sustain a relationship with China, while many were arguing for the opposite course. As a result of that painful experience, there was a trust built in China that paid off over the coming years. Burki also describes how World Bank President Lew Preston called him in to his office and "said that he was troubled by the Bank's uneasy relations with Brazil, Latin America's largest country and economy. 'I want you to fix that,' [Preston] said. 'I am told of the high level of trust the Chinese have in you. Create the same in Brazil.'"

The clearest lesson that comes from the reflections that many of the country directors lay out well—Alexander, Huang, Kavalsky, Nankani, Shivakumar, and others—is that, though there are no silver bullets in the development business, decentralization of country directors to country offices since 1997 is as close as it gets to a sure-fire recipe for mutual benefit. Although the Bank must remain vigilant to minimize the risk that decentralization devolves into unwarranted pro-client bias, all of the field-based country directors say how dramatically the shift has improved the Bank's relationship with clients.

Humility

Besides moving to the country in question, how can a country director build trust and gain respect? The most important way, for many country directors, is to be humble, both in interpersonal interaction as well as in overall approach. An anecdote from Kavalsky illustrates:

DHAKA, BANGLADESH, October 1972, on a plane returning from my first visit to independent Bangladesh. Henry Kissinger has called this country a "basket case," and it is hard to disagree. The sheer density of the population, the difficult physical environment that raises the cost of construction and infrastructure, the limited resources other than water—these seem overwhelming problems. I recite this list of disadvantages to a colleague who is by chance on the same flight. He tells me that 10 years previously he had participated in the first Bank mission to another postconflict country, and that Bank team had similarly concluded that the situation was hopeless. Corruption was rampant, natural resources were almost nil, exports were a tiny share of gross domestic product (GDP), and the government was surviving only through large aid inflows. The country was the Republic of Korea.

"It is banal but perhaps important to reiterate," he reflects, "that the overwhelming lesson is humility in the face of the complexity of the development challenge." Just as few economists predicted that the Korea of 1960 or the Bangladesh of 1972 would eventually become a development success story, similarly few predicted that the high-flying Argentina of 1994 would collapse fewer than 10 years later. "Perhaps the development successes and failures merely teach us that we do not know much at all," writes Huang.

Clearly, there is no panacea for development; yet in the Bank there is still, according to Lafourcade, a "propensity to continue to search for—and sometimes claim that it has found—the ultimate answers to development." The strategies and principles that the country directors posit—selectivity, ownership, country specificity, knowledge generation, and trust—are useful safeguards against this tendency, but history still suggests a need for the institution to be more aware of its own limitations. This realization is difficult for those in what Lafourcade calls "an institution of doers," but as Lim writes, "Saying 'no' can be as powerful as saying 'yes' in certain instances."

For these country directors, humility involves not merely recognition of the World Bank's limitations, but also a shift in the manner in which Bank staff members relate to their counterparts. Sud recalls being confused at Egypt's reluctance to receive a visit shortly after he became its country director, learning only later that the Egyptians suspected another lecture on their lack of reforms, a performance other Bank officials had delivered before. Aware of similar misunderstandings, Nankani emphasizes the need to temper one's expertise with humility, an approach that he says is valid regardless of a country's income level or institutional capacity.

Learning from the Pilgrimage

The operating principles espoused by the country directors are straightforward enough, but behind the seemingly simple maxims to pursue knowledge, build trust, and be humble are profound transformations within the institution. To be sure, the extraordinary events of the 1990s—transition, crisis, and uneven growth in the developing world, as well as a shift in development thought from a remarkable policy consensus to a more heterogeneous mix of perspectives—left a profound mark on the World Bank.

The country directors who contributed to this volume and witnessed these events as they unfolded simultaneously advocate and reflect this change. In commenting on these essays, Andrew Steer, the current country director for Indonesia, said that the country directors resembled a group of priests who had been on a pilgrimage and emerged radically transformed. For those who were the first field-based country directors to represent the "development church"[4] of the World Bank in their respective countries, it was quite literally a pilgrimage. For all, a personal transformation occurred that made them query the creed with which they had set out. As Poortman wrote, "I could summarize my experience as country director in the Balkan states as the permanent education of an economist."

The essays in this volume are bold attempts to sort out the lessons learned about policies, politics, and principles during this pilgrimage. They shine light on the thought processes of formerly faceless officials, many of whom are still struggling to determine which of their former tenets of faith are central and which should be amended or discarded. There is no longer a sacred text, if it ever existed. Many express a sort of repentance, acknowledging their mistakes and hoping that they, and others, will learn from them. As Pomerantz says, "I have contributed to some successes, but probably to an equal or greater number of failures. It is clear, at least to me, that there is no magic bullet to help the world's poor. Most of us who work in development agencies readily acknowledge that many of our past formulas for success have not worked despite our good intentions. The important thing is that we keep trying." The unfortunate reality is that wide segments of society, particularly the poor, bear the burden of policy mistakes, regardless of whether they are made by the World Bank, the country, or both. The country directors' emphasis on the commitment and credibility of reform indicates that decisionmakers' accountability to these constituencies helps to anchor good policy decisions.

Steer, on reading the essays, noted both the powerful effects of the development experience during the past two decades and the open-mindedness of the participating country directors, summarizing their transformation as follows:

> Rather than priests, the country directors have all become Methodist ministers. There has been a radical shift in our faith. There is still a lot of talk about morality and teaching and principles, but very, very different from a theist, rigorous orthodoxy. That is the number one thing that comes through. Two sets of principles permeate these reflections first, a set of principles that are required for a country to develop but, second—and this is the really interesting thing—a set of principles to guide the way that we behave and operate, and words and concepts such as *humility*, *trust*, *patience*, a *sense of journey*, a *pilgrimage*, if you like, occasionally repentance on the part of some of these people, and the occasional glimpse of glory as well.

Every church, no matter how divinely inspired, is ultimately a human institution, and, therefore, fallible. The World Bank is no different. The honest introspection represented in these essays recognizes this fallibility and explores its dimensions. We hope that the country directors' lessons are considered thoughtfully and channeled effectively to improve the lives of the world's poor.

Notes

1. Historian Thomas Carlyle (1840) wrote, "The history of the world is but the biography of great men."

2. For purposes of this trilogy, we consider the Argentina crisis of 2001–02 as the effective end of the 1990s.

3. Economist John Williamson (1990) coined the term *Washington Consensus* to describe a set of 10 economic policies widely thought in Washington-based policy circles (principally the World Bank, International Monetary Fund, and U.S. Treasury Department) to be desirable in Latin America. The term soon came to stand for a universal prescription for development based on free-market fundamentalism, contrary to its author's intention (see Williamson 2005).

4. The notion of World Bank as church first appeared in George and Sabelli (1994).

Basil Kavalsky

*Former Country Director for Armenia, the Baltic States,
Belarus, Georgia, Moldova, and Ukraine (1993–97) and
Poland and the Baltic States (1997–2000)*

Basil Kavalsky got an early introduction to the professional flexibility required to survive in the World Bank. After being sent for two months of intensive Spanish language training upon joining the Bank in 1966, he received his first assignment: economist in the South Asia Region. "The Bank was much smaller then, and I liked the casual nature of it," he laughs.

But economic development has always been a serious matter for Basil. "Being brought up in a country [South Africa] where you saw huge amounts of poverty around you, I was frustrated that I couldn't contribute to the welfare of the population at large," he recalls of his youth. After completing his master's degree in economics at the London School of Economics, Basil applied to government and university positions in various African nations. When he found all of them wary of hiring a white South African, he joined the World Bank as a Young Professional.

Among the highlights of his first 15 years in the Bank, spent largely as a senior economist in the South Asia and the Middle East and North Africa Regions, were landmark reports on Bangladesh (part of the first Bank team to work there following its 1971 independence) and Afghanistan. Ironically, each report was published shortly before tremendous upheavals: first the major political turmoil in Bangladesh in the years following independence and then the Soviet invasion of Afghanistan in 1979. "I got a reputation in the Bank for dooming governments when I worked on them," Basil jokes. Nonetheless, his work proved influential once relative stability returned; Bank staff members working in post-Taliban Afghanistan have told Basil that they still find much relevant material in his now quarter-century-old analysis.

Leaving the regions in 1981, Basil held various corporate positions in the Bank until 1992. Among them was a five-year period as director of the Resource Mobilization Department, where he oversaw a major capital increase in the institution. Because of the widespread effects of this increase in resources, he describes the position as one of the most satisfying he has held.

With extensive experience in operations and management, in 1993 Basil embarked on his most challenging roles: country department director for one-half of the republics of the former Soviet Union and, later, in Warsaw as country director for Poland, Estonia, Latvia, and Lithua-

nia. As he worked to steer those former state-run economies through their transition to capitalism, Basil found that he possessed an unexpected asset: his surname. Accustomed to
patiently spelling *Kavalsky* for perplexed scribes, in Warsaw he found himself treated with
more familiarity, and the region's culture and cuisine brought back fond memories of his
upbringing as the son of Lithuanian Jewish migrants. "I thought, 'Oh, I'm home!'"

Returning to Washington, D.C., in 2001, Basil retired from the Bank soon thereafter—at
least on paper. "In practice I've just continued," he says, working as a full-time consultant to
country directors under the auspices of the Operations Policy and Country Services Department
and Operations Evaluation Department (OED). Nearing 40 years of service to the Bank, he has
seen many changes to the once-small institution he joined, but he views the Bank as heading
in the right direction: "Increasingly we see the objective as working with countries," rather
than dictating their direction for them. "The country has to provide the leadership."

2 Pictures and Lessons of Development Practice

Basil Kavalsky

Gathering Experience

COLOMBO, SRI LANKA, June 1966, the office of the head of the Planning Ministry. I am on my first Bank mission, and the team is reviewing the foreign exchange budget. The Sri Lankan government has inherited an extensive social welfare system that is increasingly unaffordable with declining world market prices for its main exports—tea, rubber, and coconut. Aid has become a critical part of the financing package, and donors want assurances that it is being spent only on essential items. We scrutinize the import needs in great detail and calculate that the projected quantities of imported bags for cement are double what would be required for the expected production of the public cement enterprise. Our counterparts are committed and able but, like us, focused on the short term. The "strategy" seems to be one of muddling through until some exogenous factor propels the economy forward.

DHAKA, BANGLADESH, October 1972, on a plane returning from my first visit to independent Bangladesh. Henry Kissinger has called this country a "basket case," and it is hard to disagree. The sheer density of the population, the difficult physical environment that raises the cost of construction and infrastructure, the limited resources other than water—these seem overwhelming problems. I recite this list of disadvantages to a colleague who is by chance on the same flight. He tells me that 10 years previously he had participated in the first Bank mission to another postconflict country, and that Bank team had similarly concluded that the situation was hopeless. Corruption was rampant, natural resources were almost nil, exports were a tiny share of gross domestic product (GDP), and

---

I have tried to fit the mental snapshots I have taken over the years with some of the broader lessons I have drawn from my experience. I apologize to the reader for the fact that the fit is often less than ideal.

the government was surviving only through large aid inflows. The country was the Republic of Korea.

WARSAW, POLAND, April 1999. The success of the transition in Poland is extraordinary. Friends who visited Warsaw in the late 1980s compared it very unfavorably with other parts of the Soviet empire. Yet a decade later Poland is booming. The number of cars in Warsaw is going up at the rate of 40 percent a year, and my commute to the office takes slightly longer every month I spend in the country. Many things seem to have contributed to the success. First, there are the common purpose and vision provided by potential membership in the European Union (EU) and the recognition that macrostability is part of that package. Second, there is Poland's location in the heart of Europe. For the first time in history, it seems to be an advantage to be sandwiched between Germany and the Russian Federation. Third, there is size. Poland is large enough to have a domestic market on which small businessmen can cut their teeth before venturing into the export field. Furniture exports seem to have grown in this way. Fourth, there is a productive and well-trained work force. Fifth, Poland has some genuinely visionary leaders. Sixth, Poland has struck the right balance between opening the domestic market and maintaining a hard budget constraint for former state enterprises. Thus, Poles with access to funds through remittances or other means have been able to acquire productive assets, with the result being that employment in small and medium industry rose at about the same speed as employment in the large-scale state enterprises declined. Last, and perhaps most controversial, Poland is now 98 percent Polish. Joseph Stalin's ruthless ethnic cleansing has turned out to be a long-term advantage, which has saved the country from Balkan-type conflicts. Much has been lost, of course, but for the moment this homogeneity is working to Poland's benefit. I attend a special event for Pope John Paul II, who is visiting Warsaw, and am struck to see the various generations of Polish leadership, including former adversaries like Wojciech Jaruzelski and Lech Walesa, chatting and joking with each other. I feel as if I am sitting in on a family gathering.

TIRANA, ALBANIA, March 2003, the mayor's office in the newly restored municipal building. The current mayor lived and worked as an artist in Paris before he was asked to return home as minister of culture. He later won election to become mayor of Tirana. The city was in the worst phase of post-Communist blight, with the usual wide dreary streets lined with squatters' shacks in many areas. His single-minded determination has led to the clearing of the streets, the gray buildings have been painted in the bright colors of a Mediterranean seaport, trees have been planted, and funds have been allocated to keep the city meticulously clean. Since there was not even a movie theater in town, he invested in one himself with a group of shareholders. The result of those efforts has been extraordinary: there is a new vibrancy in Tirana. Hundreds of small coffee bars and restaurants have opened, and in the summertime, life moves into the streets. The next challenge is to deal with the large periurban settlements. There has been substantial migration in recent years from the rural areas to chaotic communities on the periphery of the cities. The mayor complains that rather than fund new infrastructure in those areas, the donors have romantic notions of rural Albania and are building schools in villages where there are no longer any children. "You go to these villages and all that is left are two old ladies and a don-key," he says.

It is banal but perhaps important to reiterate that the overwhelming lesson is humility in the face of the complexity of the development challenge. The history of the second half of the 20th century provides no blueprints that pin down the necessary or sufficient conditions for successful growth and poverty reduction.

Perhaps the closest we can get to a necessary condition is macroeconomic stability. There have been countries that continued to grow with large budget deficits and high rates of inflation, coupled with strict controls on imports and capital flows— Turkey and Brazil are two that come to mind. In general, however, all evidence is that this strategy is not a viable in the longer term. It brings political instability in its wake and steers investment into a set of goods and services that may not reflect the country's longer-term comparative advantage. Above all, it diverts the focus of economic agents toward exploiting the gains and avoiding the losses from financial transactions and away from creating growth in the real economy.

The Bank's focus for much of the period—and during the 1980s and early 1990s in particular—has been on getting better structural policies. This goal is more ambiguous than macrostability. The size of the budget deficit is more tangible and the implications more clearly understood than the range of trade, pricing, and competition policies. For most countries (except perhaps India) a consensus has evolved around the idea that deficits of up to 3 percent of GDP are likely to be sustainable and not to cause undue problems, while deficits above that level need to be reversed as soon as possible. There is no such consensus on structural policies. The role of the EU in setting the norms in both these areas has been very strong. The continued existence of the common agricultural policy has made it difficult to argue against protection by developing countries; indeed, some of the most bitter and unpleasant arguments I have had with counterparts have related to the Bank's urging the reduction of agricultural subsidies.

NEW DELHI, INDIA, November 1967 to February 1970. I am assigned to the India Resident Mission as a fiscal economist. While the work is interesting, living in and experiencing India yields the highest returns. The richness of the past and the complexity of the troubling present dominate day-to-day experiences. The questions of where the country is headed and what it will take to get there seem almost never on the table. The focus of our efforts is to persuade the government to liberalize external trade. We are making very little progress since this approach runs counter to both philosophy (memories of what Manchester, U.K., did to Indian textiles in the 19th century) and realpolitik (an alliance of inefficient state enterprises and the oligarchy of powerful private industrialists). The complacency is extraordinary, and we discuss endlessly whether it is in spite of or because of the high quality of India's economists.

It soon becomes apparent to me that I need to study what is going on in the Indian states as well as at the central level. My managers agree to my going down to Bangalore to look at how the state government of (then) Mysore works and to report on its role and financial situation relative to the central government. Delhi and its workings seem very remote from there. The state government almost defines the word bureaucracy. Its function is to keep in place a system seemingly little changed from the days of the raj and the maharajah of Mysore. Indeed, the official entertainment laid on for me is a trip to the horse races at the Gymkhana Club and a visit to Nandi Hills Resort, where I am proudly shown the signatures of British royalty in the guest book. Government officials go through the motions of planning, but there is nothing strategic in the way things are done. If development takes place, it will be in spite of, not because of, the state government. I prepare a report on finance, planning, and administration in Mysore that goes onto the shelves among other unnoticed and unread documents.

VILNIUS, LITHUANIA, November 1993. I have roots in Lithuania. My father and maternal grandparents migrated from here to Cape Town, and many of my relatives died here in World War II. Vilnius's old town is remarkably intact, and one can well imagine the days when it was a center of Polish, Jewish, and Lithuanian culture. The Lietuva Hotel is not, however, in the old town. It is the tallest building in Vilnius, built in a nondescript fashion, and located, perhaps, so that one can keep an eye on whatever is going on in the city. We arrive late and go to the restaurant, where we are given a 10-page menu and go through the familiar game of asking for about 20 dishes on the menu, none of which are available. We eventually give up and simply ask what they have—it always turns out to be a pork cutlet. The second-highest building in the city is the Ministry of Agriculture. Rather curiously for such a small country, Lithuania has one of the largest shares of agriculture in gross national product of any country of the former Soviet Union, 25 percent. We have had good responses in getting the beginnings of agricultural transition in Estonia and Latvia, and we have decided to try our hands in Lithuania as well. The ministry is very powerful and staffed mostly by holdovers from the preindependence era. We organize a meeting with ministry officials to discuss agricultural policy, and the temperature in the room gets higher and higher as we try to explain the importance in the long run of opening the markets, privatizing, and reducing subsidies. It is apparent that we are questioning a set of deeply held beliefs, and it is unlikely that we will make headway with this particular group. We decide to break off the meeting, given the unpleasant atmosphere. We will have to focus our support on other areas of the Lithuanian economy.

The particular difficulty with structural policies is that the groups that lose from reductions of subsidies and protection tend to be readily identifiable, and the effect of such reductions tends to be a measurable decline in their income. In contrast, the beneficiaries and the scale of their benefits are uncertain. Therefore, the political economy difficulties of reducing subsidies can be enormous. It is often worthwhile for the losers to provide rents to politicians and officials for keeping subsidies or policy distortions in place. To deal with such conduct, the Bank developed adjustment lending with policy conditionality in an effort to tip the scales in favor of taking action to reduce economic distortions. The government can derive the benefit of increased resource flows in the short term, and the longer-term efficiency gains from the policy change can be used to repay the loans.

In recent years the received wisdom is that conditionality only works when it supports actions that the government is committed to taking anyway. Something being done simply to get access to the adjustment loan or credit will likely be reversed. Experience in Moldova—reversal—and Lithuania—continuation of adjustment even when the Bank had ended adjustment support—is consistent with this argument. The problem is how to tell beforehand whether the commitment is genuine. In the early 1990s, when we were providing substantial adjustment support to both countries, we did not see deep-rooted differences in the level of commitment. With hindsight, it seems evident that political economy factors in Lithuania, such as the greater imminence of EU accession and the political and ethnic coherence of the population, were far more favorable. But at the time this call was much more difficult to make. Moldova, for example, had a strong agricultural base and a better-managed central bank in the period up to 1995.

While we are generally aware of political economy factors, we tend to file them away as background information rather than incorporating them into the strategy for engaging with the country. Our mistakes are almost never those of inadequate technical analysis, but almost always of underestimating the influence of the political economy on the willingness to undertake structural reforms.

That being said, the Bank has been quite successful in supporting structural reform. There is a huge difference in the policy regimes of countries now compared with those of 1980. The Washington Consensus model has entered the consciousness of most policymakers in developing countries, so that even where high levels of protection or consumer subsidies continue to exist, they are usually defended as temporary, and the perversity of the incentives they create is acknowledged. The problem, of course, is that the evidence of the benefits of these better policies remains somewhat mixed—depending on whether you believe William Easterly or David Dollar. Many beneficiaries of open-trade policies, for example, are large developing countries that built up a manufacturing and services base behind a high level of protection and then opened their economies and benefited from the growth in world trade. Large countries have the advantage that their markets can support multiple producers and that domestic competition allows for increasing efficiency, even with limited competition from imports. This is not the case for smaller countries; indeed, the success stories among small open economies are few and far between—for every Mauritius there are two or three Malawis. Not surprisingly, location seems to be a major factor here. Switzerland sets the marker for landlocked countries impossibly high. In the 1990s, we used to talk about the distance from Stuttgart, Germany, as the primary determinant of transition countries' success. The Russian oil boom has reduced the reliability of that indicator, but location is still a variable that deserves more attention.

The focus of Bank efforts has been mainly to try to reduce distortions in product markets, putting much less emphasis over the years on factor markets, especially the labor market, which, I think, has been a mistake. The brain drain, of course, reflects the efficient functioning of the international market for services, but it has produced a situation in which, for example, every single African country now has more trained doctors living and working abroad than inside the country. The other side of the coin is the importance of remittances, which have become the fastest-growing area of foreign exchange earnings for many countries. Bangladesh's ability to defy the pundits and keep growing despite its poor record on governance is to a very large extent a function of remittances. Yet we have done very little analytic work on the effect of these remittances on the economy, on strategies for maximizing flows of remittances, on their potential volatility, and so forth.

Since good macro and structural policies are necessary but not sufficient conditions for growth and poverty reduction, the development community has turned to institutions as the missing variable. For institutions read anything other than economic policies. This is very close to a tautology. Development will succeed when everything is in place for development to succeed. I will not add to the many lists and definitions of institutions that have been offered, but the Bank is trying to focus its efforts to support particular institutional improvements in areas such as anticorruption programs, judicial reform, banking sector reform, privatization, and regulatory frameworks.

KABUL, AFGHANISTAN, August 1976, the office of the secretary for finance. The Bank has been active in Afghanistan for about 10 years, working closely with two institutions—the agricultural and industrial development banks. We have seconded staff members for a number of years to those institutions and have provided credits for on-lending and training for their staff. The agriculture bank has one of the best repayment records on its loans of any of the many specialized banks we are supporting worldwide. These two institutions have become incubators for first-rate personnel, who can be funneled into other institutions in Afghanistan. The secretary mentions how impressed the Ministry of Finance is with what has been done at these two banks and asks if the World Bank can take the same approach in developing the capacity of the Ministry of Finance. But these operations are costly, and we are already very thinly spread in Afghanistan.

Aside from supporting the agricultural and industrial development banks, we are focusing our efforts on improving health and education. This is the era of basic needs in Afghanistan, and we are trying to set some goals in those areas and address them through our program. The secretary tells me that his government is "sick and tired" of being lectured about basic needs. What the government really wants is our support for the cement factory and for infrastructure development. Later, on a field visit outside of Kabul near the town of Tashkurgan, we walk into the fields and talk with a young shepherd boy. A piece of paper on which he has been writing falls from his hand, and I ask about it. He has been attending literacy classes and is practicing writing his name.

The question arises whether one can in fact achieve piecemeal institutional reform. The interrelations between the various parts of the institutional framework make it very difficult to improve just one area. Nepal is a good example of this. Our efforts to improve the functioning of the banking system have found that it provides a source of rents for corrupt politicians and their associates. The institutional weaknesses of Nepalese society are so intertwined that we may not be able to improve banking without addressing some fundamental governance issues at the same time. Doing so in the absence of committed leadership seems a hopeless task. But perhaps this outlook is too negative. To argue that we can do nothing unless we can do everything is surely not right. The problem is that we still do not know what works in this area and where the payoff to our efforts is likely to be the highest. In addition, we have some natural constraints. For example, the Bank has never worked with police forces, which are often the core of the corruption problem.

In reviewing my experience, I was surprised at how early we discovered the importance of good governance. We treated corruption, however, as a given, a part of the environment to be factored into the calculation. We did not treat it as a variable that we should make a concerted effort to address. The change in the mid 1990s has been to take an active approach to trying to help countries address corruption. This effort is perhaps the most complex challenge the Bank has taken on, because the people whom we must work with in government are often themselves part of the culture of corruption. Their interest may well lie in securing a larger share of the rents for themselves and their supporters.

MANILA, PHILIPPINES, August 1966. We enter the outer office of the minister of public works. It is crowded with contractors, suppliers, and job seekers, all soliciting the largesse of the minister. We are ushered into his inner office, and we find an equally large number of people there. They have secured this choice position through a payment to the minister's private secretary and are not about to move, so they remain in the room throughout our meeting with the minister. I am on my second Bank mission, and it is a shock to encounter a country where corruption is not an aberration or a distortion of the system— it is the system. After the mission I am asked to draft a note to the Bank's Board of Executive Directors submitting a project document, and I state the obvious fact that corruption is by far the country's most serious economic issue. I discover that the rule is that corruption is not explicitly discussed in Executive Board documents.

DHAKA, BANGLADESH, November 1973. A senior government official has asked to visit me at the hotel. We have prepared a lengthy report on Bangladesh some two years after its independence, laying out a blueprint for future growth based on rural development. He tells me of the cancer of corruption that in a very short time has begun to destroy the commitment and morale of the civil service, and he asks that I reflect this situation in the report. He gives detailed information on the mechanisms of corruption and their consequences, and my colleagues and the mission team decide that this problem is an important part of the story that should be flagged for public discussion. On our return, we work this theme into the report, and it is published and distributed with the new sections. Two weeks after publication, I am called into my director's office and informed that the government has complained; we need to edit out the references to corruption and reissue the report. Eighteen passages are removed from the report, and it is distributed with a request to destroy the previous version. While angry and frustrated, I take solace in the fact that this censorship will, if anything, draw more attention to the issue.

CHISINAU, MOLDOVA, February 1997, a restaurant where we are dining with a senior government official. We are listening to a familiar but sad refrain, one that has been a

counterpoint in many different countries I have visited. The official is describing how cor-
ruption has become the way of life in Moldova and how rare it is to find an honest politi-
cian or official. The buildup was gradual, but at some point in the mid 1990s it became
evident to those who were trying to play the game according to the rules that this was no
longer the way the country worked and that there was nothing to lose and everything to
gain from joining their colleagues on the take. When corruption has metastasized to this
point, there is almost nothing that can be done to stop it short of the leadership equiva-
lent of a bone-marrow transplant. It is not a matter of shoring up defenses here or there.
Why did we not see this earlier? When I look back there were straws in the wind—
rumors of government officials getting homes in Houston, Texas, as payoffs from oil com-
panies, and the evidence of collusion or coercion in the first privatization auction, where
only very limited bids at very low prices were received for the companies offered—but we
tended to judge each of these instances as problems we could deal with in the specific con-
text through fine-tuning the approach. Over coffee in the restaurant, I have little comfort
to offer except to observe that these are still early days in the transition process.

Ethnicity, Nationality, and Political Economy

KABUL, AFGHANISTAN, September 1977. I have prepared my second Bank basic report.
The Bank's chief economist asks me at a meeting which of the two countries we have
studied—Bangladesh and Afghanistan—had the better development prospects. I respond
that Afghanistan looks far more promising: it has a good export base for horticultural
products and is better located for serving the Middle Eastern and European markets. I do
not factor into the equation the political economy of Afghanistan and the difficulty of
accommodating the divergent interests of various tribal and ethnic groups. Shortly after we
complete the report, the king is deposed in a government takeover by his cousin Muham-
mad Daoud. Shortly after the Bangladesh report was produced, Sheikh Mujib Rahman
was assassinated in that country. I am getting a reputation in the Bank of dooming
whichever government I write about.

One of the great problems that many developing countries face is the maintenance of political stability in the face of demands from rival ethnic groups. The
development of the nation-state in Europe was based largely on an identification of
language, religion, and ethnicity with the military, political, and economic apparatus
of the state. Many, if not most, countries in the world are multiethnic, and the state
comes to represent the interests of the dominant ethnic group. The successful states
are those that are able to persuade minorities that the benefits to them of working
together with the majority outweigh the real or imagined loss of ethnic identity. In
those states where minority ethnic groups come to feel that they are not represented
adequately, such groups may react by attempting to make life so unpleasant for the
majority that the majority will allow them to secede with the territory that they
occupy or by provoking the majority to commit such atrocities that the rest of the
world will feel compelled to intervene. There is no simple formula for a successful

multiethnic state. It takes hard and constant work to stop ethnic feelings in either the majority or the minority community from being stirred up by the unscrupulous.

RIGA, LATVIA, March 1993, in the parliament building. The prime minister of Latvia has asked to spend a full day with the Bank team that has prepared the first economic report on the country. The thirst for knowledge is extraordinary, and the potential role of the Bank as a mentor is a very exciting one. Transition will be an uphill battle for Latvia, and the situation at the moment is very unstable. The population of Latvia has a small majority of ethnic Latvians but a very large Russian minority, and in Riga 70 percent of the people are Russian, mainly factory workers. The factories are now producing very little and are unable to pay their workers, yet they are not shedding labor because of the health, housing, and other services provided to factory workers. Alcohol abuse is a serious problem, and we are accosted on the street at night. Our local representative comes to the office with a black eye from an attempted robbery. The husband of one of our colleagues has opened a small bakery and has been approached by the local mafia to pay protection at the rate of 10 percent. He has decided to hold his ground and not make the payment, but he tells us that he has heard of another storekeeper who made the payment but whose premises were subsequently vandalized by a rival gang. The group to which he had paid protection money compensated him for the attack. We later get a letter alleging corruption in using the proceeds of a World Bank loan. Apparently a shipment of wheat valued at half a million U.S. dollars was never actually received. Our investigation uncovers a trail of phony documentation and leaves no doubt of the accuracy of the allegations. We declare misprocurement and require the government to refund the money. This is the wild, wild East.

Nowhere is the poor fit between the apparatus of the state and the multiple ethnicities of populations more serious than in Africa. The nexus between the access to rents that derive from control of the state (especially where there are mineral resources) and the complex patchwork of tribal and language groups that make up most of the African continent has created an environment of instability. In country after country, effective leadership emerges for a spell and seems to be pulling things together, only to be overtaken by the buildup of corruption and the desire of other tribal or ethnic groups to get their share of the spoils. The probability of forging meaningful national identities in many African states seems very low, yet without such identity the prospects for stable nation-states are bleak. At some point, it will be necessary to resume the discussions of pan-Africanism or at least some kind of subregional groupings. It is very difficult to see how a country such as Malawi will be able on its own, even with generous aid flows, to generate the income surpluses needed to support expanded consumption and production levels.

One of the great absurdities of our century is the continued obsession that many nations and ethnic groups have with the possession of land. In the 21st century, land is no longer an important element in a nation's wealth or international stature. Small economies such as Korea and Taiwan, China, have been able to achieve substantial income and influence. Yet countries are still willing to go to war to gain possession of small coastal islands or disputed border-land areas of little or no economic value. Our vulnerability as human beings to the exploitation of politicians who seek to inflame national feelings around land is one of the most depressing aspects of the human condition.

BELGRADE, YUGOSLAVIA, October 1978. We are dining with a group of Yugoslav officials in Belgrade. While many think that Yugoslavia will not survive after Tito goes, I am convinced that the things that unify Yugoslavs will outweigh the traditional ethnic considerations. After all, Serbo-Croatian is a lingua franca, all young men do military service together in the Yugoslav army, and most of the people I am dining with seem to have wives or girlfriends from one of the other republics of the Yugoslav federation. I am much more concerned about the strange economic system that has evolved. The factories are essentially collectives with different guilds (they call them BOALs or basic organizations of associated labor) contracting with each other. They are producing for a protected domestic market, and the quality is very poor. I visit one of these factories and am given a gift of a pair of underpants. I happily wear them the next day, only to find by evening that the elastic holding them up has lost its tension (not, I may add, on account of my waistline, which is still modest at that stage). The difficulty for the Bank in working in the Yugoslav system is finding out who is in charge. Which people are actually making decisions, and where are they getting their information?

BUCHAREST, ROMANIA, March 1979, the main railway station. I have asked the interpreter on our current mission what had happened to the interpreter on our previous mission, and he had nodded to me to follow him into the station. As the train passes and the background noise is at its maximum, he tells me that his predecessor had defected during a trip to Washington, D.C., and that, since he had shared a room with his predecessor, he was also under suspicion and had to be very careful. We have been struggling to support the efforts of those in the Romanian government who want to liberalize the economy in the hope that such efforts can also produce some political liberalization, but it is evident that they are going nowhere. The government statistics are largely fiction, and we are red-faced when someone points out that there is a huge inconsistency between the relatively low income level that our reports show for Romania and the very high growth rates that the government says have been achieved year in and year out and which we have been happily reproducing in our analysis and projections. If the growth rates had been correct, then Romanian incomes would be at about the Japanese level. We are a lifeline for the beleaguered officials. At dinner in a noisy restaurant, one of them leans over to me while the music is playing and says that they are enormously appreciative of the efforts of the Bank because "nous sommes tres isoles ici [we are very isolated here]."

At the closing session of a Poverty Reduction and Economic Management conference two years ago, Johannes Linn, the former vice president of the Europe and Central Asia Region of the Bank, summed up the lessons of his Bank career with these words: "It's the politics, stupid." Perhaps the most important gap in the Bank's work is that our frequent naiveté about political economy leads to a failure to factor political realities systematically into the economic equation. For too many years, it was practically an article of faith of the International Monetary Fund and the Bank that we did not take political considerations into account. It was regarded as unprofessional to speculate on political realities and on how our economic advice could affect or be affected by them. Because the Bank cannot and should not take an active role in the political scene in a country, civil society and the nongovernmental organizations (NGOs) become the proxy for such a view. But they create an additional dynamic and can increase the unpredictability of the environment. In many of OED's country studies, the political economy factors come through strongly, and with hindsight the question arises of how the Bank could have acted in a particular way. The trouble is that at the time it is extremely difficult to predict which way a political situation will evolve. As a consequence, we are reluctant to write off countries or governments in which we interact with some committed individuals who seem capable of acquiring a strong enough power base to provide leadership for change. Our biases run in favor of doing something and of supporting those who speak our language. So more analysis is needed, but we should not expect much change in the way we do business until we have internalized many years of lessons.

One Size Does Not Fit All

PHNOM PENH, CAMBODIA, May 2003. With 32 aid donors in Cambodia, coordination becomes difficult. There are a limited number of government officials to interact with, and the donors compete for their attention. This situation has taken the form of a pervasive system of salary top-ups. Everything requires an extra payment—attending meetings and seminars, writing reports, and supervising programs. The average salary of a Cambodian government official is US$20 to US$40 a month. The average family in Phnom Penh requires something like US$200 a month for subsistence. It is evident that salary levels are unacceptably low, and indeed lecturers in private universities in Phnom Penh can earn US$1,000 to US$2,000 a month. Government salaries need to be increased, but how? Numbers could be reduced, yet 140,000 government officials for a country of 12 million people is not unreasonable. The government hopes to reduce this figure by 10 to 20 percent, but that reduction will not make much dent on salary levels. The dilemma is terrible and constrains the effectiveness of the Bank, which has a policy of not providing salary top-ups to government officials. This is part of the reason the Poverty Reduction Strategy Paper (PRSP) process that we are helping the government put in place has not achieved more traction.

"You Bank people always say that one size does not fit all, but when push comes to shove, that is the way you act." An NGO representative in Phnom Penh said that to me recently, and there is much truth in his statement. The diversity of countries is an obvious lesson, yet it is one on which we often do not act. Basic models need to be adapted to meet the needs of particular countries and even parts of the same country, yet doing so is difficult for a large bureaucracy. Our headquarters-based structure with a very heavy oversight function of the executive directors makes it even more difficult. In Phnom Penh, our discussions on the PRSP process are good examples of the problem. The PRSP model fits countries that have achieved certain levels of capacity and have a degree of motivation and leadership commitment to development. It is much less suited to a country such as Cambodia, where neither of these conditions exists. Instead of trying to put in place some of the preconditions through education and training, the Bank and others jumped straight into a PRSP, which in many respects was an empty shell with its likely effect being very limited.

Public and Private Ownership

We work with the public sector, and our basic development model is one in which the government strategizes and puts in place the conditions for development. Until the 1990s, we never had the slightest doubt that physical and social infrastructure was part of the government's role and responsibility. During the 1970s, the Bank actively supported the development of public sector manufacturing enterprises with an industry department to provide assistance in this area. A great deal of analysis was devoted to how to make public enterprises efficient. For a while, the French *plan-contrat* (upfront, agreed-on outcomes with incentive payments associated with achieving them) was the rage, and the Bank was trying to persuade enterprises throughout the developing world to adopt this approach. The interest in privatization did not derive from ideology so much as from desperation. Nothing seemed to work. Public enterprises everywhere were a fiscal drain, and even loss-makers had their cash flow prey to rent-seekers. For this reason, the Bank climbed on the bandwagon of privatization in the mid 1980s.

In general, few would now question that privatization of enterprises operating in competitive markets has been a genuine success story. The real controversy relates to the privatization of infrastructure. Some of the designs that the Bank pushed for infrastructure privatization would have been cutting edge, even in the major industrial countries. Telecommunications seems to work quite well in the private sector, perhaps because it has less historical baggage than some of the other areas, but even here the availability of mobile telephone connections makes privatization of traditional telecommunications services far less important than previously. Most rents in large-scale infrastructure accrue at the procurement end rather than at the production end. The Bank needs to focus much more on national procurement systems and try to put in place the kinds of checks and balances we have in our own projects. If this can be done, then reliance on public sector–owned infrastructure may prove viable. Despite the efforts of the Bank, there is very little evidence that the lower-middle-income and lower-income countries will be able to put in place the kind of regulatory environment needed for efficient functioning of private infrastructure services. At the same time, the transaction costs for the government of the privatization process and the risks of its yielding substantial rents are very high. The Bank has proceeded as if the burden of proof were on the government as to why public infrastructure should not be privatized. This attitude needs to be reversed, and it must be demonstrated quite clearly that the efficiency gains are likely to outweigh the potential costs of privatization.

To some extent, the focus on privatization diverted the Bank's attention from the much more important need to develop small and medium enterprises (SMEs), which are the engine of growth and employment in most developing countries. That effort was a primary focus of Bank work in the 1970s and early 1980s, with financial intermediary lending used as an instrument for supporting SMEs. But with the shift from specialized banking, the Bank relinquished the main instrument available to support this sector and, in effect, left the task to the International Finance Corporation (IFC). Because private sector development was no longer a primary lending activity for the Bank, there was a weakening of the analytic support and not enough focus on ensuring the right environment for private sector activity. Through the years, the division of labor between the Bank and the IFC in this area became stronger. That partition needs to be reversed if we are to do a more effective job of internalizing the needs of private sector development in country programs. Although there have been some token efforts to strengthen the integration of the Bank and IFC, if anything the drift is toward increasing separation as IFC expands relative to the Bank and as the IFC's corporate profile becomes more prominent. From the perspective of a country director, the case seems overwhelming for integrating the strategic dimension of the Bank's and IFC's work in a country and putting it under the purview of a single country director.

SEROWE, BOTSWANA, January 1985. We have asked to talk with some local entrepreneurs and see some small enterprises in operation. We are taken to one enterprise that imports large packages of sugar from South Africa and breaks these up into smaller packages for the local market. South Africa produces these small packages and at a considerably lower price than the Botswana producer, but the government, by applying differential taxes to larger bulk sugar quantities and smaller packets, has made this local enterprise profitable. Later we visit Francistown in the north of the country, and here we meet with local businessmen. I am especially impressed by a former mailman, who had taken early retirement three years ago and invested in a small construction firm with about nine employees working for him. I ask him why he is not expanding and what he would require to do so. I expect him to talk about access to bank credit or skilled labor, but instead he looks me in the eye and says, "Rome wasn't built in a day."

Population Growth

KATHMANDU, NEPAL, March 1970. We are not in a country where economic policy is a relevant topic for review and discussion. Here the Bank is concerned about helping to build key development institutions, particularly the banking system. As I step out of the government offices into the streets of Kathmandu and visit the villages around the valley and towns in the hills, I begin to understand the difference between low income and poverty. There is richness to the cultural and natural environments that makes one wonder if development will bring better lives to these people. But already we are aware of a serious concern on the horizon—the population in the hill villages is growing at rates that cannot be sustained by the limited agricultural land.

The Swiss have a special interest in Nepal as a kindred, landlocked, mountainous country. They have an integrated development project in the Jiri Valley, which is some distance from the capital. The project has forestry, livestock, health, education, and other components, and with Swiss assistance, the villagers are now producing a very passable cheese served in the hotels in Kathmandu. I am talking to the United Nations Development Programme resident representative, who has just returned from a visit to the project and has asked the villagers about the benefits of the various components. On the forestry component, the villagers replied, "We have had no benefits. Before they came we could simply go into the forests and chop the wood we needed. Now we are no longer allowed to do this." On the livestock component, the villagers said, "Before they came we could graze our cattle anywhere. Now we are no longer able to do this." On the health component, the villagers simply stated, "Before they came we had no sickness here!"

KATHMANDU, NEPAL, April 2001. After more than 20 years, I am back in Kathmandu. It is a saddening experience. The population of the valley has grown from 100,000 to 1 million, and it is hard to find a tree or a green space. Garbage is strewn on the sides of the roads, and many of the handsome traditional buildings have been torn down and replaced by featureless new ones. Large amounts of donor funding seem to have served mainly to provide rents for politicians and consulting opportunities for former civil servants, who are now running NGOs. Nepal must have the largest number of NGOs per capita of any country in the world. Meanwhile, much of the country is under the control of Marxist rebels, and few jobs are available outside the tourism sector. I speak with the Planning Commission and discover that it has no way of tracking whether the aid received is actually resulting in outcomes on the ground. I suggest that the commission consider a monitoring and evaluation system and that the Bank would be willing to provide support. The head of the Planning Commission thanks me for my offer and explains that such systems have already been provided on three previous occasions with donor support, but that they fell into disuse within months because no one showed the slightest interest in the information that was generated.

In recent years, population growth has become the topic that "dares not speak its name." There is an alliance of the right, which has concerns about birth control and abortion, and the left, which sees population planning as a racist effort to limit the numbers of the nonwhite populations of the world. Even the environmental NGOs have been silent on this issue, yet the expansion of the global population is surely the greatest contributor to environmental pressure and degradation. The impact of population growth in much of the developing world has been devastating, yet we have moved population growth back to where corruption was in the 1980s—something we wring our hands about but not a variable to be addressed. The demographic transition is supposed to take care of too rapid population growth. And so it has but, unfortunately, not at the pace required to enable countries' economies to grow as rapidly as they require to make a significant dent on poverty. The Polish economy has grown at only about 4 percent on average in the past decade, but given its zero population growth, that 4 percent translates directly into increases in real income. Many

African countries have managed economic growth of around 4 percent, but coupled with 3 percent population growth, their achievement has hardly made a dent on living standards, especially when some worsening of income distribution is factored into the account.

LILONGWE, MALAWI, February 1981. When I came to the Bank in 1966, I had assumed that I would be working on Africa, underestimating the difficulties for a South African national at that time. Malawi and Botswana are two of the few exceptions, and I am glad for the opportunity that they provide me. Malawi is under the sway of the extraordinary Dr. Hastings Kamuzu Banda. He rules with an iron hand, and government officials respond to every question we put with a pause that seems to factor in how their response will be interpreted by the ruler. He has created an elite educational institution for boys. At the institution, they are treated as future rulers, with first-class food and services—all paid by the state. Meanwhile, most of the population has no access to education or medical services. Still the tradeoff relative to many other parts of Africa is the evident peace and stability, and it seems on the surface to be a reasonable one.
Lilongwe—which Banda has made his capital, since it is in the center of the country—is a charming town, with flowers everywhere, and the South Africans have provided funding for the construction of simple and functional but attractive government offices. I walk into a village near the shores of Lake Malawi and talk with some young boys, who tell me of their ambitions to be lawyers and doctors. The fish from the lake and the ample supply of naturally growing tree fruits and root crops mean that the population around the lake has scarcely any need for cultivation.

LILONGWE, MALAWI, December 2002. Once again I return to a country after a 20-year absence. It is perhaps even more saddening than Nepal. At each meeting I attend, there is a brief exchange among the officials present asking who has been to the hospital, how a colleague is getting along, and whether anyone went to the funeral last week. This is testimony to the impact of AIDS, which has left scarcely a single government office untouched. The government has arranged to import drugs and an adviser to the president tells me of the plan for distribution. The highest priority will be for doctors, then for senior government officials, then for teachers and health workers. Malawi had around 4 million people when I was last here, and now it has 12 million. In a country where, at that time, it was possible to live well from hunting, fishing, and gathering, there is now malnutrition and hunger. Government expenditure works out at US$50 per person. That amount is the total available for foreign embassies, the police force, health and education services, and whatever else needs to be done. Malawi seems to have spent 20 years running just to stay in the same place, with little likelihood of forward movement in the years ahead.

Process Is as Important as Substance

Since the 1980s, when the Bank reached the conclusion that projects alone could not promote development in the absence of a policy environment that created incentives for efficient growth, we have operated on the basis of a very simple, probably simplistic, business model. The starting point was to carry out analysis of the economic situation in a country and identify the key issues. We discussed these with the government and designed adjustment loans that incorporated both institutional and policy measures to address these issues in their conditionality. This business model of analysis—conditionality—worked well initially. Countries were struggling to deal with the debt crisis of the late 1970s, and many had major policy distortions for which corrections could often yield quick benefits. Over time, however, the effectiveness of this approach diminished. It proved less effective in dealing with the kind of policy fine-tuning and institutional support that was needed to consolidate the broad policy changes that had taken place earlier. We found it much harder to argue that these changes needed to be of a particular kind or to associate very clear outcomes in terms of income growth, poverty reduction, or employment with them. In the absence of major policy changes, we tended to use a large number of conditions to defend the case for the value of our policy interventions. Then we found ourselves banging the table to argue that we could not go ahead unless some condition that we argued was vital and the government saw as peripheral was met. This scenario made for a very difficult relationship with governments and an increasing perception of the Bank as arrogant.

This perception of arrogance came directly from the business model. Many of us were deeply hurt by the imputation of personal values to a professional approach. This outcome was perhaps inevitable—for example, debt collectors are almost invariably called heartless, even though debt collection is an important part of the system, and there is no evidence that the individuals doing that job care less about humanity than anyone else. So we became the arrogant enforcers of what was caricatured as the Washington Consensus model—a one-size-fits-all set of policy prescriptions for borrowing countries.

As the 1980s and early 1990s wore on, we found ourselves increasingly squeezed between the views of the right—the Bank was a massive global subsidy scheme set up to support governments to do things much better done by the private sector—and the views of the left—the Bank was the puppet institution of powerful Western political and business interests willing to despoil the environment and coerce developing countries to follow policies leading to further environmental degradation to secure repayment of loans that should not have been made in the first place. (The environmental NGOs were ambivalent about coercion of developing countries; they were quite content to see it take place if it matched their agenda.) The corrosion of international public opinion and client support for the Bank brought morale in the institution to very low levels.

We needed some strong medicine, difficult though it was for insiders to identify that need, and we got it in the form of World Bank President Jim Wolfensohn. What Wolfensohn has brought to the Bank, above anything else, is the awareness that *how* we do things is as important as *what* we do. Years of OED evaluations had drummed home the importance of country ownership of the development strategy and the supporting policies and programs, yet we had been unable to find a way to incorporate that in the business model. Indeed, it can be argued that we have still not succeeded in doing so.

At least in poor countries, we now have a process overlay through the PRSP process, which has the potential to become an alternative business model. The process elements of the PRSP model emphasize ownership of the strategy (the country in the driver's seat), transparency of the strategy process (participation), donor coordination (partnership), and careful monitoring of implementation outcomes (results focus).

The constant repetition of these principles, like a mantra, has seeped through into the consciousness of most Bank employees, so that there is a real attempt to embody them in what is done. But the basic business model has not been rethought in terms of these principles. The rhetoric, for example, of project appraisals and supervision still echoes the approach of a quite different period in the Bank. It still implies a separation from the country at a time when we need to see ourselves as being part of the same team. OED often points out that there are cases in which it rates the Bank's performance as satisfactory but the country's performance as unsatisfactory. I find this objectionable. If the country is not performing satisfactorily, then I have failed, and the Bank has failed. It may not have been our fault, and we may have done our best, but it is failure nonetheless. I have been to too many meetings where the objective seems to be how can we save some honor in defeat?

BEIJING, CHINA, April 1983. We are in a meeting room in the Beijing office. A 16-member Bank mission is here to look at trade issues. The government has assigned a 16-member Chinese team to work with us as part of the mission. Each of us has a counterpart who is to watch and learn. At the initial meeting, we each present our ideas about the area we are covering, and our counterparts take notes. By the end of the mission, they are participating much more actively, and it has evolved into a genuine team. I regard my counterpart as a colleague and talk with her about policies and whether they are moving in the right direction. I am moved when, at the end of the mission, she turns to me and says, "Thank you, you have been my teacher." Of course, I have learned equally as much from her. We visited a number of new factories set up by foreign investors where everything except unskilled labor is imported. The Chinese seem eager to learn from the experience of others, unlike the Indians, whose approach is that one should learn by reinventing the wheel.

WARSAW, POLAND, September 1998, a conference room in the World Bank office. As country director, I am being debriefed on the results of the negotiations on the coal sector adjustment loan. The coal industry is one of Poland's most serious problem areas, and to his credit, Deputy Prime Minister Leszek Balcerowicz has decided to take it on. He has asked for the Bank's help—not as a matter of securing money, since Poland can fund the program from its own resources, but rather for the independence, structure, and discipline that the Bank can bring to programs it supports, especially those that cut across individual ministries and are difficult for governments (especially coalition governments) to manage. Poland provides a substantial subsidy for every ton of coal mined, keeping about 140,000 workers employed at very heavy costs to the budget. The miners have a life expectancy that is 13 years shorter than the other men in their community, yet they cling to those jobs and even want to ensure that their sons will have an opportunity to work in the mines. The government has designed a voluntary program offering generous packages to those willing to leave. The Bank's efforts are (a) to ensure that the buyouts are part of a comprehensive program leading to a viable, commercial coal sector and (b) to deal with the social and environmental issues that restructuring will raise. My colleagues tell me that something exciting had happened during the negotiations. The four deputy ministers—economy, finance, labor, and environment—who barely knew each other at the beginning of the week, had, in the days that followed, begun to understand the synergies from their working together on this common problem. By the end of the week, they had indeed become a team—an unexpected, but vitally important, benefit of our involvement.

VILNIUS, LITHUANIA, May 1999. We are discussing the conditionality for the upcoming structural adjustment loan with the deputy minister of finance in her conference room. The transformation in Lithuania has been striking. The country has confounded predictions and caught up with its Baltic siblings in the race to prepare for EU accession. We have played a modest but useful role in this process, particularly in helping to get the energy and banking sectors up to speed. We are supporting a package of reforms with the government that will strengthen the program in these and other areas. With only months to go before a new election, I am concerned about the attitude of a new administration (the incumbent government is well down in the polls). I propose that we actively consult with the opposition and other members of parliament about the proposed measures. The deputy minister opposes this suggestion. She argues strongly that the timing will almost force the opposition to take issue with a set of measures that ordinarily would not raise any difficulties for them. She suggests we go ahead and present them with a fait accompli when they come into office. I have mixed feelings about this. There is some truth in what she says, but she is underestimating both the extent to which the opposition can take a balanced view of the proposed policy changes and the risks of reversal in the absence of consultation. In terms of short-term realpolitik, it seems the right decision, but in the longer run, it is not the kind of relationship we want to build. In the circumstances, we decide to limit ourselves to some discreet one-on-one consultations with opposition politicians whom we have worked with in the past. They are very supportive of the measures that will be part of the agreement. I discover from my successor after the election that there is indeed a new coalition, but the deputy finance minister has been elevated to the position of minister and is now quite unhappy that we are insisting on some of the conditionality that she herself had agreed to in her previous position.

Has the Bank Added Value?

YEREVAN, ARMENIA, April 1993. I am on my first visit to Armenia. Even in April it is cold, and the guesthouse I am staying in has enormous draughty rooms. I am told that Leonid Brezhnev stayed in the room I am using, which may have been fine when there was heating, but Armenia has no money to pay for Russian oil. I gingerly wet the towel in the mornings and put some soap on it to try to keep myself clean. Colleagues who visited earlier have had to bring some of their own food, and one told me of waking up to find that some water left in the bathtub had frozen overnight. But more depressing than the cold is the devastation of the past two years. All the trees in the city have been chopped down for firewood. The prime minister takes me to visit some parts of the city, and while we are walking, an elderly woman comes up to us. She is well groomed and elegantly dressed, but her eyes are burning. She says to the prime minister that this is her last coat, and she is going to have to sell it for food. "You have made a country where only the wolves will survive," she cries. It is difficult to get these words out of one's mind. The encouraging part is how committed the people we work with are. Our own staff members feel more passion about trying to assist Armenia than I have seen in any other country where I have worked.

In general, the Bank has been most effective when it can work with a government committed to the objectives of growth and poverty reduction, with a substantial level of capacity to implement programs and policies needed to achieve those objectives. It is easy to caricature this observation as saying that only countries that do not need the Bank can benefit from it, but the witticism would not explain why so many countries that have commitment and capacity continue to judge that they need the Bank's financial resources, policy advice, and technical expertise.

The financial resources of the Bank are no longer as good as they once were. Borrowers in emerging markets can often match or even better Bank interest rates, at least for short-term money. The big advantage Bank financial resources continue to offer is the availability of 15- to 20-year money. Rather curiously, some countries actually view long-term funding of development as undesirable, as limiting the choices of future generations. The Bank has done a poor job of communicating the usefulness of a country portfolio that includes some amount of longer-term funding. Such a portfolio is useful both because of the reduced vulnerability through the increased stability it provides and because future generations will be better able to repay these debts. That position is not inconsistent with prudent debt management and efficient use of borrowed funds.

The International Development Association (IDA) continues to be one of the most important innovations of the last half century in terms of development funding. It is a pity that, after all these years, we are still on a treadmill of three-year replenishments. One understands the desire of the donor community for a short leash, but there must be more efficient ways of handling this wish than endless negotiations. For much of my career in the Bank, we tended to treat IDA funds as grants. We recognized that countries would need to repay the principal, but we felt secure in the view that we could always refinance the annual amortization through new IDA funding. Eventually, we paid a price for our failure to recognize that, for countries that are not growing, the burden of principal repayments can be unsustainable. We are beginning to assess the creditworthiness implications of IDA credits, as well as of Bank loans.

BERNE, SWITZERLAND, May 1990, the ballroom of a hotel in the Swiss capital where we are holding the final sessions of the IDA negotiations. Switzerland is in the process of joining the World Bank Group. It has always contributed to IDA, but with its impending membership comes a desire to take a more prominent role—thus the invitation to come to Berne. The negotiations have been long and complex, as usual. IDA donations are governed by the concept of burden sharing, which means that each donor wants to set a limit on the share of the total it is willing to provide. In essence, this means that any donor that tries to reduce its total contribution will, by definition, cause everyone else's contribution to decline as well, given that shares must remain constant. On top of this, since donors commit in their domestic currencies, the shifts in exchange rates can mean large variations in contributions to keep shares constant. Our job as the staff team is to come up with increasingly far-fetched and creative ways to maintain the shares of each donor while trying to push up the total. The way we are doing this is essentially to leave a gap so that the total of every country's contribution adds up to considerably less than 100 percent. Our problem is then how to fill this gap, and with each replenishment we find a new gimmick to do this.

On top of the mechanics of funding, each country has its own agenda that we need to incorporate. The Nordics want assurances that the share of IDA assistance used for social purposes will continue to increase; the Americans want reference to the private sector in practically every paragraph; the Canadians are concerned that the Caribbean islands, which are part of their constituency, continue to get IDA assistance even though some have per capita incomes of around US$10,000; the French have negotiated a minimum of 45 percent of IDA aid for Africa; and the British are concerned lest the share of adjustment lending go above 25 percent. But we have a trump card. For a year now, we have been meeting with the deputies from the IDA donor countries, and over that time, we have gradually begun to feel ourselves as part of a team. By now, at the end of the negotiations, there is a common desire to be able to return to capitals with an agreement that can be proclaimed a success. At the 11th hour, it all comes together, and we are able to drink champagne with our Swiss hosts.

Over the years, Bank investment lending has become weighted down with numerous safeguards and fiduciary management requirements. One borrower government recently estimated those costs as being equivalent to 300 basis points. This pattern raises very real questions as to whether project investment lending is still a viable instrument for the 21st century. The Bank needs to consider whether it should move all its lending to a more macro level, where it finances government budgets and uses conditionality to try to improve country systems for managing environmental costs, procurement, and financial management. This approach is not inconsistent with focused sectoral program support. Our support for coal sector restructuring in Poland was carried out entirely through adjustment loans, but it brought major changes in environmental management and in the financial accounting and procedures of the coal companies. The time has come to consider moving entirely from projects to programs with clearly defined objectives and the measurements associated with them.

TALLINN, ESTONIA, October 1994, the prime minister's office. The prime minister is in his early 30s and is one of the oldest members of the cabinet. He is very appreciative of the role of the Bank in helping get the transition process started and says that our ana-

lytic work particularly has played an important role in providing a clear sense of direction for policy reform. A few days later, we leave the capital on a car trip to visit some rural areas and pass by a simple but solid-looking house of a local government official. We ask if we can go and talk with him about some of the challenges he sees in transition. We are welcomed into his home, and when he hears the name of one of our colleagues, he exclaims that he is delighted to meet him since he has just been reading his book. He takes out the Bank economic report on Estonia, which does indeed have our colleague's name as principal author on the inside front cover. Given the sophistication and intellectual attainments of the Estonian population and the rapidity with which transition is taking place, it is little surprise (though disappointing) when, a year later, the prime minister tells me that the government wants to limit borrowing from official sources and that he sees little future role for the Bank.

BRATISLAVA, SLOVAK REPUBLIC, October 2003, the office of the deputy prime minister. We are discussing, as part of the Bank's quality assurance function, the contribution our work has made to the Slovakian "miracle." In about five years since the departure of Prime Minister Vladimir Meciar, the Slovak Republic has been transformed. It is now attracting the largest per capita levels of foreign direct investment of any Eastern European country. The deputy prime minister gives a great deal of credit to the Bank for its help in this turnaround. In particular, our lending and conditionality for the banking sector seem to have been instrumental in helping the Slovak Republic get on its feet. Other work by the Bank on poverty and social issues has also been very helpful. Among the most interesting things we are doing is our work on the Roma. It is evident in our discussions that the Slovak authorities have mixed feelings about the spotlight the Bank is shining on the problems of the Roma. I am beginning to understand how difficult this issue is. There are problems in educating Roma children in the public school system, and the investments that have been made to upgrade the housing and infrastructure in the Roma settlements have not been maintained. I hope the Bank will move carefully in this area and try to learn from approaches with which the countries themselves are experimenting, rather than simply charging ahead with projects and loans as we are too often inclined to do in our eagerness to solve difficult problems that have been around for many years and will be around for many more.

Clients consistently indicate that they value the analytic work of the Bank, and it is easy to point to Bank reports that have had a significant effect on policies and public opinion in countries. In Poland, for example, the work on corruption brought to public attention an area about which the Poles had been relatively complacent. The work on exports helped to head off a new wave of protectionism that was building steam in the country. The work the Bank has done on the Roma in Central Europe has been unprecedented in looking across countries at a significant issue in the subregion and helping to share approaches and problems. I have little doubt that these examples can be multiplied for every country the Bank works with. That said, we have no objective basis for judging the cost-effectiveness of this work, which is a free good to the country. For every successful study, there is probably one that had little effect.

A couple of decades ago, a colleague told me of passing by a government office in Cairo and seeing a familiar-looking logo on a carton on a shelf inside. On entering, he found a large number of unopened boxes of World Bank economic reports on Egypt stored there. One hopes things have improved, but too many of our reports are still prepared with little reference to the likely interest, readership, and effect in the country. We need to do more upfront to build a constituency in the country for particular Bank analytic exercises. This effort means much more involvement of country counterparts. Why are country counterpart teams of the kind that China sets up not the routine way of doing business? Why are we not preceding our analytic (or project and program work for that matter) with joint learning events at which Bank staff members and country counterparts are exposed to similar efforts elsewhere, drawing on the institution's global knowledge, and then work through together what would be required to make the task at hand more useful?

An important benefit that countries derive from the Bank—the reason that many middle-income countries still come to us—is that we provide a structure and coordinating framework for key programs. The more complex the program and the more it requires intersectoral coordination, the more likely it is that the Bank can add value. The Bank provides a temporal framework, a timeline for various activities to be undertaken and completed, a managerial framework, and a clear indication of which actors are necessary to meet the objectives and what their respective inputs are. In addition, the Bank provides regular monitoring services and reports to the government to allow it to assess progress. In the late 1990s, when Latvia no longer needed Bank adjustment lending, we were asked to provide a shadow adjustment loan so the government could have the benefit of benchmarks set up by the Bank as a way of measuring whether it was managing economic change effectively. Latvia subsequently became the first country to use the development drawdown option.

The most difficult problem for the Bank is how to operate effectively in the gray middle—that is, the large group of countries between the committed, competent states and the failed states. In this area, there is probably little alternative to patience. We need to be in for the long haul and not to read too much into either the short bursts of progress after elections or the long periods of stagnation or backsliding leading up to the next election. Looking back, I have too often let myself be taken in by ministers or officials telling the Bank what they knew we wanted to hear and then making myself believe the empty promises, even when all the evidence suggested that there was neither the will nor the capacity to follow through on them. We need to put more emphasis on track records and more reliance on what is done than what is said. But in countries such as Moldova, Georgia, and Ukraine —and initially even in Belarus—from 1993 to 1996, my colleagues and I so badly wanted the government to take decisive measures and succeed in moving the country through the transition process that we confused the rhetoric of a few individuals, who were often handpicked to deal with the Bank, with a serious commitment to change. On balance, we would have done better through greater skepticism, less lending, and more serious efforts to build country capacity and work collaboratively.

TBILISI, GEORGIA, June 1994, the office of the minister of finance. The minister of finance seems to have little sense of the fiscal problems facing the country and his appointment is understandable only in terms of President Eduard Shevardnadze's eagerness to keep a balance among powerful political and ethnic groups within Georgia. Unfortunately, this is a key appointment, and in a country where the share of revenues in GDP has declined to about 3 percent, it is difficult to foresee much progress while he is in office. We are extremely concerned about the potential for disaster in Georgia through the lack of maintenance of basic infrastructure. A number of dams and bridges are in such fragile condition that a serious accident could result. Georgian food is the best I have had in the countries of the former Soviet Union, and we are taken to a delightful restaurant with traditional Georgian music as accompaniment to an excellent meal. When I get up to visit the men's room, I pass the kitchen and see a large number of bags of flour that indicate in large letters that they have been provided as relief assistance by one of the donors.

MINSK, BELARUS, December 1993. I meet Prime Minister Vyacheslav Kebich, who explains why he is reluctant to take the kind of measures that transition will require, in particular to impose a hard budget constraint on state enterprises. He contrasts the situation in Belarus with that in Lithuania, where income levels have fallen by 50 percent since the breakup of the Soviet Union. He discussed this with the Lithuanian president, and they agreed, he says, that the difference was that Lithuanian nationalism made people willing to accept that level of sacrifice. Belarus, by contrast, has very little national identity, and he does not feel that his government could survive an austerity program. His successor, President Aleksandr Lukashenko, whom I meet a year later, is convinced that all the reforming countries are out of step and that he alone is right to maintain the structures and policies of the ancien régime. Only heavily subsidized energy from Russia makes it possible to sustain this position. Nevertheless, Lukashenko is eagerly seeking foreign direct investment from Western companies. "I told the CEOs that whatever they need, they only have to come to me, and I will see that they get it." He seems surprised at the lack of response and attributes it to political intervention. I try without success to explain that what is needed are rules of the game that are fair and stable.

KIEV, UKRAINE, September 1995, on a minibus. We are traveling out of Kiev to visit some collective farms. Ukraine is perhaps the greatest disappointment I have had to deal with because the gulf between its potential and its achievement is so huge and we seem unable to persuade the government to unleash the potential. The administration is woefully weak for a country of this size and educational achievements. The unwillingness to move away from collectivized agriculture is perhaps the biggest problem we have encountered. The heads of the collectives are extraordinarily powerful. On the way back on the bus, I observe the government officials who came from Kiev and the interpreters, all getting angrier and angrier as they discuss among themselves the way of life on the farms. I ask what the issue is. "The people who work on these farms are slaves, and the director is the tsar," they reply. "They need his permission to go to the dentist."

We have been struggling to find an entry into the Ukrainian economy, some area where we can support committed reformers and try to achieve visible changes. Our good experience in helping the Russians to reform the coal sector has led us to propose this area to the

Ukrainians. They seem eager for our help given the huge fiscal drain that inefficient coal enterprises represent—many of them are very deep mines with outdated equipment, and hardly a month passes without a newspaper report of a mine accident. We visit a mine in the Donetsk area and are taken first to the mine museum, where they show machinery, which is no longer in use. We are then taken to the mine. The machinery in the museum looks in far better condition and more trustworthy than the machinery in use. It is the end of the shift, and the workers come to the surface huddled together on the elevator, faces black and eyes glazed. It is a scene from the 19th century. The government has promised some critical actions on reform but has not followed through. As a consequence, we are holding up funding for the mining program. We continue to support a pilot program for closing three mines, a way of combining environmental and social services for the mines and the workers who will be laid off. The program is going well, and we are very optimistic that it will be a model for future actions. But when I later visit the deputy minister of planning, he screams at me that the World Bank is not providing the support we have promised and that all we are doing is some technical assistance for closing three mines. In the conference room in our office in Kiev, we are listening to a presentation by a professor from a local university on the economy of Ukraine. Our office has been holding these sessions every Wednesday evening for two years and inviting Ukrainian journalists to come and listen to discussions of important economic topics. This activity is not dominated by the World Bank agenda. The object is to help provide journalists gain literacy in the concepts of a market economy, so that they can create greater understanding among their readers. The journalists are impressive young men and women. If only the offices of government could be staffed with people of this caliber.

One of the more important lessons I have learned is the value of closeness to the client. I was a country director in Washington, D.C., from 1993 to 1997 for Armenia, the Baltic states, Belarus, Georgia, Moldova, and Ukraine, and then in Warsaw from 1997 to 2000 for Poland and the Baltic states. There was no comparison in terms of job satisfaction and effectiveness. In the field, the accountabilities seemed so much clearer, and the feedback loop was so much shorter. Decentralization forced the Bank to give far more responsibility to the country director, even though the pre-1997 system ostensibly integrated both the program and sector functions under the country director. Being on the spot enables the country director to identify demand and needs as they arise and to organize responses to them. At the same time, being on the spot enables the country director to call a halt to foundering programs where the client has withdrawn support. Program teams are often reluctant to cut their losses for fear that doing so will be interpreted as failure. At the same time, the country director in the field can have a direct effect on public opinion through a communications strategy and can judge firsthand how to position the Bank effectively in the country context.

The Architecture of International Development Support

PARIS, FRANCE, February 1991, a room in the Ministry of Finance. The donors have been discussing the possibility of earmarking part of IDA funding for programs to improve the global environment. We are very concerned about this because it means that money would be taken out of poverty reduction programs for this purpose. We are arguing that funding for this purpose should be additional. We have prepared a note identifying funding for biodiversity and reducing global warming as appropriate items for a new fund. We also argue that some of the countries that are currently not eligible for funding for eliminating ozone depleting substances under the Montreal Protocol—the transition countries—should be eligible to use these funds. The French have somewhat unexpectedly become our chief allies. They are concerned that IDA not be eroded for special purposes and have thought through our proposals very carefully. They suggest one addition to our list—marine life protection. A difficult issue is whether these new funds should be used only for the costs associated with the portion of the benefits that do not accrue to the country. We discuss at some length whether a country converting from coal- to gas-based electricity generation, for example, would receive full funding from the facility even if it would have made the conversion anyway on the basis of a least-cost plan for the energy sector. The discussion is inconclusive, and it is clear there will need to be much fine-tuning in the months and years ahead. A few months later we ask donors to participate in the first meeting of what we have decided to call the Global Environment Facility. There is much enthusiasm inside the Bank for our increased involvement in environmental issues, and one senior manager suggests renaming the institution the International Bank for Environment and Development.

The international system to support development is not a thing of beauty. It has evolved over the past 60 years in a way that defies logical explanation. The relationships between the World Bank Group and the International Monetary Fund, between the World Bank Group and the regional development banks (RDBs), between the international financial institutions and the United Nations (UN) development agencies, are all opaque. The costs in terms of overlapping administrative systems, funding, representation, and transaction costs for developing countries are enormous. We probably have to live with these costs because there is no consensus view of what a more rational and clearly structured system might look like, and the short-term political costs of changing the system seem daunting. That said, there is surely no excuse for not trying to reduce those costs at the margin. The current harmonization initiative that the Bank is spearheading, which goes beyond the international agencies, is a very worthwhile effort in this direction, but there is a strong argument for a more aggressive approach. For example, an integrated and planned approach to economic analysis would save a great deal of resources. There could be much greater sectoral specialization, considering, for instance, that it may not be worthwhile for the RDBs to duplicate the World Bank's capacity in areas such as health, education, and social welfare. In the UN system the integration of United Nations Development Programme and United Nations Conference on Trade and Development is an obvious step that would benefit both agencies. Reducing the transaction costs of the international system is not a matter for a one-off task force or study but should be an ongoing effort with a standing group of representatives from the different agencies with a clear mandate to move in this direction.

However, there are still gaps in the international system. In one important respect, the architecture seems incomplete—the absence of an analog for developing countries to the Organisation for Economic Co-operation and Development. The perspective on aid levels, modalities, and policies is lacking in those countries. There is no instrument for forging a consensus among developing countries on the major international issues of our day—this is done ad hoc, and the interests of small groups of highly vocal developing countries often dominate the overall dialogue. The large, relatively wealthy, developing countries—Brazil, Chile, China, India, and Mexico—can afford to devote resources to setting up and maintaining such a body. It would need a high degree of political independence to have the requisite credibility and would have to be staffed with the best and brightest analysts so that it is able to underpin policy positions with solid technical work.

Postscript

GUJARAT, INDIA, November 2003, a village in northern Gujarat near the Rann of Kutch. I am spending three days as the guest of Gauri and her husband. Gauri is the village coordinator for the Self-Employed Women's Association (SEWA), a remarkable organization that helps its members to improve their economic situation and the quality of their lives. She describes the events in her life, and I begin to see a pattern of life at the margin. I have often heard and used the word vulnerability but never really understood it until now. It means that in most years she and her family can earn what they require for their lives and even have a margin of resources for the small luxuries of village life. But every five or six years—the pattern is remarkably constant—an extraordinary event, such as a drought, a flood, an earthquake, or a wedding, wipes out their capital stock and what they have earned for the year and forces them to start over again and struggle for three years to get back to some sort of equilibrium. She has had two main jobs, one as a salt worker and the other as a sharecropper in the cotton fields. I ask her which of these jobs she enjoys more, fully expecting her to say that the work in the fields is much more pleasant than the desolate life on the salt pans. She clearly does not understand my question. She simply does not think about work that way.

Gauri has eight children and cannot read nor write. I am puzzled to find that she has no interest in her children attending school beyond the first four years in the village. Surely, further education is the key to breaking out of the cycle of vulnerability. She patiently explains that first it would be costly to send her children to the middle school in a village 9 kilometers away and would require substantial bus fares over the course of the year. Second and more importantly, she has seen what happened to a neighbor's son who was educated and has come back to the village after trying unsuccessfully to get a job in town. He refuses to work in the fields. Except for the youngest daughter, who is six, her children are all important contributors to the family's income or welfare. The teenage daughter cooks and cleans so that her mother can spend the day working. When she marries, the youngest daughter will take her place. Gauri has a sharecropping arrangement that gives her 30 percent of the income from some cotton fields, and her four sons are all living and working at the site some distance from the village. I find it very difficult to cast aside my belief that education is the lifeline for families like this, and I encourage her to keep the two youngest children at school as long as she can do so.

The day I am to leave the village, an elderly woman comes by, and I see Gauri take a small bag of flour and hand it to her. I ask why she has done this and learn that the elderly woman's children have gone to Ahmedabad and are no longer taking care of her, so Gauri and other villagers help her out with her daily needs. Later that evening, some of the women and young girls come over to visit. I ask about music in the village and am treated to an impromptu concert and dance. All of us have a good time. I had expected to feel pity and to be moved by the plight of the poor. Instead I find that, despite poverty, there is real quality to the life that Gauri and the villagers lead. What I feel above all is respect and admiration. Gauri and the ladies of SEWA are building better lives in the present brick by brick. I am doubtful that my years in development add up to theirs in terms of achievement, but the experience of meeting these remarkable people leaves me with no doubt that the task of trying to help people help themselves out of vulnerability and poverty is the most important of our time.

I recall wandering through a village in Bangladesh in the early 1970s and having a young girl come up to me, her eyes red and streaming with tears, an obvious case of conjunctivitis, easily curable with ointment. The only other foreigners she had seen had all been doctors, and she had assumed that I was one, too. I remember thinking to myself how much more satisfying it would have been if I were a doctor and had the means available to treat her. For economists, the connections between the medicines we prescribe and the patient's health are rarely so clear-cut and demonstrably effective. In the end, what matters is that we use our best judgment and work in good faith to assist countries to achieve better economic and social health and that we learn from both the things that go right and the things that go wrong. The most important lesson is to be open to learning and continuing to learn. It has been a privilege for me to spend nearly all my working life with colleagues and with counterparts who have been my teachers. I thank you all.

Phyllis Pomerantz

Former Country Director for
Mozambique and Zambia (1996–2000)

As the World Bank's chief learning officer (CLO), Phyllis Pomerantz is well versed in the latest technologies for communication and knowledge sharing. Yet she expresses nostalgia for her early years at the Bank, when landline telephones and carbon copies of documents were state of the art: "When you were on mission, nobody could find you!"

An American national, Phyllis's awareness of the developing world blossomed as a teenager, when she spent summers in Panama with her older brother, a former medical director for Latin America in the Peace Corps. After completing her Ph.D. in international development at the Fletcher School of Law and Diplomacy (Tufts University) in 1978, she taught political science for a year at Hartwick College in New York but found that academia did not satisfy her desire for engagement with the real world. "I wanted to do something about the problems I taught about," she says, and she left to join the World Bank as a Young Professional.

Phyllis spent much of her early career in the Bank as economist in the Brazil Agriculture Division of the Latin America and Caribbean Region, becoming its division chief in 1989 and maintaining a heavy schedule of travel and involvement in rural projects. "I still know North-east Brazil better than I know the United States," she says. She notes that, because communications technologies were more primitive then, an unintended consequence was to encourage more travel and face-to-face interaction by Bank teams with clients. Though the 1980s in Latin America are often dismissed as a "lost decade" for development, Phyllis takes a more optimistic view: "In the 1980s, we saw a resurgence of democracy in the region. There were the beginnings of more participation and a more active civil society. Clients were becoming more engaged in our projects, and I think that contributed to a rising tide of civic engagement and democratization."

Phyllis left the Latin America and Caribbean Region in 1992 to become division chief of infrastructure for southern Africa and then for country operations of that region two years later. Though she found that many of the lessons from her prior development experience translated to the African context, "The linear vision of progress was gone." Her role in the region was made even more challenging on her appointment as country director of Mozambique and Zambia in 1996 under a new pilot structure for country directors. "I was a guinea pig," she chuckles. Lacking many guidelines in the new system, "we had to make things up," crafting new procedures that were later adopted for country directors as a group. Though disappointed that Africa did not make greater strides toward sustainable growth during her years working there, Phyllis says that "witnessing Mozambique's transition from war to become one of the more hopeful countries in the region was very satisfying."

In 2000, Phyllis spent a year drafting a manuscript on aid relationships in Africa. Allowing her to "crystallize thoughts" on her experience in the region, "it was a logical progression" to her next job as the Bank's first CLO. "I was an academic, then a practitioner, and now as CLO I need to use a combination of analysis and experience." This combination of ideas and action is what attracted Phyllis to the Bank in the first place, and it is the reason she is still there, hoping to influence the next generation of Bank staff and managers.

3 A Little Luck and a Lot of Trust

Aid Relationships and Reform in Southern Africa

Phyllis Pomerantz

I HAVE SPENT NEARLY 30 YEARS—25 OF THEM AT THE WORLD BANK—THINKING about and working in international development. I worked for over a decade on Latin America—mostly on Northeast Brazil—before switching over to work on southern Africa. I went from being a generalist to a rural development specialist and then back again to generalist. I have supervised projects, prepared and appraised projects, negotiated projects, and written project completion reports. I have also written sector reports and Country Assistance Strategies (CASs), managed policy and debt relief operations, chaired consultative group meetings, and led the aid dialogue in two African countries. The work has been worthwhile, exciting, and gratifying. There have been times when I have been disillusioned and weighted down by failures, fatigue, and frustration. Other times, I have been buoyed by optimism, sometimes warranted, sometimes not. The biggest lesson I have learned is humility. I have contributed to some successes, but probably to an equal or greater number of failures. It is clear, at least to me, that there is no magic bullet to help the world's poor. Most of us who work in development agencies readily acknowledge that many of our past formulas for success have not worked despite our good intentions. The important thing is that we keep trying.

The Experience

My earliest years in the World Bank, working on integrated rural development programs in Northeast Brazil, laid the foundation for my later experience as country director for two of the poorest and most heavily indebted countries in Africa: Mozambique and Zambia. The Bank has been involved for several generations in poverty reduction projects in Northeast Brazil. I worked on both the so-called first generation and second generation, where the Bank supported statewide projects in all 10 Northeast states. The projects were big, complex, and—in many ways—innovative. For example, as far back as the mid 1980s, the Bank assisted in the financing of the program as a whole, including, as necessary, salaries and other recurrent costs, much as the sector investment programs do today. The program also channeled part of the funds to small rural communities for investments and services that the community would decide on and help implement. This was some time before the first social fund projects were approved elsewhere in the Bank. The projects were plagued by poor disbursement rates, long implementation periods, and anemic economic rates of return. But they were also the training ground for many of Northeast Brazil's technocrats and politicians. The projects' alumni became some of the most prominent architects of Brazil's new federalism. And as democracy returned to Brazil, the Bank and the government were able to transform the programs into more agile vehicles for poverty reduction.

The Bank's longstanding commitment to Northeast Brazil, including continuity of key staff members, remained with me as I moved away to work on Africa. Northeast Brazil came to mind when a country economist described Mozambique and its poverty to me as an "interwoven morass of interlocking problems." And when drought hit southern Africa, as it did several times during my 10 years working in Africa, I remembered the *industria da seca* (the drought business) of Northeast Brazil, where some firms profited while families literally starved. And when people talked about the need for capacity building in Africa, I flashed back to my early days teaching state government technicians in Piaui, Brazil, how to do cost tables and discussing with rural cooperative officials how to keep their agricultural input store from going bankrupt in the face of spiraling inflation.

So there were themes that united my work in Latin America with my work in Africa. But in many other ways, the experiences were radically different. My first trip to Mozambique was in July 1992, right before the peace accords were signed after a 15-year civil war. Mozambique was a classic postconflict situation, something I had never encountered before. It urgently needed humanitarian aid, infrastructure, and basic health care. The government had to convert itself from being mainly a fighting organization to one engaging in the day-to-day problems of governing and planning for the future. And outside of Maputo, the signs of nearly two decades of destruction and neglect were everywhere. At the time, our staff members were used to bringing food, water, and sleeping bags whenever they left on field trips. Some of the field trips we took in 1992 and 1993 represented the first time some of our local personnel had been outside of Maputo since childhood.

Pervasive poverty and neglect were also evident during my first trips in Zambia. This time, the culprit was not war but failed economic policies heavily reliant on state ownership. By 1993, it was hard to imagine that Zambia had been a middle-income country and an International Bank for Reconstruction and Development borrower in the 1960s. Copper, the country's main export, still dominated the economy, but increasingly, instead of being an engine of growth, copper was dragging down the rest of the economy. The government was forced to subsidize the operations of the state-owned Zambia Consolidated Copper Mines Ltd. (ZCCM) as copper production dwindled and prices fluctuated. Zambia was a shock to me. Up until then, I guess I assumed development was like a car with no rear gear; you could go forward, but not back. Working in Zambia, I realized that economic sustainability was not just about going forward at a steady and, it is hoped, increasing pace; it was also about ensuring that you did not slide backward.

I spent from mid 1994 to March 2000 as first country manager and then country director for Mozambique and Zambia. In that capacity, I watched—perhaps contributed to—Mozambique's struggles and success, and I watched—perhaps contributed to—Zambia's struggle and basic failure. Both countries were fledgling democracies with economic reform programs supported by the World Bank and the International Monetary Fund (IMF). Both countries had an active and large international donor community eager to provide support. Both countries began attracting international investor interest: Mozambique because of its natural gas resources and the potential to produce aluminum cheaply, and Zambia because of the imperative of revitalizing the copper industry. Both countries had unsustainable debt levels and were prime candidates for the HIPC (Heavily Indebted Poor Countries) initiative. Mozambique managed to achieve among the highest, if not the highest, growth rates during the period, not only in Africa, but worldwide. Zambia, in contrast, sank further into poverty. Granted, Mozambique started from an exceptionally low base, but it has now sustained growth over a 10-year period.

There were big reforms, big issues, and big projects in both countries. In Mozambique, these included its first-ever democratic national elections; central bank reform and privatization of state enterprises, including the state-owned banks; exchange rate stabilization; fiscal reforms, including the introduction of a value added tax (VAT) and improvement of public expenditure management; the privatization of the cashew industry; the Pande Gas Project, including a gas pipeline to South Africa, which involved Enron; the Mozal aluminum project, which is the International Finance Corporation's largest investment in Africa to date; and a host of Bank-supported adjustment and investment operations, including sectorwide programs in several sectors, most notably roads, education, and agriculture. In Zambia, the list was equally long: constitutional amendments and contested presidential elections; exchange rate and trade policy reforms; fiscal reforms, including public spending limits and VAT; privatization of hundreds of state-owned enterprises; the liquidation of Zambia Airways; civil service reform; and—overshadowing all the others—the privatization of ZCCM, the state-owned copper conglomerate. As in Mozambique, in Zambia the Bank had an active adjustment and investment portfolio, including sectorwide programs in health, roads, and agriculture.

In both countries, the Bank and the IMF had extensive dealings with each other and with the country. In both countries, the Bank's local presence grew during the period, especially through the addition of local staff members and consultants. In Zambia, the Bank's country office moved into larger quarters. In Mozambique, the Bank added a story to its office building while staff members kept working on the floors below. The Bank was the acknowledged leader of the aid community, which included at least 20 bilateral and multilateral aid agencies in each country. During the period, the Bank's CAS grew to be an increasingly important and participatory process and document. Mozambique also completed the requirements for HIPC debt relief and its first Interim Poverty Reduction Strategy Paper (PRSP) while I was country director. And in Zambia, as part of a CAS process, we began a discussion about the country's future prospects, using the Comprehensive Development Framework (CDF) in a multiparty dialogue among donors, government, and civil society.

The Lessons

As I look back, I personally remember those years as the breathless ones. I had the distinct feeling that if the government, assisted by the Bank, just made a concerted push, each country could get itself on a sustainable growth path. I now view that as overly naive. Hard work is perhaps a necessary, but hardly a sufficient, condition for sustainable growth and poverty reduction. So what else did I learn from the experiences—both complementary and contrasting—of Mozambique and Zambia in the 1990s? There is little new in what I have to say, and maybe that is a lesson in and of itself. The lessons fall into two categories: those related to the overall reform environment and those related to the aid relationship.

The Overall Reform Environment

Pushing Reform: The Perils of Privatization

Much has already been said about perhaps an overzealous emphasis on privatization in the 1990s, especially in Africa. Yet in countries such as Mozambique and Zambia, privatization was key to changing the overall role of the state. Privatization was not driven by ideology, but by practicality. Where there are severe capacity constraints, the government needs to focus on overall planning, policymaking, and service delivery to its citizens, particularly in those sectors that are not attractive to or desirable for private sector involvement (such as rural roads, schools, and health posts). Privatization is especially important for the introduction of new ideas and new technologies, both of which are critical for rapid growth. Although there are notable exceptions at the industry or firm level, privatization brought benefits to both the Mozambican and Zambian economies.

But in the push to privatize in both Mozambique and Zambia, some elements were not well thought out—or, at least, well implemented. On the policy front, there may have been too little investment in thinking through and publicly debating what the government expected from privatization. Neither getting ready cash nor getting the enterprise off the public accounts was a convincing argument for most of the public. And even out of the public eye, it was not always clear what the motives and prospects were for the industries being privatized. In Zambia, where the copper industry desperately needed new technology and sound management, some of ZCCM was sold off to firms that came up with seemingly high purchase prices but had neither the long-term cash nor the expertise to manage the investment. And in Mozambique, where the cashew industry had dubious medium-term prospects at best, the new owners assumed—or claimed they were led to believe—that subsidies and protection would shield them from international competition indefinitely. In reality, at the time of the cashew privatization, the government had given little thought to the medium-term prospects of the cashew industry and the appropriate regulatory framework; it just wanted those cashew factories out of the public sector. By the time the Bank and the government were engaged in a serious discussion about policies and regulations for the cashew sector, the factories were already in private hands, and the scope for policy reform was limited.

Because the objectives and prognosis for specific privatizations were not clear, not enough attention was paid to impacts and to programs tailored to help mitigate those impacts. In Mozambique, it was assumed that rapid overall growth would create new jobs faster than jobs lost because of privatization, and generally that has been the case. But in specific sectors, such as cashew processing, that did not happen. A declining export tax on raw cashews, coupled with antiquated technology and dwindling production, raised production costs and forced cashew processors out of business. Belatedly, the World Bank offered to assist those out of work with retraining programs and other forms of assistance, but the government never took the Bank up on its offer. In Zambia, the World Bank helped to support retraining and job-search programs, but the programs did not do much good because of the general economic malaise.

The lesson here is that both the objectives and effects of specific privatizations need to be clearly analyzed in order to anticipate negative impacts and plan actions to mitigate them. But a deeper lesson may well be in the reason this was not done. In some sense, a lack of clarity helped form a coalition, with various motives and objectives, to support privatization. Calling attention to and discussing specific objectives *and* specific winners and losers could well have called into question or delayed the entire privatization program. Instead, privatization proceeded, but with controversy after the fact and largely without the support of trade unions and the general public—and with workers and owners in some sectors caught in unprofitable businesses.

As a result, privatization today hardly enjoys an unblemished reputation and probably has become harder to do, despite the benefits it *can* bring. I think the international aid agencies, including the World Bank, at best, were unwitting accomplices. In our anxiety to see rapid policy reform, we were not particularly sensitive to the potential fallout and its effect on the medium-term sustainability of reform. For me, at least, the lesson is clear: in the haste to make progress—regardless of external pressures—governments and their aid partners should not short-circuit a full and transparent discussion of objectives and effects of reforms. Perhaps privatization would have been slower and more selective, but it would have taken place on surer footing. And today, neither governments nor aid agencies would need to be on the defensive regarding one of the most useful and successful tools for redefining the role of the state and kick-starting the economy.

The Double-Edged Sword of Leadership

In my time as country director, policy reform was king. The easiest stroke-of-the-pen reforms required only an executive order or an administrative decree. In that context, the personal and leadership qualities of the minister of finance were paramount. I was privileged in Mozambique and Zambia to work with several effective and committed ministers of finance. With two of those ministers, close working relationships evolved. I knew that if they told me something would be done, it would be. There was trust and respect between us.

I continue to believe that sound and committed leadership makes a big difference. But I think that World Bank staff members (myself included), as well as personnel from other development agencies, have to some extent relied too heavily on and invested too much based on extraordinary individuals, almost to the point of developing a cult of the individual leader. That tendency gives rise to several problems. It creates a bias in favor of policy reform rather than the harder and longer-term work of institutional development. It leads to a rush to get things done while the individual is still in power, with less attention paid to sustainability. It sometimes results in too much optimism and blinds us to the bigger picture, in which the commitment to and direction of reform may be considerably less favorable. And in some cases, our public alliance with those individuals actually makes it harder for them to get some things done. Finally, when the individual we have relied on leaves office, uncertainty and disruption can enter the aid relationship.

It may be that our reliance on individual leaders—and the attendant problems—are inevitable in countries where democratic institutions do not exist or are still young. Perhaps this is a problem that will disappear as democracy takes root over the next several generations. In the meantime, I think this issue reinforces the need to move strongly in some of the directions that the World Bank and other organizations have started to go. Development staff and managers need to get out much more and talk to people both inside and outside of government to have a more realistic reading of the situation, priorities, and future prospects. And more important, public and meaningful consultations on development policies and programs, such as those now conducted by governments as part of the PRSP process, are essential to create an ongoing and expanding constituency for reform. In some countries, those consultations are seen as window dressing or impositions by international development agencies. Although the process undoubtedly needs to mature, a constituency for development that extends beyond the leader and the "inner circle" is critical for sustainability of development efforts. Without this constituency—even with a brilliant policy reform record—a leader has no legacy.

Another prerequisite for sustainability is an increasing emphasis on institutions and institutional capacity. In general, this area has not been given sufficient emphasis in our operational work. We talk about the importance of institution building and capacity enhancement. But in our rush to get things done, we do not, in practice, always take the route that will lead to institutional strengthening because we know it will be longer and harder. Importing foreign technical assistance and creating project implementation units are classic examples of opting for the easy way. We are moving away from this habit but are not always sufficiently proactive. We need to work with the country's leadership to create the next generation of leaders. The best example I encountered was the national roads director in Mozambique. He knew that opening roads was an urgent priority in postwar Mozambique, and he used and successfully managed a host of foreign consultants and construction firms. But at the same time, he also insisted on funding scholarships and internships for Mozambicans studying to be civil engineers at the university in Maputo. Within a few years, the number of Mozambican civil engineers grew from the single digits to dozens. Among them, undoubtedly, is a future national roads director.

I continue to believe in the importance of leaders and leadership. The lesson I have learned is that we need to work more with those leaders on ensuring sustainability. We and they need to balance the imperative of getting things done and showing results with the equally important and less visible task of ensuring that things will continue to get done after the leader has departed.

Understanding the Political Economy of Reform

When President Joachim Alberto Chissano of Mozambique appointed his first postelection cabinet, he named a number of young technocrats to key ministerial positions. And when one analyzes the professional backgrounds and career paths of most World Bank staff members and managers, one will find something not dissimilar. Most have technical backgrounds, with a heavy concentration on economics. For the macroeconomists, the lure of data analysis and economic policy formulation is irresistible. For those who have development project experience, getting involved in project formulation and implementation details is equally fascinating. In a number of instances, the marriage between the young technocrats of the government and the personnel of the World Bank was a happy one, and we learned from each other. But in other circumstances, our combined lack of political acumen and understanding caused big problems.

The best example of this is the cashew story. Both before and after the postwar privatization of the cashew industry in Mozambique, the government imposed an extremely high tax on the export of raw cashews, at one point reaching an effective rate of 45 percent. The tax was aimed at ensuring a cheap supply of raw cashews to the cashew factories. The agricultural and macroeconomic staffs of the Bank were extremely concerned about the tax. At the time I became country director, several mainly technical studies had already been done, pointing out that farmers—and the economy as a whole—would be much better off if the tax were removed and raw cashews were exported for processing elsewhere (mainly India). One of the technical studies clumsily concluded that Mozambique would benefit from giving up its cashew industry. The new owners of the cashew factories were outraged, as was organized labor because cashew workers (about 10,000) made up the predominant portion of the formal labor force outside the public sector. The Bank team was unanimous in its view that the tax needed to go. Confronted with Mozambique's overwhelming poverty, it felt that this was the one stroke-of-the-pen reform that could bring some immediate benefit to more than 1 million rural poor—the cashew farmers and their families who, with the elimination of the export tax, would receive higher prices for their product.

After negotiating with the industry, the government proposed a phaseout of the tax over a 10-year period. The Bank's initial position was that the tax should be immediately eliminated. After some discussion, the government reluctantly proposed to the Bank a phaseout period of five years, with a declining scale that went from a 25 percent tax to 18 percent to 12 percent to 7 percent to 0. Contrary to popular belief, this arrangement was never a formal condition in any Bank document. The CAS at the time had something like "satisfactory liberalization of the cashew industry" as an indicator for the base case for Bank assistance. The Bank also recommended a series of other measures to improve the quantity and quality of cashew production because there were major technical problems with both on-farm production and the cashew factories. The discussions of those measures dragged on, with little or no action.

The cashew export tax was reduced over the next two years to 14 percent, before the policy was first stalled and then reversed. By then, Mozambique was already showing dynamic growth, and the fate of the cashew industry became relatively less important compared with other poverty reduction efforts. Whether the reduction in the export tax brought substantial benefits to poor farmers is not clear. Declining production because of weather and technical conditions and middlemen profits mitigated the effect on the poor. Many cashew factories closed, and many workers were laid off. A few factories that had adopted cost-saving technology or new production methods survived.

Overwhelming the story of what *actually* happened is the commotion that ensued after the government announced that it was reducing the export tax. The cashew factory owners made common cause with the political left in Mozambique and orchestrated an increasingly vocal national and international campaign. They accused the Bank of coercing the government to accept the policy and being completely insensitive to the need to promote industrialization and protect workers in developing countries such as Mozambique. The Mozambican cashew story became the equivalent of an urban myth in development circles and became one of the poster children for the antiglobalization movement, essentially demonstrating how the international financial institutions supposedly blackmail governments with their conditions and ruin industries with disastrous policies. The *Washington Post* printed a story criticizing the Bank; an op-ed piece by a prominent economist supporting the Bank appeared in the *New York Times*. Bank management was openly critical of the country team, whereas the Operations Evaluation Department said that, if anything, the Bank should have pressed harder for the total elimination of the export tax sooner. The government viewed the Bank as largely responsible for the problem and did not assume public ownership of the policy. Both the government and the Bank expended substantial effort doing damage control.

From where I sit, the lessons are not about whether the policy was good or bad. The lessons are really about the need for thorough understanding of the political environment in which reform takes place. The cashew factory owners were prominent members of Frelimo, the government's political party. The government ministers were not politicians; new to their jobs, they were also relatively inexperienced in dealing with the Bank. The Bank's country team, including myself, had little understanding of the dynamics of politics in Mozambique. We did not understand some of the unlikely alliances that had been forged as a result of fighting side by side in the civil war, and we did not understand that cashews were an emotional lightning rod in the country. Although the government ministers who were involved in the decision understood that there would be opposition, they never anticipated its extent. As one minister told me, "I knew there would be noise. If we adopted the policy, the cashew owners would make noise. If we didn't adopt the policy, the Bank would make noise. From where I was sitting at the time, I thought that the noise from the cashew owners was more manageable. I was wrong." He also told me that at the time he had not understood that the Bank would have been capable of flexibility had he and his colleagues been able to present a convincing argument about the extent of opposition.

The Bank and the government vastly underestimated the need to analyze the situation and the various stakeholders and to share their information and analysis with each other. We were not familiar enough with each other to be candid. At that point, both the Bank and the government did not properly understand how important it was to sell reform and increase public understanding of the reasons that the reforms were needed. And neither the Bank's team nor the government really understood that the policy decision was being made just as a worldwide movement protesting globalization was getting under way.

Perhaps the hopeful part of this story is that both the country team and the government learned from the cashew story and were able to put the lessons to good use in subsequent reforms, including Mozambique's successful completion of the prior actions needed for debt relief. In many ways, the experience made the Mozambican government a more careful consumer of Bank policy suggestions; it strengthened our interest and our ability to engage in candid dialogue with each other; and it made the Bank sensitive to the need to be more flexible and consultative. For me, understanding the political economy of reform became central to improving the Bank's partnerships and achieving results.

The Need for Luck

Many development economists have written about the need for luck. I saw this over and over again in my work. Bank staff members have a tendency to overanalyze and sweat the details. We share with many government officials a belief in our ability to make a difference and affect outcomes. We believe that it matters what we do or do not do. We spend an enormous amount of time trying to forecast outcomes and considerable, although relatively less, time analyzing and evaluating results. We agonize before, during, and after.

It is hard for us to accept that stuff happens. It seemed while I was working in Mozambique that every time the country was getting on an even keel, another natural disaster would occur. In Zambia, after more than five years of struggle to privatize ZCCM and years of negotiation, the bulk of the copper company was finally sold to the Anglo-American Corporation, a highly respected international mining company. Who could have imagined that, after fewer than two years, Anglo-American would walk out? The events of September 11, 2001, and the ensuing plummet in commodity prices, including copper—no doubt a factor in Anglo-American's decision—could not have been foreseen. And as anyone who has been involved in the policy and aid dialogue can attest, sometimes success comes down to personalities. It seems entirely random and unfair that things unravel because key country and donor officials take an immediate and visceral dislike to one another. Yet it happens.

As with everything else, luck matters more to the poor than to the rich. The extreme vulnerability of poor countries like Mozambique and Zambia allows them very little room for maneuver. Western European countries and the United States also have natural disasters, but they are able to weather them much more easily. But what about a failed privatization like ZCCM? Isn't that fundamentally more a question of bad policies—a protracted delay in privatizing that made a marginal investment even more marginal—rather than bad luck? The Operations Evaluation Department thinks that, paradoxically setting aside the entire question of country ownership, the Bank should have insisted on an earlier privatization. I have a different view: there was so much effort put into the ZCCM privatization, and there were so many factors responsible for the delay, and so many examples of even more marginal investments becoming successful that it is hard to ascribe what ultimately happened to any one thing other than bad luck.

Luck is not always bad. Although geography and history link Mozambique and South Africa, who could have predicted that Nelson Mandela, once released from prison, would marry Graca Machel, the widow of Mozambique's first president? The links between the two countries, strengthened by that union, have brought opportunities and advantages to Mozambique that relatively few poor countries have. And while the Bank encouraged ties between South Africa and Mozambique, it cannot claim to have played a role in introducing Nelson Mandela and Graca Michel.

What are the lessons associated with this discussion of luck? At least two are important. The first is that we need to be exceedingly careful in attributing successes and failures in the countries where we work to things that the Bank did or did not do. There are so many factors involved, including luck, and there is so much context that it is hard to draw definitive conclusions about what we did right, what we did wrong, and what was the ultimate value of our role. Also, if not everything can be controlled or even known, that also means that not everything can be planned or anticipated. This reality argues for simpler and shorter planning periods and a shift in effort away from preparation and toward implementation. All these points are well known and widely discussed within the World Bank. Although nothing here is new, we have difficulties putting this policy into practice. The need to continually reaffirm our value as an institution, the analytical bent and training of the staff, internal processes, and finally sheer habit all conspire against moving boldly in this direction.

The second important lesson is that the existence of both good and bad luck is no excuse for passivity or ignorance. As the cliché says, to a greater or lesser extent we all make our own luck. It is our role to help governments make their own luck by helping them, to the extent possible, in defining and investigating issues and supporting solutions. To do that, we need to be more attuned to emerging trends in the countries where we work. Just as the Bank has recently instituted a risk-opportunity scan internally, Bank country teams—preferably together with governments and other aid partners—need to look systematically for emerging trends and issues and take a fresh look at what is already happening. PRSP and CDF processes do this to some extent, but they need to be complemented by regular scans of what is happening outside of our usual business. We need to take time to identify and discuss issues that may not be at the forefront of the agenda today, but that will be tomorrow. During my time as country director, I think my country teams—including myself—needed to do more of this. For example, I think we, along with many other organizations, were not quick enough to recognize the absolute economic and social devastation that HIV/AIDS would bring to southern Africa. By the time I left in 2000, it was clear, and we were increasingly active. Perhaps had we systematically done a risk-opportunity scan, we would have been able to pinpoint HIV/AIDS sooner as the single most important threat to economic and social development over the medium term in Zambia. Possibly, we could have then helped support the Zambian government to move faster and more decisively on HIV/AIDS prevention and treatment.

Aid Relationships

The economic reform process, leadership, politics, and the role of luck are all complex topics in and of themselves. Together, they underline the difficulties involved in economic development and underscore the need for humility on the part of development agencies and their evaluators. My experience has taught me that simple causal formulas seldom exist outside of textbooks. Maybe, as a result, I have grown increasingly interested in *how* aid and development agencies do their work, as opposed to *what* they do and the related financing aspects. What works and how much it will cost are both critical and receive considerable attention. Less attention, although it is increasing, is paid to aid relationships.

The Need for Trust

Fundamentally, development agencies are trying to be catalysts for change, acting through money or ideas to try to influence outcomes and help achieve poverty reduction. It seems clear that money by itself will not achieve desired outcomes and can even be counterproductive in some circumstances. Zambia, at least up until the 1990s, is a frequently cited example. It is also clear that coercion does not work terribly well, and the use of conditionality has had a mixed record at best, even, I believe, when conditionality has been adhered to and enforced, as it was in Mozambique and Zambia during my tenure as country director. Although sometimes conditionality can change hearts and minds—a form of institutional behavior modification—most of the time it cannot. The need for country ownership of policies and actions is something few of us, at least in the World Bank, would now question.

This consensus places new emphasis on the quality of aid relationships. In fundamental ways, the quality of the relationship will determine the ability to influence and, in turn, to be influenced by the governments with which we work. And that, in my experience, brings us to trust. Without trust, it is hard for others to hear what you have to say, let alone adopt your advice. Without trust, open and frank dialogue, which leads to mutual influence, is impossible. Over the years, a cynicism has built up around development efforts in Africa. Certainly among some of the aid partners, the phrase "the government can't be trusted" is all too common—and sometimes well deserved. What is harder for us to hear are the governments saying "the donors can't be trusted," or even "the World Bank can't be trusted."

Trust is a big concept, and this is not the place for a lengthy discourse on the topic. It is clearly something that is not automatic, and it frequently takes time to develop. It implies changes in how development agencies go about their business, a theme I will return to briefly at the end of this chapter. But I think that two key elements of trust are fundamental: the need for shared purpose and the importance of reliability.

The Need for Shared Purpose

The cynics and agency theorists among us take for granted that the World Bank, bilateral aid agencies, and recipient governments all have different objectives—hence the need for legal contracts and conditionality. My experience has taught me to be less cynical. We all have multiple objectives, but I think there is sufficient common ground or complementarity to forge a common purpose around poverty reduction. That is not to say that other interests and incentives will not get in the way or that it will be fast or easy. But I think forging a common vision is unavoidable if development efforts are to succeed. Only when the various parties are convinced that we are working toward the same objectives will there be sufficient trust among us to work on the difficult questions surrounding strategies, timing, and pace of reform.

To me, creating a common understanding and a basis for trust is the fundamental aim and value of the PRSP and CDF processes. I believe we still have a rather long road ahead of us. For those processes to succeed, the government needs to exercise true leadership, and there needs to be an intensity of involvement internally as well as externally. We in the Bank need to base our assessments less on the quality (according to us) of the product and more on the quality of the process. Our moving in that direction explains the recent interest I have seen in areas such as strategic communication, participatory processes, and client engagement skills. But it is difficult for us because our expertise—plus, for many of us, our intellectual interests—lies much more in the *what*, as opposed to the *how*.

It is also difficult for us to take a back seat. And indeed, the pressures on the Bank seem a bit contradictory, at least in the short term. The World Bank is being called on to show concrete results for its work and to justify how it operates and how much it spends. At the same time, the imperative of country ownership demands that we and other aid partners no longer lead the aid process. The only possible way of reconciling those two is for the government to exercise leadership but within a common framework with common goals. In other words, we need to be part of a relationship of mutual trust that permits us to exercise influence and add value where we can. Again, we are moving in that direction, but I think that the World Bank and the other aid partners need to move a bit faster. In that respect, I do not think that it has been helpful to link the completion of PRSPs directly to approving loans or granting HIPC debt relief. What that link does is to mix the new paradigm with the old paradigm and bring us right back into the old world of conditionality, imperfect compliance, and lack of trust. I recognize that this transition is difficult. In many cases, none of us, governments and development partners alike, are ready yet to make the full transition. Nonetheless, in our direct work with countries, we need to be particularly vigilant that short-term pressures and incentives do not sabotage the ultimate value of some of our new instruments and processes.

The Importance of Reliability

Reliability is fundamental to trust and sound aid relationships. You cannot trust someone on whom you cannot count. Much has been said and written about the need for reliability on the part of the governments with which we work. Much less has been said about the reliability of development agencies.

We are less than perfectly reliable partners for many reasons. Our relatively complicated processes and procedures are among the principal culprits. I recall that at least half of the visits by country team members to my office were not about substance at all, but about how to go about getting something done in the bureaucracy. In the past few years, when we have had a relatively rapid turnover of staff members and managers, new personnel find it particularly hard to figure out how to get something done. Not only does this confusion cause delays, but it also creates misunderstandings with our clients. Staff members sometimes provide incorrect information about how long something will take or what it will involve because they do not know the correct answer. This problem, of course, argues for the importance of core operational skills training and easy access to information guides on the intranet. It argues even more eloquently for the simplification of our procedures.

But simplifying our processes and procedures is not the whole answer. There is unquestionably a conspiracy of enthusiasm. Team leaders from the World Bank and other development agencies and government officials consistently underestimate the amount of time it will take to get a project properly planned, approved, and started. Ministers of finance and country directors rarely delve into the details of individual projects; they, in turn, make commitments based on what the technical teams are telling them. Delays are almost inevitable, even when preparation schedules are carefully thought through. We then sometimes start pressing our team members to maintain something close to the original schedule. Everyone gets stressed and looks unreliable. Fingers start pointing. We do not want to look inefficient, and our team members blame government preparation delays. The government does not want to look inefficient and blames Bank internal delays.

The only way to survive this as a Bank manager is to have two sets of books, one with more realistic timeframes than the other and the more realistic schedules shared with senior government officials and senior Bank management. It feels duplicitous, but the alternatives are worse. If you base what you do entirely on the teams' plans, the Bank's reliability can be called into question, and you can also create serious difficulties for governments in their planning and public information efforts. If you widely share the more realistic schedule, you take away some of the incentive for improved efficiency: it is important to have stretch goals. We do not want to stifle the innate optimism of many of our staff members; it is what keeps them going year after year in difficult circumstances. But the leadership in the Bank needs to be able to manage the process in a way that does not create the perception of delays and lack of reliability. Over the medium term, simplifying and shortening preparation requirements will help eliminate this source of irritation and bolster aid relationships.

The way development agencies sometimes handle conditionality also undermines reliability and, consequently, trust. Zambian government officials during my tenure spoke openly about their perception of changing conditions and evaluation criteria (moving the goalposts). They felt that they did not know where they stood with some development agencies. They felt that sometimes they met conditions only to be faced with another set of conditions. They looked at neighboring countries and larger countries elsewhere and concluded that they were being held to a different standard.

In my experience, there is some truth to that perception. At various stages up until project and program approval, technical reviews may determine that additional safeguards are needed to ensure project success or protect people or habitats. Policy reviews may determine that economic reforms are unlikely to yield expected results unless additional measures are taken simultaneously. External stakeholders, either nongovernmental organizations or governments, may insist that additional or changed conditions are necessary. Also, in recent years, the broadening of the scope of conditionality to include areas such as governance can sometimes lead to differing implicit perceptions about the meaning and compliance standards of a particular condition. And it is a fact of life that larger and somewhat more prosperous countries have more room to maneuver in their relationships with international financial institutions and development agencies.

The lessons here are also well known. Simplifying conditions and agreeing explicitly on what constitutes compliance are essential. We have a responsibility to have early, candid consultations with internal stakeholders within our agencies. Together with the government, we need to do that with external stakeholders as well, both within the country and internationally. Sometimes there are unavoidable and irreconcilable differences of opinion. In those circumstances, it is obviously better to know sooner than later. A clear no, with a frank discussion of the reasons why, is better than stringing someone along or providing reasons that either are vague or stretch credibility. And though it is admittedly difficult, given the political realities that the World Bank and other development agencies face, I believe we have to think hard about adding or changing conditions at an advanced stage in the approval process. At advanced stages, I think the burden of proof has to be that either the addition or the change is unquestionably fundamental for project or program success or that approval cannot take place without it.

Even in countries where there are relatively strong aid relationships, we should not take the risk of chipping away at the foundation of trust. We talk a lot about *reputational risk* at the broader level; we need to give greater consideration to reputational risk at the country level. I believe our effectiveness ultimately depends on our ability to influence and support change through lasting, trusting aid relationships.

Conclusion: Are We Prepared to Change?

We have a wealth of lessons to guide the future business of development. We are gaining an impressive amount of information and analysis on what works and why;

what are realistic goals and what they will cost; and what constitutes good aid processes, practices, and relationships. This piece has focused on the last set of issues, what some might call the *software* of aid. Without the right *hardware* (in this case, effective solutions and funds), software is useless. But without the right software, the hardware is equally useless.

This is not the place for an extensive review of all the proposals related to improving development and aid processes and relationships. But my experience tells me that we are at least headed in the right direction. The push for increased listening and consultation with a more diverse set of stakeholders; programmatic approaches; pooling arrangements and multiyear funding commitments; simplification; and government leadership on country strategy, policy, and procedural harmonization all bring the possibility of improved results and increased aid effectiveness. The power of those process changes lies not only in their ability to improve aid relationships, but also in their power to improve the formulation and implementation of policies and investments that lead to results.

That being said, I wonder about the extent to which we have a common understanding of what those changes, if implemented in a committed and widespread manner, would mean to the World Bank and to other development agencies. The implications are far reaching in terms of staff qualifications, administrative budgets, location of work, the daily work routine, and the measurement of results and our contribution to them. How far and how fast we—and our shareholders—are prepared to go is an open question. My usual unbridled optimism is tempered when I contemplate possible answers to this question. But it is too important for the lives of the poor not to keep trying.

One final note: I started this piece claiming that the biggest lesson in development I have learned is humility. I have to end it on a similar note. Some of the lessons I have discussed here I understood well while I was country director; others only became clear after I had an opportunity to reflect. Reflecting on lessons is invaluable, and it is hard work. Even harder is actually practicing what one has learned. Doing so requires a lifetime of effort.

Gobind Nankani

Former Country Director for Brazil (1997–2001)

Growing up in Ghana, Gobind Nankani found it easy to spot poverty and its effects. But his upbringing in a family of businesspeople also enabled him to spot the dynamism of his surroundings. "I was very impressed by the entrepreneurship around me," he recalls, attributing his interest in economic development to his desire to harness that entrepreneurship in the fight against poverty.

After completing his Ph.D. in economics at Harvard, Gobind joined the World Bank as a Young Professional in 1976. "I was attracted to the Bank not only because it was analytically serious, but because it provided an entrée into policy dialogue in developing countries." Working first in the International Finance Corporation, then the Development Economics Department, Gobind won notice when a background paper he wrote on issues facing mineral exporting countries became the basis for a chapter of the 1979 *World Development Report* (World Bank 1979). "This was before there was talk of a 'resource curse,'" he says.

Always as much interested in policy and operations as in research, Gobind enthusiastically accepted an invitation from the Ghanaian government in 1981 to serve as economic adviser to the vice president. "I took a lot of hard knocks, but it was a terrific experience," he recalls. After six months in Ghana, Gobind came back to the Bank as senior economist in the West Africa Region, but he returned to Ghana in subsequent years for two additional stints as a government adviser. When the government offered him the position of governor of the central bank, Gobind found himself torn between remaining in his home country and continuing at the World Bank. Family concerns led him to choose the Bank.

Back in Washington, D.C., Gobind shifted to the Latin America and Caribbean Region in 1986, where over a period of five years he served first as departmental senior economist, then as division chief of country operations for Brazil, and then as chief of infrastructure, for Brazil, Peru, and Venezuela. With such a wide range of countries and job responsibilities, he says, "I saw the Bank from many different angles." During his stint on the project side of the Bank's work in the region, Gobind placed major emphasis on strengthening the quality of associated analytical work. His overall efforts earned him a promotion to chief economist of the South Asia Region, a position in which he served from 1991 to 1994.

Gobind then returned to the Latin America and Caribbean Region, this time as country director for a group of countries including some he had worked on in his previous positions in the region, among them Argentina, Brazil, and Chile. The contours of his work changed greatly when, in 1997, he was appointed country director for Brazil and sent to manage the field office in Brasília. In the field, analytical and operations work were no longer sufficient hallmarks of success. "You also had to be cognizant of the politics of the situation, and invest in strong relationships" with multiple stakeholders, Gobind says, a task "reminiscent of my experience in Ghana."

Leaving Brazil to assume the vice presidency of the Poverty Reduction and Economic Management (PREM) Network in 2001, Gobind says that, although he found himself responsible for the Bank's approach to a range of interesting issues—among them poverty reduction, growth, gender, trade, debt relief, and governance—he at first faced a tough adjustment away from field-based work. "I had withdrawal symptoms!" he laughs. Indeed, Gobind says that though his stint as PREM vice president, a position he held until becoming vice president of the Africa Region in 2004, gave him a richer global perspective on development, his work in Brazil and Ghana has been the most fulfilling of his career, "because it offered me the chance to engage in attempts to help implement policy in real-world situations"—exactly his aspiration from the outset.

4 Acting Strategically and Building Trust

Reflections on Brazil

Gobind Nankani

FOR ROUGHLY 12 OF THE 15 YEARS BETWEEN 1986 (MY FIRST ASSIGNMENT IN LATIN America) and 2001 (my last), it was my privilege to work in and with Brazil, always a challenging country for development economists. Built on rapid state- and debt-led growth in the 1960s and 1970s, Brazil achieved the highest average growth rate of any country in the 20th century. It also had one of the worst indices of inequality in the world and an arid Northeast that had spawned many new theories of under-development and state schemes to redress its abject poverty. In 1986, when I became departmental senior economist for the Atlantic countries of the Bank's Latin America and Caribbean Region, plus Bolivia, the fight against hyperinflation occupied much of the space on the regional policy agenda.

During the 1980s and 1990s, the Bank's relationship with Brazil was characterized by periods of harmony interspersed with some tension. A period of maturation that began in the 1990s continues today. The changing relationship reflected the difficulties that the Brazilian economy confronted as it entered the debt crisis of the 1980s; struggled with that crisis while losing the battle against inflation; and then—in its own way—gradually clawed its way back into a period of low inflation, some growth, significant poverty reduction, and a gradual and strongly owned reform effort that still continues. In its recent assessment of the Bank's assistance to Brazil during the 1990–2002 period, the Bank's Operations Evaluation Department (OED) concluded "that the Bank can still play a relevant role in a middle-income country such as Brazil" (World Bank 2004, p. 37).

In what follows, I will try to give a personal account of what, in my view, helped make the Brazil-Bank partnership a relevant, dynamic, and mutually beneficial one. I will focus on the period between 1997 and 2001, during which I was the country director in Brasília.

Many thanks to Indermit Gill, Joachim von Amsberg, Homi Kharas, Angela Furtado, Alfred Friendly, and, last but not least, Todd Pugatch for their insightful comments and suggestions. All remaining errors are my responsibility, as always.

My four years in Brasília beginning in September 1997—together with my three short assignments as an economic adviser on Ghana's reform programs, at home on leave from the Bank—stand out as the most rewarding professional experience I have had in development. I had the good fortune to work with outstanding individuals in the countries and the Bank and with dedicated, committed teams, whose efforts explain all of what was achieved. I made many mistakes and learned much. These experiences, mistakes, and lessons have been for me a journey of discovery.

Three Personal Lessons

The journey, with hindsight, had three major guideposts that made a difference. I put them in the form of three simple propositions that I suggest country directors and their teams consider in reflecting on their work of leading the Bank's partnerships. Underlying each of these propositions is a corresponding tension inherent in the job of a country director, which country directors may find helpful to bear in mind.

First, *focus on a few strategic thrusts in your partnership and keep your eyes relentlessly on the ball.* Obviously, these strategic thrusts have to emerge from the country's policy dilemmas. Yet the Bank's cross-country perspectives should also help to enrich the policy agenda and policy debates, without supplanting the home-grown exigencies. Strategic thrusts will provide the framework for a more selective country program, but there will be constant tension between maintaining this selectivity and making room for Bank-wide initiatives, a reflection of the more generalized tension between local and global agendas.

Second, *invest big time in strategic analytical and advisory activities (AAA) and recognize that the Bank has much to learn from your countries.* Strategic AAA is related to the strategic thrusts above: it is the investment needed to bring Bank knowledge and the country's knowledge to policy questions before the window of opportunity for their pursuit opens or before a crisis hits. Do your AAA work always in collaboration with national researchers or analysts, and build in strong mechanisms for consultation and dissemination. Share the Bank's global analytical work with the policy and research community in your countries. And showcase national analytical work in the Bank for use by others in different situations. Although rigorous AAA is the foundation for effective lending and participation in policy dialogue, it can also generate tension between our expertise and the need for humility in our approach.

Third, *build trust and live up to it, both in the country and in the Bank.* Trust is a characteristic of a good relationship. It is absolutely vital for the Bank's partnership with countries. But underlying this trust must be the right strategic thrusts and the right strategic AAA. Without all three elements, the partnership weakens over time as it is subjected to the normal ups and downs of any relationship. Trust is not without cost: it means that, on some occasions, when there are risks or costs, the Bank takes on those risks and shares those costs and does not always take the risk-averse route of shifting them to the country or staying on the sidelines. Trust also means being able to explain why, in some situations, the Bank is unable to help and having that explanation understood, however painfully, by our partners in the country. It requires that we assume a posture of humility, not of arrogance. And even a successfully trusting relationship carries the risk that one party will be reluctant to point out the other's mistakes, reflecting the tension between trust and complacency.

Although I have offered these three broad lessons sequentially, over the years I have begun to see them as strongly interrelated: good AAA is needed to identify and keep our strategic thrusts current, and our strategic thrusts influence what AAA we undertake. Similarly, both the strategic thrusts and good AAA are the foundation for building and maintaining trust. And without trust, it is difficult to reach a consensus on the strategic thrusts or to undertake AAA that will fit into the policy dialogue and be owned and implemented. Selectivity is necessary to ensure that we can deliver what we promise and earn our clients' trust, but it involves risks. Solid analytical work helps to mitigate those risks. In practice, of course, the process is messy and the tensions are ever present, but the point is that each of the three elements draws on and feeds the other two.

Strategic Thrusts: The Brazil Experience

The search for strategic thrusts stemmed from my realization that, helpful as our three-year Country Assistance Strategies (CASs) were, they did not provide a long enough timeframe to deal with the tough developmental issues that a country typically faces. Because no major development challenge was likely to be licked in three years, we needed to think of a longer time horizon in designing an assistance strategy that did not miss the real challenges.

The five strategic thrusts that I describe in this section are less important in themselves for this essay than the fact that, in the management team and the broader country team, we set about defining them in a systematic and sequential way. The Bank's CAS approach typically has a three- or four-year time horizon, although it builds on previous CASs, of course. What we discovered was the need to look much farther forward, asking ourselves what the enduring developmental challenges were over this longer time and then working backward into the CAS period. Of course, many potential issues can be drawn from to establish such strategic thrusts. This is where selectivity comes in: selectivity was driven not only by our understanding of what we thought the major levers for growth and poverty reduction would be, but also by the nature of our policy dialogue with our Brazilian counterparts and, indeed, the policy debates more generally in Brazil. Finally, it was driven by some notions on our part of what we thought the Bank's comparative advantages were.

Determining Strategic Thrusts: Merging Technical Analysis with Country Priorities

Perhaps no strategic thrust has dominated the Bank's partnership with Brazil as much as *reducing poverty in the Northeast of Brazil*.[1] I know from talking to Olivier Lafourcade, who became the first World Bank representative ever in Brazil when he opened the Bank's office in Recife in 1976, that the Bank's operational interest in the Northeast was ignited after a visit by Bank President Robert McNamara in 1974. By 1994, when I began my assignment as the country director for Brazil (and the Southern Cone), there was a sense that we had found a new and successful instrument for reducing poverty in the Northeast, centered on rural community-driven projects.

It was against this background that Bank President Jim Wolfensohn visited the Northeast, almost exactly 20 years after McNamara did. In a very elegant dinner in the home of the governor of Bahia, in Salvador, all nine governors from the Northeast plus the highly influential ex-governor of Bahia (Antonio Carlos Magalhães) met in a separate room with Jim Wolfensohn, Javed Burki (the Bank's vice president for Latin America at the time), and me. Most of the governors suggested that the Bank needed to redouble its efforts with rural poverty loans.

At the meeting between President Wolfensohn and the Northeast state governors, the lone dissenting voice was that of Tasso Jereissati, then governor of Ceará, who said the future of the Northeast lay in a massive program of investment in education that the Bank needed to support as a complement to its rural Northeast strategy. *Education* became, in fact, a second strategic thrust of the Brazil program. Its identification arose both from the country team's view that it was an essential building block for higher growth and lower inequality in Brazil and from strong representations on the issue by many of our counterparts in Brazil, such as Governor Jereissati, and at the federal level, Education Minister Paulo Renato Souza. At a memorable meeting of the departmental management team in 1995, we debated what the strategic thrusts for Bank support in Brazil might be over, say, 10 years, and all the sectoral division chiefs, not just the country and social sector chiefs, supported the issue of education. And a 2002 report on economic growth again identified education as one of the most important ingredients of sustained growth in Brazil (World Book 2002b). At the rhetorical level, education has always been regarded as key for growth and inequality both in Brazil and in the Bank. The difference here was that it became a de facto laser-beam focus for the Bank's CASs and for our program of support, thus determining managerial attention and resource allocation decisions during the day-to-day implementation of the CASs and the policy dialogue. This strong focus does not characterize very many Bank programs.

A third strategic thrust that the failures of the various anti-inflation plans in Brazil had helped identify as essential was, of course, *structural reforms for medium-term fiscal adjustment*. The Cruzado (1986), Bresser (1987), Verão (1988), and Collor (1990) anti-inflation plans had all foundered on this same design flaw. And while the Real anti-inflation plan (1994) had been designed to have such a structural fiscal program, it was clear that its implementation would need sustained efforts over many years. As it turned out, it was not until the 1998 crisis occurred in the Russian Federation and the effects of that crisis were felt in Brazil that the issue was seriously confronted. And not until early 1999, with the crisis in Brazil itself, did it become possible to claim that an understanding of the need for structural fiscal reform was hardwired into the executive and the Congress. The obstacles to reform were substantial, including Brazil's many bouts with inflation and debt default throughout the 20th century, a constitutional bias in favor of rising expenditures, and lax governance of state-level borrowing.

A fourth strategic thrust that was identified more clearly after the success of the Real Plan in 1994 was the need to *reestablish the conditions for high and sustained growth*.

Brazil had seen periods of high growth until the 1980s. Although lowering inflation in the mid 1990s had very salutary effects on reducing poverty, it was clear that deeper reductions in poverty would, among other things, need to be built on a growing economy. Brazil became, after the mid 1990s, one of the world's major destinations for direct foreign investment. Countries such as France, Spain, and the United States invested in many sectors—such as telecommunications, banking, and energy—as the privatization program of the Fernando Henrique Cardoso administration took off. Brazilian investments also picked up, particularly in steel and airplanes, as well as in the more traditional agricultural areas of oranges, soybeans, livestock, and poultry.

And yet there was a sense that the growth potential of the Brazilian economy was being held back, particularly for small and medium enterprises. The so-called *custo Brasil* ("Brazil cost"—the idiosyncratic costs of doing business in Brazil) was deemed a major impediment to investments. And the extremely high real interest rate, driven by the anti-inflation plans, had a strong dampening effect on all investments.

A final strategic thrust—one that also had a global dimension—was the *environment*. Since the 1970s, the Bank had sought to help Brazil to pursue its development goals while managing its forest resources with due regard for sustainability. The tension between extant and future generations was complemented by a similar tension between national and global perspectives. This tension is one of the challenges for the Bank relative to other multilateral development banks, which are less able to take a global public goods point of view. The Bank's role in the environment sector had languished during the 1980s, in the face of strong nationalist sentiments. The 1992 Rio Environmental Conference led to a rethinking by Brazil of its role as a global player on environmental issues, reopening the door for strong Bank involvement in the 1990s and beyond. The Bank acted as a partner on many levels—with the federal government, with key states, and in support of the donor-financed Rain Forest Trust Fund. Our relationship has drawn on all Bank instruments—AAA, lending, grants, outreach to civil society organizations, and honest brokership. It has been a difficult role, and selected successes have been offset by slow institutional progress and continuing high rates of deforestation. It is only from a longer-term and more global perspective that the Bank's involvement in the environment can be embraced. For Bank country directors, there is no easy escape from the need to recognize that, because of our global reach and mandate, strategic thrusts often have to include those that are global, not merely those that are national.

The Difficulty of Selectivity: The Challenge of Maintaining Strategic Thrusts

Defining these five strategic thrusts allowed us to be selective in our priorities as a country team. But selectivity has become difficult to manage in the Bank since the mid 1990s and, in particular, since the Bank began outreach efforts toward civil society groups and the issues of concern to them. We have become adept at adding new and oftentimes critical issues to the development agenda. (I believe, for example, that the emphasis on empowerment and participation is transforming our ways of thinking and assisting with poverty reduction.) The problem is that we have not been able to drop lines of activity as we add new ones, and in this all are to blame: management, staff, and indeed the Board of Executive Directors, despite its frequent calls to management to be more selective. And yet I dare say that in the Brazil program our sense of the strategic thrusts was crucial in helping us to stay focused on the broader issues that had to be central to our work. That sense helped us to keep our eye on the ball whenever there was a client or internal Bank overture to consider new areas of interest. We did not always succeed: sometimes the pressure was too difficult to deflect. But we were able, I estimate, to spend 80 percent of our effort on the most important 20 percent of the issues, and invariably, the strategic thrusts were what helped us do so as a team.

It is worth giving examples of some thing we did not deflect successfully, which then turned out well, and vice versa. A good illustration of the former was the pressure placed on us from an Executive Board CAS discussion to look at gender in Brazil as a developmental issue for possible Bank support. This discussion had arisen from a plea to some Board members from a nongovernmental organization in an industrial country. At the Board meeting, we responded that Brazil did not exhibit some of the labor force nonparticipation characteristics found in other countries. But when Maria Correia, then gender manager in the Latin America and Caribbean Region, offered to work on gender issues in Brazil, we took up her offer on the condition that she focus on a review of existing work and then organize a workshop with Brazilian experts in the field. As it turned out, this exercise proved to be very useful. The report was well received by the gender researchers in Brazil, and it helped contribute to the gender policy debate in Brazil.

A less favorable example arose in the context of a visit to Brazil by a senior Bank official who promised the University of Rio de Janeiro Bank support for a culture-related effort to rehabilitate the university's museum. We struggled to find ways of supporting this effort because a Bank promise had been made. But I recall how frustrating it was for me as the country director to be told by this Bank official, after the fact, that we would need to find a way to honor his promise.

This episode, of course, raises the issue of selectivity at the institutional level. Former Bank Chief Economist Nick Stern's two-pillar framework—set forth during the 2001 Strategic Forum focusing on the climate for investment in the private sector and for human capital—was an attempt to get at selectivity. But, like previous attempts, it too proved very difficult to implement. The pillars grew broader and broader, as every constituency in the Bank argued for including certain topics or areas. The matrix structure, one benefit of which is the incorporation of both geographic and functional expertise, also has the unintended consequence of empowering each technical function to perpetuate itself, given its independent structural existence beyond the reach of the client test. In this environment, it is particularly important for each country team to make a serious attempt to grope intelligently toward a few strategic thrusts, using Bank experience, comparative advantages, and the clients' policy and institutional spaces. Only with such an approach is it possible, at least at the country level, where the budget constraint is indeed large, to achieve selectivity of sorts.

It is important to note here that selectivity at the country level is essential if the Bank is to support growth and poverty reduction using its comparative advantages. Selectivity is not just a mechanism for shielding country directors from global or corporate priorities. Indeed, it must, for a global institution like ours, also include those global or corporate priorities that make the most sense in the country-specific context, as was the case with environmental issues in Brazil. Judiciously adapting the global agenda to the local context is the challenge facing the country director in managing the tension between the two.

Building on the Bank's Real Comparative Advantage: Analytical and Advisory Services

There is an often-quoted view of the Bank's comparative advantage that originated with Roberto Jaguaribe, who was my counterpart at the ministry of planning in Brazil in 1994–98. During one of our annual consultations, he remarked, "When we need financing for something on which we know exactly what to do, we go to the Inter-American Development Bank. But when we need financing and we do not know exactly how to go about addressing an important issue, we seek the World Bank's help." This view has been restated in many ways, but the key point is that it is the combination of lending and knowledge for which many clients—certainly middle-income clients—look to us.[2]

The specific project that led to Jaguaribe's comment was the Bolivia-Brazil gas pipeline project. It emerged as a fine example of Bank work: bringing together the private sector, two countries, and the Inter-American Development Bank and, within the Bank, combining a loan with a guarantee, while ensuring that broader concerns such as the environment and social and indigenous issues were handled soundly. Many civil society organizations had expressed concerns about the environmental and social risks posed by the pipeline. The Bank's handling of these concerns was seen as one of the Bank's major contributions and has been validated by the relatively smooth implementation of the project. Underlying this whole effort was the Bank's professionalism in relation to undertaking not only the project's analysis but also the entire sectoral context.

Similarly, a model that emerged from our work in Brazil was a product life cycle that moves from being strategic thrust-driven AAA that is done with partners, through consulting and disseminating our findings, and ending in many cases by helping with implementation through finance. But the important foundation needed for this product life cycle to work was our ability to undertake AAA work of relevance, timeliness, and high quality. This ability is the Bank's real comparative advantage, and the recent emphasis on the Bank as a knowledge institution has to be understood in this way.

Managing AAA for Strategic Impact: How the "Knowledge Bank" Should Function

In the Brazil program, the commitment we made to making AAA the bedrock of our relationship was unwavering. In hindsight, it is clear that we used a model that developed as we went along but that had three main characteristics: first, AAA had to be a strategic element of our assistance; second, it had to be done in partnership with key Brazilians or Brazilian institutes that had interests or had worked in the same areas; and, third, as part of the design of the AAA, we needed to work out outreach and partnership strategies that were aimed at ensuring consultation with key audiences during and after the work. That model evolved most significantly after the decentralization of the Country Management Unit (CMU), because the partnership and consultation dimensions were facilitated by our location in Brazil. What was also noteworthy was that, depending on the issue, we ended up on most occasions helping to shape the policy debate on the issue, and in many cases, although this was not planned or part of the design, we ended up providing financing—loans, projects, Institutional Development Fund grants, Development Grant Facility support—to help implement some of these ideas.

That we were able to do a lot in Brazil does not mean that we are well placed to do so in every other setting. There are, indeed, many other examples of effective AAA cycles that have been developed in the East Asia and Middle East and North Africa Regions. Even so, effective AAA cycles are certainly not the norm around the Bank, and the recent middle-income country report identifies the need for the Bank to find ways of ensuring that our AAA stance in middle-income countries is strengthened beyond the current more spotty approach, which, from a broader Bank point of view, is what the Brazil and other successful AAA experiences really are.[3]

The Many Uses of AAA: Five Examples from Brazil

It is useful to look at a few examples of areas of policy interest that arose in our work on Brazil, how we addressed them in our AAA work (or did not), and with what consequences.

Example One: AAA Helps Provide the Foundation for Successful Reform

Perhaps the most positive example of AAA work, done along the lines of the product cycle referred to above, was our program of analytical work on social security reforms. The Bank had identified this area as the core structural fiscal issue as early as 1994, and Homi Kharas and his team then arranged the presentation of the Bank's Policy Research Report on pensions (World Bank 1994a) to a congressional technical group, creating a wave of interest among congressmen. One of the most prominent congressmen of recent history in Brazil, Antonio Carlos Magalhães, the senator from Bahia, was full of compliments. Many years later he commended the Bank in a conversation with the Bank's vice president for Latin America, David de Ferranti, and me for the quality and relevance of the report.

In the Brazil program itself, we began further work on the issue in the mid 1990s by using the Bank's Pension Reform Options Simulation Toolkit (PROST), which permits easy analysis of the fiscal implications of alternative social security reforms in relation to a baseline unchanged policy scenario. This effort led to a request for an Institutional Development Fund grant to help train state-level civil servants on the use of toolkits such as PROST. It was later the subject of a learning and innovation loan led by Indermit Gill and Chris Parel, which is now considered to have been among the Bank's most influential recent loans. Indermit Gill then began analyzing social security reforms for Brazil; working closely with key officials in the Ministry of Social Security, such as Minister Waldeck Ornelas and Vinicius Pinheiro; and bringing in Bank expertise from the Human Development Network as needed.

The result was a major piece of work that was very carefully attuned to the institutional realities of Brazil, that brought international experience to bear on the choices Brazil faced, and that allowed Brazilian counterparts to adapt the PROST tool to analyze alternative scenarios (see box 4.1). They saw the completed report as a joint product, and, as the subject of numerous workshops over a few years, it informed the legislation that was sent to Congress to initiate a social security reform program after the 1998–99 crisis. The study then also provided the policy foundations for the bulk of the Bank's special structural adjustment loans, which were designed to help finance the transition out of this crisis. As Brazil continues with its program of reforms in this area, the analytical foundation provided by the Bank's entire support program—from disseminating global reports to training in the use of analytical tools through learning and innovation loans, to contributing to the shaping of policy debates and choices in the reform program, and then to financing the costs of transition related to reforms—all stand as testimony to how the Bank's AAA can be catalytic under the right circumstances.

The lesson is that strategic AAA must be done, with close country collaboration whenever the intellectual and policy environment allows for it—and sometimes the Bank can play a catalytic role here. When AAA will feed into policy decisions is hard to predict—sometimes during crises, and sometimes when the right political circumstances appear in noncrisis situations.

It is also noteworthy that the work on social security in Brazil has influenced the Bank's own views on pension reform. Probing questions by Brazilian counterparts on the suitability of the Bank's prescriptions have been instrumental in encouraging the World Bank's chief economist for Latin America and the Caribbean, Guillermo Perry, to commission a regional report to assess social security reform in Latin America. Brazil may indeed have taught us more than we could teach the Brazilians.

Example Two: AAA Demonstrates Our Initial Mistake

Quality AAA can also help us change course when necessary, as was the case with an issue that was brought to us for support by Cristovão Buarque, who was then governor of the federal district of Brasília, and that we wrongly turned down. In 1996, Governor Buarque approached us with the idea of Bank financing for what he called the *bolsa escola*: a cash transfer to mothers, which was based on an income means test, for enrolling and keeping their children in school. The idea seemed very interesting, but we were so concerned about the fiscal costs of the proposal that we declined to work further on it. Governor Buarque had talked of a stipend of one or more minimum wages, and simple back-of-the-envelope calculations suggested to us that the total cost could be as high as 4 percent of Brazil's gross domestic product per year.[4]

BOX 4.1

On the Value of Bank AAA: A View from Brazil's Press

These days, everything that comes from the World Bank . . . . is received with mistrust by a large portion of public opinion. Injustice is . . . . done with regard to the World Bank. The resources the Bank invests in sanitation, housing, education, and poverty reduction may seem insufficient for the needs of the poorest communities. But without Bank loans and grants, many Asian and African countries would not have the means to alleviate the suffering of their populations.

Another aspect that we need to highlight is the diagnostics of extremely high quality made by the technical staff of the World Bank. With independence and autonomy from local power, IBRD economists usually put their fingers right on the wounds of mistaken or prone to failure public policies.

The World Bank study on Brazil's Social Security system . . . . is especially noteworthy. According to the Bank's analysis, Brazil cannot afford the current system, and the deficit of the public sector pension system should reach R$53 billion in 10 years, "unless profound reforms take place." The worst problem is the high level of retirement pensions of civil servants, equivalent to 100 percent of their last salary . . . .

The World Bank touched a sensitive chord. It dared to talk about the civil service's perks. "To make cuts in the General Regime without also reforming the RJU [civil servants regime] will exacerbate income inequities, even if it helps contain the general fiscal burden," says the report.

Whether one likes or dislikes the World Bank, the report exposes the crystal clear truth. And the truth hurts. The question is how long do private sector employers and employees intend to put up with the privileges of the public sector?

Source: Excerpted from one of Brazil's leading dailies ("Luz no Privilégio" 2000).

Buarque pursued his idea with missionary zeal and implemented it on a small scale in Brasília, as did many other Partido dos Trabalhadores (Workers' Party) mayors in other cities. By 1998–89, it was clear that the idea was a winner. It was apparently increasing enrollments even though the stipends remained relatively low in order to meet fiscal criteria. At that point, we realized our mistake and offered to review the scheme for possible use on a broader scale. The federal government also adopted the essential idea, with another name (Programa de Garantia de Renda Minima) and it became a major part of the social response to the 1998–99 Brazil macroeconomic crisis. The Bank, in partnership with the United Nations Children's Fund and Brazilian researchers, prepared a report of AAA on the scheme. Although the report was not conclusive (because there was no survey that could separate the effects for an experimental and a control group), it found lots of evidence to suggest that enrollment had increased in response and some evidence suggesting that scores, too, had improved over time for children from poorer families.

After much discussion, the government decided not to seek Bank financial support for this effort, while encouraging us to undertake continuing analytical work.

The reasons had more to do with the government wanting to be seen as in the driver's seat on these effective and popular schemes, which it was, and not as pursuing these programs at the behest of the Bank.

Example Three: AAA Demonstrates a Potential Government Mistake

A somewhat different example of the Bank's advice being sought, this time to examine a controversial project, with at least some in the government being open to Bank financing, was the São Francisco project. This ambitious idea involves major irrigation works in the Northeast around the São Francisco River, which were advanced as the real answer to the drought conditions in the states of Bahia and Pernambuco, as well as in many other states in the Northeast. The Bank's involvement was sought because of the hot debates in the government about the advisability of this project, with respect to both its design and its economics. Our knowledge had suggested that the project had many problems and, indeed, that the array of incomplete smaller irrigation projects in the same areas, financed in part by the Bank's Proagua loans, deserved first priority because of potentially huge rates of return. We also saw our role, where necessary, as providing the analytical basis for *not* doing a project, even if the government planned to finance it entirely by itself.

We speedily assembled a first-rate team, profiting from being based in Brasília. The sector leader, Bob Schneider, and the task manager for Proagua, Gabriel Azevedo, plus the principal country officer, Antonio Magalhães, managed the work, and got excellent support from the Environmentally and Socially Sustainable Development network. The conclusion was not in favor of the project, and the sponsoring ministry not only rejected the work's findings but also sat on it. The Planning Ministry, however, as was routine, received a copy and was able to use it in the debate that ensued within the government and that resulted in downgrading the project. Apparently the project has been revived recently in debates in Brazil, and use is being made again of the Bank's research from 2000.

Example Four: Subnational AAA Generates New Policy Debates

In 1998, the Bank also introduced State Economic Memoranda (SEMs) in Brazil, focusing on the states in the Northeast, where we felt that the challenges posed by the troika of growth, poverty reduction, and fiscal reform required that each state assess its options. The foundation for the work in the SEMs had been laid in the mid 1990s, when the Bank had played a catalytic role in analyzing the issue of state-level debt in Brazil. This work, done in close collaboration with the Ministry of Finance, led to the establishment of a new state finance–debt unit in the ministry. It also helped provide the analytical foundation for a series of subsequent renegotiations of federal-state debts, which ended up hardening the heretofore soft budget constraints to which state governments had become accustomed.

One example of a new policy debate generated by the SEMs was that many states were not convinced that our critique of industrial policy was well founded. They pointed to the success of similar policies in East Asia, Ireland, and the United Kingdom. With the help of the PREM Network, we sought to bring the Bank's best knowledge on these issues to the table. But we did not convince our counterparts. They were instead drawn to the "cluster" idea—an idea that had been given credibility by Michael Porter and had been used by the Bank in such other countries as Morocco—and we ended up helping finance and supervising cluster analysis work for three Northeast states, focused on three products and services: grains, tourism, and information technology. The experience is a good example of the Bank's overreliance on textbook-like advice, even when the institutional conditions are quite different. The states were convinced that without some state role—and they were sensitive to the risks of rent-seeking—the private sector would underinvest in areas of comparative advantage. Although the experience illustrates how textbook-based advice by the Bank can fail to engage and influence policymakers, the jury is still out on the merits of the case.

Example Five: AAA Supports Strategic Thrusts of Poverty and Inequality

Finally, our AAA work on the broad issue of poverty and inequality has helped shape policy debates and choices and has featured a strong partnership approach. The central planks in our work in this area were the reports on rural poverty (World Bank 2001b), urban poverty (World Bank 2001a), and inequality (World Bank and Institute for Applied Economic Research 2003). The participation of key Brazilian economists—such as Ricardo Paes de Barros (also a Yale visiting professor on many occasions)—and of international experts—including François Bourguignon and Francisco Ferreira (a Bank employee who was on leave at the time)—under the task leadership of Joachim von Amsberg for the poverty work and Carlos Velez for the inequality work gave the work substantive and policy content. The reports made extensive use of background work done by Brazilian experts, drew deeply on census and survey data, and brought to the fore the dimensions and characteristics of poverty and inequality in Brazil, while integrating those policy efforts in a manner that the Bank appears to be unique in providing.

In this area, a key role of Bank AAA was to bridge a gap between excellent analytical work done by Brazilians on poverty and inequality and the policy choices that had to be made by officials in the finance, planning, and budget ministries and in the subnational governments. Distilling the policy options from a complex body of academic work, making it actionable for policymakers, and creating a forum for dialogue between analysts and policymakers turned out to be a critical role.

One particular focus of Bank work was the untargeted nature of most of Brazil's very ample social spending. Not everyone liked the stylized fact that better targeting of only some of Brazil's social spending could make a large difference in poverty reduction. But it became a critical argument in the national debate and facilitated dialogue between those concerned with social justice and those concerned with fiscal stability. In this case and others, the Bank can facilitate a productive dialogue between opposing groups within the country, in this particular instance moving the debate between those recognizing the need for fiscal adjustment and those opposing it to the critical question of the quality of fiscal adjustment and expenditures.

Importantly, the most effective venue for influencing public debate has often been through the national collaborators in joint AAA: national academics and researchers who participate in national discussion forums and write in local newspapers with a frequency that Bank personnel are unable to match. This was again the case on issues as diverse as targeting of social spending, formulation of social indicator targets, and reform of social security.

The result was to highlight the racial, gender, and spatial dimensions of poverty and to widen the poverty focus in the Northeast, with recognition that poverty was also a major issue in the outer urban areas—in particular in the "dormitories" in the periurban areas surrounding cities such as São Paulo, Rio de Janeiro, and Brasília. In the aftermath of the Brazil crisis in 1998–99, the effort to ensure that the response was as socially benign as possible and especially protective of the poor derived much from our poverty reports, which, because of their mode of preparation, were seen as joint reports, much as the social security reports had been.

The work on inequality in Brazil was seen in the Bank as a good pilot, encouraged strongly by Guillermo Perry, the Bank's chief economist for Latin America. In 2003–04, Guillermo and his team, including Mike Walton and Francisco Ferreira, produced a Latin America and Caribbean Flagship report on inequality (de Ferranti and others 2004), which is now proving to be a stepping stone for the 2006 *World Development Report* on equity and development. While discussing the Flagship report, Guillermo remarked that the Latin America and Caribbean Region of the Bank had learned a lot from work on inequality in Brazil. In the Brazil program, the country team had identified the issue as central to the strategic thrust of poverty reduction. And thus, as with the work on social security, the cycle of two-way learning took another positive turn.

Making AAA Strategic: Emphasizing Outreach in the AAA Product Cycle

My brief references to the consultation and dissemination part of the product life cycle need to be rounded off by a fuller discussion of the integral part that outreach played in our AAA strategy. In its recent favorable assessment of the Bank's role in Brazil during the '90s, OED singled out our dissemination efforts as an area in which we could have done a lot better. We could have done even more than we did; certainly our Brazilian counterparts thought so. But might it be that they appreciated our errors of omission and commission because we were engaged in an outreach strategy that compares favorably with others in the Bank in the first place?

The strategy was geared to our most consequential AAA pieces, in which, at the concept paper stage, we would agree on what partnership, consultation, and dissemination approaches were most appropriate. Thus, for example, for the water privatization report (World Bank 2000a), municipal-level workshops in key municipalities and with groups of mayors were highlighted, because concessions for water were a municipal responsibility. For the growth report (World Bank 2002b), we had a pre–concept paper workshop with key government officials and researchers and then shared the draft report with the same group. For the poverty report (World Bank 2001b), we included state civil servants from some Northeast states in the concept paper meeting, and their involvement led us to change important aspects of our study. To support such outreach efforts, we had a special outreach fund in the CMU to which task managers could apply for funding, and we also had, in the person of Angela Furtado, a very dedicated and able external affairs–communications officer in the CMU to provide advice, guidance, and support for the agreed outreach strategy.

The other element in our outreach strategy was a focus on broader communications with the media, Congress, civil society, academia, and research and policy institutes. The centerpiece of this effort was the annual World Bank Development Forum, for which there was always a theme such as poverty reduction, growth and inequality, and others. Well attended by key government officials, the forums had themes that were always chosen to be responsive to key policy debates. We brought to bear in the sessions global or regional Bank reports on the issue, as well as the AAA work done on Brazil. Soliciting input and participation from multiple stakeholders in those sessions is a key element in managing the tension between demonstrating our expertise and remaining humble in our approach. Nonetheless, the government's comments to the OED team that assessed our work show that we failed to do enough. Certainly it was not easy to get task managers outside the CMU always to see the potential gains from a strong outreach strategy.

A working hypothesis is that their view had more to do with incentives than with a lack of appreciation: they were rewarded for completing their AAA reports, but the outreach part, though attractive from a professional point of view, often got crowded out by the need to deliver other products, such as supervision missions or projects. Clearly, the failure to have in place an AAA cycle, similar to the project cycle—an argument that has been made systematically by both the East Asia and Middle East and North Africa Regions in the past few years—has meant that outreach efforts have been given short shrift in the Bank. Our renewed focus on results and on effects should be leading us to follow the insights from the East Asia and Middle East and North Africa experiences: without an AAA cycle equal in importance to the project cycle, our role in knowledge will remain mired in conflicting incentives.

Building and Retaining Trust: The Glue

We increasingly take the view that development, in the words of Ricardo Hausmann and Dani Rodrik, is "a journey of self-discovery" and one that involves risk-taking at all levels (Hausmann and Rodrik 2003). It is also a journey undertaken in a world of imperfect institutions, an understanding that supplements the concept of development as the judicious use of markets on the one hand and the capacity of the state to more than offset market failures on the other. Given the large political and economic influences on state actions, this latter condition is hard to ensure. Amid the pressures of uncertainty, risk, and particular influences, the Bank—with its technical expertise, cross-country experience, and ability to finance the implementation of accepted policies—has a potentially strong role to play. The role is that of honest broker, convener, adviser, and potential financier.

Although the Bank as an institution has, over the years, carved itself a reputation for being able to provide this range of functions, the degree of success in any given

situation is driven by the degree of trust that the country team and its principal interlocutors build and retain with country counterparts. Such trust, as is well known, is
hard to build and easy to lose. It is characterized by a relationship in which, because
motives are not suspect, it is possible both to provide strong support for good initiatives and to discourage doubtful initiatives without harming the relationship, overcoming the tension between trust and complacency. In short, it is fine to disagree
without paying a price, because the overall trust supersedes the discontent that disagreement generates. This does not mean that such situations do not often involve
frustrations on both sides. It does mean that the relationship overcomes them.

The Importance of Trust: A Tale of Two Crises

There were many examples of situations in Brazil in which the trust issue developed
and was tested and through which it grew sometimes in fits and starts. Such examples included the strong partnership in policy analysis—supported at times by lending—that we developed with sectoral ministries such as those for social security, land
reform, and the environment and water resources. We also developed similarly robust
relationships with many states, notably Ceará, Bahia, and Mato Grosso, combining
policy dialogue with selective lending support.

Perhaps one of the most important times in the relationship between countries
and the Bank when trust comes into play is whenever the country hits a currency or
debt crisis. Such a crisis happened twice in Brazil in the latter half of the 1990s, and
the two experiences are instructive.

The first was in January 1995, a few weeks after the Tequila crisis had hit Mexico.
In response, the central bank of Brazil introduced a new exchange rate policy, with a
preannounced crawl, as a way of gradually exiting from the fixed exchange rate policy that had been the cornerstone of the Real Plan. At the Bank, we were puzzled by
this policy: experience with such preannounced crawls in the early 1980s in Latin
America (for example, in Argentina) had led to their abandonment after heavy reserve
losses. The same quickly began to happen in Brazil. At that time, the Bank's relationship with Brazil had been heavily focused on rural poverty and infrastructure projects,
following the failure of the Collor plan. We did not have a very active dialogue on the
macroeconomic front, although we had issued a favorable review of the Real Plan in
a 1994 Country Economic Memorandum (World Bank 1994b). I was then based in
Washington, D.C., as the director for Brazil, Argentina, Chile, Uruguay, and Paraguay.
The sum total of our crisis-period interaction with the Brazilian government was a
phone call I made to Minister of Finance Pedro Malan, to understand how the government interpreted the market's rush to sell reals and learn what its policy response
was likely to be. Malan was very communicative, explaining that the government was
revisiting the policy and hoped to calm the markets that way. After losing some
US$10 billion in reserves, Brazil abandoned the scheme and introduced essentially a
quasi-fixed scheme, a very narrow band within which the currency could float.

This minimal contact contrasts with the quality of the interactions with the Bank
in 1998, after the Russian crisis, and in early 1999, when the real hit a confidence cri-

sis. In both cases, as a result of our much stronger relationship after 1996—which went beyond project lending to include state-level economic policy dialogue with the federal government and a very strong AAA work program on a wide range of economic issues, such as social security reform, state debt, privatization, and regulation—the quality of our interaction was of a totally different kind. By the time of the East Asian crisis, the Brazil country unit had just been decentralized. So when the Russian crisis hit, and there was an attack on the real, both Malan and I were trying to reach each other. When we connected, he wanted to give us his take on the situation and to know what kind of support the Bank could give if Brazil were to make a request. Our talk was followed by a request, and the Bank set aside up to US$4.5 billion in special structural adjustment loans to support reforms.

Because we had developed a rich array of AAA work on key structural issues, and had done so in collaboration with key Brazilian researchers and with strong government involvement, it was relatively effortless to support these "owned" reforms in our special structural adjustment loans for social security, fiscal adjustment, and social protection. There was no attempt on our part to suggest that Brazil undertake reforms that had not been studied by us together. This restraint was important to the Brazilians, who had remarked to us that the Asian countries had complained bitterly about external pressure to undertake reforms of which they had no ownership. Larry Summers's (2005) view, in his lecture at the Bank on practitioners in development, that in times of crises countries must be urged to dust off all possible reforms and implement them, was decidedly not our approach. What made our course possible was that we had invested up front in AAA that we knew would be needed whenever Brazil came to the point of addressing the fiscal weaknesses of its program.

Interestingly, when the real was again attacked in January 1999, this time because the market did not believe that the quasi-fixed exchange rate policy was sustainable, and the central bank decided, with the president's approval, to let the real float, Malan called me before I could get to him. We had lunch to discuss Bank support and options, as well as the Bank's policy views, even as the real was falling and he was getting calls telling him what the latest developments were. We made statements of support, reaffirming our financial backing, even as similar statements of support were made by other bodies such as the International Monetary Fund and U.S. Treasury. The key point is that, between 1995 and 1999, a stronger relationship of trust had been built, which permitted the Bank to support Brazil's reform efforts with jointly done analytical work, just-in-time policy advice, and financial support. That progress was made possible by decentralization and by the investment in strategic AAA and the style in which it was undertaken, as well as by our stance of not pushing for reforms that had not been developed or for which there was no apparent ownership.

Conclusions

The three elements I have focused on—strategic thrusts, strategic management of AAA, and trust—were, I believe, the underlying factors of our successes in Brazil. By maintaining our focus on a few key areas, as determined by both technical work and country priorities; using AAA to build the body of country knowledge and support key reforms; and building strong relationships with clients to improve our mutual understanding and ultimate effectiveness, we helped the Bank play a useful and appropriate role in Brazil. By the same token, I believe that had we not performed well in those areas, our performance would have suffered and our relationship with the country would have been strained. The three issues seem most relevant to country directors elsewhere—perhaps especially in middle-income countries, where the Bank's role is more in flux.

I conclude with some further observations on several tensions to which I have alluded that are inherent in how we engage our clients and with some thoughts on what can be done to make this engagement more effective. In a sense, these are the implications for the Bank's internal processes and the mindset that it fosters in our service to countries.

One: The Tension between Trust and Complacency

Although trust is essential to effective country engagement, there is a risk in taking a cooperative but noninterfering stance for too long. There is no doubt that in the Brazil team, for instance, we had worried a great deal about the sustainability of the quasi-fixed exchange rate policy. Given the risk of a currency crisis and its consequences for growth, poverty, and such social setbacks as decreases in school enrollment, we did not see the exchange rate issue as just a short-term macroeconomic matter. We had, in discreet ways, including in some one-on-one conversations between Malan and me, expressed our concerns about the policy. Its strongest defender was Gustavo Franco, then the president of the central bank, who held that it would be inflationary to let the rate float and that it would not have much of an effect on exports anyway. Others, in private, were less defensive. None of us touched on the obvious political issue: no change in exchange rate policy could be undertaken by President Cardoso before the election scheduled for October 1998, given that he had won the previous election on the success of the anti-inflation Real Plan, which had been based on a quasi-fixed rate system.

Did we, because of our proximity to the economic team, play this too softly? Perhaps. We were encouraged by Malan to share with him Bank policy work—either on other countries or on Brazil—that we felt was pertinent for policy issues being confronted by Brazil. In fact, we had shared with him a policy options note after the Russian crisis, giving a floating rate system as one scenario.

When Guillermo Perry visited Brazil in the period before the Russian crisis, he saw Malan and was strongly critical to him in private about the exchange rate policy. A big risk of decentralization is that key policy issues will not be raised or will be raised too late because of the proximity of the country director to the policymakers. It is important that such risks, which offset decentralization's benefits, be managed carefully, and one of the key roles here is that of the chief economist. In this case, Perry was playing a key role by adding his voice and was doing so at the right moment. All country directors should certainly be on the lookout for such slips in the making and should rely strongly on their colleagues to help them avoid complacency.

Two: The Tension between the Global and the Local

The Bank's global reach and mandate generate many kinds of tensions—albeit valuable ones—for the country director and country team. The first kind relates to global public goods that pose difficult tradeoffs at the national level. The Bank's support for environmental policies and investments in Brazil was noted earlier. It is easy—and wrong—for a country director to argue that all global issues are an imposition on what is a client-driven model of engagement. Clearly some are. But others may require the Bank, selectively, to play a key role at the country level to help find win-win solutions that promote superior national and global outcomes. This concept has been the underlying rationale for the Bank's engagement in the environmental sector in Brazil. Such engagement is difficult and sensitive—yet every country director needs to be ready to lead such efforts where they make the most sense.

A second kind of tension here is that between global "best practice" and country-specific approaches. When working across many countries, as many of us do, one gets a strong sense that each successful country finds its own institutional approaches and policy sequencing to make progress, rather than following a standard approach and doing it all at once. This is also one of the key conclusions of the PREM director's study, *Economic Growth in the 1990s* (World Bank 2005). You cannot look at the experiences of Bolivia, Ghana, and the Philippines, on the one hand, and of Botswana, Chile, the East Asian successes, and—more recently—China and India, on the other, without coming to this conclusion.

Moving from this recognition to policy advice is still the challenge. The country-specific approach makes sense only if there are still some global footholds that allow one not to slide down the slippery slope of the post hoc fallacy. We can identify some of those footholds: as a general principle, macroeconomic stability is necessary; similarly, openness to trade is necessary; extensive but not exclusive use of markets is warranted; but depending on the institutional capacity of the state, differing and qualitatively more sophisticated use of state instruments is also important. In Brazil, the policy experiments of the 1990s were pregnant with such lessons as the state was extricated from many sectors (such as banking, telecommunications, and energy). At the same time, the role of the state was strengthened in certain social programs such as the *bolsa escola* and now *bolsa familiar*, HIV/AIDS curative and preventive programs, primary enrollment incentives, and child-labor alleviation. The success with improvements in social indicators in Brazil, despite at best tepid growth and limited progress in the reduction of poverty and inequality, owes a lot to public policy innovations that were based on experiments. And as inequality becomes a policy issue, policies such as affirmative action enrollments in universities and in employment are being increasingly discussed and implemented.

Those global footholds must be paired with mindfulness of a country's institutional capacity in order to make country specificity more than an empty slogan.

Institutional capacity has an important bearing on the effect of policies. We need to ensure (a) that policies are designed with due regard for institutional capacity; (b) that institutional capacity building—about which we have still to learn the basics and about the necessary timeframe for which we are typically unrealistic—is still a conscious part of the broader country partnership strategy in a multiyear framework; and (c) that the interaction of policies and institutions is recognized as requiring political economy analysis, particularly with respect to reforms and how the constituencies for them and against them change over time.

The interplay of global best practice with country-specific approaches, plus the role that institutions and political economy play in those approaches, poses tough choices for the country director and country team. There is much more ready support within the Bank for global best practice approaches. It takes good country-specific AAA—done in a timely way and with in-country partners—to create space for tailored country approaches. An effective country director and country team have no real option here—they must take the more difficult route.

A final element of successfully managing the global and local tensions is to continue to promote the voice of developing countries at the global level. The Bank has increased its activity greatly in this area through its advocacy of developing countries in global trade talks, its creation of the Global Development Network, and its support for the G24 and G20 initiatives. But in our own country work, we do not systematically use our projects and AAA work to strengthen the capacity of our client countries to undertake more analytical work on their own. The World Bank Institute does take on this role, but its effectiveness is not easy to evaluate. There is a need for the Bank to think about how to have an overall strategy to contribute to increasing the voice of developing countries in global governance, using all available instruments and doing so in a manner that is obviously supported by our shareholders as a group. This job is still to be done. And the effective country director and country team will—indeed already can—be a key lever in this effort.

Three: The Tension between Expertise and Humility

A final lesson—one that is implicit in much of the foregoing—is that of the strong need for humility on the part of the Bank and of economists and policy advisers such as we are. The Brazil experience, as well as my experience in similarly large, highly human capital–intensive (at the higher levels of government and business) and confident countries, such as India and Nigeria, makes it clear that the Bank is forced to be more of a partner in these countries, more of a listener, and more of a purveyor of additional perspectives. In less well-endowed countries, such as International Development Association–only countries, where the dependence on external aid is high and capacity more limited, our counterparts have exactly the same degree of resentment against us when we are didactic and act as if we have all the answers. The difference is that they do not protest.

In crises, some organizations take advantage of countries' dire straits to demand policy reforms in areas that countries are not yet ready or able to reform, and similar resentment sets in. Yes, we can bring an additional perspective to the table. But it is only useful if we are also listening and providing the relevant comparative perspectives. The record of failures, where we got it wrong in terms of picking countries that we thought would do well (Burma, Bolivia) or not (Bangladesh, India, Mozambique to date); the frequency with which we suggested to countries that, if only they got the policies right as we advocated them, each would grow at 6 to 8 percent per year irrespective of initial conditions, exogenous shocks, and institutional capacity; and our failure still to understand how countries can do a mediocre job on growth and poverty reduction but make excellent gains in social indicators (Brazil in the lost decade of the 1980s, and also in the 1990s)—all these require that we bring to our work a dollop of humility. We need to recognize the strong role of institutions, shocks, and initial conditions, and the weak foundations of much of the country-specific policy advice we offered in the 1990s because we did not recognize those factors. We need to search for country-specific approaches with the right footholds because these footholds themselves will have elements of country specificity. Country directors must be at the forefront of efforts to enhance the country specificity of Bank support.

Managing the tensions inherent to the job of a country director is a tremendous challenge. Country directors who successfully balance global and national perspectives, build trust, and remain humble play an essential role in our clients' efforts to foster shared growth and reduce poverty.

Notes

1. The Bank's concern with poverty reduction was seen as both the framework for our overall work in Brazil—not just the Northeast—and the focus of specific concerns, such as land reform, microcredit, child labor, conditional cash transfers (such as *bolsa escola*), and the strong presence among the poor of Brazilians of African descent (the *negros* and *pardos* in the census and survey data). In addition, it was clear that the issue of inequality would need some attention—but clearly as a second priority after poverty reduction—given the highly unequal distribution of income and wealth.

2. This view was strongly reinforced in our recent consultation with middle-income country clients as we reexamined our approach to them for a Bank-wide exercise.

3. I should mention that we also took pains to disseminate the Bank's regional reports (for example, the Latin America Regional Flagship reports) and global reports (for example, *World Development Reports, Global Economic Prospects, Global Development Finance*) in a major way, involving members of the government (both federal and state), as well as academics and policy analysts. The annual World Bank Development Forum in Brazil was a major contributor to the policy debates on key issues, including influencing congressional discussions on issues such as poverty reduction, social security reform, and the *custo Brasil*.

4. Apparently this idea traveled in some way to Mexico, where it became the kernel of the Progresa program, which has become a model for conditional cash-transfer programs. I am also aware of the Bangladesh government having used a similar program to spearhead girls' education in the early 1990s very successfully, using food baskets in place of cash transfers.

Edwin Lim

Former Chief of Mission for China (1985–90)
and Country Director for India (1997–2002)

Edwin Lim was born in a small village outside Zamboanga City in the southwestern tip of the Philippines; he grew up in Zamboanga and, later, Manila. His education took a major turn when he won a scholarship to do undergraduate study at Princeton. "Although I started as a physics major, Princeton's liberal arts curriculum allowed me to explore a wide range of subjects and discipline—from opera to art, from existential philosophy to geological engineering. I was like a kid in a candy shop, and that's how I discovered my interest in development and public policy," he recalls. That experience led to a year as a research student at the London School of Economics immediately after Princeton and subsequently to a Ph.D. in economics from Harvard. After Harvard, Edwin returned to Asia to teach at the University of Hong Kong.

After five years in Hong Kong, China, Edwin joined the World Bank as a Young Professional in 1970. Like many in the Bank then, Edwin came expecting to spend a couple of years to gain some development experience. He stayed for 30 years, virtually the rest of his professional life. Soon after completing his Young Professional rotations, Edwin was assigned to Lagos as the country economist of the field-based Nigeria Program Division, part of the Bank's first experiment in decentralization. The experiment eventually failed and was not attempted by the Bank for another 20 years, but that did not prevent Edwin from discovering that field-work was what he wanted to do in the Bank. He proudly points to the fact that, in the last 17 years of his life at the Bank, he spent only three-and-a-half years at headquarters.

Another feature of Edwin's career was that it was spent entirely on country work, the bulk of it on three of the most populous countries in the world: Nigeria, China, and India. "I can't say that working on large countries was by choice. It just happened that way. Nigeria was my first assignment after the [Young Professional] program so there was not a wide range of choices available to me. Now, China in 1980, who would have turned down an opportunity to be part of the team to develop and manage the Bank's program for this new member? The opportunity to work on India came late in my career, and I could not resist the challenge of being the first field-based country director in such an important country. The six years I lived and worked in India turned out to be one of the most rewarding times of my life."

In addition to his 30 years with the Bank, Edwin spent 2 years in the private sector, on leave from the Bank from 1994 to 1996, during which time he initiated the establishment of China's first international investment bank, China International Capital Corporation (CICC). Started as a financial sector reform initiative with Edwin as its first chief executive officer, CICC has become an enormous commercial success. "I am proudest of the fact that CICC today is managed entirely by Chinese nationals," Edwin says.

Since retiring from the World Bank in 2002, Edwin has divided his time between homes in Cape Cod, Massachusetts, and London, with frequent visits to Asia. He has recently organized a team of economists, mostly former colleagues from the World Bank, to advise the Chinese authorities on economic policies. Though Edwin has taken his commitment to development and public policy well beyond the Bank, he still credits the Bank with opening the door to his long and varied experience in development: "Where else in the world would this have been possible except in the World Bank?"

5   Learning and Working with the Giants

P32 P21
O13 O19
F53
Q18

Edwin Lim   (China, India)

I AM SURE THAT ALL THE AUTHORS OF THIS SERIES BY BANK PRACTITIONERS SHARE MY overwhelming sense of gratitude at having been a country manager in the World Bank over the past two decades. It was truly an exciting and challenging time for the Bank, as well as for the countries we served. I feel particularly privileged to have been—for quite an extended period—a member of the management teams for China and India. Not only are these countries the two most populous in the world, but during those two decades both countries went through remarkable transformations. After decades of limiting itself to the so-called Hindu rates of growth, India began to grow at a pace that meant a substantial improvement in the standard of living of the population within a generation. The change in China was even more remarkable. From a country deeply rooted in communism, China launched itself in the late 1970s and early 1980s onto a path of reform and development that resulted in a double-digit average growth rate over the following two decades, dramatically increasing the standard of living of the average Chinese and reducing the incidence of poverty.

I was fortunate not only in having worked on these two countries but also in living in them for a total of more than a decade. In China, the Bank and I personally were very much part of the development process in the 1980s. We participated in the debate, the formulation, and the implementation of reforms and development policies to an extent few other foreign institutions or individuals were able to achieve. In China, I also had the unusual experience, while on external service leave from the World Bank between 1994 and 1996, of initiating the establishment of the country's first international investment bank, China International Capital Corporation (CICC), and acting as its first chief executive officer. Although I would never regret this professional opportunity in the private sector—the only one in my life—my experience in investment banking also showed me how much more rewarding my career in the World Bank had been in terms of real values.

Actually, there was a third giant in my life at the Bank. It was in Nigeria that I started my Bank career, including three years in Lagos. Nearly 15 years later, I had another opportunity to work on Nigeria, as director of the Western Africa Department from 1990 to 1994. I will, therefore, begin my reflection with a brief account of my experience in that country. It will be brief because, despite two assignments of significant length, I still do not feel I understand what happened in Nigeria, nor how the World Bank might have done better in that country over the past three decades. Then, in the rest of the chapter, I will summarize my perspective on the development experience in China during the 1980s and the role of the Bank over that decade. Finally, I will conclude with my experience in India and, where possible, contrast it with my experience in China.

Nigeria in the 1970s and 1990s

Just as those who did not know China before 1980 cannot truly comprehend the changes that have taken place in the country since, those who know Nigeria only in recent years will find it difficult to imagine how it was in the 1970s when I had my first encounter with the country and from which time I hold the strongest memory. The Nigeria Program Division was my first assignment after my Young Professional rotations in 1971, and two years later, as one of the Bank's earliest experiments in decentralization, the entire division was transferred to Lagos. As part of the transfer, I moved with my family and lived in Lagos for three years.

Nigeria, in the early 1970s, was full of hope, as was all of Sub-Saharan Africa. The country had just emerged from a civil war, but reconciliation was remarkably successful. The country seemed determined to stay together as by far the most populous and powerful country in Sub-Saharan Africa. Agriculture was the mainstay of the economy and was being quickly rehabilitated. What seemed even more important at the time, large oil reserves had been discovered, and the country was well on its way to becoming one of the world's major oil producers.

As the resident economist of the World Bank, I worked closely with the government's Planning Office. I distinctly recall one long day working with two of the directors of the office. One was an Ibo and personally a symbol of the remarkable reconciliation after the civil war. He had been head of the Biafra Central Bank during the war but was restored to his former position in the federal government immediately after the war ended. The other was a Yoruba of noble birth. The three of us had spent long days trying to work out the balance of payments and fiscal projections for Nigeria's next five-year plan. The critical variable was, of course, oil prices. At the end of that particular day, the three of us had come to one conclusion: if oil prices were to reach US$2 a barrel, Nigeria's financial problems would be over. How wrong we were! How inadequate we were as economists, despite our excellent training!

In retrospect, the rest of the Bank's program in Nigeria during the 1970s was not a success either. The experiment at decentralization failed. The Bank was simply not ready to delegate substantial responsibilities to the field, and after several years of continuous tension between the chief of mission in Lagos and the programs director at headquarters, the Program Division was returned to headquarters. Although the Bank financed some useful projects, a core element of its program in Nigeria was a series of Integrated Rural Development Projects that copied the "successes" of similar projects in East Africa. Those projects, which sought to create an island of good agricultural practice served by privileged allocations of inputs and extension workers, became quite controversial in the 1980s. Instead of serving as good demonstrators, they were found to be quite damaging to agriculture and rural development in the surrounding areas.

I left Nigeria in 1976 and returned to work on the country only in 1990. After completing my 10 years on China, I was anxious to return to work again on Africa's most populous and promising country and had asked for the assignment as director of the Western Africa Department. The reality was sobering, as I found that the country had clearly fallen behind, with a lower standard of living and an even sharper fall in the quality of life over the two decades during which some other countries, particularly in Asia, had launched themselves onto the path of rapid and sustained growth.

Oil prices, of course, went not just over US$2 a barrel, but well over US$30. By 1990, however, Nigeria found not only that its oil revenues had disappeared, but also that it was saddled with billions of dollars of external debt. Agriculture had been devastated. A lot of the oil and debt money went into infrastructure, but it was not at all clear how that infrastructure had benefited anyone but contractors and suppliers. Even as the economic decline of the country seemed obvious, multibillion-dollar industrial projects—steel mills, aluminum plants—were being initiated. In each of the projects, both the corruptors—the American or European companies involved—and the corrupted—an army general, a minister, or even a permanent secretary—were well known, but despite the enormous harm the proposed projects were to bring to the economy, they seemed unstoppable.

Corruption is found all over the world, but I found corruption in Nigeria then particularly tragic because of the enormous harm it brought to the economy. One of the industrial projects we in the Bank fought against during my tenure as country director was a huge steel project promoted by European steel companies and contractors. The mill had to depend on imported ores and coal, which also had to be transported a long distance inland. The project, therefore, would cost the country billions it could ill afford and would never be economically sustainable without the protection of high tariffs. Moreover, the protection required to keep the mill going would condemn all downstream steel-using industries in Nigeria to high-cost and low quality steel for decades to come. The Nigeria team in the Bank spent most of its time trying to kill such projects—not exactly a pleasant task.

I had reasons to be optimistic about being able to effect some changes in the Bank's dialogue and programs in Nigeria in the early 1990s. The country departments created in the reorganization of 1987 brought under one department all the necessary elements of a country program—economic analysis, dialogue, strategy formulation, and project preparation and implementation capabilities. The director of the department had capabilities unprecedented in the Bank. (Such coordination prevailed only briefly—until the 1997 reorganization dismantled the country departments.) I personally also had advantages because my previous assignment in the country meant that I knew many of the senior officials well. Indeed, of the two directors in the Planning

Office in the 1970s who had shared my naiveté about the benefit of higher oil prices for Nigeria, one was minister of petroleum when I returned in the 1990s, and the other was minister of finance and later a presidential candidate.

Despite those advantages, my tenure as director of the Western Africa Department can be described only as a process of continuous disengagement from Nigeria, because we could not find a way to work with the country constructively during those three years. My first task as director was to stop preparation of a second structural adjustment loan. Then we stopped preparation of large infrastructure projects, leaving only a core program of social sector projects. Then we began to cancel undisbursed balances of projects, the implementation of which was unsatisfactory. Finally, we stopped lending altogether and aggressively reduced the portfolio to manage the risks to the Bank. In the last year of my tenure as director, our efforts in Nigeria were entirely focused on preparing a program of debt relief conditional on reforms and policy changes that would be acceptable to the official creditors, the so-called Paris Club. Although some progress was made, in the end this effort, too, failed.

What lessons can I draw from this experience? First is the limitation of the Bank. Nigeria in the 1990s desperately needed Bank lending and, more important, the endorsement of the Bank for its development programs and policies. This need gave us the illusion of tremendous influence over economic policies. In retrospect, it is obvious how little influence we really had. Economic policies were the products of a confluence of social, economic, and political forces in the country that, unfortunately, we did not fully understand, much less have the ability to influence. In countries smaller than Nigeria—I was also responsible for Ghana, Sierra Leone, and other West African countries—we may have great influence over a longer period of time. In the long run, though, it is forces within the country itself that will determine economic performance, and the Bank can play at best only a marginal role. That role can be very beneficial to the country, but we should never ignore our limitation.

Being realistic about our limitation means that, in some situations, the best the Bank can do is to walk away. Saying "no" can be as powerful as saying "yes" in certain instances. In Nigeria, in the 1990s, we might have been able to help the country more by saying "no" earlier and louder. In fact, despite all the rhetoric about selectivity and all the analytical evidence that we should concentrate our efforts on the good performers, saying "no" is probably the most difficult thing for Bank staff members, as individuals, and for the Bank itself, as an institution, to do. As individuals, our instinct is to stay and find ways to help, even in situations in which, obviously, the Bank cannot do anything to help. At the institutional level, it is politically almost impossible for the Bank ever to walk away from any country, even when that seems the best course for the Bank and the country.

Toward the end of my tenure as director of the Western Africa Department, I had a conversation with a senior minister who was very close to the military leadership then ruling the country and whom I also knew well from the 1970s. I shared with him my thoughts that, because the Bank could not support what was going on in the country and because all our major initiatives in development assistance and advice seemed to have failed, perhaps the best course for Nigeria and the Bank was to agree on a period of disengagement. He disagreed violently. The relationship between the World Bank and Nigeria was like that of a Catholic marriage, he explained. Although it was true we were no longer true partners at that time, separation was not something we could contemplate. Nigeria would always need the World Bank. And how could the World Bank exist without the most populous country in Africa? Sooner or later, Nigeria would find its way to development and growth.

The minister, of course, was correct. Nigeria's day will come. However, the 1980s and 1990s belonged to India and China. Before I turn to my experiences in those two countries, it might be useful to examine their performance in the international context during those two decades.

The Growth Performance of China and India in an International Context

Neither China nor India fits economists' standard prescription for growth. Particularly in China's case in the 1980s and 1990s, orthodox economic thinking had great difficulty explaining what was clearly becoming a great success story of economic growth. So, until recently, little was written about the Chinese experience in development literature. An illustration of this omission is the World Bank (1993) report on East Asia, titled *The East Asian Miracle*. Despite the facts that China represents more than half the population of East Asia and that the World Bank itself had been deeply involved in Chinese economic reforms for more than a decade, China was not included in the study, the title of the report notwithstanding.

Indeed, the development experiences of both China and India over the past two decades were not at all consistent with the standard prescriptions that were emerging among Western economists, later to be known as the Washington Consensus. Nonetheless, the achievements of China and India were impressive. One benchmark is the growth of per capita income in the industrial world over the last four decades of the 20th century: an annual rate of 2.7 percent, somewhat slower in the last two decades compared with the previous two. This rate of growth means that every 30 years a new generation would experience a doubling of income, certainly a reasonable aspiration.

In comparison, the "miracle" countries of East Asia, excluding China, were able to sustain a growth rate in the 1980s and 1990s comparable to that of the previous two decades, averaging a per capita growth of 4.4 percent a year over the four decades despite the financial crisis toward the end of the period. However, in Latin America, the region of the developing world that most closely followed the prescriptions of the Washington Consensus—fiscal discipline, liberalization, and privatization—per capita income fell in the 1980s, and despite a recovery in the 1990s, growth remained at only half of the nearly 3 percent achieved in the two decades before 1980.

Even more to the point are the experiences of the former Soviet Union and Eastern European economies that followed the "Big Bang" and "shock therapy" strategies recommended to them by some Western economists. Most of those economies witnessed a dramatic output collapse of about 60 percent after 1991. The collapse of output and real incomes was unprecedented in modern history: the scale and the length of the recession (8–10 years) were far greater than those of the Great Depression of 1929–32, when output fell by about 35 percent, and the breakdown lasted about 4 years.

Sub-Saharan Africa, too, followed orthodox economic policies, although reforms were much less extensive than in Latin America. Per capita income in those countries also fell over the past two decades.

In fact, it is in India and China—the two most populous and, in 1980, two of the poorest countries in the world—that the success stories of economic reforms can be found. In the 1980s, India, for the first time since independence, was able to break out of the "Hindu rate of growth"—1 percent per capita gross domestic product (GDP) per year—and income per capita grew by more than 3 percent a year over most of the 1980s and 1990s. China's achievement was even more impressive. Over the 1980s, per capita income growth averaged nearly 9 percent, dropping slightly in the 1990s to 8.3 percent. This rapid growth was able to lift an estimated 200 million people out of poverty over the period. Statistics may lie sometimes, but anyone who has been visiting China since the 1980s can testify to the remarkable transformation of the economy over the past two decades and the prosperity it has brought to the bulk of the population.

China, 1980–90

Reform and Growth in China

The reform and growth of the Chinese economy over the past two decades were quite unusual compared with those of most developing countries, even with those countries undergoing a similar process of dismantling the Soviet-type command economy and building a market economy. In the initial stage of reform in China, the strategy was not so much to restructure the existing state sector as to allow a market-based nonstate sector to emerge at the margin—the now well-known two-track system. For instance, instead of allowing market forces to determine all agricultural prices immediately, the state continued to control the prices of products within the set quota. If farmers could produce beyond their quota, they could sell their output at market prices. The same was true for basic commodities such as coal, steel, and lumber. Over time, the volumes set by quota, or subject to planned allocations, were reduced, thus allowing prices to move gradually to market levels.

Thus, two economic systems coexisted—the centrally planned system and a market-based arrangement—in what was known in the 1980s also as the two-bloc approach. In economic terminology, the Chinese strategy sought to gain the allocative efficiency of market-based prices at the margin, while minimizing the adverse effect of changes on the existing economic structure and income distribution.

The concept of two—and often even more than two—sets of prices for all basic commodities and of two supply distribution systems—with the opportunities thus created for illegal arbitrage, rent-seeking, and corruption—was a source of major concern to all. Observers also feared that vested interests would be created that would impede reform. As it turned out, the potential abuses of a partially reformed system were relatively well contained because of the stability of the political institutions over this period and the continued effectiveness of the bureaucracy. This performance was in contrast to that of the Russian Federation, where radical reforms were undertaken at the very same time that the political and public administrative systems were collapsing.

In the context of this incremental transition from a planned economy to a market economy, new sources of wealth and growth emerged, resulting in the remarkable growth of the economy and in the reduction of poverty. What were considered weaknesses of the economic structure were transformed into strengths during the reform period.

First was agricultural growth. Large volumes of rural assets had been created in the prereform decades, such as an extensive irrigation system, land development, and rural infrastructure. When proper incentives were generated under the household responsibility system, the existence of those assets led to an explosion of agricultural growth.

With rapid agricultural growth came substantial increases in rural incomes, which led, in turn, to incremental demand for agricultural and nonagricultural goods. The unleashing of agricultural productivity gains was not without risk, however. The challenge then was how to manage the political consequences of hundreds of millions of unemployed peasants.

Ten years later, this weakness of the economy had been turned into a strength with the development of the township and village enterprises (TVEs). The labor force freed up by agricultural reforms, as well as the growing demand for consumer goods fueled by rising rural incomes, became the dynamic factor leading to the creation of the TVEs throughout the country. In fact, by about 1990, TVEs were employing almost 100 million workers. By the mid 1990s, they accounted for over half of China's industrial output.

The growth of TVEs in the rural areas was followed by the growth of nonstate enterprises of various forms in the urban areas. With the opening up of the markets and the availability of semiskilled but low-wage labor, foreign direct investment poured into China, making foreign-invested enterprises a major factor in the growth of the economy. The creation of the special economic zones was another element of the two-track strategy, allowing a radically reformed structure at the margin while not changing the core of the economy. The phenomenal growth of exports, combined with foreign direct investment, also allowed an annual growth in imports of about 18 percent. This growth, in turn, led to inflows of technology and know-how embodied in imported goods and capital equipment at a level unprecedented in China—and in virtually any other country in the world. Thus, the reform process triggered a virtuous circle of change and growth.

What Are the Key Elements of the Chinese Reform Strategy?

Crossing the Stream by Groping for the Stones

To me, the best description of Chinese reforms is that phrase used most often in the 1980s: "Crossing the stream by groping for the stones." As the phrase implies, the reform process in China has been gradual and without any precise idea of what the path should be. There was a great deal of experimentation, many trials and errors. Experiments were usually at the local level, but when success was found in a locality, the experiment was replicated quickly throughout the country. Above all, there was great determination to cross the stream, to get to the other side, even though the other side was most of the time so far away that it was not visible.

That will to progress was most obvious in rural reforms, with the introduction of the household responsibility system in the late 1970s and early 1980s. Tremendous drive and initiative for reforms were coming from the local levels, particularly because in many regions the disastrous consequences of the Cultural Revolution and its aftermath were making even subsistence increasingly precarious. There was not only intense competition among provinces and localities to innovate but also a willingness to learn from each other. There was no clear vision at the center except to allow these local initiatives to continue groping their way across the stream. Often the central government did not even know what was going on, especially because the information and statistical system had been weakened during the 1960s and 1970s.

This characteristic of Chinese reform was obvious to us even during the first Bank economic mission to China in 1980. We were very conscious of the size and diversity of China and decided that we would visit three selected provinces—Gansu, the northwest province among the poorest in China; Hubei, an average province on the Yangtze; and Jiangsu, a relatively well-off province on the outskirts of Shanghai—as well as Beijing and Shanghai as urban centers. In Beijing, the central authorities in their "brief introduction" gave us tons of meaningless statistics dating back to 1949 and outlined what the country had achieved over the past few years in the rural areas and what they intended to introduce in the next few years: lower-level production units would be given some independence in determining the crops to be planted. Then we went to the provinces, and there the provincial authorities revealed to us that, unknown to the central authorities, they had already implemented what the central authorities intended to introduce in the future and that, under the household responsibility system, households in the next few years would be given autonomy in deciding what to grow, how much fertilizer to use, and so on. This revelation went on and on as we traveled to lower levels of the rural areas. Only when we got down to the village levels did we discover that the villages had already divided up the land among the families and that the families were effectively working family farms, though without formal ownership of the land.

Although the vertical flows of information seemed limited, perhaps because of political fears, there seemed to be no shortage of horizontal flows of information on successes and failures in experimentation. During the mission, we learned a popular jingle among the peasants at that time: "If you want to have grains, find Ziyang. If you want to eat rice, find Wan Li." Zhao Ziyang, the secretary of the Communist Party in Sichuan Province, and Wan Li, the party secretary in Anhui Province, were then the pioneers in introducing rural reforms, giving farmers autonomy in managing their farms. It was obviously known throughout the country that the reforms were transforming those hitherto grain-deficit provinces, which had been plagued with widespread poverty, into provinces with surpluses. Within a few years, the household responsibility system pioneered in Sichuan and Anhui was introduced throughout the country. By then, Zhao Ziyang had become China's premier and Wan Li his vice premier.

Another example of crossing the stream while groping for stones relates to the issue of rural workers. In 1982, we had organized a team of Eastern European economists and practitioners to talk to the Chinese about economic reforms of the Soviet-type command economy, particularly price reforms (discussed later). Late one evening, many of us were in a large seminar room, with all the Eastern Europeans glued to the small black-and-white television set watching the flickering images of the World Cup. At the other side of the room, some of us began to talk about the biggest economic problems confronting the Chinese leadership. The eminent Chinese economist Xue Muqiao—then one of the key thinkers behind the reform process—surprised us by saying that his biggest worry was not about areas where reforms had been stalled, such as price reforms, but about reforms that had been remarkably successful, such as the household responsibility system and the effect it was having on agricultural production. He estimated that if agricultural productivity growth unleashed by the household responsibility system continued, only 100 million of the 300 million peasant workers in China would remain fully engaged in agriculture: 100 million would become underemployed, and the remaining 100 million would become unemployed altogether. Although agricultural growth would undoubtedly be welcome, the resulting rural unemployment would create such social and political problems that reforms would undoubtedly be reversed, and even the political situation would be destabilized. Migration was ruled out because China was not ready to cope with a vast influx of population into the cities. The only solution, therefore, was to create employment opportunities for the workers outside agriculture. China already had a history of promoting rural industries, and the discussions turned to how increased incentives could be provided. The Chinese also acknowledged that the most effective means of promoting rural industries was allowing such activities to operate outside the deadly reach of the planned economy.

This informal conversation may not have been critical to the issue of rural employment or to the eventual policy response. It provided, however, a glimpse into how Chinese reformists are continuously anticipating the next step of the reform process, constantly groping for the next piece of stone to step on, and watching out for the waves that may be forming in the stream. Often the solution found was very simple. Many years later in India, Indian economists and government officials often asked me what the Chinese government did to promote the TVEs. My answer was always "nothing." This answer was not facetious. The policy response to the risk of massive unemployment in the rural areas was for the government to withdraw, to allow the natural entrepreneurship of the peasants to find their own solutions, and to allow the traditional institutions of the townships and villages to play their roles. Basically Chinese policy was to allow an unplanned, market economy in the rural areas to compete with the planned economy. It was no contest. As noted previously, the TVEs were employing some 100 million rural workers by the end of the 1980s.

"Black Cat, White Cat, It Doesn't Matter, So Long as It Catches Mice"

Chinese reforms have always been characterized by pragmatism, as summarized in Deng Xiaoping's statement, "Black cat, white cat, it doesn't matter so long as it catches mice." The response to a reform problem was designed according to Chinese conditions and capability, not according to any economic theory or principle. Of course, ideological constraints existed, but pragmatism was always the guiding principle under the overall objective of building socialism with Chinese characteristics. In fact, the term *with Chinese characteristics* allowed reformists effectively to overcome many of the ideological constraints that existed. Of course, there were powerful ideologues in the early 1980s, but they lost their influence rapidly as reforms unleashed the forces of growth and development. The challenge then became one of finding a direction for change and assessing the institutional capacity for managing the change. Today we may take this pragmatic principle for granted, but unfortunately, too many countries still follow textbook prescriptions or external advice with inadequate considerations of their own capabilities and conditions.

What Matters Is the Right Institution with the Right Policy

Development experiences in nearly all countries have increasingly demonstrated the importance of institutions in furthering development. This realization has led sometimes to this question: is it institution that matters, or is it policy? The Chinese experience clearly shows that what matters is the right institution combined with the right policy. The right institution with the wrong policy can lead to disastrous results. Nowhere is this clearer than in the example of Chinese rural institutions.

The Chinese rural economy consists of several layers, with the townships at the top in economic terms but usually serving at the same time as the lowest level of government. Below the townships are the villages; below the villages are the hamlets and the neighborhoods—clusters of farm families. The political base of the Chinese communists was rural—unlike the urban base of the European communists—and when they took over in 1949, they were very conscious of the importance of these rural institutions. They built on the institutions, though giving them the revolutionary names of communes, brigades, and teams. The communes were the basis for the Great Leap Forward movement in the late 1950s—China's attempt at pure communism, with common ownership of land, communal food halls, and backyard furnaces. The disastrous results are well known: millions starved to death. The same institutions continued under the extreme leftist policies of the Cultural Revolution. However, the traditional rural institutions made possible the local, collective self-reliance that achieved so much in basic education and health during that period as well as the investment in rural infrastructure such as irrigation work and land development.

The same rural institutions were responsible for the explosive growth of rural enterprises, probably the single most important factor for growth and poverty reduction in China over the past two decades. These institutions made possible the collective decisionmaking; the pooling of physical, financial, and human capital; and the sharing of risks that enabled the creation of thousands of enterprises serving the needs of the agricultural economy. Hence, they met the demands of rising rural incomes and absorbed workers made surplus by agricultural reforms. Although the rural enterprises initially were known as commune and brigade enterprises, they soon reverted back to the traditional names of township and village enterprises.

Indeed, with the growth of the markets in the rural economy, the rising levels of private enterprises, and the increasing complexities of financing and credits, rural institutions are proving inadequate for the further development of the rural economy. Once again, the institutions pose challenges to further growth, and their further evolution is necessary if they are to continue to power China's development.

Another example of the relationship between institution and policy is the two-track pricing system that was the hallmark of Chinese reforms. As a policy, the concept of multiple sets of prices for all basic commodities was obviously undesirable, because it would create enormous opportunities for rent-seeking and corruption. We at the Bank strongly advised against it. The Chinese, however, had greater confidence in their institutional capacity to contain those problems. Today the transition has been successful, and prices are again unified and largely determined by the market. Strong institutions overcame the defects of a flawed policy. Undoubtedly, the two-track system to some extent left a legacy of rent-seeking and corruption. Was there any other policy that would have completed the transition without such a legacy? Certainly no counterfactual is available in China. The only experience that may be considered as a counterfactual to the Chinese experience, that of Russia, would suggest that the Chinese made the right choice.

If We All Want to Be Rich, We Have to Let Some Become Rich First

In 1987, as part of our program of economic dialogue and assistance through conferences (which I will describe later), the Chinese authorities asked us to organize a conference on plans and markets, mainly to understand how Asian countries managed their economies. The main interest then was the Republic of Korea, with which China had no direct relationship but whose experience in state-directed growth was the object of much curiosity from Chinese policymakers. So we organized a conference in Bangkok, Thailand, with all participating countries obviously giving it quite a bit of importance. The host-country delegation was headed by the finance minister. The Korean participants were headed by the deputy prime minister. From India came Dr. Manmohan Singh, then chairman of the Planning Commission, and Montek Singh Ahluwalia, the economic adviser to the prime minister. The large Chinese delegation was headed by the vice minister for the System Reform Commission, the agency responsible for formulating the reform program and strategy.

After the other delegations presented their experiences in managing a market economy, the Chinese vice minister presented an outline of the Chinese reform program. At the end of this presentation, Manmohan Singh, in his usual gentle but forceful tone, asked, "Would not what you are trying to do result in greater inequality in China?"

To that the vice minister replied, with firm conviction, "We would certainly hope so!"

As economists, we have all struggled with the issue of equality and growth. Many of us would see a degree of equality as an end in itself; empirical evidence also shows that economic growth can be sustained only if the benefits of growth are fairly distributed among different segments of the population.

There are, however, instances in which greater inequality has to be possible to create the incentives necessary for work and entrepreneurship. Actually, my first encounter with this situation came not in China, but several years earlier, on the first economic mission to unified Vietnam. On a visit to the Mekong Delta, I was shocked to find that this area, long known as the rice bowl of Asia, had reverted to subsistence farming almost overnight. It appeared that the new regime had imposed such a harsh tax and procurement regime that farmers no longer had any incentive to produce more than what they required for their own consumption.

The deadly effect of extreme equality on incentive was also evident during our first mission to China. It was not that income distribution throughout China was highly equal. In fact we were surprised to find high degrees of disparity as we traveled from cities to rural areas, from province to province, and even within provinces. China was clearly a country with a huge regional income disparity. Within each locality, however, the standard of living of the population was highly equal. Indeed, any attempt by families or individuals to better themselves was frowned on. With limited communication and movement of people between regions, the prereform political leadership could preach the philosophy of egalitarianism while allowing large income disparity among regions to persist.

With reforms, a different approach to extreme poverty became necessary. In Gansu, one of China's poorest provinces, the first economic mission asked to see and was taken to visit an extremely poor village, the poorest of the poor. The village was on top of a hill, and over centuries of cultivation, the farmers had lost their source of water and the capacity to feed themselves. The provincial authorities proudly explained to us that, under their social welfare programs, a truckload of water was delivered to the village every day and all villagers were provided with a minimum subsistence level of grains. Our hosts were not at all happy when we pointed out that what they were doing was nothing more than condemning these villagers to many generations of absolute poverty. Should they not consider allowing these people to migrate? I thought I could convince them with the story of my grandfather, who also came from a very poor village in Fujian, a province almost as poor as Gansu but had the foresight (and the opportunity) to stow away on a boat to the Philippines. Even this story, so common among the poor Chinese who migrated out of poverty, did not move them to believe that migration could be a powerful means of poverty alleviation.

Fortunately, it was Deng—not those officials—who was leading the Chinese reform and development efforts. He immediately saw egalitarianism as incompatible with reforms and attacked what he described as "the equal distribution of poverty." As it turned out, reforms led to a major improvement in income distribution in the country. By far the largest disparity in China at the end of the 1970s was between the rural and urban populations. Chronic poverty was largely a rural phenomenon.

After more than 20 years of reforms and a quadrupling of per capita income, income inequality and the persistence of absolute poverty among some groups are issues that the present government needs to address. There is no question, however, that the acceptance of a greater degree of inequality was a necessary element of the reforms initiated in the late 1970s. To many of us, the images today of China's new millionaires, weaving their Ferraris among the cyclists in Beijing, drinking 100-year-old cognac mixed with Coca-Cola at elaborate wedding banquets, and buying Rolex watches by the dozens in New York and Paris, may seem the uglier side of Chinese reforms, but we must not forget that it is the existence of these nouveaux riches and the possibility of becoming rich in the new China that they represent that are motivating millions of ordinary Chinese to work long hours, to save for their children's education, and to exercise their entrepreneurship and take risks.

The World Bank and China

As China transformed itself after 1980, so did it transform the World Bank. China was a founding member of the World Bank and the International Monetary Fund (IMF), but until 1980, it was represented by the authorities of Taiwan, China. It was only in 1980 that China assumed membership in the Bank and the IMF and became an active member. With that, and with the entry of the former Soviet Union and Eastern European countries a decade later, the Bank became truly a World Bank.

The entry of China into the Bank and the activation of our program in the country represented an exhilarating time for those of us fortunate enough to participate in that process. As one would have expected from Robert McNamara and Shahid Husain, then the regional vice president for East Asia, the first cycle of activities was completed in an impossible timetable of a little more than a year.

The initiative came almost out of the blue. In 1979, there were indications that China was exploring the possibilities of "joining" the Bretton Woods institutions. Those of us in the Bank working then on Vietnam were finding excuses to make stopovers in Beijing, that being the most convenient way to get to Hanoi. I had negotiated permission with the Chinese liaison office in Washington, D.C., for Bank personnel to pass through Beijing on the way to Hanoi and came to know some of the officials in the office. On one of my stopovers in Beijing in 1979, I found myself invited to dinner with a group of Chinese officials obviously charged with the responsibility of learning about the Bank Group. What is the difference between the Bank and IMF? I was asked. (As John Maynard Keynes said, the Bank is a fund, and the Fund is a bank!) What is the International Finance Corporation? What are the differences in lending terms between the International Bank for Reconstruction and Development (IBRD) and the International Development Association (IDA)? Would China be eligible for IDA? What is required to process a loan? What is the purpose of an economic study? I, of course, explained to the Chinese officials that the very first step toward initiating a program of assistance would be to prepare an economic report.

The invitation for McNamara to visit China came in February 1980. Reflecting the cautious Chinese approach at the time, the invitation came from the Bank of China—responsible only for foreign exchange and trade—and not from any government agencies. It was agreed that the visit would be in April, two months later.

I was at home on a Sunday that February, preparing for a mission to Thailand the next day, when I received a call from Shahid Husain's secretary that I was to cancel the mission and come and see Husain on Monday. Husain was quite clear in his instruction. The situation was completely fluid. The China program could end up anywhere in the Bank, although East Asia was the obvious choice, and Husain would be accompanying McNamara on his visit, along with the head of finance and the legal counsel. Husain, therefore, wanted the following documents on China prepared: a Country Economic Memorandum, a Country Assistance Strategy (CAS) paper, and an IDA eligibility paper, all of which had to be done in time for the McNamara mission in less than two months. Moreover, because this whole exercise had to be done in absolute secrecy—the Bank did not want to be perceived as jumping the gun where extremely sensitive geopolitical issues were involved—I was to work alone, without a team. I was, however, given the use of the office of the chief economist, who was then on home leave, and a secretary of my own. I am happy to say that the three papers were completed on time, to the satisfaction of both Husain and McNamara.

The McNamara mission that April was successful in reaching agreement with the Chinese authorities on their assumption of China's membership in the IMF and the Bank, a measure formalized in June 1980 (see box 5.1). Then began an even more impossible schedule. The reason was that McNamara was to turn 65 in 1981, and although there was no formal retirement age for the president, he wanted to follow the rule that governed the rest of the staff. Because he was undoubtedly the force behind China's entry to the Bank—without him the process would have required at least another 5 to 10 years—we on the China team, as well as the Chinese government, wanted to complete a cycle of activities before July 1981, when he would retire. This schedule meant an operational mission went to China in July 1980, led by Shahid Husain, to agree on the work program for the coming 12 months, with an economic report set as the first task to be completed. A Country Economic Memorandum would not have been sufficient to launch a lending program. We needed instead what was then called a Basic Report—a full economic report with annexes on all major economic and social sectors.

So an economic mission was scheduled to be in China for three months, from October to December 1980. I was to lead the mission in the field and be there the entire period. During the three months, sector and general economic teams would rotate, each for one month at a time. The chief economist of the East Asia Region—formally the chief of the Economic Mission—as well as the Bank's chief economist would join the mission at the end, just before Christmas 1980, to participate in the wrap-up discussions and subsequently to supervise the drafting of the report. The Green Cover draft had to be ready and translated for discussion with the authorities in March 1981 so that a Gray Cover could be issued in April.

The April 1981 completion date for the economic report was critical because the July 1980 mission led by Husain had also agreed to initiate the preparation of a number of projects. At first we thought infrastructure would be the priority—as was recommended in the CAS prepared for McNamara—but the Chinese decided that the first project would be in education. Preparation for this project was, therefore, started in October 1980, too. The April 1981 completion for the economic report was

> **BOX 5.1**
> ## A Personal Note about Robert McNamara
>
> I never knew McNamara personally when he was president of the Bank, but I came to know him to some extent after his retirement from the Bank. In recognition for his personal role in bringing China into the Bank, the Chinese government invited him to spend a couple of weeks in China after his retirement. I was fortunate enough to be given the responsibility of accompanying him on the trip. For two weeks, therefore, the two of us traveled throughout China, including to the Three Gorges, the First Emperor's tomb in Xian, Beijing, and Shanghai. We were alone a lot of the time, and I came to know the personal side of this truly remarkable man. Since then, McNamara visited me when I was the head of the Bank Office in Beijing and again later in Delhi.
>
> It was in Delhi, in 2000, I think, that McNamara had an evening engagement canceled at short notice and ended up spending an evening alone with me at my house. This visit gave him the opportunity to reminisce about his meeting in 1980 with Deng Xiaoping, China's supreme leader at the time, and to compare his experiences with Chinese and Indian leaders. McNamara told me that in his private meeting with Deng, Deng made one simple point very forcefully: China was determined to modernize and develop its economy. With the World Bank's assistance, China would be able to achieve its goals faster and more efficiently. Without the Bank, China would still do it but it might take longer.

essential because the Board of Executive Directors had to have the report before we could even contemplate inviting the government for negotiation in May, thus making it possible for Board presentation of the first loan to China in June, just before McNamara's retirement. This schedule was impossible in any circumstances. In addition, China was a country that we knew very little about; its government had never dealt with us and knew hardly anything about the Bank.

Nonetheless, the schedule was met, and we went to the Board in June 1981 and received strong support for the First China Higher Education Project. McNamara, however, broke his arm playing tennis the weekend before and missed the Board meeting.

One month after the McNamara visit in 1980, Caio Koch-Weser, then McNamara's personal assistant, and I were appointed as the core of the China management team, Caio Koch-Weser becoming the program division chief and I the lead economist responsible for managing the economic and sector work and for leading the policy dialogue. Adrian Wood then joined us as the principal economist. I remained in this assignment for a decade, from 1980 to 1990, taking on the added responsibility of heading the Resident Office in Beijing, which I established in 1985.

A Marriage Made in Heaven

True to the sentiment expressed by Deng, China made full use of the World Bank in its reform and development programs. Although the Bank program in any large country would be diverse and rich, the China program in the 1980s seemed particularly so. Apart from the traditional activities of lending and project supervision, economic and sector work, and policy dialogue, the Bank program included the following:

- A China-specific Economic Development Institute (EDI, the precursor of the World Bank Institute) program. In addition to Chinese participation in Washington and regional activities, a series of EDI courses were conducted in China every year, in collaboration with Chinese training institutes. The courses were tailored to Chinese requirements and were conducted in Chinese as well as English. This program was funded partly by the United Nations Development Programme (UNDP).

- A 1-year economics training program at Oxford University for senior economists in government think tanks and agencies. The program included a crash course in English for those participants without the required language skills. Participants were taught by regular Oxford tutors and professors. Funded by UNDP and later the Ford Foundation, the program trained nearly 70 economists, many of whom are in senior government and research positions today.

- A China-specific publication program. We did not suffer from the usual dissemination problem of the Bank's economic work simply because our counterpart agencies were very keen to disseminate the Bank's economic and sector work widely. All major economic and sector reports were published in Chinese and sold in retail bookstores throughout China. The 1985 economic reports, for instance, which outlined a possible path for China's reform and development over the following 20 years, were published and sold at an equivalent of US$0.50. Tens of thousands of copies were actually sold. The report of the *Bashan* Boat Conference (discussed later) became part of basic university reading in economics. Major Bank reports on development issues were also translated and published in China.

- Collaborative economic research. A program of collaborative research between the economic research staff of the Bank (the development policy staff) and several Chinese economic research institutes was initiated soon after the first economic mission. Following the tradition of the first economic mission, every economic and sector mission in the 1980s worked with a counterpart team that shared responsibility for research and analysis.

From the first education project approved in June 1980, the lending program expanded rapidly and reached nearly US$2 billion a year by the end of the decade—one of the largest lending programs in the Bank Group. Contrary to early expectation, the program was not concentrated on infrastructure but was a broad-based, diversified program: from education and health to water supply and sanitation; to agriculture, forestry, and rural development; to oil and gas; and, of course, to highways, ports, and thermal and hydroelectric power. There was only one adjustment loan, and it was based on rural reforms already achieved. Conditions were never a major element in our lending, but through project lending, the Bank nonetheless made major contributions in areas such as investment analysis and decisionmaking, international competitive bidding, infrastructure construction and supervision, cost recovery, and other aspects of investment discipline. The management of the Bank's lending program was always the responsibility of the State Planning Commission, which decided how Bank lending would fit in China's overall investment programs.

Within this large and diverse program of assistance, I think I can objectively say that the Bank made the greatest difference in China in the economic and sector work program and the policy dialogue built on it. I personally had the major responsibility in this part of the program, so I may be biased, but I think most senior Chinese officials knowledgeable about the China program in the 1980s would share this view. We were very deeply involved in the reform process, not just an external observer commenting on the process. Together with the Chinese, we learned about the Chinese economy; the devastation of the Cultural Revolution meant that even Chinese economists knew little about the economy in the early 1980s. We pushed the envelope of what was feasible alongside the Chinese reformists, but we were never far enough ahead to be irrelevant.

The following account of the economic and sector work program of the Bank and the process of policy dialogue will better illustrate the nature of the partnership between the Bank and the Chinese in China's reform process. The program comprised two parallel tracks: (a) preparation and dissemination of economic and sector reports and (b) conferences—that is, a forum for international experts and practitioners to present the lessons of international experience and to discuss and comment on Chinese development and reforms. Above all, the objective was to transfer knowledge.

The objective of the first economic report—a main report and 10 annexes on economic and social sectors—completed in 1981 was to analyze the Chinese economy for the Bank, as well as for the international community and the Chinese, to benchmark their economic achievements and structure against the rest of the world. Although outside scholars on China assisted in the preparation for the mission, we decided that we needed to rely mainly on Bank staff members, not only because they seemed best qualified but also because of the need for different parts of the Bank to learn about China. The mission, therefore, was drawn from all parts of the Bank, including both economists from the central economic complex and sector experts from the different sector departments (see box 5.2).

BOX 5.2
The First Mission and the Future Premier

This first mission from the World Bank attracted the interest of a Chinese economist who was just reentering government at the time. He volunteered to be the counterpart on industry to the Bank team and wrote a short piece on Chinese industry for the mission. His name was Zhu Rongji, later China's premier during the late 1990s and early 2000s.

This mission was the first instance of a large external team (some 20 persons) coming to China to study its economy, and there was a great deal of concern within China about what the visit entailed and whether we might be foreign intelligence agents. In response, we suggested to the government that it should appoint a counterpart team to attend every meeting, see every statistic we would receive, and read every draft. Indeed, we expected the counterparts to draft parts of the report. This arrangement proved extremely useful and became a practice for all future economic and sector missions.

This first report of the Bank attracted the attention of Chinese senior leaders, who since then have paid much attention to the work of the Bank. Zhao Ziyang, China's premier during most of the 1980s, paid particular attention to Bank reports. In 1983, President Alden W. Clausen visited China and met with Deng Xiaoping, who explained that China was interested in the economic work of the Bank. China had just decided to launch a development program aimed at quadrupling its per capita income from the US$200 of 1980 to US$800 by 2000. Deng invited the Bank to send a mission to assess the feasibility of this program and to offer suggestions on how the objectives might be achieved. At the end of the meeting with Deng, Premier Zhao took me aside and told me that he personally liked the first report very much and hoped that the Bank would produce an even more useful second report.

In response, the Bank sent a second comprehensive mission to China in 1984. Unlike the first report, the report of this mission (World Bank 1985a) was forward looking, in accordance with Deng's request. The report, *China: Long-Term Development Issues and Options*, was published with six sectoral annexes. Since we wanted to bring to China some of the best economic thinking available, the second report was prepared by a team of Bank staff members as well as external consultants.

The Bank also served as a conduit for international knowledge and expertise through a series of conferences. The subjects of these conferences, in fact, reflected the rapid progress made in Chinese thinking on reforms.

The first, held in 1982, took place in a politically sensitive period when even Soviet-type reforms were in question politically. Other than Adrian Wood and myself, all the other international participants were East European practitioners in Soviet-type reforms, particularly price reforms. Two major conclusions came out of this conference. First was that price reforms of the type attempted in the Soviet Union and Eastern Europe—more price adjustments than fundamental reforms of price-setting mechanisms—were not seen as true reforms. China thus began to look beyond the Soviet Union and Eastern Europe for its reform strategy. By the end of the decade, China was far ahead of the Soviet Union in moving toward a market economy. Second was the consensus among both international and Chinese participants that China simply did not have the margin of error to consider rapid reforms or shock therapy.

Gradualism—in the sense that elements of reform came sequentially rather than simultaneously—may be the signature characteristic of Chinese reforms, but the pace was certainly rapid. Three years later, following the publication of the second Bank economic report, the question the reformists faced was how to manage a market economy and, particularly, the transition to it from a command economy. To address that question, we organized what has become known in China as the *Bashan*

Boat Conference. The premier attached a great deal of importance to this conference and wanted many of the senior economic policymakers to participate. To ensure their complete attention, the conference was held on a boat (the *Bashan*) that floated slowly down the Yangtze River through the Three Gorges for seven days. Spouses of the international participants were invited, and each day the boat would dock to allow them to go sightseeing while the conference continued.

The foreign participants to this conference, in addition to Adrian Wood and myself, included Jim Tobin, the Nobel Laureate from Yale, who explained the basic principles of macromanagement in a market economy; Sir Alec Cairncross of Oxford, who talked about management of a market economy, particularly the postwar experience of the United Kingdom in dismantling the wartime price control and rationing systems; Otmar Eminger, former president of the Bundesbank, who talked about the role of an independent central bank in macromanagement as well as the German experience in dismantling the wartime control economy; Michel Albert, former head of the French planning commission, who talked about indicative planning in a market economy; and Janos Kornai of Hungary, who talked about behavior of a planned economy that may persist in a reformed scenario.

After 1985, we organized annual conferences on increasingly detailed topics as reform deepened in China and a market economy began to emerge. The conferences included one on enterprise reform and corporate governance, with participants including Peter Drucker and the chief executive officers of Petrobras and Volkswagen, and other conferences on central banking, banking reforms, and so on.

What lessons would I draw from the first decade of the Bank's relationship with China?

When I returned from the first operational mission to China in July 1980, I was asked at the East Asia Departmental Meeting how I would characterize this new relationship. I replied, "It was a marriage made in heaven." Nearly a quarter century later, I would still describe it as such. But there was no question who was the lead partner. China drove the agenda and decided what the country needed from the Bank. The economic dialogue was always within the Chinese ideological and political limits. It was China that decided on the lending programs, which formed a part of its overall investment plans.

The Bank was a much-valued partner. By effectively responding to China's needs, we did make a real difference to China's transition from a Soviet-type command economy to a market economy, to the country's achievements in lifting more than 200 million people out of poverty and in more than quadrupling the average income of more than 1 billion people over the past two decades. But we never lost sight of the fact that the program belonged to the Chinese.

India, 1996–2002

The Travails of an Arranged Marriage

If the relationship between China and the Bank could be described as a marriage made in heaven, flushed in the 1980s with the excitement of newly discovering each other, then that of India and the Bank should be seen as an arranged marriage. By the 1990s, this marriage was well into its fifth decade. India has always been a reluctant partner. IDA had been created by the pooling of bilateral funds, the most important of which were the economic aid from France and the United Kingdom for their former colonies. Being by far the most populous of these colonies, India understandably felt entitled to the lion's share of IDA resources. It was the donors who arranged for India to obtain its share of the concessionary funds through the Bank Group.

As to the other services offered by the Bank, many in India, including many politicians, felt the country could do without them. Sovereign India never borrowed from the international capital markets, and for many years it borrowed from the IBRD most reluctantly. India has some of the world's best economists, including a Nobel Laureate and world-renowned professors. What had been needed was not advice from external agencies but simply the political will in India to do what was necessary. As for the requirements that come with borrowing, many Indians saw them only as nuisances to be circumvented whenever possible. One such example was international competitive bidding. For many years, for instance, the Indian agencies responsible for highway projects to be financed by the Bank would slice up the highways into such small construction contracts that hardly any international contractors would be interested in bidding, leaving the field open for domestic firms. Bank bashing was a favorite sport among some Indian politicians, and only their ignorance caused them often to target the IMF for alleged sins of the Bank.

There was always agreement between the two partners that the Bank should make a greater contribution to Indian development than it actually had. The disagreement was over whose fault it was. Like many arranged marriages, however, the relationship has endured and grown stronger over time, despite the absence of romance in the beginning and the persistence of irritating behavior on both sides over the decades. Compared with the relationship with China, the Bank's relationship with India was actually deeper, more solid, and based on a high degree of knowledge—if not always understanding—of each other. It was this relationship that I inherited in the middle of 1996, as the first country director to be stationed in Delhi.

From the onset, it was obvious that my task was going to be very different from that in China. I found my counterpart to be Montek Singh Ahluwalia, already a star economist in the Bank when I joined as a Young Professional. By 1996, he was an economist and bureaucrat renowned both within and outside India. He and we in the Bank by and large shared the same views on what was needed to accelerate reform and growth, as well as on the frustration in persuading the politicians to act. The task of the Bank clearly was to work in partnership with Indians like Montek to persuade the politicians to introduce the right policies and implement the necessary programs.

Challenges of Development in India

In 1996, there were reasons for optimism that the Bank could finally make a difference in India. Reforms of one form or another had been in progress for nearly a decade. Growth had clearly accelerated, and the incidence of poverty had finally begun to fall after years of persistence. Some states were breaking out of the pack by pursuing aggressive reform and growth policies, led by a new generation of politicians. Moreover, even then, India was still considerably ahead of China in the strength of its market infrastructure; in the rule of law and property rights; in the size, dynamism, and discipline of the private sector in the smaller state sector; and in the depth and diversity of the financial system. In several areas, however, the challenges were formidable.

Agriculture and Human Resource Development

In 1980, India statistically was at about the same level of development and per capita income as China. In both countries, the bulk of the population, particularly the vast majority of the poor, lived (and still live) in the rural areas. Reforms, therefore, needed to be initiated, or at least to be based, on agricultural growth and rural development to lead to rising incomes and declining poverty among the rural population. As noted previously, this situation paralleled that of China, where rapidly rising rural incomes triggered a virtuous cycle of growth and reforms. That response did not occur in India, despite reforms being launched probably not much later than in China.

To begin with, for several reasons agriculture did not serve as the launch pad for reforms. First, the degree of distortions in India's rural incentive system was never as high as in prereform China. The distortions were so large in China that their correction led to an explosion of growth. In India, however, the potential agricultural response to reforms was much more limited. Second, at the initiation of reforms, India did not have the benefits China had from the vast investments in rural areas that took place in the decades before reforms. Perhaps most important of all, the level of human resource development among the rural population at the start of the reform period was much lower in India than in China. Literacy in India in 1980 was below 50 percent, with female literacy only half that of male. Only a little more than half the population had easy access to safe water, and health indicators were closer to levels in Sub-Saharan Africa than in Asia. The capability of the rural population to take advantage of the opportunity to raise rural incomes was, therefore, much more limited in India.

The inability to stimulate rapid agricultural growth meant that rural poverty fell only very gradually, especially during the 1980s. The persistence of widespread poverty exerted enormous pressure on the government to provide subsidies. Thus, a two-track system for such basic commodities as grains, fertilizers, water, and power also emerged in India, but in a very different way from in China. In addition to market prices, governments at both the federal and state levels provided large subsidies to distribute commodities at below-market prices to poor households. As might be expected, abuses and leakages were widespread.

The inability of these antipoverty programs to reach the poor became quickly known. Not surprisingly, little was done to change them, because the real beneficiaries were often the very same bureaucrats who managed the programs, as well as vested interest groups with powerful political ties. The number and size of such programs grew rapidly, eventually crippling governments, especially at the state level.

Over time, pressure to provide subsidies to the poor, especially in rural areas, became a main feature of Indian politics. Indeed, the political process at the state level had become one of "competitive populism," with the political parties promising in each election to provide free water, electricity, kerosene, and other essential commodities to rural households. At present, subsidies for power, food, fertilizer, and petroleum come to more than 3 percent of GDP. With such a huge burden on the budget, some states are facing difficulties even in paying wages and salaries, much less in funding any form of development expenditures.

Infrastructure

Another consequence of persistent poverty in India is the political pressure against reforming the public utility sector, where public financing has had to cover huge losses. The magnitude of the problem can be best illustrated by the case of the power sector. In the late 1990s, its total financial losses came to more than US$5 billion a year. The Indian prime minister himself has estimated that theft alone in the sector amounted to US$4 billion a year. To put this figure in perspective, note that US$5 billion is half of what all the state governments in India combined were then spending on all levels of education every year. The sum was double what they were all spending on health, and three times what they were spending on water supply.

Those huge financial losses borne by every Indian every year would perhaps be more tolerable if they led to a high quality of power supply. On the contrary, the losses have led to inadequate investment and maintenance. As a result, India is among the worst developing countries in terms of reliability of power supply. India's manufacturing sector suffers twice over from India's power sector policies. It not only receives low-quality power, but is also forced to pay tariffs above cost to cross-subsidize residential and agricultural consumers. Industrial tariffs in India, at US$0.07 to US$0.10 per kilowatt-hour, are among the highest in the world. A particular irony is that, though most of the theft and subsidies to the power sector are allegedly attributable to efforts to help the poor, nearly three-quarters of poor households, especially in rural areas, do not even have access to electricity.

There is no disagreement in India that any attempt to reform electricity distribution requires—as critical elements—governance reforms to stem the theft and corruption that plague the power sector and tariff reforms to ensure that tariffs more closely reflect costs and are more predictable. But those who benefit from the current situation and somehow pocket the US$4 million to US$6 billion lost in the system every year represent powerful interests strongly opposed to reforms.

Other aspects of infrastructure have suffered from equally inadequate investment and maintenance. Increasingly, the lack of or the inadequacy of infrastructure services is contributing to slow growth below the levels that could be achieved otherwise. The difference in infrastructure development between India and China is most striking. In 1980, electric power and highways were probably better developed in India than in China. Two decades later, India has fallen far behind. The 1998 *Global Competitiveness Report*, for instance, rated India last among the 53 countries surveyed in the adequacy of infrastructure (World Economic Forum 1998). In the same survey for 2004, India was rated much higher than in previous years in all categories of competitiveness—macroeconomic performance, business efficiency, and government efficiency—except infrastructure, where it stood 57th of the 60 countries surveyed (World Economic Forum 2004).

Thus, in India, low agricultural growth and a low level of human resource development in the rural areas have led to enduring rural poverty. The persistence of this poverty has created political pressures to subsidize the rural population and other poor, draining resources away from development expenditures and from investment in infrastructure and growth-promoting activities. These poorly targeted antipoverty programs, which suffered from substantial abuses and leakage and did little to help the poor, led to growing fiscal deficits and reduced overall levels of savings and investment, making rapid growth difficult to sustain and the decline of poverty very slow. The challenge is for the government to design a reform strategy consistent with the conditions and the capabilities of India—particularly its political structure—that would promote growth, reduce poverty, and thereby build popular support for reforms. Indeed, in my view, no attempt to understand the economic challenges of India can conclude without an examination of India's politics.

The Politics of Reform

In many discussions about the failure of India to pursue reform in certain areas, such as the power sector, a common argument has been "but we are a democracy." Indeed, in some circles, democracy is used almost as an excuse for the difficulties of reform and growth and for the poverty that still exists in the country. Although it is incorrect to use a generic term such as *democracy* in such a context, any evaluation of the record of democracy as practiced in India since independence against the record of poverty reduction and human development of the bulk of the population would produce at best a mixed verdict.

The key question is whether politics in India present an advantage or an obstacle to reform and development. In India, politicians did not seem to have an ideological bias for or against reform. Reforms over the past two decades, however, have been largely top down and government led; there is little evidence of grassroots-based reforms similar to those in rural China. The ruling politicians and their technocratic advisers have initiated and pushed reform in India. Where it has started, however, the process of reform is not unlike the Chinese experience. Reformers have improvised as they have gone along, pausing and reviewing at every stage. Incremental reform has enabled them to erode or chip away at opposing interest groups, most clearly where reform has made considerable advances—telecommunications and external liberalization, for example. Nevertheless, in areas such as basic education and health, progress has been limited because the local elites who controlled such services apparently had no incentive to improve them.

Indeed, telecommunications is a sector where reform has clearly been successful. Today, compared with the early 1990s, government control is less, a regulator is in place, day-to-day political interference is reduced, services have improved, and pro-reform constituencies—consumers and corporate interests who have benefited from competition—now exist. An optimistic view of such experience could hold that the process of gradualism has allowed India to plan and sequence its reforms coherently, ensured democratic buy-in, prevented policy reversals, and made all major political parties associate themselves with the reform agenda through the election cycle, which has seen them all govern at the center. A more pessimistic view would be that special circumstances were at work in the external and telecommunications sectors that may not apply to the rest of the economy. Reforms of the external sector in 1990–91 were undertaken in response to an economic crisis and to a large extent involved stroke-of-the-pen measures. In telecommunications, the process was essentially one of dividing up a rapidly growing pie, with incremental resources being generated alongside improving services to the consumers.

There can be no disagreement, however, that to accelerate reform and poverty reduction, India must break the vicious cycle that now exists in areas such as power reform and create a virtuous cycle of reform and growth. Attempts made in the recent past gave cause for optimism. Since the early 1990s, we saw the emergence of young, technocratic politicians at the state level, the most conspicuous of whom was Chandrababu Naidu in Andhra Pradesh. Naidu's technocratic credentials and records once won him the "Businessman of the Year" award in India. Not only was he attempting to pursue a comprehensive reform strategy in his state, but also he had run his election on the platform of reform and economic performance. Throughout India (in Madhya Pradesh, Karnataka, and Tamil Nadu), signs began to appear of performance becoming one of the criteria for the election contests. Recent state and national elections have, however, demonstrated the difficulty of maintaining such a course in the face of resistance from deeply rooted vested interests able to counter reformist programs with hard-core populism.

Indeed, increasingly better articulated aspirations for jobs, infrastructure, health, education, and other social services are changing the nature of Indian politics. The growing middle class, especially in urban areas, represents an informed and increasingly powerful political force. The maturity of Indian democracy is inevitable and will create the conditions for accelerated growth and poverty reduction. In my view, however, the change will be slow, and worse, occasionally reversed, unless a major effort is made to improve the basic education and health of the masses. Indian education projects an impressive image to the world, with Indian managers running some of the world's largest companies, with the elite graduates from the Indian Institutes of Technologies much sought after by multinational corporations all over the world, and with the country's global leadership in knowledge-intensive industries such as information technology and pharmaceuticals. This image obscures the appalling conditions of basic education and health among large segments of the population, especially among women. For as much as 40 percent of the population, basic human development is no higher than in Sub-Saharan Africa. Indeed, my biggest question about India continues to be why the world's most populous democracy did so little for the education and health of its masses. In my view, this failure is the primary explanation of the vicious cycle that exists between reforms and politics in India. As long as a large part of the electorate remains illiterate, uninformed, and impoverished, the worst features of Indian politics will persist and continue to be an impediment to accelerated growth and poverty reduction. The challenge will be to transform this situation into a virtuous cycle, based on accelerated human development among the masses and democracy being the asset it should be to the country's development.

A New Approach for the World Bank in India

When I became country director for India in late 1996, there were persuasive long-term as well as short-term reasons for a new approach for the World Bank in India. From a long-term perspective, few in the Bank or in India would disagree that the Bank's contribution to development and poverty reduction in India over the preceding five decades had been disappointing relative to India's needs and potential. A short-term reason also existed. When the worst of the 1991 crisis was over and the first wave of reforms focusing on the external sector was under way, the need for balance-of-payments financing from the Bank began to fade. However, India's economic performance continued to be hampered by unsustainable domestic policies (for example, power, food, and fertilizer subsidies, as well as civil service wages), which in turn fed large fiscal deficits at both the central (federal) and state levels. However, we were unable to articulate a program of assistance that would provide an effective and coherent response to those policy issues, thus greatly diminishing India's appetite for borrowing from the IBRD for what was a relatively disparate program of isolated operations. As a result, our lending to India dropped and softened considerably (two-thirds IDA, one-third IBRD). This situation began to concern some of our major shareholders, prompting them to call for India—as they had for China—to graduate from the IDA.

The desire of both the Indian authorities and the Bank to increase IBRD lending also seemed to be leading to some undesirable trends. The pressure to include a particular large loan for a power project in a particular fiscal year, for instance, apparently led to an accelerated processing schedule that drew strong criticism from the World Bank's Inspection Panel, which heard the appeal from some project-affected groups. Preparation of a large infrastructure loan seemed to have been launched without sufficient thinking about the rationale of the proposed operation other than to boost IBRD lending.

As it turned out, the beginning of my assignment to India coincided with James Wolfensohn's first visit to the country as president of the Bank. In fact, my very first day in India was the day I accompanied him on his arrival in Mumbai to begin his official visit. The discussion with the Indian authorities during that visit clearly indicated both an opportunity and a desire for an expanded relationship on the Indian side.

The need for a new approach was, therefore, compelling. Although I was very new to India, I was fortunate in having on the management team individuals with long experience and a deep understanding of India. Together we began to formulate a new strategy, the key elements of which I outline in the following paragraphs; however, I would not be so presumptuous as to refer to these elements as "lessons." The experience is much too new, and results are not yet apparent. These elements should be considered only as features of our programs in India in the late 1990s and early 2000s that might also apply to other countries served by the Bank.

Learning How to Work in a Democratic System

At least during most of my career in the Bank, the staff had been directed to be completely nonpolitical. Until I came to India, it was also very much my personal belief that Bank staff members should not be concerned with politics. My Indian experience showed me how wrong this attitude was. It did not take long for me to realize how ill equipped the Bank, as an institution, and I personally were for our mandate in India as a result of our lack of understanding of politics in the country.

The reality of the Indian democratic system became quickly and simply clear. Soon after my arrival, I found that we had completed an appraisal of a rural water supply project that seemed well prepared, with the borrower committed to significant reforms of water policy, including pricing and supply management. We were ready for negotiation. The only problem was the timing—immediately before the election of a new state assembly. In this election, the opposition party, which had run on a platform of giving free power and free water to farmers, won. Although the new government was extremely anxious to proceed with the project and had promised that it would "ring-fence" our project area to adhere to the agreements on water pricing reached with our appraisal mission, there was no possibility that we could proceed with the project.

In fact, the policy of the new government on free power and free water was so against the direction of reforms throughout the country that we decided that we needed to make the position of the World Bank absolutely clear. Accordingly, we advised the state government that not only would we drop the water supply project, but also we would not consider any lending to the state as long as the policy of free water and free power remained. Having learned about the dominance of politics, one of my first trips within India was to travel to the state to deliver that message directly to the new chief minister. This trip breached the strict protocol that the central government bureaucracy had imposed, stipulating that no Bank staff member should have direct contact with politicians. Fortunately, our counterparts in the central government at the time supported what we were doing and raised no objection. From this unhappy beginning, dialogue with the chief ministers of states became a very important part of our relationship.

In response to our discovery of the importance of Indian politics, we first added capacity in political analysis to the Delhi office. We made much greater use of conditionality in our operations in order to help the technocrats resist political pressure. In many states, we had an understanding that we would not process any sensitive operations the year before local government elections. In states where the Bank had a high profile in supporting a controversial reform program, we would, in fact, agree on a hiatus in all our operations and dialogue in the year before local elections. For particularly difficult policy measures, we would no longer accept the agreement of the bureaucrats as sufficient. We required that the state assembly debate the policy measures as a condition of project appraisal or negotiation. Increasingly, we required explicit political endorsement of the programs we supported. The electoral cycle was explicitly built into our operations. In Andhra Pradesh, for instance, we prepared a large multisectoral project. Although it was an investment—not an adjustment—operation, the various sectoral programs were linked closely to a number of policy measures. We knew that, in the course of project implementation, a state election would occur, with the possibility that a new government might result. We, therefore, scheduled—and provided for in the legal agreements—a midterm review of the project a few months after the planned election and required that the existing state government confirm its commitment to the programs before the project could continue (as it turned out, Naidu, the incumbent chief minister, won reelection on a reform platform, and implementation continued without interruption).

I knew from my experience in Nigeria how difficult it is for the Bank to withdraw from any country, particularly a large, important one, even if conditions no longer exist for an effective Bank role. This difficulty was much less acute for states within the country. In India, therefore, we began to withdraw from states where the government had opted for policies that were clearly against reform. We never gave these decisions any publicity, but this being India, the media and the public soon became aware that the Bank was increasingly allocating its resources to reforming states and withdrawing from nonreforming states.

Shifting Our Relationship to the Subnational Level

Changes in India were also conducive to our new approach. The mid 1990s witnessed a change on the political front in India: with the decline of the Congress Party, the only real national party, regional parties gained in individual stature and influence in the states, and the central government—a coalition of these regional parties—gradually lost its leadership. As a sign of the growing influence of regional parties, India started to witness the emergence in a few states of reform-minded political leaders who were willing to confront critical economic issues in their states, such as state finances and power sector reforms. Under India's constitution, most of these issues require policy decisions at the state level.

At the same time, we were inevitably frustrated in our effort to initiate a policy dialogue with the central government or to influence policy at that level. Decision-making was quite inefficient and was accomplished through a protracted process of internal negotiations and horse-trading. By contrast, in many states the context was very different. Chief ministers were clearly in charge and functioning as political leaders as well as chief executives. A much greater chance of following through existed after an agreement was reached with the chief minister at the state level than with any senior official in the central government. With the relocation of country directors to the field, the Bank also made working with the state governments much more effective. Increasingly, therefore, we shifted the Bank's relationship in India, including both policy dialogue and lending operations, to the states.

Selectivity and Demonstration Effect: The Focus-State Strategy

The Bank obviously cannot deal with all Indian states simultaneously. We therefore adopted a new strategy, known as the *focus-state strategy*, which governed our work from 1998, when the Board approved it. The core of the new strategy was to be selective in our engagement with the states and to concentrate our resources on a few focus states. The main criteria that we used to select them were (a) their relative poverty, (b) their willingness to undertake comprehensive reforms, and above all (c) their invitation to the Bank to work with them and help them formulate and implement reforms. As soon as the Bank was able to articulate what it meant by comprehensive reforms—namely, to include at least fiscal, governance, and power sector reforms—the states basically selected themselves to become focus states.

As we saw it, the strategy had many advantages: it helped us increase our influence and leverage, look at state development issues in a comprehensive way, engage at the highest political level, and create competition among states. But it also involved a few risks, some of which may have become more visible over time.

We increased our influence and leverage in several ways. The strategy allowed us to gain substantial leverage and influence in the focus states. Although it implied that we might end up limiting our engagement to only a few states, the scale of such engagement within each state would be quite significant, much more so than ever before. This involvement gained all the more significance given the fiscal crisis faced by those states, particularly because the Bank was able to provide a mix of investment lending and budget support. Equally important were the analytical contributions and knowledge that underpinned the formulation of the reforms. The respective state governments appreciated our role as a knowledge bank much more than the central government did. The strategy also enabled us to get into sensitive issues that would have been difficult to tackle up front with the central government. Governance, for example, became a central feature of our dialogue with the focus states with which we discussed anticorruption strategies, freedom of information, deregulation, and so on. In Uttar Pradesh, India's largest state and one of its poorest and most notorious for poor governance, we initiated our program with a comprehensive study on governance in the state and with a first adjustment operation focused on governance reforms.

We pursued a comprehensive approach in our relationship with individual states. Probably the greatest benefit of the strategy is that it enabled the Bank to take a comprehensive approach to the development challenges of a state. Looking at a state as if it were a country, we would first carry out a comprehensive analysis of its economy, finances, and development prospects. We would then formulate a State Assistance Strategy (SAS, sort of a mini-CAS) that encompassed both sectoral and cross-sectoral priorities and laid out the rationale and sequencing of our proposed interventions. In doing so, we set the tone early for a multisectoral approach and carried out our policy dialogue through frequent multisectoral missions. We were also better able to exploit synergies and support reforms across the board in an integrated manner. For example, through adjustment operations, we supported broad governance reforms, and through investment lending, we supported the application of these reforms to individual sectors (for example, public works, social sectors, or irrigation). The multisectoral approach also allowed us to influence sector policies even in sectors where we had had no lending, the centrality of reforms in such sectors determining the overall assistance strategy in the state (SAS triggers).

We were able to engage at the highest political level. As mentioned earlier, becoming a focus state began very much as a process of self-selection. However, proceeding with the reforms and, hence, the Bank's program required a continued engagement by those who made the final policy decisions. In all the focus states, the chief minister, the political head of the government, led the dialogue with the Bank, ensuring not only ownership and clarity of engagement (or nonengagement at times) but also a good understanding of the comprehensive nature of the strategy and the adoption of SAS triggers.

We promoted competition among states. From the very beginning, a rationale for the strategy was that extensive Bank support for reforms in focus states would encourage other reform-shy states to follow suit, thus creating demonstration effects and competition among states for receiving Bank support. The manner in which the first three focus states selected themselves is evidence that such demonstration effects worked. The competition among the three states continued as they moved further in their reforms. The Bank's involvement was increasingly regarded as providing a sort of Good Housekeeping Seal of Approval, a sign of significantly increased influence on policymaking. Some states even approached the Bank to engage in a comprehensive policy dialogue with no immediate prospect of a large lending program given the uncertainty of reforms. Even at the sector level, increased competition for Bank funds among states was visible. In rural water supply, for instance, the Bank and the Ministry of Finance actually held a competition among states and selected state projects for support according to agreed criteria of reforms.

There is no question that the strategy had its own risks, costs, and limitations. Understandably, the central government expressed growing political concerns about the concentration of Bank resources in a few states, which led to some tension in our relationship with India. At the same time, the central government recognized the economic rationale behind the strategy and, in fact, started to introduce performance-based assistance to the states. We still did not have a seat at the table at the center for engaging in broad, all-India macroeconomic issues, even if we were able to make some headway in a few selected areas. A large set of policy issues remain uncovered. A critical gap in our strategy is the negligible effect we have had on the very poor, nonreforming states, where the prospect of the Bank's providing financial assistance is still quite remote given serious governance problems. We accepted the reality of a growing disparity among states in India. Internally, the focus-state strategy is quite resource intensive because each state's program takes progressively the shape and size of an active country program. All three states in which we were at some point involved simultaneously are very large. However, the budget resources available were a fraction of what they were for countries with much smaller populations. We were achieving economies of scale as we progressed further in the implementation of the strategy, but it was not possible to cut the investment required for policy dialogue. The United Kingdom's Department for International Development, one of our strongest partners, made available to the Bank an India-specific trust fund of UK£4 million (about US$5.8 million) for a three-year period to help the Bank continue its focus-state work and expand it to poorer states.

Although this strategy was first articulated in 1997, implementation was still at an early stage when I left India in 2002. It would be difficult to describe it as a success or a failure. The strategy continued to be controversial, both in India and within the Bank. Particularly after the 2004 election in India, the Bank will be challenged to hold firm to the principles of the strategy. What seems to be beyond debate, however, is that the World Bank must always have a clearly defined and well-articulated strategy in India. Given the persistence of large-scale poverty in India, the country's dominance in determining the possibility of achieving the Millennium Development Goals worldwide, and opportunities that exist of achieving a real breakthrough in poverty reduction comparable to the achievements in China in the 1980s and 1990s, India's performance in the coming decades will continue to be critical to the rest of the world. The contribution of the Bank's program to the country's poverty reduction effort will continue to be a key measure of the Bank's performance.

Concluding Remarks

The past two decades not only have given me an enormously satisfying professional experience but also have provided me with a rich opportunity for learning. This final section briefly summarizes the major lessons that I have learned. Like much of economic science, the most important principles are often the simplest and will sound almost tautological, except that they are not always the principles followed.

From my personal experience, the overriding lesson of the past two decades must be that there is no unique path to economic growth and poverty reduction. Each country has the opportunity and the need to determine its own strategy, depending on its own capacity and conditions. Although this pragmatic principle may be obvious, unfortunately too many countries still try to follow textbook prescriptions or external advice with inadequate considerations of their own capabilities and conditions. Equally unfortunately, too many economists still try to develop standard prescriptions for economic success and to advise countries without adequately understanding the country's capabilities and conditions.

There are, however, conditions without which, in my view, sustained economic growth and poverty reduction seem impossible. One is a minimum level of basic human development—basic education and health of the bulk of the population. Without these conditions, economic progress and political progress would not seem to be possible. Another is a reasonable level of governance and of institution. These conditions are necessary but not sufficient for economic progress. Effective institutions with the wrong policies can lead to disastrous results, as the Chinese experience demonstrates.

The need for a pragmatic approach, which is based on actual country conditions and capabilities, is true for a Bank's assistance program as well as for a country's development strategy. The requirement for effective country management is not unlike the advice Bob Hope had for effective comedians: timing is everything. A comedian must be able to deliver his message at precisely the right moment and to the right audience. The right assistance strategy for China today is unlikely to be the same as in the 1980s. The right strategy for India is unlikely to be the same as for China. And how do we ensure that the timing is right and the audience correct? Only through timely and continuous analysis of our client country's economic, social, and political conditions.

A time will come when conditions no longer exist for an effective role for the Bank, and the best strategy for the Bank is to withdraw. Some of the best contributions we can make to a country are those projects we refused to finance; the Bank can be as effective by saying "no" as by saying "yes." The opportunity of saying "no" as well as saying "yes" will be greater if the Bank is willing and able to work with subnational governments as well as national governments.

In a democracy, the Bank needs to work within the political cycle of the country rather than in our own fiscal year or CAS cycle. To attempt to agree on operations with high policy content soon before or after an election would seem highly imprudent. The Bank also needs to accept being told "no" by a country's electorate. There will be times when the outcome of a particular election will test the Bank's conviction about the correctness of the policies it was supporting in the country.

The Bank also needs to be realistic about the extent of its influence. It needs to have the humility to accept that, even though it may have made a difference, it cannot take the credit for the successful performance of a client country. Neither should it take the blame for a client's failure.

Shahid Javed Burki

Former Country Director for China (1987–94)

It took one of the most influential macroeconomists of the 20th century to convince Shahid Javed Burki to become an economist. While Javed was studying physics as a Rhodes Scholar at Oxford University, Professor Roy Harrod took note of Javed's previous training in the civil service in his native Pakistan and saw the potential for Javed to put his technical skills to good practical use. As Javed recalls, Harrod told him, "The Pakistani government won't appreciate an academic physicist. Why don't you try economics?"

Javed took Harrod's advice and returned to Pakistan in 1960 to serve in various administrative positions, rising to become chief economist of the government of West Pakistan in 1970. Although he left in that same year to become a senior fellow at the Harvard Institute for International Development and pursue his Ph.D. in economics, he continued to serve as an adviser to the Pakistani government, and in this latter capacity, he traveled to China to study communal agriculture. The data Javed collected in China were of great interest to Western researchers for whom China was still closed, so he decided to write not a dissertation but instead a book, *A Study of Chinese Communes* (Burki 1970).

Also while at Harvard, Javed worked on a World Bank project for employment generation in rural areas and found that his skills were in demand as Bank President Robert McNamara turned his focus on rural development. Javed joined the Bank as a senior economist in the Policy Planning and Review Department in 1974, later becoming its division chief. He found his government experience in Pakistan invaluable to his effectiveness at the Bank. "I recall a report on Pakistan that made 12 recommendations, 10 of which I knew were politically impossible," he says. "It made me realize that it's very necessary for Bank staff to have knowledge of the field."

Javed served as director of the Bank's International Relations Department from 1983 to 1987 before taking on the pivotal role of country director for China and Mongolia. Although China's prior economic reforms had done much to stimulate growth, Javed entered the scene at a time when many basic institutions were still not in place. "We literally taught *macroeconomics* to the Chinese," he says. "The word didn't exist in their language before." Javed's team helped the Chinese government learn the essentials of macroeconomic management, including the establishment of a central bank. A turning point during Javed's tenure as country director came when he made the politically risky decision to maintain the Bank's program following the turmoil in Tiananmen Square in 1989, a controversial move that earned him the government's trust and led to an enormous expansion of the Bank's China portfolio.

Following his time as country director, Javed became vice president of the Bank's Latin America and Caribbean Region in 1994. He took a sabbatical in 1996, however, to return to Pakistan as interim finance minister. Whereas his time at the Bank had taught him the importance of politics in economics, Javed says that in his return to Pakistan he sought to teach the "understanding that without sound economics, politics does not work." Javed returned to his role as vice president of the Latin America and Caribbean Region in 1997, but he left the Bank in 1999 to become chief executive officer of Emerging Markets Partnership–Financial Advisers, a private consulting firm. Reflecting on his career, he notes that his time at the World Bank offered him the most varied experience, spanning all regions of the world. "It's this global view that makes the Bank unique."

6 World Bank Operations
Some Impressions and Lessons

Shahid Javed Burki

THIS CHAPTER IS A BRIEF OVERVIEW OF THE OPERATIONAL LESSONS I LEARNED DURING the time I held two senior management positions at the World Bank. From 1987 to 1994, I was the director of the China Department, and from 1994 to 1999 I worked as vice president of the Latin America and Caribbean Region. The chapter's main purpose is to provide some insights gained by a former World Bank manager on various aspects of the institution's stated and unstated missions. I hope that what I have to say will be of some use for the institution's current managers as they go about doing developmental work in the countries for which they are responsible.

Before I proceed further, it would be useful to define two terms used above. The phrase *operational lessons* refers to what I learned about making the World Bank's operations more effective in the countries in which I worked in the 12-year period between 1987 and 1999. Operations cover a wide *developmental front*, the second phrase to be defined. This term encompasses not only the Bank's lending program but also the economic and sector work the Bank carries out and the technical assistance it provides. The Bank's operations managers should consider their work successful not only when their stated objectives are realized but also when they have contributed to improving the lives over the long run of the citizens of the countries in which the World Bank operates.

I present this work in four parts. The second is a biographical note on how I got to be appointed to two of the most attractive jobs in the Bank—department director of China and vice president of the Latin America and Caribbean Region. I tell

---

The first draft of this chapter was prepared for the Poverty Reduction and Economic Management Network's "Practitioners of Development" analytical initiative. It was read by a number of former and present managers of the World Bank, including Gobind Nankani, Alexander Shakow, Richard Stern, and Roberto Zagha. I have benefited from their insightful comments in reviewing this draft. The views expressed in this chapter, however, are mine and do not in any way reflect those of the people who were generous with their time in reading and commenting on the first version.

this story to make what I think is an important point. In spite of all the commitments the senior managers made—and, presumably, continue to make—about career development and succession planning, most appointments to senior management positions, at least during my time at the Bank, were made for opportunistic reasons. People were put into important slots because they happened to meet some requirements the appointing managers had in mind at the time the decision was made. The biographical note also serves another important function: it details how one particular manager made decisions that had considerable consequences for the Bank's operations on the basis of his personal beliefs and not according to carefully developed institutional criteria. This assertion may be a controversial one. I say this not as a criticism of the Bank's personnel management policies but as my reading of the way a number of management decisions were actually made.

The next part of the chapter discusses a number of lessons I would draw from my 25-year stay in the Bank. In this part of the work, I look not only at my experience as an operations manager but also at the period between 1974 and 1987, when I was deeply involved in policy work, first as a member of the Development Policy Staff (DPS) and later as director of the International Relations Department.

The concluding section provides some advice to the Bank's current management—three things I consider paramount for the institution's future—for maintaining its relevance in a fast-changing world.

A Biographical Note

I joined the Bank in April 1974, largely at the urging of Hollis Chenery, who had taught me development economics at Harvard University, and Mahbub ul Haq, whom I had come to know not while he was in Pakistan but when he joined the Bank. Because my relationship with Mahbub ul Haq remained a critical part of my work in the Bank on several policy issues, several anecdotes about him, of which the following is the first, will appear throughout this work.

In 1969, while at Harvard, I wrote a critique of Haq's famous "22-family speech," in which he had asserted that a good part of the benefits of economic growth during President Ayub Khan's much analyzed and appreciated model of development had accrued to a couple of dozen households that controlled large chunks of Pakistan's large-scale industry and finance. He made that speech in 1968 while President Ayub, who governed the country from 1958 to 1969, was still in power and when Haq himself was still Pakistan Planning Commission's chief economist. The speech created quite a stir both in Pakistan and at Harvard. In Pakistan, it provided the justification for the nationalization, six years later, of all large-scale industries and financial institutions by the left-leaning government of President (later Prime Minister) Zulfikar Ali Bhutto. Pakistan has still to recover from that shock to its economic system.[1]

At Harvard, Haq's analysis led to some rethinking about the institution's reading of Pakistan's economic model. In fact, Pakistan was used as a case study of success in the courses on economic development I was taught. Its experience was discussed in two influential books, one by Gustav Papanek (1969) and the other coedited by

Papanek and Walter Falcon (1972). Reading my rejoinder to his analysis, Haq invited me to visit him in Washington, D.C., at the World Bank. That meeting resulted in a long period of deep friendship and an equally long period of professional association. I joined Haq's Policy Planning and Review Department (PPRD) as senior economist; a year later I was promoted to be one of the department's two division chiefs. The other division chief, incidentally, was Arun Shourie, Indian Minister of Privatization in the Bharatiya Janata Party's government headed by Prime Minister Atal Bihari Vajpayee.

I left PPRD in 1981 to take up a position as senior adviser to Munir Benjenk, who had taken over as vice president of external relations. One of Benjenk's conditions for moving over from Operations was to have President Robert McNamara create a senior policy adviser position in his front office. Benjenk did not know me; he chose me for the job based on a three-page memorandum I had written and sent to McNamara arguing that the Bank should take a more activist position in the deliberations that were then being held in a number of international institutions on issues pertaining to developing countries' relations with the industrial world. I had suggested that the Bank should engage itself more fully with institutions such as the General Agreement on Tariffs and Trade, the United Nations Conference on Trade and Development, the International Labour Organization, the United Nations Children's Fund, and the Development Department in the United Nations. It was while working in the External Relations Department that I, together with Alexander Shakow, built the Development Committee into an important forum for policy-making at the World Bank.[2]

In June 1987, I was appointed to head the newly created China Department, one of the 19 country departments formed following the 1987 reorganization at the Bank. The entity I was chosen to lead was one of the three single-country departments. The others were Brazil and India. I stayed in that position for six-and-one-half years, until January 1994, when I was promoted to head the Latin America and Caribbean Region, a position I held for five-and-a-half years. I left in July 1999 to take up a position in private equity banking, which is where I remain to this day.

My two appointments in operations were unusual in the sense that I had not prepared myself to hold either of them. On the DPS, I worked in close proximity to McNamara and Haq. In that position, I wrote, or oversaw the writing of, a number of policy papers on a wide variety of subjects, ranging from the World Bank's support for primary education and primary health care to the Bank's sponsorship of development finance institutions. For a couple of years, I spearheaded the Bank's effort to define its role in meeting the basic needs of the citizens of the countries in which the institution was active. My team looked at five such areas: food, drinking water, sanitation, education, and health; wrote policy papers in each area; and also produced half a dozen country case studies to demonstrate the kind of policy changes needed for the governments to meet their citizens' basic needs and to describe the burden that such action would place on those governments' budgets. Our principal conclusion was that, given the presence of political will, it was entirely within the reach of most developing countries to meet their people's basic needs.

Our effort split the Bank's policy staff into two opposing camps. One subscribed to the view that a development institution such as the World Bank had to explicitly promote the production of and access to at least five basic needs. The other group believed that such needs would be met more or less automatically with growth in gross domestic product that exceeded the rate of increase in population by a comfortable margin. Those of us who held the first position were supported by President McNamara and by some, though not all, operational vice presidents. Those who promoted the second view looked to Ernie Stern, who was at that time vice president of South Asia Region, for leadership. McNamara's departure in the summer of 1981, followed soon after by that of Mahbub ul Haq, brought the basic needs project to an end. The work that we had done was published in a book titled *First Things First*, which I coedited with Paul Streeten (Streeten and Burki 1982).

Although the conceptual work on basic needs did not have any significant effect on the Bank's operations, it led to some further studies. It resulted, for instance, in the writing of the Bank's first *World Development Report* on the subject of poverty (World Bank 1980). The report was written by a team headed by Paul Isenman, who was a member of the basic needs team that I had headed. The Bank updated its thinking on poverty in 1990[3] and again in 2000–01. Some of the controversy in which we were engaged in the late 1970s—pushing for economic growth versus a direct attack on poverty—was revisited during the preparation of the 2000/2001 *World Development Report*.[4] In 1982, the Bank set up a task force to assess its work on poverty alleviation with a view to providing policy guidance to the staff. Alexander Shakow, who had succeeded me as the main coordinator of policy work after I moved to become senior adviser to the vice president of external relations, was the principal author of the report (see World Bank 1982).

By the time China chose to regain entry into the Bank, the country had been extraordinarily successful in alleviating poverty and in laying the ground for most of its citizenry to meet their basic needs. In 1980, Syed Shahid Husain, then vice president of East Asia, invited me to join an informal task force he had assembled to prepare for China's entry into the World Bank. I worked closely with Caio Koch-Weser, who was then McNamara's assistant, and Edwin Lim, an economist of Chinese background. I made some contributions to the writing of the terms of reference of the Bank's first major economic study on China, supervised by Hollis Chenery, then the World Bank's chief economist, and produced by a team led by Pervez Hasan, chief economist of the East Asia Region.

The other reason for my choice to head the China Department was the decision by Barber Conable, the World Bank president, to appoint Moeen Qureshi as senior vice president of operations. I had, by then, developed a close relationship with Qureshi, a fellow Pakistani whose previous job was senior vice president of finance. In 1985 I had, at his request, overseen the preparation of *IDA in Retrospect* (World Bank 1985b), a report that celebrated the first 25 years of the International Development Association (IDA). The report was requested by the IDA deputies to facilitate the deliberations on another replenishment of funds for the association.[5] My work on the report earned me a spot on the Finance Policy Committee headed by Qureshi, which, in turn, resulted in a close working relationship with him.

Qureshi's appointment as senior vice president of operations was a part of the organizational and management shakeup to which the Bank was subjected every time a new president took office. In 1986, the U.S. government decided not to invite Tom Clausen, McNamara's successor, to stay on for another term. Instead, the Republican administration in Washington chose Barber Conable, a highly respected congressman from New York who had retired from politics. Conable had little knowledge of the Bank when he took up his position but quickly became aware that under his predecessor the institution had lost some of its momentum and grandeur. He wanted the Bank's revival as a meaningful development institution, and in promoting that vision, he appointed a task force of middle-level and senior managers to come up with an organization plan that would better serve the Bank to achieve its stated objectives—promoting development and alleviating poverty.

At this time, Moeen Qureshi persuaded me to move over to the operational side of the institution. Qureshi's main argument in getting me into operations was bringing a strong policy content into the Bank's dealings in China. He believed that China would benefit much more from our involvement in helping shape its policies than simply from large loans. He thought, given my China and policy experiences, I was the right person to do that job.

My second move within the Bank's operational side was equally unplanned—it was not a part of the career path that I had envisaged for myself or the one that the Bank's senior managers had in mind for me. The move came in January 1994 after a long conversation a few weeks earlier with Lew Preston, then president of the Bank, whom I had accompanied a few months earlier to China, where he was told of the role I had played in keeping the World Bank's lines of communications open during the Tiananmen Square crisis and its aftermath.

At that time, the G-7 (Group of Seven) was putting pressure on the Bank's management to stop lending to China—a pressure that I resisted on the ground that the Bank's mandate was to promote economic development among its members and not to pursue the political objectives of its large shareholders. A week after the Chinese army's crackdown on the demonstrators camped in Tiananmen Square, I was dispatched to Beijing by President Conable to ascertain whether the Bank could continue to operate in that country. He made the decision following a discussion at the White House with President George H. W. Bush. I was told to travel immediately to Beijing and meet with China's senior leaders. I drafted my own terms of reference for that mission. I told Conable and Qureshi that the Bank should resist G-7's pressures if it determined that China (a) remained creditworthy to borrow money from the International Bank for Reconstruction and Development (IBRD); (b) was pursuing the policies, both macroeconomic and sectoral, that the Bank was advocating; and (c) continued to implement the Bank-financed projects effectively. After spending a week in Beijing and Shanghai—a week during which I found Beijing, in particular, empty of people, especially foreigners—I determined that in spite of the political upheaval caused by Tiananmen, China's performance on those three scores remained entirely satisfactory.[6] My message to the Bank's senior management was clear: there was no reason for us to suspend our operations in that country.

Before I left for China, President Conable had said that I should report my findings to the Board after completing my mission. On my return, and hearing my report, the president decided that a presentation on the lines I wanted to make would be much too contentious to be politic for the institution. Instead, he asked me to brief each of the Board members individually about my conclusions, which I proceeded to do over a period of a week. The directors representing the G-7 were not particularly happy to hear what I had to say. One of them was agitated enough to say that I would regret the day that I chose to visit Beijing so soon after the Tiananmen Square incident.

That prediction, of course, did not come true. I did not have the occasion to regret it, nor did the World Bank's senior management. My efforts to keep the Bank's program going in the country created an enormous amount of trust for me, as well as for the Bank, in Beijing. The case was not the same with China's relations with the International Finance Corporation (IFC), which, reacting to the same pressure from the G-7, decided to disengage. At that time the IFC had an active program in the country aimed at building capital markets, helping the fledgling private sector, and getting the public sector to disengage from some of the functions that it was not well equipped to perform. It took years for the IFC to regain the confidence and trust of Beijing and to rebuild its program.

Reserving the subject of trust for discussion later, I will continue with the circumstances that resulted in my promotion to vice president of the Latin America and Caribbean Region. The Chinese authorities told Lew Preston of the efforts I had made to stop the G-7 from interfering with the Bank's program in their country. When he summoned me to his office to offer me the Latin American job, he said that he wanted to place the region in charge of a person who had demonstrated the ability to work with large countries. He said that he was troubled by the Bank's uneasy relations with Brazil, Latin America's largest country and economy. "I want you to fix that," he said. "I am told of the high level of trust the Chinese have in you. Create the same in Brazil." That was the reason for my assignment to the Latin American job and the terms of reference for my new position.

The reason for recounting this bit of personal history is to make the point that, at least in my case, all appointments to senior positions in the Bank were not anticipated by me nor planned for me by the institution. I have no idea whether other people who held similar positions at the Bank while I worked at the institution would come to the same conclusion if they, too, had the occasion to look back at their careers.

A Dozen Lessons Learned from My 25-Year Experience at the Bank

The discussion that follows is highly subjective and based on the experience I had in various positions, both as an operations manager and on the policy side during my reasonably long career at the Bank. I present the lessons under the following 12 headings:

1. The Importance of Staying Relevant
2. Building the Borrower's Trust

3. Obtaining the Borrower's Commitment and Ownership

4. Laying a Solid Analytical Base

5. Disadvantages of Staying in a State of Constant Flux

6. Vacating the Commanding Heights

7. The Need to Return to Basics

8. Communicating Lessons Learned Elsewhere

9. Working with the NGOs

10. The Need to Build Institutional Memory

11. The Need to Maintain Focus

12. Is There Life after Service in the Bank

The Importance of Staying Relevant

Over the past few years, the World Bank Group has defined its mission and its mandate in ways that were not envisaged by its founders some 60 years ago when they created the institution that is still at its core. What is the Bank Group today was originally the IBRD. It now has a number of other affiliates—the IFC, the IDA, the Multilateral Investment Guarantee Agency, and the International Centre for Settlements of Investment Disputes.

All organizations must either evolve to stay relevant or else atrophy. It was necessary for the Bank to change over time, and it did change. However, looking back on the way the Bank has reshaped itself, one may note that most of the time the institution was responding to pressures from its major shareholders, the G-7 countries.[7] Following the founding of IDA, the World Bank Group progressively became more beholden to the wishes of the donors. A lot of the change that contributed to developing the shape in which the institution exists today reflects the desires of the major IDA donors. That was the price they exacted to continue to fund the IDA.

It was the IDA deputies who forced on the Bank the Inspection Panel, which required the Bank management to begin grading projects according to their likely effect on the environment, to rely more on project financing from private sources to build infrastructure, to work more with civil society institutions even when that relationship was not appreciated by the borrower, and to require the Operations Evaluation Department to examine the effectiveness not only of the projects the Bank financed but also of the way the institution advised the governments to manage their economies. The list is long, but the items that I have mentioned illustrate the main point I wish to make. In getting the management to buy into those and many other changes, the donors did not consult the borrowing countries. The borrowers, therefore, did not buy into many of the policies that the World Bank came to advocate, especially those adopted to placate the large shareholders. Two sets of policies were particularly important in shaping the Bank's lending program: the emphasis on policy reform and the concern with environmental and settlement issues. I will treat the Bank's relations with the nongovernmental organization (NGO) community as a separate lesson I learned during my tenure at the Bank. Here, I will say a few words about the Bank's focus on policy.

The emphasis on policy reform began in the late 1970s when the oil-importing developing world came to feel the full weight of the increase in oil prices by the Organization of Petroleum Exporting Countries. A number of middle-income countries got into serious troubles after building up large external imbalances by continuing to import expensive oil and then, later, financing the accumulated deficits by careless borrowings from international financial markets. Commercial banks were awash in liquidity because of the large deposits the oil-exporting countries placed with them. The banks were eager to lend, and the capital-short middle-income countries that were creditworthy enough to access the capital markets were eager to borrow. Not unexpectedly, a number of oil-importing countries ran up huge exposures to the banks that they could not service. Mexico was the first country to default in 1982, followed by several others.

Along with the International Monetary Fund (IMF), the Bank stepped into the breach, equipping itself with a new instrument called the structural adjustment loan (SAL). Gradually, the SALs began to dominate the Bank's portfolio in many countries. I have no problem with structural adjustment lending—or any form of policy lending—per se. But, enamored of this new instrument, the Bank moved away from its original purpose—financing projects. Policy loans appealed to the staff and also the managers—such loans could be prepared quickly, thus cutting down the staff costs for working on development loans and credits. This form of lending became very attractive to the managers when the Bank formally moved to dollar budgeting.

My real concern over an excessive focus on the increasing emphasis on policy lending was that the staff members who had the responsibility for preparing such loans were not always well equipped to handle major policy issues. Three things were required for policy-based lending to be effective. One, the staff members needed to fully understand the sociopolitical environment in which they were operating.[8] Two, they had to be fully confident that the policies they were pursuing were the right ones and would really support development. They could only have such confidence if all policy loans were backed by robust analytical work, which was not always the case. Three, the policy loans could not come encumbered with a vast number of conditions that had little relevance to achieving the desired policy reform. That also was not always the case. I recall one conversation Prime Minister Percival Patterson of Jamaica had with Jim Wolfensohn during Wolfensohn's first visit to Latin America and the Caribbean. Patterson complained that one of the policy loans his country was not successfully implementing came with more than a hundred conditions. One of them was to privatize two drug-sniffing dogs used by the country's customs authorities.

Building the Borrower's Trust

I spent a few days recently at the Asian Development Bank (ADB) in Manila, where I met with Vice President Liqun Jin, whom I have known for nearly 20 years. He spent several years at the China office in the World Bank, including representing his country as executive director on the Bank's Board, and after returning to Beijing, he held several positions in the Ministry of Finance. His last position in the ministry was as vice minister in charge of China's international financial relations. In that capacity, he oversaw the programs of the World Bank and the ADB. In 2003, he was appointed one of the four vice presidents at the ADB.

I interacted with Jin throughout my six-and-one-half years working on China. He was deeply involved in helping me devise a strategy that would keep the World Bank's lines of communication open to China following the Tiananmen crisis. Meeting with him in Manila, I told him that I was working on a paper detailing the lessons I had learned as a manager at the World Bank. I sought his view of the World Bank's work during the time I was in charge. He said that one lesson the Bank should draw from my experience was the importance of building trust between the managers at the Bank and their counterparts in the country in which they were working.

He said that when I did not buckle under the G-7 pressure, the message to the Chinese authorities was clear: they could trust that I would work diligently to pursue what I considered was best for China. This lesson does not mean that Bank managers have to toe the line laid down by the borrower; all it implies is that the only agenda the Bank officials should pursue is that of promoting development in the countries for which they have the responsibility. There can be serious differences between the Bank and the borrower—as was the case while I managed the China Department—but they should be honest differences in what the two sides consider the right approach for handling a specific developmental problem. Only when trust has been built will the borrower be fully committed to implementing what it has signed up to do with an aid agency. "If you are looking for borrowers' commitment and ownership, they must have complete trust in the motives of the Bank officials they are working with," said Jin.

Obtaining the Borrower's Commitment and Ownership

One of the most important lessons I draw from my tenure at the Bank is the importance of recipient governments' commitment to development—adopting the reforms the Bank advocates, implementing projects in a way that the Bank thinks would produce the best results, accepting technical assistance to help with the design of new policies, strengthening institutions, and also fully owning all of the above. Another anecdote from my time at the Bank illustrates this point.

In the spring of 1995, I accompanied President Jim Wolfensohn to Latin America. This 11-day trip was the second regional visit the new president had undertaken after a first visit to Sub-Saharan Africa. The Latin America and Caribbean Region had prepared a very elaborate briefing book for the president, including detailed write-ups on the performance of the Bank-financed portfolios in the six countries he was to visit. Our itinerary included stops at Argentina, Brazil, Colombia, Haiti, Jamaica, and Mexico. While on the long leg of the trip from Kingston, Jamaica, to a city in the northern part of Brazil, Wolfensohn read the brief prepared by the staff working on the country. To his dismay, he discovered that the Bank's Brazil portfolio was rated one of the worst in the institution. Visibly upset, he sat down next to me in his small plane and asked me why I had allowed that situation to develop. "Why don't you do what Russ Cheetham is doing in China?" he asked me. "You know Cheetham's China portfolio is the best in the Bank?" I told him that my managers and I had drawn up a detailed plan of action to rectify the situation. We wanted the Brazilians to take full ownership of the program we were funding and then work with us to improve the implementation of the various projects. In fact, we had recommended that, in his discussion with President Fernando Henrique Cardoso in Brasília, Wolfensohn propose setting up a joint Brazil-Bank commission on project implementation. The commission should recommend a line of action to the two presidents after a period of three months.

In Brasília, Finance Minister Pedro Malan asked for a one-on-one meeting with Wolfensohn at which he wanted to discuss his country's relations with the Bank. Malan and I were old friends; at one point in our careers we had worked on issues that fell within the ambit of what was called the New International Economic Order. Later, he moved to the Bank as Brazil's executive director, a position from which he gave me enormous support as I struggled with the G-7 directors on the post-Tiananmen Square crisis. He was, therefore, very familiar with my work on China and how I had worked with the authorities of that country to build robust and extremely well-implemented lending and economic and sector work programs. Malan mentioned all of this to Wolfensohn while expressing the hope that I would be able to bring my China experience to reflect on the Bank's programs in Brazil.

After the lunch with Malan, Wolfensohn asked me to ride with him on our way to the president's house to meet with Cardoso. "I am sorry I gave you a hard time over the performance of the Brazilian portfolio. Pedro Malan tells me that you were the author of the program in China for which I was giving Russ Cheetham so much credit," he said. I told him that it was not correct to label China's portfolio as Burki's program or to call the Brazil program Shahid Husain's portfolio. (Shahid Husain was my predecessor as vice president of Latin America and the Caribbean.) I then told him what Wang Bingqian, China's finance minister during most of the 1980s, said to me when I took over the management of the China Department: "I have been told that more than a hundred professionals work for you in your department. I want to say to you that they also work for me—for the Chinese authorities. We should take joint responsibility for their work program." And he did—not himself directly, but through his vice minister, who had the responsibility for overseeing the Bank's China program. Consequently, if the Bank task managers ran into any problem that needed the involvement of a senior official, a telephone call from me to the vice minister normally solved the problem. During my six-and-one-half years working on China, we financed 102 projects for a total of US$12 billion. Of those projects, only one was a problem, a program loan that we had forced on the unwilling Chinese in order to satisfy the Bank's Board, which was very interested in those types of loans.

My main point to Wolfensohn was that the health of the Bank-financed portfolio depended to a considerable extent on the commitment and ownership of the borrower of the policies that were embedded in the various projects. The Brazil portfolio improved over time because a number of projects that were doing poorly were restructured and aligned more closely with policies with which the authorities were comfortable. I do not wish to imply that the Bank should completely follow the borrowers' preferences. If it did so, it would not be fulfilling its purpose and its mandate. Borrowers can—and should—learn much from the Bank, which is the subject of the final lesson, but it is important to ensure that the borrower is fully committed to what it signs up to do and also completely owns the project.

Laying a Solid Analytical Base

Senior-level commitment and ownership certainly help make a success of the Bank's involvement in the countries that it is assisting, as the examples from my Chinese and Brazilian experiences well illustrate. But borrower commitment and ownership are helped by firmly anchoring the lending in analytical work. In China, largely as a result of the wishes of the authorities, the Bank adopted a sequential approach. In twice-a-year meetings with the Ministry of Finance, we defined the various subjects to be studied; once studied, many of the findings were incorporated in the designs of the projects the Bank financed. Sometimes the Chinese authorities identified the subjects; at other times the Bank's staff and managers did. An example from each category will help underscore my point.

Some people working on China's health sector wished to study the consequences of the very high incidence of smoking on citizens' health. The Chinese officials were not particularly keen for the Bank to delve into this subject, but we prevailed. When the report was completed under the leadership of Richard Bumgarner (a staff member who later moved to the World Health Organization and became an ardent anti-smoking crusader in that organization), the Chinese were troubled by its principal finding: that unchecked, smoking at the rate prevalent in the country not only would begin to adversely affect the quality of life of the Chinese elderly but also would reduce the life expectancy of the citizenry. This finding was particularly devastating for a population that was rapidly aging and for a government that had spent so much effort on health care over a long period of time. One component of the Chinese health care system—the barefoot doctors—had become famous the world over. These medics were essentially villagers trained in basic hygiene and health care who went from house to house delivering their message and dispensing some rudimentary care. The Chinese government was upset that some of the gains it had made were quite literally going up in smoke. After the report was prepared and disseminated, antismoking provisions were incorporated into several health projects financed by the Bank. The Bank's work also led to the smoking ban on internal flights in China.

Another example of analytical work laying the ground for operations was a study done by the Bank on the availability and use of water in the Yellow River basin in northern China. This time the initiative came from the Chinese, who were increasingly worried about serious water shortages they could foresee in the not-so-distant future in the country's northern areas. Water availability was becoming a problem because of the significant increases in urban and industrial consumption as China continued to urbanize rapidly and, at the same time, saw a dramatic change in the structure of its economy.

We accepted China's request and assigned Daniel Gunaratnam, an irrigation engineer from Singapore with deep knowledge of Asia's river systems, to undertake the study. Gunaratnam was one of several Asian irrigation engineers who did numerous innovative projects for the Bank in several parts of the world. His work laid the basis for some mega-projects in China, including the Bank-financed Xialongdi Dam on the Yellow River as well as the massive civil works project the Chinese plan to undertake to transfer water from the Yangtze River in the country's center to the Yellow River in the north. This massive engineering project is still on the drawing board, and with emphasis returning to lending for infrastructure—as I discuss later—it is probable that it will be included in the World Bank's China lending program.

In emphasizing the importance of anchoring the lending program in sound analytical work, I believe that it is important that the work be done by people who remain involved with the country or countries they are studying. This method was possible after the 1987 reorganization, when people who did economic and sector work, such as Gunaratnam and Bumgarner, also had heavy responsibility for doing or overseeing operations. It was not possible, however, after the reorganization of 1996–97. Because I have continued to maintain a strong interest in China, I continue to follow some of the analytical work the World Bank is currently doing. I am particularly impressed with two recent studies. The first one evaluates the economic effect of China's accession to the World Trade Organization (Ianchovina and Martin 2002); the other looks at the consequences of China's emergence as the international production systems' workshop (Martin and Manole 2003). My assumption is that these studies were not done by the staff of the small China Department. If so, their authors will not have the opportunity to influence policymaking in China, as would have been the case if those doing analytical work were fully embedded in country operations departments.

Disadvantages of Staying in a State of Constant Flux

The World Bank is a pioneer in development in the sense that it invented multilateral development banking. Pioneers, by necessity, have to break new ground as the Bank has continued to do throughout its nearly 60-year history. Development is a constantly changing field, and an institution such as the World Bank must be supple enough to adapt continuously to changing circumstances. There is one area, however, where the Bank needs to be in a state of constant flux. I refer to the way the Bank should be organized to achieve its mission and use the enormous amount of expertise available to it for the benefit of its developing member countries.

During my 25 years at the World Bank, I saw four major reorganizations—in 1973, 1982, 1987, and 1996.[9] All of them sought to determine the best way of delivering financing, development advice, and technical assistance to countries of the developing world that were eager to receive support from the Bank.

In deciding on the right mix between what the Bank calls "country focus" and availability of development knowledge to its clients, it has failed to find a happy combination. In reorganizing the Bank's operational and policy arms in 1987, those of us who were involved in that effort may have erred too much in the direction of country focus. As I indicated previously, when I was appointed to head China operations, my department was one of the 19 that had program, policy, and project responsibilities for the more than 100 borrowers. That arrangement served the client well. It was also popular with staff members—at least those of my department—because it gave them the opportunity to concentrate their attention on learning about the country, their only client. Of the more than 100 professional staff members who worked in the department, about 40 were macro- and sectoral economists. As Professor Dwight Perkins, a China expert at Harvard University, said to me on learning of the skill mix in the department I headed, "I don't think there is any other place in the world outside China that has under one roof such a rich talent working on the country."

My deep conviction born of that experience persuaded me to resist the pressure brought to bear on me in 1995–96 to create small country departments in Latin America. Several other regional vice presidents did adopt that pattern. I believe that by the time that particular reorganization had run its course, the Africa Region had more than 30 country directors, some of them heading single-person departments consisting of the department director himself or herself. The only concession I made to that pressure was to increase the number of departments in the Latin America and Caribbean Region to seven from four. Two of these seven were responsible for only one country each: Brazil and Mexico. Each department had about a dozen core staff members, who could specialize in the countries for which they had the responsibility. This arrangement was still way short of the quantum and quality of skills that were available to China when I headed that particular department, but it was much better than the single-member departments in several other parts of the institution.

For as long as I have worked in the area of development, I have been a strong believer in acquiring what anthropologist Clifford Geertz (1963, 1973) once called "thick" knowledge about countries and cultures. In this context, another personal experience is relevant. I believe it was some time in the late 1970s when Bevan Waide, then the chief economist of South Asia Region, invited me to speak at an economists' retreat he had organized in Annapolis, Maryland. I was asked to talk about the political economy of reform, a subject on which I had been working in the context of Pakistan. (That was the theme of the book I authored a couple of years later [Burki 1980].) To prepare for that presentation, I read cover to cover some half-dozen country economic reports Bank staff members had written on Pakistan over several preceding years. From this reading, I drew up a list of a dozen policy recommendations the Bank had made to the decisionmakers in Islamabad. I placed these recommendations in a matrix. One column of the matrix explained why the policy advocated would have support in the country; the other column indicated the opposite—why considerable opposition meant that the policy had no chance of being implemented. Of the dozen or so policies that I subjected to that kind of political economy examination, I concluded that about 10 had little chance of being adopted. Because the political and social environment was hostile and because there was no official ownership for recommended policies, they would not get implemented. In fact, as it turned out, those policies were not adopted.

My presentation had a positive response from the audience. The economists at the meeting were intrigued by the methodology I had used, but as I summed up, I was aware that Bevan Waide did not share in the enthusiasm. He said that, although my analysis of the recommended policies reflected a deep knowledge of the Pakistani situation, it could not be duplicated by the Bank's "normal" staff. I differed, saying that it was incumbent on all policy analysts to develop the kind of understanding I had of the Pakistani situation. A person did not have to belong to a country to develop the Geertz type of "thick" understanding. Any social scientist, including a World Bank economist, worthy of his or her salt had to have that kind of appreciation of the local situation he or she was dealing with. You did not have to "go native" to be well informed.

It is my view that the 1987 reorganization's country focus allowed staff members the opportunity to gain a deep understanding of the situations with which they were dealing. This benefit was lost by the 1996–97 reshaping of the operational side of the Bank. Conversely, did the emphasis on accumulating development knowledge and applying it to the operations the Bank was called on to deliver improve as a result of the shift in focus? Did the creation of the networks help in that context? Because this change was still in its infancy when I left the Bank, I cannot offer a definitive conclusion about it. What I can say, however, is that for a variety of reasons, the Bank vacated the commanding heights of development analyses—its great forte during the 1970s and, to a lesser extent, in the early 1980s. I now turn to that subject.

Vacating the Commanding Heights

When I joined the Program and Policy Review Department headed by Mahbub ul Haq in 1974, it was one of the four departments that together constituted the Bank's Development Policy Staff. The DPS was headed by Hollis Chenery, who had done some pioneering work in the field of development before taking up his Bank position.

Hollis left a deep effect on the Bank. He had strong views of his own, but he appreciated as well the strong views of others. Mahbub and I often clashed with him, particularly on the question of the most appropriate way of alleviating poverty and improving income distribution. Hollis and several of his close associates, including Jack Duloy and Montek Ahluwalia, placed their confidence in alleviating poverty by accelerating growth. They coedited a book, *Redistribution with Growth* (Chenery and others 1981), which was for many years widely read by the development community. The book laid down the case for concentrating a good part of development effort on increasing aggregate incomes in the developing world. This effort was to be achieved by improving such fundamentals as savings and investment rates, bringing fiscal and external balances into line, opening the countries to greater external competition through international trade, and concentrating the attention of the state on the provision of public goods.

But macroeconomic issues were not the only ones that received the attention of Chenery's DPS. Dozens of well-known development economists with a variety of

WORLD BANK OPERATIONS: SOME IMPRESSIONS AND LESSONS

microeconomic expertise produced seminal works on a number of subjects: issues pertaining to movements in commodity prices; the best way of managing public financing; the most appropriate relationship between federal and subnational financing; rural-urban migration, the growth of large cities, and the pressures they put on public services; the role of international trade in promoting economic development; dynamics of demographic change in developing societies; and the role that education and knowledge accumulation played in promoting economic growth and alleviating poverty. At one point, such luminaries of economic science as Jagdish Bhagwati, Paul Streeten, Frances Stewart, T. N. Srinivasan, and Michael Lipton worked as advisers in the various DPS departments. Even a quick analysis of the bibliographies of the books published on various aspects of development economics in the 1970s and 1980s compared with those of more recently published books should persuade people who maintain that the Bank continues to produce high-quality work that the institution is no longer at the center of development thinking.

A case can be made—as did one of the commentators on the first draft of this chapter—that "Chenery's period coincided with the one in which developing countries did not have the Edman Bachas, the Carlos Antonio Rodriguezes, the Kaushik Basus, the Abhijit Singhs . . . . a whole generation of bright, among the brightest, economists from developing countries. Isn't it natural that with more competition the Bank would necessarily be less of a center of concentrated knowledge about development?"[10] This point is a fair one. In fact, the Bank has in many ways made impressive contributions to the development of many centers of excellence, some of them staffed by people who once worked for the institution. However, I do not see knowledge accumulation as a zero-sum game: the use of dozens of institutions doing pathbreaking work does not mean that the Bank should not be in the lead as it was in the 1970s and 1980s. One more example of the type of work that was undertaken by the Bank in that period is the book *Pioneers in Development* (Meier and Seers 1984). That book was based on the assessment provided by such pioneers as Gunnar Myrdal, Arthur Lewis, Albert Hirschman, and P. T. Bauer on how their thinking had changed since they did their original work. It was natural for those stars to assemble in the Bank to provide such an overview. I cannot find a similar example of this kind of exploratory work done by the institution in recent years.

It was also during Chenery's stewardship that the institution made the decision to launch the series *World Development Report* (WDR). That report, first produced under the direction of Ernest Stern and D. C. Rao, became the Bank's annual publication—its flagship on development issues. The first WDR was published in 1978; the 1980 report, by focusing on poverty and basic needs, set the tradition of dividing the book into two parts. The first part was devoted to describing the state of development of the developing world and its prospects in the next few years. The second dealt with a special subject chosen for the year—poverty, agriculture, trade, urbanization, infrastructure, finance, and so on.

The WDR spawned a new industry worldwide. Soon most international organizations had annual reports of their own: the United Nations Development Programme (UNDP) on the state of human development, the United Nations

Conference on Trade and Development on foreign direct investment, the United Nations Children's Fund on the state of the world's children, the International Labour Organization on the state of labor markets, the Food and Agriculture Organization of the United Nations on the state of agriculture and world food production, and so on. Now, a quarter century after the World Bank launched that effort, the development community pays much less attention to the WDRs than it does to some of the other institutional reports. For instance, the UNDP's *Human Development Report* receives much greater notice in the popular press and is referred to more frequently in the academic literature than the *World Development Report*. The Bank is no longer at the cutting edge of development, in large part because it does not commit a sufficient amount of resources to basic and operational research, as it did during the McNamara era.

There are many development issues on which the Bank's senior managers need to have positions that can be communicated to the leadership in the borrowing countries at appropriate times. One such issue is trade, on which the institution did some pioneering work while Nicholas Stern was the chief economist. Another is technology and how it affects productivity in the developing world. A third is demographic asymmetry—the sharp differences in the rates of fertility in the industrial and developing world, which have left the former with rapidly aging populations and the latter with the young still the dominant cohort. What are the consequences of this asymmetry for migration, brain drain, or outsourcing? Yet another is the way that several developing countries are picking up fiscal contingent liabilities as they engage the private sector in developing infrastructure by providing it with incentives. All these areas—and many more—should be properly researched, not only to have informed general debate on them all around the globe but also to equip senior managers with the analytical insights they need to conduct dialogues with leaders in the developing world.

And then there are the issues about which the Bank's managers must have an informed opinion even if such issues do not fall into the Bank's territory. I am aware of the sensitivity the IMF has about the Bank's involvement in monetary policy and exchange rate management. Perhaps a new concord is needed that would have the IMF recognize that both areas have a direct bearing on development. Illustrating this point, I recall two conversations on critical issues I had during my tenure as vice president of Latin America and the Caribbean.

The first one was with President Lew Preston in February 1994, after I had done a fair amount of reading on Argentine economic history and the country's current economic situation. At that time, Argentina was a darling of the financial world. Much of its success was based on practically eliminating inflation by fixing the exchange rate of the peso at parity with the U.S. dollar. It had done so by adopting what it called the Convertibility Law, meaning that the rate at which the peso was converted into foreign currencies could not be established by the central bank. Instead, the rate had to have legislative approval. My view, after getting acquainted with the country's economy, was that the law had outlived its utility. It had produced the economic stabilization that the country craved and the international financiers loved. But by maintaining parity, the managers of the economy were introducing serious distortions, in particular into the financial sector. I was of the view that the Argentines needed to use a more flexible system, perhaps a crawling peg. I mentioned this view to Preston, who was not convinced to support my position in the absence of evidence. I might have persisted had my position been supported by analytical work in the Bank that told me what is an appropriate exchange rate policy for a country in Argentina's position. Later, of course, my intuition was tragically proven correct, as Argentina plunged into financial crisis.

The other conversation was with Finance Minister Pedro Malan and Central Bank Governor Chico Lopes of Brazil in January 1999 in Washington, D.C. This conversation took place two days after Brazil began to float its currency. That decision was implemented on Friday, and Malan and Lopes traveled to Washington to hold discussions with the IMF and the Bank over the weekend. I met with the two on Sunday after they had already seen Michel Camdessus, IMF's managing director. At the meeting with Camdessus, the Brazilian officials were told that the IMF preferred to have the country's currency "defloat" and placed within a wide band. Malan and Lopez wanted my view on that proposal.

I had already had a disagreement with Stanley Fischer, who was IMF's first deputy managing director at the time, a few weeks earlier when he had broached to me the idea of suggesting a currency board arrangement for Brazil. My view was that, although such a device might work for small economies such as Hong Kong, China; Israel; and Panama, it would be totally inappropriate for Brazil. Obviously the IMF officials, in their conversations with the Brazilians, had given up that idea and had suggested movement within a band rather than a free float. I was also surprised to learn that the reason Malan and Lopes had traveled to Washington was that, at the IMF's insistence, the Brazilians had floated their currency for only a day, telling the market that the final exchange rate policy would be announced three days later, on Monday.

Floating the currency for a day was a strange thing to do, anyway. To get back to a band would create total lack of confidence on the part of the financial markets in Brazil's capacity to deal with the run on the currency, I told the Brazilians. Malan wanted to know how Joseph Stiglitz, chief economist at the Bank, would react. We called Stiglitz; he came over and gave the same advice I had given. Now that the Brazilians had floated the currency, it was prudent to keep it floating. The Brazilians took our advice and stayed with the float. Once again, good analytical work on these issues would have been very helpful in this debate.

The Need to Return to Basics

IBRD, IDA, and IFC were founded as institutions for financing projects. The first two, however, have moved away from that original purpose. Policy lending became the theme in the 1980s and 1990s, particularly after the countries of Latin America faced a series of debt crises. It was as a response to those crises that the Bank became an enthusiastic contributor to the Washington Consensus, an approach to development that advocated a radical change in the policies pursued by the developing world.[11] In the late 1980s and most of the 1990s, the Bank made two decisions: to phase out lending for infrastructure and to concentrate on bringing about policy reform. The first decision was based on the belief that the copious amount of foreign capital that became available to the developing countries would flow into project financing. The second decision was anchored in the assumption that policymakers in the developing world could be bribed with large program loans to institute policy reforms. Both beliefs were mistaken.

Private sector infrastructure investment in developing countries reached US$128 billion in 1997 but slumped to US$58 billion by 2002. Not only are the private sector flows erratic and volatile, but they are also concentrated in a handful of countries. For the rest, multilateral development banks and bilateral aid agencies remain the only viable source of project financing.

From my own experience, the Bank scored real success when it provided its financing for discrete projects or for well-focused sectoral reform. One of the most lasting development effects in the Bank's history is the massive Indus Water Replacement Project in Pakistan implemented in the 1960s. Working over a period of a decade and a half, the Bank was able to find a solution to the difficult water-sharing problem between India and Pakistan. The Bank acted as an intermediary, and after it had brokered a deal between the two countries, it led the consortium of donors that poured some US$5 billion (in 1965 prices) into constructing a series of linked canals that brought water from the northern to the southern rivers in the Indus system. It also financed the construction of two massive dams on the Jhelum and Indus Rivers—the Mangla and the Tarbela Dams.

The Bank was equally successful in helping China develop its infrastructure. The Bank financed the building of roads, highways, and motorways; the rehabilitation and improvement of the country's vast railway system; the building of new ports, one of which was dedicated to the intercoastal transport of coal; the building of three large dams (Shuikoh, Ertan, and Xialongdi); and the construction of a number of coal-fired power plants. In all those projects, financing was not the only input provided by the Bank. I recall what Prime Minister Li Peng told Moeen Qureshi during the latter's visit to Beijing in the spring of 1990. He said that the most valuable input the Bank had made to project development in China was introducing the country to international competitive bidding. He said that the Chinese had begun to use international competitive bidding in the projects they financed from their own resources.

One valuable consequence of the Bank's emphasis on financing infrastructure projects was to build within its staff an impressive cadre of expertise. The Indus Water Replacement Project resulted in the recruitment of world-class irrigation engineers trained in India and Pakistan. They were to play important roles in transferring technical know-how to the Middle East, China, and East Asia. I have already mentioned the important work done by one such engineer—Daniel Gunaratnam—in China. But he was not alone. There were several other people with considerable expertise whose work was highly valued by the borrower. I recall a mission with one such person—a staff member named Otto Ragambi, a highway engineer from

Hungary who had worked for a number of years in the Bank's Latin America and Caribbean Region but who had transferred to China when the region phased out lending for infrastructure. Ragambi once traveled with me by car on the yet-to-be opened Beijing-Tianjin Expressway, which the Bank had financed. At one point during the journey, he asked the driver to stop and go over a patch of road we had traveled on. He had felt—quite literally by the seat of his pants—that the contractor had not put a cushion of sand under the road pavement. This cushion was required by the design the Bank had approved. He asked me to suspend disbursement for the project unless the problem was addressed. I threatened to do precisely that, but the Chinese argued that the entire length of the road had been built to the specifications agreed between them and the Bank's technical experts. But Ragambi was not impressed by that argument, and at his insistence, the Chinese agreed to dig up a part of the suspect portion of the road. They found that Ragambi was right. The problem was fixed, and disbursement continued.

Although the Chinese authorities were not particularly happy with my intervention at that time, they later cited it as an example of the expertise they really valued. Unfortunately, over time the Bank has seriously depleted its ranks of people such as Ragambi and Gunaratnam.

Getting back to basics does not mean that the Bank should do project financing exactly the way it did this kind of lending in its early days. A number of things have been learned since that time, including the importance of working closely, at times, with the private sector in raising resources for the projects and managing implementation with the help of private firms. The Bank has also acquired a number of fiduciary responsibilities, particularly in the areas of environment and resettlement of the people displaced by the projects it finances. Finally, the Bank has become sensitive about the question of the borrower's acquiring fiduciary liabilities contingent on the terms on which the private sector was brought in as a partner in development in the first place. I discuss the second and third parts of this relationship with the private sector in other parts of the chapter. Here I deal with the question of how the Bank could work with private players in doing structural financing for large infrastructure projects.

Because the private sector has focused a great deal of attention on developing specific lines of financial products for specific clients and specific circumstances, structured financing has become an important part of the way it provides capital for investment. Every transaction has many components: straight lending, convertible bonds, contingent convertible bonds, zero-coupon bonds, private equity, various kinds of guarantees—the list is long and getting longer by the day. The reason for providing various forms of financing for the acquisition of the assets being privatized or for mergers or for greenfield projects is to cover different kinds of risks and different appetites that various investors have for the activity in question. Structural financing, therefore, spreads the risks around and saves both the borrowers and the lenders the pain associated with failed projects.

Now that the World Bank has decided to go back to basics and start lending for large infrastructure projects, the skills associated with making structured finance deals will be as important for the borrowers as are the technical and project management skills that the institution was so good at providing in the past.

Communicating Lessons Learned Elsewhere

The World Bank, a pioneer in development financing and still the most prominent player in this field, has one distinct advantage over regional and subregional multilateral development banks. The edge comes from its global reach—it works in all corners of the developing world. Unfortunately, the Bank does not systematically exploit this advantage.

My experience in Latin America suggests that policymakers are very interested in learning about the experiences of countries in other regions of the world. They have an enormous appetite for information on what works and what does not work in other environments. This information gains considerable credibility when it comes from the people who have direct experience of distant places. In the scores of meetings I had with the senior leaders of Latin America, I found presidents, prime ministers, finance ministers, and other senior officials greatly interested in what I had to tell them about China and East Asia.

I have a vivid recollection of one long conversation with President Carlos Menem of Argentina as President Enrique Iglesias of the Inter-American Development Bank and I traveled with him to Bariloche to attend the annual Summit of the Americas. We were on President Menem's private plane and were invited to join him in his well-appointed office after the aircraft took off from Buenos Aires. Menem wished to talk about the need for improving educational standards in Latin America, something he planned to touch on in his opening remarks at the summit. Iglesias asked me to tell President Menem why I thought China and several other countries of East Asia had done so well in educating their people. I used some data from the two regions to make my main points: The systems in East Asia were much more egalitarian when we looked at the Gini-coefficient of educational expenditure, although the two regions spent about the same proportion of gross domestic product on education. Also, by emphasizing teacher training, textbook preparation, small class size, and so on, the East Asians had focused much more on quality than the Latin Americans had done. Finally, I said that the East Asians had put considerable emphasis not only on primary education but also on secondary, tertiary, and technical education. The Argentine president used some of the information I provided him in his speech at the summit.

I used my China experience to drive home to my interlocutors in Latin America several other lessons I had learned before moving to the region. One of those was the importance of the role of the state, a concept that was understood very differently in East Asia and Latin America. In fact, I used to argue that the emphasis on the Washington Consensus policies served to weaken the Latin American state. It did not create the environment through investments in physical infrastructure and human development that had laid the basis for the rapid growth of the East Asian "tiger" economies. The East Asian state was also much better equipped to regulate the private sector than was the state in Latin America.[12]

In designing its personnel policies, the Bank has done little to encourage its staff members—in particular the institution's managers—to move from one region to another in order to better disseminate the knowledge they have accumulated. There is, of course, a tradeoff between the acquisition of deep knowledge about particular countries and regions and the advantage to the borrowers of learning about development experiences in other parts of the world from the Bank staff. A balance can be struck between achieving these two objectives, but only if the Bank deliberately factors them into its personnel policies.

Working with the NGOs

On many environmental issues, there was a widespread impression among several countries receiving World Bank funding that the institution had been forced to adopt the agendas of northern nongovernmental organizations—the institutions that operated out of the industrial world. These NGOs were able to exert considerable political pressure on large shareholders, especially at the time of various IDA replenishments.

I was fully exposed to the politics that motivated a number of northern NGOs from two vantage points: when I was appointed to chair the Bank-NGO Committee in 1984 and when I dealt with the complaints filed by the NGO community about some of the projects the Bank financed in Latin America. It was in the first position that I developed a good sense of the enormous gap in the interests pursued by the northern and southern (developing country) NGOs. In fact, when I took over as the chairman of the committee, no southern NGO was represented on it. Initially, members of the northern community resisted my efforts to bring in the developing countries' NGOs. I soon realized that many powerful NGOs in industrial countries pursued agendas that helped them with their fundraising activities. This divergence in views was one reason the governments of developing countries were not always willing to buy into the policies the Bank pursued, especially those related to environmental protection and resettlement of the people affected by Bank-supported projects.

My second impression of the power the NGOs could bring to bear on the Bank, if the senior management was receptive to it, was in the context of the crisis over the implementation of the Yacyreta Dam Project on the border between Argentina and Paraguay. The Bank had been involved with this dam for several years before some NGOs formally expressed their unhappiness with the way the various components of the project were supervised. The NGOs were concerned in particular with the resettlement of the people displaced by the huge lake created behind the dam. The Inspection Panel came into the act, and I led a mission, accompanied by three directors from the Latin America and Caribbean Region, to the dam site to see for myself what had really gone on.

Without doubt several features of the complex resettlement program were not well implemented. But the problem was basically with the entity doing the work on the Paraguayan side. The Bank had two options: to put pressure on the government using the leverage of its entire financing program in the country (which was my position) or to remove the various Bank managers involved with the project (an action the senior management wanted). My position was that the Bank staff members and managers were operating in a very difficult political and social environment. Any precipitous action against them would cause further NGO interference with the Bank's management of operations and demoralize the staff. In the end, we agreed to use our leverage and not come down hard on the staff.

Two unhappy consequences of the Bank management's willingness to give in to the pressures of the northern NGOs are worth noting. One, it has made the managers who are responsible for operations risk averse; most managers do not relish the prospect of facing the Inspection Panel. That outcome is singularly unfortunate because economic development is a business full of risks. Mistakes have been made and will continue to be made. By scaring the staff, the Bank has hurt its ability to do innovative work.

Second, largely because of the pressures from the NGO community, the Bank has loaded its project work with extra fiduciary responsibilities. Some of the conditions that the Bank is now required to impose on the projects it helps design may be important for industrial societies. However, they neither are relevant for many developing countries, nor is there political consensus around them. In this context, I should mention a conversation I had with some Mexican authorities about putting together a large highway construction program to be financed by the Bank. We were talking about putting US$500 million into the program. However, some of the environmental and resettlement conditions we wanted the Mexicans to accept posed serious difficulties for them. The minister in charge of highways said to me, after a long discussion on the subject, "You are not financing the construction of an intercounty connector in Montgomery County near Washington." (He seemed well aware of the series of problems the planners keep encountering in trying to build the intercounty connector between Interstates 270 and 70. Most of those problems are related to environmental concerns. The intercounty connector project has been stalled for two decades.) "You are offering to help with the construction of roads in Mexico," he continued. "There may be political consensus in Montgomery County or in other places in the United States for these types of conditions. This does not exist in Mexico. Regulations must be the product of politics."

That was a very fair point, and the Bank should pause and think about it. I suggest that this may be a good time to review, with the assistance of the borrowers, all fiduciary responsibilities the Bank has accumulated over time and determine their political viability in the developing world.

The Need to Build Institutional Memory

Although the effort being made now to turn the Bank into a knowledge institution is to be applauded, this transformation will not happen unless the institution undertakes explicitly to build institutional memory into its processes and practices. The Bank loses so much because it does not systematically tap into the knowledge acquired by staff members who have served in the institution a long time. This case is particularly true for staff members moving from one region to another or retiring.

I am aware of the oral history program the Bank has in place and under which scores of senior staff members have been interviewed on their retirement. I was also interviewed for several hours by a historian whom the Bank has hired as a consultant. He was accompanied by a staff member who runs the program. They did a good job asking me the right questions; they had prepared themselves well by asking a number of people who had come to know me while I was at the Bank. However, the impression I gathered from talking to my interviewers was that the program was not fully owned by the senior management and, consequently, was starved of budgetary resources.

I gained a strong impression about the absence of institutional memory at the Bank when I served on the 1987 Reorganization Task Force. As I have already noted, one of my tasks was to design a new department responsible for policy and strategic planning. In preparing my proposal, I found that I was the only person left in the institution who had knowledge of the way the policy planning and review functions worked in McNamara's day (discussed in the next section). Even the documents from that period were not readily available—they were deposited in some underground space (an old mine) in Pennsylvania. It took a week to get some of the files from that period to my desk.

With the advent of e-mail, the problem has become even more acute because so much of what gets exchanged among staff members is not automatically stored. Gone are the days of white, pink, yellow, and blue pages, each color destined for a different filing space.

The Need to Maintain Focus

When policymaking was a more formal process, the Bank took time before launching new initiatives. During Robert McNamara's time, each policy recommendation was developed by the staff in a policy paper. The first draft of the proposed initiative was reviewed in a meeting chaired by the director of the Policy Planning Department, with all regional program and project directors and chief economists participating. Also taking part were the directors in DPS and what was called the Central Policy Staff, in all a group of some two dozen senior staff members.

After the staff review, the policy proposal was revised and sent for final comments or approval to the Policy Review Committee, which was chaired by McNamara. I was the secretary of the committee. All 17 Bank and IFC vice presidents were the members of the Policy Review Committee. I recorded its final decision, which was circulated to all Bank managers. Thus, the Bank's policy was made—revisions in what was already being done or the new initiatives the Bank wished to take on.

This process may have been time consuming and highly bureaucratic, but it had two advantages. In the lesson immediately following, I argue about the need for speed in preparing projects. But those two thoughts do not contradict one another. Speed becomes possible when those engaged in implementing policies are totally comfortable with them. The type of process that governed policymaking in McNamara's day provided the opportunity for reflection and the incorporation of all points of view. And it created staff and management ownership of changes in policy or a new policy initiative. Of late, the Bank's management has been very willing to change policies and practices without much consultation and—at least it is my impression— without much thought. This seeming lack of studied process has resulted in the introduction of new ideas that, at times, caused confusion and at other times produced unhappiness in the institution. Some of the recent policies adopted by the Bank did not have the full ownership of the staff and management.

Is There Life after Service at the Bank?

I took early retirement in August 1999 to join the Emerging Markets Partnership (EMP), a private equity firm that—as its name suggests—made investments in emerging markets. The firm was founded in 1993 by two former senior World Bank officials, Moeen Qureshi and Donald Roth. Roth had served as the Bank's treasurer and vice president, reporting to Qureshi. Most of the senior managers at EMP were once senior officials at the Bank. The roster included, in addition to Qureshi and Roth, Kim Jaycox, Will Kafenberger, Sam Santos, Rauf Diwan, and Thierry Baudon. I joined the group in 1999 and was later followed by Richard Stern.

There are many things I have learned about the private sector that I did not know while I was at the Bank. There are also many things about the Bank that I have begun to appreciate now that I have the occasion to look at it from a different angle. Not surprisingly, the thing that strikes me the most about the difference between a multilateral development institution such as the World Bank and the private sector is the motives of the people who work in these two parts of the international financial system. I will never meet as many smart and committed people in the private sector as I came across during my quarter century at the Bank. What drives the private sector is a relentless focus on the bottom line—at the end of the day, what really matters is the size of the paycheck and bonus that people take home. That, of course, is not what motivates Bank employees.

Nonetheless, there are things the Bank could learn from the private sector that would help it in its own work on development: speed, relevance, appetite for risk, and innovation. I deal briefly with each of these four.

First, the need for speed: I remember once a discussion with a senior Brazilian official about the policy the Bank began to push, following the 1994–95 Mexican peso crisis, to price its emergency loans on the basis of a new formula. The Bank proposed a higher-than-normal charge. "Don't do that," was his blunt advice. "I have a rule of thumb that I follow. If I can raise money from the private sector at a price 300 basis points lower than the Bank charge, I will not borrow from your institution." In other words, in his mind there was a 3-percentage-point premium that he was prepared to pay for private sector capital because of the speed at which it came. Private money was also accompanied by fiduciary considerations that the lenders had to follow, but they were understood by the borrower. Sometimes, as discussed in "Disadvantages of Staying in a State of Constant Flux," the Bank's fiduciary responsibilities dealt with issues of no concern to the borrower. Transactions made by the private sector are almost always done with speed and come with very few conditions attached.

Second, the need for relevance: Borrowers would not welcome lenders in the private sector (a group that also includes those who provide equity) unless they provided financing for activities the borrowers considered relevant. Private operators must always be in search of the opportunities that borrowers consider attractive. It is difficult for them to push on the borrowers lines of products that they do not want or to get invited to participate in activities in which borrowers have no interest. Along with other development institutions, the Bank has at times found itself pushing lending for activities with little or no demand among the borrowers.

Third, the willingness to take risks: One skill that is highly valued in private financing is risk assessment and pricing of risk: the higher the appetite for risk, the higher the returns for those who do not get burned in the process. Ultimately, as finance theory tells us, all risk-adjusted returns gravitate toward what is regarded as the norm. In a meeting with a group of venture capitalists a couple of years ago, I was told that the firms they worked with had made 20 investments in India, of which 18 resulted in bankruptcies, while 2 provided annual returns of more than 100 percent, fully compensating for those that had failed. Understandably, the venture capital firm was looking for skills that made it possible to distinguish the good from the bad and the ugly.

Over the years—in part because of the fiduciary responsibilities that have been loaded on it and in part because the senior managers frown on projects that fail—the Bank, as a development institution, has become excessively risk averse. The ability to take risks in the area of development has high rewards. A risk-averse person, for instance, would not have launched the Grameen Bank, or promoted the cultivation of high-yielding seed varieties in the late 1960s, or supported the manufacture of retroviral drugs for AIDS treatment, as several Indian companies did, without waiting for the expiration of patents.

Finally, a word about the need for innovation: I did not see the kind of restlessness expressed in the search for new ideas and products in the Bank that I come across in the private sector. Innovation is undertaken mostly for the purpose of dealing with risk—that is how various forms of financial derivatives get constantly invented and offered to the markets so that risks get broadly shared. Much less innovation is done in the field of development. One function the networks could serve, for instance, is to help the Bank evolve into an institution where the risks of development work are understood, evaluated, and then developed into lines of new and innovative products.

Conclusion

If I had, at this time, some say in influencing the Bank's policies with respect to development and also some way of influencing the way the institution does business, what three pieces of advice would I give to the senior managers? Why do I say three and not ten or a dozen? My advice does not cover all the subjects explored above for the simple reason that not too many things should be done at the same time. Change should be focused and not so widely distributed that it becomes chaotic.

First, the Bank should return to what I have termed the basics. It should, once again, concentrate on financing the development of physical infrastructure. To do this, the institution will need to re-create the staff expertise to undertake project work and, whenever possible and necessary, work with the private sector to establish consortia for financing large undertakings. The Bank should, in this context, adopt some of the features of investment banking, as the term is understood in the United States. By this I mean that it should do more structured financing, rather than take the entire burden of financing projects onto its shoulders.

Second, the Bank should develop a real sense of partnership with the borrowers. At times, this policy may bring it into conflict with the NGOs, in particular those operating out of the industrial world. Rather than bending over backward to cultivate the NGO community, the Bank should spend the same amount of energy working in harmony with the community of borrowers.

Third, it should re-create the capacity to do serious research and analysis on cutting-edge development issues and, thus, regain the commanding heights of intellectual work that it has abandoned over time—and perhaps without fully realizing that it was doing so—to a variety of other players in the field of development. This rededication to research and analysis will require that new skills be brought into the institution and new processes be developed to ensure that the subjects chosen have a bearing on the institution's overall mission.

What I have presented in this chapter are a few thoughts drawn from a quarter century of experience in various places and positions I occupied at the Bank between 1974 and 1999. Most of the time I have used the first-person singular to tell the story in order to underscore a simple point: the observations made in this chapter are based on personal experiences that may or may not be shared by other people who were at the institution at the same time as I was a staff member. That notwithstanding, it is my hope that what I have said may interest some people who currently occupy management positions and face the types of challenges I had to deal with when I served the institution.

Notes

1. I have dealt with this episode in Pakistan's history in several books I have written on the country. See, for instance, Burki (1991)

2. How the two of us were able to turn a moribund committee into an effective institution is itself an interesting story, for which I do not have space in this chapter.

3. See World Bank (1990), the *World Development Report* for that year. The report was prepared by a team led by Lyn Squire.

4. See World Bank (2001c). The report was prepared by a team initially led by Ravi Kanbur, who resigned his position while the report was still in preparation because of differences with some of the managers who were supervising his work. They wanted greater emphasis on growth than Kanbur was prepared to place in advocating the strategy mix for poverty alleviation. He was succeeded by Nora Lustig.

5. The deputies are a group of officials representing the governments who provide funds to IDA. The group meets every three years when IDA's funding needs to be replenished.

6. I was explicitly instructed not to meet with Premier Li Peng, whose name was associated with what the West called the Tiananmen Square Massacre. Instead, I met with the three vice premiers and Zhu Rongji, the mayor of Shanghai. Zhu later became China's premier.

7. In alphabetical order, the group comprises Canada, France, Germany, Japan, Italy, the United Kingdom, and the United States.

8. I pick up this point in the lesson on "Disadvantages of Staying in a State of Constant Flux."

9. The 1973 reorganization took place before I joined the institution. However, there was enough corridor and coffee-shop talk in the Bank for me to realize that the changes that had been made were very unsettling for some of the staff people and managers.

10. Personal communication in e-mail to the author from Roberto Zagha.

11. The term the *Washington Consensus* is attributed to the economist John Williamson, who used it in a paper written for the Institute of International Economics (Williamson 1990). He elaborated on the subject in several later articles. See for instance, Williamson (2000).

12. Some of the speeches I gave on these and other comparisons between East Asia and Latin America were later published in the form of a book by the World Bank (Burki 2000).

Yukon Huang

*Former Country Director for the Russian Federation
and the Former Soviet Union (1992–97)
and China (1997–2004)*

Yukon Huang quite literally came of age in the World Bank. His father was a Bank economist specializing in commodities markets, making Yukon among a select few second-generation Bank managers today. But if economics came naturally to him, his interest in development was not solidified until a stint in Tanzania as a visiting lecturer at the University of Dar es Salaam in 1972–74, shortly after receiving his Ph.D. from Princeton. Yukon says a central topic of his time in Africa was the debate between growth and equity, which led him to shun an "either-or" approach in favor of recognizing their complementary nature. "A country that cannot grow well cannot deal with poverty issues," he says. "Growth doesn't guarantee equity, but it makes it feasible."

Yukon joined the World Bank in 1976 as a country economist for Southeast Asia. This work was followed by service as deputy chief of Mission in Bangladesh from 1981–84. From there he returned to Washington, D.C., to serve as division chief for bank assistance policies and later as lead economist and country operations chief for Asia.

In 1992, Yukon assumed what was arguably the most challenging job in the World Bank during the 1990s: division chief and then department director for the Russian Federation and the Central Asian former Soviet republics. As the former Soviet Union began its heady embrace of capitalism, Yukon oversaw a project portfolio accounting for nearly a quarter of the Bank's total lending program in an environment of political and economic collapse.

After five tumultuous years, Yukon became country director for China from 1997–2004. During this period, Yukon has supervised work on a scale befitting the world's most populous nation and an emerging economic power: on average nearly 100 ongoing projects with a value of some US$10 billion, plus 10 to 15 major studies of Chinese economic development annually. He is the first China country director to be based in the field, which he says greatly contributes to the Bank's effectiveness: "In the field, we have a much better understanding of country conditions and a better ability to respond," making the Bank a more agile institution to resolve project issues, to provide core services like disbursements and procurement, and to transfer knowledge.

Despite the apparently divergent paths of Russia and China—both enormous, formerly state-run economies encountering very different results in their adaptation to markets—Yukon bristles at comparisons between the two. "A country's approach is heavily influenced by its history and political legacy," he says, cautioning against attempts to draw simple lessons. "Russia had no other choice in the 1990s," as the political disintegration of the Soviet Union triggered an economic collapse that was inevitable, not the result of a failure to adopt gradualist policies. On the other hand, "China had a different starting point," needing to economically and politically unify 25 to 30 different provinces while ensuring equity and reviving growth. "Politically divergent objectives lead to divergent economic policies," he concludes.

Reflecting on his work at the World Bank, Yukon laments the frequency with which the Bank's objectives fail to mesh with a country's objectives or political constraints, leading to missed opportunities for development. His most fulfilling moments have occurred, he says, at those special times "when the Bank's role fits exactly into a country's needs."

7   On Good Policies and Great Men

Reflections on China and Russia

Yukon Huang

As a naive graduate student at Princeton University, I asked my thesis adviser, Sir W. Arthur Lewis, a seemingly simple question: "Why do some developing countries grow faster than others?" Professor Lewis, a 1979 Nobel Laureate and arguably the founding father of development economics, appeared to me as the wisest man around, and I was hoping to learn the secret for success before preaching what I would eventually have to practice.

He responded that, after countless debates with both practitioners and academics, he found that two factors stood the test of time. The first was a variant of historian Thomas Carlyle's Great Man thesis:[1] the presence of a great leader can shape the course of economic history. The second was that good policies do matter: where good policies are applied, rapid growth follows.

But lest he mislead me into thinking that this answer was so simple, Professor Lewis then explained that the conditions necessary for either of those factors to emerge were rarely present and little understood. Because so few of the political systems in developing countries were truly democratic (and even fewer at the time of our conversation), most nations would have to rely on a Great Man to rise and lead them. But such men do not emerge often in history, and when they do, their emergence seems largely a matter of luck.

In well-functioning democracies, Professor Lewis continued, the existence of a Great Man may help, but then the issue is likely to be more about how the administrative system generates the broad support necessary to implement good policies. Thus, the emergence of good policies seems to rely as much on luck as does the emergence of the Great Man.

After three decades of working in development, I still think of Professor Lewis' comments when I am pressed to answer why some developing countries succeed and others do not. His simple, intuitive notions may explain why sustaining growth is so difficult and why so few countries have managed to do so.

I began my development career by debating with my Marxist teaching colleagues in Tanzania in the early 1970s. Most recently I dealt with the consequences of the fall of Marxism as the World Bank's country director for Russia and China over the past decade. Throughout that period, the underlying messages in Lewis's approach still resonated.

Tanzania was blessed with a Great Man, Julius Nyerere, but his well-intentioned, village-based *ujamma* socialist policies did not turn out to be good policies. In Russia, as well as in many of the other republics of the former Soviet Union (FSU), initial conditions in the early 1990s militated against good policies emerging, and although many notable political figures have taken center stage, we are still waiting to see if a Great Man will pass the test of time. In China, initial conditions in the late 1970s were apt for the emergence of good policies launched under the auspices of a Great Man, Deng Xiaoping. This essay will focus largely on China and, to a lesser extent, Russia, while drawing on other country cases that I have worked on over the years. It concludes with thoughts on the implications of those experiences for the World Bank.

Explaining Russian and Chinese Development: Understanding Their Objective Functions

Many people ask me to explain why China's economy has performed so well in recent decades, while post-Soviet Russia's economy has encountered so much difficulty. Some think that this debate is between the virtues of shock therapy versus a gradualist approach to reform for transition economies. Because both are large countries in transition from centrally planned to market-based systems, people ask, "Shouldn't Russia have followed China's path to development?"

I find this query frustrating to answer, because it is the wrong question. Despite their superficial similarities, Russia and China started their transitions from very different points. Accordingly, the objectives of each government at the outset of each period—China in 1978, Russia in 1992—were diametrically opposite. Although China's objective in the post-Mao era was to unify disparate interests under a central authority and to restore stability, Russia's was to break down the centralized political structure of the FSU, an aim that provided the environment for a free-for-all struggle. Therefore, the right question to ask about Russia and China is, "Why did they have such different objectives, and what were the consequences?"

As economists, we have been taught that, to understand behaviors and outcomes, we must first understand what the objectives were. Consumers maximize utility, firms maximize profits, but governments maximize objectives depending on the broader political context.

China was ripe for change in 1978. Mao Zedong had died in 1976 after ruling the country for 27 years, and whatever one might feel about the unfortunate consequences of his divisive actions in the latter years of his regime, he fostered a political system that was still genuinely concerned with the plight of the rural poor and was founded on the objective of creating a unified nation. The challenge for Deng Xiaoping, who assumed the leadership role in 1978, was to reestablish central authority over disruptive factions within the party and to ensure that China's diverse regional interests did not undercut national unity. China was thus ripe for a message of stability and consolidation with the promise that an opening to the outside world would bring the return of rapid growth.

Deng probably never heard of Lewis's (1954) classic article, "Economic Development with Unlimited Supplies of Labor." If China's leader knew the work, which formed the basis for Lewis's Nobel Prize, he would have realized that the Lewis model would well characterize China's impressive economic successes in the 1980s and 1990s. In particular, moving forward to deliver progress to the rural poor, who provided the foundations for the Chinese Communist Party's rise to power, laid the basis for surplus generation. This advance would, in turn, free excess rural labor for more nontraditional activities and create the industrial markets that formed the basis for trade expansion and more rapid growth. Deng was both pragmatic ("It does not matter if the cat is black or white; if it catches mice, it's a good cat") and willing to experiment ("Crossing the river by feeling the stones"), as well as politically astute enough to ensure approval for his reform agenda. The first wave of reforms focused on providing incentives for rural productivity gains by allowing peasant farmers to sell surplus crops at market prices but without the wholesale liberalization of agriculture that could risk stability. It was the first step of a Great Man initiating appropriate policies.

Contrast this first step in China with that of Russia in the early 1990s. The Soviet Union had collapsed, but less understood at the time was that it was also in the new ruling class's interest that disorder continue—at least for a while. "Why not be president of my own country and not play second fiddle as the titular leader of one of the many republics in the Soviet Union under Gorbachev?" was the tantalizing question racing through the minds of those who came into their own with the dissolution of the FSU. The shared objective function of the new political interests was thus to facilitate the collapse of the old political regime and dissolve interrepublican links. Doing so made an economic collapse inevitable.

Thus, the issue for the genuine reformers was never a choice between shock therapy and gradualist reform, but rather how to ameliorate the destructive consequences of a political disintegration inspired by parceling off Russia's vast natural wealth to those who would support the dissolution of the FSU. Although development practitioners, including World Bank officials such as myself, were preaching the importance of establishing functioning institutions and a sound legal system as a basis for reforms, Russia was engulfed in a chaotic and inequitable process of redistributing assets from the state to those who happened to be around at the right time. Stability and a new-found respect for the rule of law would eventually return, but only after the process of asset redistribution had run its course, because only then would the new owners share a common interest in protecting property rights and fostering a stable investment regime.

These sketches of China and Russia at their respective initial crossroads are admittedly simplistic, but they illustrate the primacy of the historical and political context in determining subsequent economic outcomes. At that time, the regimes of China and Russia were maximizing entirely opposite objective functions. To suggest—with the benefit of hindsight, revisionist history, or both—that one country could have followed the path of the other is simply not worth debating.

Gradual or Rapid? Comprehensive or Selective?

Another common misinterpretation is to characterize China as taking a gradualist approach in contrast to some of the episodic rapid experiences elsewhere. The erroneous conclusion of this comparison is that China succeeded by proceeding slowly with reforms, while others went too fast and too far ahead of the pace of essential and complementary institutional reforms.

For anyone who has witnessed the speed of China's development over the past two decades, *gradual* is not an adjective that comes to mind. The magnitude and diversity of the change under way are staggering, and in fact there is a growing sense that those changes may be exceeding the capacity of institutions to absorb them.

The process under way in China has neither been slow nor gradual, but rather it has been selective and in many aspects rapid. Increasing market orientation and openness, growth with stability, and pro-poor processes has guided China's policymakers over the past 25 years. True, economic outcomes have not always been perfect, and there have been times when progress has staggered, but in historical perspective, those objectives were consistent drivers toward unprecedented achievements in reducing poverty and establishing the foundations for accelerated and sustained growth. Moreover, China's leaders recognized that comprehensive approaches did not mean that one should or could tackle everything simultaneously and with equal intensity. Instead, they saw that complex systems as well as committed leaders can take on only a limited number of reform priorities at any given time. There may be a logical sequence for reforms guided by economic postulates, but equally important for success are political acceptability and opportunism, which are often dictated by exogenous factors. China since 1978 is a story of selectivity and seizing opportunities; it is not about the virtues of gradualism.

Since 1978, the Chinese government has had an uncanny ability to identify what needed to be done next—and to keep at it until success was achieved. And while the leaders were genuinely interested in global experiences, they also realized that borrowed approaches had to be adapted to local conditions. Hence, as discussed above, the initial emphasis was on liberating the agricultural sector, and only after progress appeared self-sustaining did the country turn to the next set of issues: emergence of village-based enterprises that provided higher-value jobs, followed by development of the coastal provinces through trade and special economic zones. Those various drivers of growth did not run on autopilot. They provided stimulus at crucial stages but often required adjustment. In due course, after they had served their purpose, the system moved on to new initiatives. This was learning by doing at its best.

Furthermore, in identifying priorities, the Chinese government realized early on that identifying a problem was not good enough; equally important was whether conditions were ripe for initiatives to succeed. The attention of China's leaders over the past five years, for example, was on achieving membership in the World Trade Organization (WTO). They recognized early on that key reforms would be much easier to handle in an expanding economy and with institutions alerted to and prepared for the consequences of a more open external regime.

In the aftermath, any potentially negative consequences of WTO membership turned out to be fewer than envisaged, thus allowing the new administration to move on to the next set of priorities, including distributional needs and financial sector reforms. The extent and complexities of poverty alleviation, for example, meant that reviving growth had to take place before distributional issues could be effectively resolved, even if, in the process, some regions benefited more than others. But, in time, distributional issues would be taken up frontally when more effective instruments and fiscal systems evolved to ensure better results. In the case of China's oft-criticized banking system, for example, the authorities have long acknowledged the severity of the problem of nonperforming loans, but they also realized that that problem could not be adequately dealt with until sustained growth was ensured, key enterprise reforms were well under way, and the institutional and managerial capacities were strong enough to deal with the complexities involved.

Contrast this approach with that of the Russian experience: selectivity of the Chinese variety is not much of a choice when the entire political and economic system has collapsed. Gradualism is even less so. Shock therapy should not be judged as an option but rather as a consequence, and Russia did not really choose this path but rather fell off a path. But even shock therapy as a reform path is a misnomer. Reform takes time; it cannot be imposed on the economic structure overnight.[2] Russians left impoverished by the economy's collapse could only hope that there existed a shock therapy that could quickly generate the economic revival that they sought!

Other Factors in China's Success: Competition and Accountability

Selectivity in policy reform is not the only reason for China's success. Many other factors have contributed, some by design and some by luck. But two factors worth emphasizing are how this system has instilled competitive pressures and how it has fostered accountability.

A remarkable paradox of the China that Deng inherited in 1978—one that continued for over the past two decades—was that, despite China's being a highly centralized planned economy, a latent but powerful ethic of competition persisted in the system. This ethic of competition was due not only to the dynamism inherent in family-based farming structures, which survived the communal pressures. State enterprises were also more easily liberated from the formal enterprise management structures than one would have surmised. We are taught in our textbooks about the inefficiencies of soft-budget constraints and quantitative output targets, and the experiences of Russia and Eastern Europe more generally showed how difficult it is to transform state enterprise sectors into globally competitive units. But despite decades of poor policies and many gross inefficiencies, China has been relatively unique in preserving competitive forces in otherwise inefficient production systems. This status is explained in part by the historical emphasis on benchmarking against global markets as an exporter. In addition, though China's provinces may often hide behind protected regulatory walls, they still have to compete with each other on both price and quality as mini-nations within a nation. Thus, when Deng began opening China to external market forces, latent competitive pressures, supported by the ability of the Chinese to adapt quickly, emerged to produce a remarkably efficient engine of growth.

China is seen as no less afflicted than other Asian countries by corruption, a vestige of the clash between market forces and controlled systems under single-party rule. Yet unlike the case in several similar countries, corruption in China has not been seen as having inhibited growth—although some studies would argue that the economic costs have been substantial. Moreover, the Bank's portfolio has consistently been rated among the best, and the frequency of fraud, in relation to the size of the portfolio, is low—an outcome that puzzles many observers.

At the project level, part of the explanation lies in a strict system of accountability applied to donor programs at local levels. External assistance is guided by the simple proposition of ensuring accountability through application of a beneficiary-pays principle. Almost all Bank-assisted projects are based on the principle that repayment obligations are passed down to those who will benefit—reaching in many cases down to county, township, and even household levels. Because each level in the chain is responsible for its own share of repayment, each level takes unusual care to ensure that proceeds are well used and accounted for. Because of sovereign guarantees and the concessionary nature of our assistance, the Bank, like many other donor agencies, is not subjected to true market tests, and accountability is harder to ensure. For most of our borrowers, a central agency such as the Ministry of Finance assumes the repayment obligations, although the benefits are typically targeted at local levels. In the process, without strong monitoring and enforcement systems in place, the incentives can encourage less-than-ideal outcomes and diversion of resources.

However, while this aspect of project administration is one of China's greatest strengths, it is also one of its greatest weaknesses. By pushing repayment obligations down to beneficiary levels, project selection ends up favoring projects with promising financial rather than social returns and reducing eligibility for financial support for poorer localities with less borrowing capacity. A major challenge thus remains to balance the benefits of accountability with broader development objectives.

At the broader political and country level, the destabilizing aspects of corruption have been tempered thus far by the particular kind of scrutiny to which the top leadership is subjected under China's particular governance system. Indeed, when commoners in the regions protest against abuse or corruption, they are more often than not sending messages for help to the senior leadership in Beijing to rectify the perceived excesses committed by local officials. In many other developing countries, when the people complain about corruption, they are as likely to be targeting their top leadership as their local administrators.

Lessons from China for the World Bank

We at the World Bank often lecture to our clients about the essential ingredients for success. In talking about reforms, we highlight the need for political sensitivity, selectivity, and accountability. China has acted on those principles. But as an institution, we have to remind ourselves constantly of the need to practice what we preach.

First, I have discussed the crucial importance of understanding the political context that shapes our clients' thinking and whether their objective function is the same as ours. Decentralizing Country Management Units to the field is a major step in the right direction, but our operational staff members are driven by a career-development model that is based on the concept of undertaking several three- to five-year country rotations with input-related outcomes that are more time bound than the longer-term perspectives needed to chart a sustainable path driven by country circumstances. We shape human resource policies more with a view to encouraging personnel to acquire multicountry perspectives than with the idea that over the course of their careers they should reengage periodically or stick with the same country or region over the 10- to 15-year time span needed for a country to really shape its developmental foundations.

Second, it is correct, of course, that a successful development strategy must be comprehensive in identifying the range of elements that need to be addressed, but we too often take that to mean that all issues are of similar importance and need to be addressed at the same time. Successful practitioners choose objectives not only on the basis of importance but also with regard to the feasibility of success. Although the Chinese have given us many excellent examples of this approach, the World Bank, like many institutions governed by diverse interests, often does not have the luxury of saying no. We are moved far too often to pursue simultaneously multiple agendas with the risk of not doing any of them well. Taking lessons from China's use of selectivity and of matching need with capacity would help the Bank put the strategy back in our strategic approach. We need to ask more often, "What is actionable?" rather than just "What is a pressing problem?"

Third, we can learn from China's experience with instituting accountability in the management of its World Bank project portfolio. We face tremendous pressure from our shareholders to do all that we can to ensure that our resources are used wisely and efficiently. Rightly so—anything less means that we are squandering the scarce global resources devoted to poverty reduction. Yet we might spend more efforts to put in systems that make our clients more accountable for the efficient use of borrowed funds—including considering those aspects of a modified beneficiary-pays principle that might promote more market tests to improve outcomes.

Conclusion

Professor Lewis died in 1990, and I often wonder what he would say today about the development experiences of the past decade. No doubt he would view the string of crises—in economies previously considered both well managed and poorly managed—and the disappointing results of reforms in Africa, Eastern Europe, and Latin America as lamentable evidence that his intuition about the difficulty of policymaking was correct.

But he might also look at the success stories—not only in China, but also in other East Asian nations, as well as Chile, Poland, and (as has been noted more recently) India and certain African countries—as at least a partial refutation of his Great Man thesis. Though all of these countries were blessed with good policies, not all were particularly democratic regimes, and surely not all have produced a Great Man. There is a temptation to attribute China's success to the leadership skills of Deng or to benefits of a fine-tuned administrative structure's ability to implement when it gets the policy right in comparison with the agonizing hesitation and debates that characterize fledgling democracies. However, those explanations prove facile when one considers the variety of historical legacies and political regimes under which successful development has occurred.

Development has occurred—and has failed to occur—under both democratic and authoritarian systems and under dynamic as well as tepid leadership. Perhaps the development successes and failures merely teach us that we do not know much at all. Let our task at the World Bank continue to be one of trying to understand the policies that allow countries to grow and develop, plus the conditions under which such policies arise.

(Postscript: This essay is about China's impressive accomplishments, not about its failures or the risks that lie ahead. But I would be remiss in giving the sense that the future is all roses and that the country's leaders can now relax. There are major problems for which solutions are not easy to envisage: widening social inequalities, environmental degradation of an extreme nature, a fragile financial system that could jeopardize macroeconomic stability—and many others. If China continues, however, to be receptive to new ideas, to promote change, and to adapt social as well as political institutions to fit the new circumstances, then there is no reason why the major accomplishments of recent years cannot be sustained. The real challenge for the new leadership is to stay open, innovative, and responsive.)

Notes

1. Carlyle (1840) wrote, "The history of the world is but the biography of great men."

2. By the same token, the only form of shock therapy that can truly take place overnight—price liberalization—is often mislabeled as "reform." Price liberalization is not reform, but merely a recognition of reality!

Olivier Lafourcade

*Former Country Director for Western Africa (1992–96)
and Mexico (1996–2000)*

As a native of the southern French region of Bordeaux, Olivier Lafourcade says, "I've always been associated with the rural sector." But rather than remain among the vineyards of his home region, a trip to the Middle East to work on a project of the United Nations Food and Agriculture Organization when he was a student spurred Olivier to pursue a career in international development. After receiving his Ph.D. in agricultural economics from the University of Maryland in 1971, Olivier worked briefly in agricultural research in Argentina before joining the World Bank as a Young Professional in 1973.

Olivier spent his early career in the Bank as a rural development economist, gaining operations experience in a number of regions. Among his favorite projects from this period was work on the first Bank study of the rural sector in the English-speaking islands of the Caribbean, which gave him the chance to travel to "all the nice places, like St. Lucia and Grenada and the rest," he laughs. But he also recalls the period as one of serious progress in rural development, as Bank President Robert McNamara led the institution to focus heavy attention on the rural poor.

In fact, McNamara's commitment to rural development and high regard for Olivier's efforts were so great that he appointed Olivier as his personal assistant in 1980, largely to ensure that the Bank would continue to focus on the rural sector on McNamara's impending departure. The strategy worked, as Olivier remained in the position for a year under McNamara's successor, Alden Clausen.

Olivier returned to agricultural operations in 1982, serving as deputy division chief in the East Africa Region and later as division chief in the South Asia Region. Of the lessons of his multiregional experience in the rural sector, Olivier says that, with respect to its technical aspects, "Agriculture is agriculture is agriculture. Small farmers face similar challenges everywhere." But the widely divergent political and economic environments among regions generate divergent needs and approaches, and Olivier has enjoyed playing a catalytic role in the Bank's rural strategy by questioning conventional wisdom.

In 1988, Olivier received "an offer I couldn't turn down" to return to France and become the Bank's Paris-based director of external affairs for Europe, a position that found him jaunting across the continent to represent the Bank to governments and other stakeholders. Four years later, the Bank "decided I'd had enough fun in Paris, and it was time to get back to work. They didn't give me much choice!" he jokes, and he was appointed director for francophone Africa, a job that later expanded to include several nonfrancophone African nations.

Olivier was appointed to an even more challenging role in 1996: country director for Mexico. "The country situation was absolutely dismal," he recalls of Mexico's first years following the financial crisis of 1994–95. Additionally, Olivier was the first field-based country director in Mexico, and although managing the transition was daunting, "it was one of the reasons why I accepted the job."

He left Mexico in 2002 to retire to France, but as a consultant to the Bank, the French aid agency, and various private companies, nonprofits, and universities, Olivier says, "I'm busy," in typically understated fashion. As a Bordeaux native, he brings a particular credibility to the issue of agricultural protectionism, which he denounces in his talks with governments and universities. Looking back on more than 30 years in development, Olivier says, "The cause of poverty alleviation is still as valid today as ever."

8 Lessons of the 1990s

A Personal Account

Olivier Lafourcade

THE FOLLOWING ACCOUNT OF MY EXPERIENCE AS A COUNTRY DIRECTOR IN THE West Africa Region (1992–96) and then in the Latin America and Caribbean Region (1996–2002) also reflects the effect of my previous job as director for external affairs for Europe in Paris (1988–92). It is also influenced by my background and work experience in the sector of agriculture and rural development, in which I spent most of my pre-Bank training and professional life, as well as a good half of my time with the Bank. While I focus my observations on the decade of the 1990s, I wish to draw some further lessons from my wider exposure to the development process and its challenges during a longer period extending over the entire length of my career (1973–2002) in dealing with development issues.

First, I discuss a few aspects having to do with the circumstances of my work with the Bank over the period under review, essentially dealing with my perception of what the realities and the challenges were at the time when I was given my respective assignments, and then detailing and explaining how I tried to address those challenges and what happened during the course of the assignment, as circumstances changed. Second, I will offer some observations on what I perceive to be the main lessons of those experiences, both from a viewpoint of substance and from a viewpoint of the ways and means through which we provided our assistance to the process. Throughout, I will enlarge my comments to broader issues covering the longer period, with a view to drawing broader, more general lessons of experience than simply those of the 1990s.

At the outset, it is important to remind the reader that such an assessment cannot be dissociated from the inherent biases and personal beliefs of the writer, not just my motivations but also my understanding of what the institution is all about. I am fully aware that I may open myself to fairly predictable criticism—being accused or labeled with being excessively idealistic, narrow minded, perhaps naive or innocent, or—worse—blind or shortsighted. So be it.

I believe in the notion of service and have always considered that the World Bank fulfills a function of civil service to the world. This was the reason it was created. This notion does immediately raise a question of whether the service is to countries, to the populations, to the governments—to Zaire or to a leader such as Nzanga Joseph Mobutu, in one instance, and to Nigeria or to Sani Abacha, in another. The debate about whom the Bank truly serves is important and figures in some of my observations below, but one point is clear to me: a civil service, be it international or national, does not deal with clients. A relationship with a client implicitly carries the notion of mercantilism. Since we are not in the business of selling stuff, I much prefer the term *partner* to that of *client*, and I am not at all comfortable with the notion of conditionality. This concept is quite contrary to that of partnership. How can I impose a condition on my partner? What sort of partnership is it where one side conditions its action on the other?

I also believe in institutional loyalty. I can certainly admit, or rather welcome, criticism of the institution, because I believe, as well, in excellence and in pursuing excellence through consistently questioning the institution, its way of operating, its idiosyncrasies, and its procedures. Our partners in the borrowing countries expect and deserve the best. The Bank must offer the best, and it often does, but not always. And if we recruit the best, as we claim we do, then why do we consistently behave as if we do not trust them? Why is there so much second guessing? Why are there so many control systems, reviews, and other mechanisms that say clearly that we do not trust the judgment of managers and individuals? What is actually needed is to unleash the capacities, imagination, commitment, and drive of the vast majority of people in the institution.

Finally, I believe in the importance of tolerance and its corollary, humility. There is just nothing that cannot be resolved with a minimum of goodwill, understanding, and compassion. Although there should be no room for arrogance, know-it-all attitudes, disrespect, intellectual oppression, or heavy-handedness, I have had difficulties with the amount of impatience, intolerance, and sometimes nastiness among people at the Bank and with the appearance that our entire culture is designed to find fault in others. My experience, to the contrary, tells me that, in general, staff members are well intentioned, competent, and professional, and everyone—I included—is entitled to make mistakes.

My entire career at the Bank has been strongly influenced by a few such individuals who helped shape these convictions about what the job is all about. First and foremost is Robert McNamara, a model to me in many respects, especially through his unmatched commitment to the cause of poverty reduction and economic development, with the highest level of personal, intellectual, and moral integrity. Additionally, I respect a number of second-tier key managers and professionals whom I have seen contributing, each one in his own ways, to the same cause and to the fulfillment of the Bank's objectives: Warren Baum, Roger Chaufournier, Burke Knapp, Moeen Qureshi, Ernie Stern, Monty Yudelman, and many others. Among the countless people with whom I interacted in the course of 30 years, I owe much to the peasants of Northeast Brazil, Cameroon, India, Mexico, Nepal, and Rwanda; to many country leaders and high-level officials; and to numerous partners from nongovernmental organizations (NGOs) and private institutions—in particular, such truly outstanding practitioners of development as Father Francisco de Roux in the Magdalena Medio Rural Development Project in Colombia, who brought his priceless contribution to development in the middle of a hotly contested conflict area.

The 1990s Experience: Salient Features

As far as my own experience is concerned, the period of the 1990s can be divided in three major parts: (a) the European period (1990–92), at the time when I was still director of the European Office, with the fall of the Berlin Wall and all of its consequences for the world and for the Bank; (b) the African period (1992–96), in my position as country director in the West Africa Region, in charge of a large group of countries, with the major event of the devaluation of the Coopération Financière en Afrique (CFA) franc in 1994; and (c) the Latin American period (1996–2000), as country director for Mexico, and subsequently (2000–2002) as country director for Mexico, Colombia, and the República Bolivariana de Venezuela.

The European Period (1990–92)

As director of the European Office in Paris (1988–92), having dealt for the previous six years with the realities of agricultural and rural development in Central Africa and in the Indian subcontinent, I observed the effect of the fall of the Berlin Wall and the start of the Bank's dealing with the former Eastern bloc. Also important were the emergence of truly European issues, the creation of the European Bank for Reconstruction and Development, the mobilization of the European Commission and the European governments, and—along with the Cold War's end—the rise of the debt issue, particularly with Latin America, and the early lessons of adjustment, especially in Africa. I gained exposure to truly global issues (environment, debt, and macroeconomic matters) and familiarity with the financing part of the institution (for example, borrowing operations in Western European capital markets). Furthermore, I learned about dealing with many diverse constituencies from donor countries, especially northern NGOs, the media, advocacy groups (for example, on environment), academic centers, and "noninitiated" people, who are generally unfamiliar with and far removed from operations and had the experience of seeing the Bank (Washington, D.C.) from a distance.

It is hard not to think about that period without underscoring the Bank's isolation from and insensitivity to the realities of Europe. For example, it was interesting to note the complete absence of reaction from Washington, D.C., when I first raised the issue of migration as a point of great concern to European countries (especially in Italy, Spain, and to some extent Germany). At the time I was told that "these are problems of the industrial countries and not something of a priority for the Bank." I found the response strange. We could have made a great argument in these countries precisely to seek their increased support to assist the countries of out-migration in their efforts toward development. Such assistance might have reduced migration and, at the very least, contributed to better educated and qualified migrants. This issue testifies in general to the lack of dialogue between the Bank and European countries on many matters of importance at that time.

The need was already clear to know and listen to other constituencies besides government—NGOs, the private sector, and academia—and to be sensitive to issues of interest to them. The efforts made by the Bank then were by no means sufficient, and the result was continued widespread ignorance of, if not outright opposition to, the Bank from various sides.[1] The Bank's physical presence in Europe was conspicuously lacking, and the very limited means of the European Office did not allow the Bank to be present in many forums. For example, I would argue that the Bank could have contributed (and still could contribute today) much more effectively to the promotion of a real information base and debate on development issues at the school level (including primary and secondary). Fifteen years later, I am still shocked at the degree of ignorance among youngsters about basic issues of development. It is no surprise, then, that there is so much misconception, misunderstanding, and negative reaction to these matters and to the Bank—witness the antiglobalization and alter-mondialization movements.[2]

Assuming that, since we do good things, everybody will know about it, the Bank neglected the education of the masses in Europe, conducting very little dialogue except with development professionals and the initiated few. Even with them, there was virtually no participation and very little debate. In fact, there was very little contribution to development thinking from a theoretical standpoint. Compared with the 1960s and 1970s, which had seen a large number of intellectual contributions (more often than not heavily biased to the left), the 1980s and the beginning of the 1990s were devoid of much intellectual debate. This outcome was not entirely surprising, as the dominant ideology prevailing until then—very much socialist or Marxist oriented—was so much discredited by the collapse of the Soviet Union and the Eastern bloc. This intellectual void, however, fed another widespread reaction and belief that perceived the Bank as dogmatic, heavily biased to the right, and tied to the interests of industrial countries and private multinational corporations. Thus, the Bank became increasingly perceived as U.S. dominated, excessively liberal, and not tuned or sympathetic to a more social vision of development. This perception is still the prevalent one in a large number of academic and NGO centers in Europe.

I became painfully aware of the serious gap between the external affairs side and the operational part of the Bank. Clearly, operations were so busy with their immediate responsibilities that they contributed precious little to the dissemination of information. Conversely, the good and well-intentioned external affairs officers in many cases lacked the concrete knowledge that comes from operations and gives much more credibility to storytelling, debating, and maintaining a constructive dialogue with so many of the Bank's partners, especially NGOs with considerable practical and field experience.

The Bank is essentially an institution of doers, in which the typical approach to development is—what is the problem? And what can be done about it? Where is the project? How much does it cost? Who is going to run it? When do we get on with the job? That approach leaves little time and patience for others who may have very different or more selective preoccupations—for example, analysis of a problem or discussion of the issues, without necessarily being able or willing or equipped to deal with all these issues. Thus, Bank staff members typically regarded the Organisation for Economic Co-operation and Development (OECD) as a waste of time—all talk and no action. This attitude resulted in an unwillingness to attend many important OECD meetings, with people staying away without realizing that the OECD is an immensely useful and worthwhile instrument for analysis, discussion, and debate. Far too often the Bank missed the opportunity of making its own case and views known in such a forum, exacerbating instead the negative views many held of the Bank as insensitive, arrogant, and isolated.

The same know-it-all attitude was also prevalent in the Bank's dealing with others such as NGOs. It reflected the arrogance of the one who has the money and the doer who has huge difficulties in communicating with the nondoers, who were often labeled, if not accused of, being poets, theoreticians, and idealists if not ideologues. Along the same lines, the relationships with other institutions—multilateral organizations such as the European Commission and bilateral cooperation agencies—were not without their occasional aspects of some distance and misunderstandings. Admittedly, things have changed considerably on this front, especially over the past few years. But the damage done at the time may have been very serious indeed, and reversing the negative perceptions takes time and effort.

The African Period (1992–96)

In 1992, I took over the management of the AF1 Department at a time of great tension over the issue of the CFA franc, the currency of 14 French-speaking countries of Africa, including the Comoros in the Indian Ocean. Starting in the mid 1980s, the Bank and a few other organizations felt that this currency was heavily overvalued, as it was tied (through a fixed-parity arrangement dating from the late 1940s) to the French franc, which itself was appreciating progressively as it was linked to the German mark. The result was that the economies of these francophone countries were becoming increasingly noncompetitive and had been sliding back dramatically over a 10-year period. It also appeared that the so-called internal adjustment measures (that is, fiscal adjustment measures and other structural reforms), which had been put in place over several years, were largely proving unable to bring about the changes that would have ensured renewed competitiveness. This subject had been overwhelming the relationships between the Bank, the 14 countries, and especially the French government, which had long opposed any monetary adjustment, largely for political reasons. Hence I took on my job as country director in a particularly tense environment and being a Frenchman did not make my work any easier.[3]

From a substantive standpoint, arresting the decline of the 14 francophone African countries through devaluation of the CFA franc was the overarching challenge of my tenure. From 1984 to 1992, Côte d'Ivoire, for example, lost approximately 50 percent of its per capita income. The situation in most of the 14 countries was literally pathetic; production and exports of traditional commodities in Côte d'Ivoire—

cocoa, coffee, and timber—had all but come to a complete stop; the standards of living in rural areas had fallen to unprecedented lows; and the gap between urban centers (largely living off trade and civil service salaries) and rural areas (living off
agricultural production and exports) was clearly increasing. Poverty was increasing
throughout the region. The various fiscal and other structural adjustment measures
designed to restore competitiveness were failing miserably, proving the limitation of
this strategy. The Bank and other organizations were issuing one adjustment loan
after the other on relatively hard International Bank for Reconstruction and Development terms, and the effects were basically to (a) enable the reimbursement of previous loans and (b) add to the debt burden with no visible positive effect on the status
of the real economy. There was a sense of *fuite en avant*, with no one able to stop the
downward spiral, against a background of mistrust and suspicion among all partners,
with strong political undertones. The French were essentially accusing the Bank of
dancing to the tune of the United States, which wanted nothing other than to reduce
French influence in Africa. The reverse argument held that the French were out to
exploit the Africans and maintain their control of the countries. And what about the
Africans themselves in all this?

Remarkably, given the circumstances, the devaluation of the CFA franc in early
1994 and the subsequent recovery produced a major success. The devaluation was
unique—an unprecedented operation consisting of a simultaneous monetary realignment in the 14 francophone countries. It included not only a mix of short-term
monetary and fiscal adjustments (including a one-time 50 percent devaluation of the
currency), but also all sorts of accompanying social and economic measures with
long-term development goals. It required the preparation of 14 separate adjustment
programs and corresponding, new Country Assistance Strategies (CASs), following
an incredibly tight schedule with considerable pressures both from the countries,
which had been less than fully enthusiastic about the measure and had good reasons
to fear its political and social implications, and from the various partners—not least
of all the French government and the International Monetary Fund (IMF). Following a long-awaited, well-planned, and well-executed operation, no negative side
effects of the devaluation materialized, especially not the social disruptions so many
feared would take place. The economies of the countries started rebounding at a
spectacular pace. Agriculture and exports recovered quickly from their previous low
levels, and a new wind of enthusiasm, optimism, production, and prosperity started
blowing in rural areas.

From an institutional standpoint, the CFA franc devaluation provided an unprecedented experience in successful cooperation among many actors: the 14 French-
speaking African governments, the IMF, the World Bank, and the French
government. This achievement was truly masterfully managed, with an intense spirit
of collective responsibility, competence, and dedication. Just think about the questions of coordination within the French government itself.[4] In Washington, D.C., the
Bank and the IMF displayed outstanding cooperation, and within the Bank there was
also exemplary cooperation between the two operational departments most immediately concerned (the AF1 Department, which I headed, counted with the heavy-

weight countries, Côte d'Ivoire and Cameroon, and the Sahel Department, which was headed by Katherine Marshall). The cooperation with the IMF is worth mentioning as a model of how things can work between the two institutions, even under—or perhaps because of—the extraordinary stakes and the heavy pressures.

The question of why the operation took place at all, when there had been so much opposition to it for so long, is a legitimate one. In my view there are two main reasons: (a) the French Ministry of Finance came to the realization that it could no longer support the cost of carrying the countries single-handedly as it had done for so long by paying for recurrent expenditures, including part of their debt, in several countries that were basically bankrupt, and (b) the coincidence of the cohabitation in France whereby Prime Minister Edouard Balladur seemed not to have the biases toward Africa of most of his predecessors and, being somewhat agnostic about the need for the monetary operation, was ready to go forward with it, provided that President François Mitterrand was not opposed. All of Balladur's predecessors, from right or left, had been vigorously opposed to the operation, as had Mitterrand. There was a window of opportunity under Balladur, which was fortunately not missed. And the preparation for the operation on the French side had been the responsibility of a handful of remarkable, competent, and courageous civil servants from a few key institutions—the French Treasury and the Prime Minister's Office.

Within the Bank, preparation was the key element explaining the swift and successful response to the enormous challenge. For months and months, the Bank was consistently being asked by its partners (especially the IMF and the French government), "Are you ready?" (that is, in case the operation takes place tomorrow). The clear answer is that the Bank was indeed ready. Years of very sound analytical work had looked at the various aspects of the currency realignment—the need for accompanying social measures, the preparation of new strategies in each country, the preparation of new operations in the economic and social areas, and the completion of new CASs. And in the end, the Bank delivered, exactly as planned, both in the nature of its support—which was heavily biased toward mitigating the social costs of the adjustment, but also took the form of adjustment measures in infrastructure and productive areas—and in financial terms. This support was a noteworthy demonstration that, under the strongest time and political pressures, the Bank can respond and deliver, provided that there has been the necessary amount of preparation.

Additionally, it is relevant to observe that the pressures from all sides justified some special internal treatment by management, often cutting some red tape, reducing the review periods for selected documents, cutting the amount of and timing for peer reviews, and shortening some reporting and hierarchical relationships (for example, I had direct access to Ernie Stern's office). The experience raises the obvious question: were these requirements necessary in the first place? I would argue that the quality of the operations never suffered from allowing staff members and managers to move very expeditiously with a hard dose of flexibility and independent judgment.[5]

The successes, however, do not erase the fact that the Bank, though absolutely right in its assessment of the extreme seriousness of the CFA franc's overvaluation and in its recommendation of a monetary adjustment, was not very effective in the way it tried to make its argument and in its attempt to convince all of its partners, including the African countries. Over a period of several years, it behaved a bit like a bull in a china shop, especially with the African countries and with the French, to the extent that there was large resentment toward the Bank in many quarters. Books are being written on this subject, but in the end, I have a strong suspicion that the Bank lacked political savvy and sensitivity for a long time on this issue. As an illustration, why did the Bank's then-regional management incite the African leaders to gang up against the French to bring about the currency adjustment? Such posturing showed a surprising lack of historical and political perspective and demonstrated a strange absence of political and sociological perceptions about the way the African leaders and people related to France. Arguably, such bullishness and insensitivity prevented the Bank from promoting the devaluation of the CFA franc earlier than when it actually took place.

The 1994 reorganization of the West Africa Region resulted in my taking charge of a very large department, with an opportunity to think and operate with consistency and complementarity across countries in terms of strategies and operations. For the first time since the 1987 reorganization, the department included both French- and English-speaking countries—from Nigeria in the east to Côte d'Ivoire in the west, as well as Niger and Burkina Faso—an impressively coherent set of countries. I will never understand why the 1997 reorganization destroyed what had been done so successfully three years earlier.

Not until I became country director of Nigeria in 1994 did I realize that one African in five—125 million in all today—is Nigerian. This is an awesome fact of immense importance. De facto it means that there will be no future or prospects for at least the western half of Africa without Nigeria getting its act together and performing its role in accordance with its relative weight in the continent. In those days, I am pretty certain that the Bank was not paying sufficient attention to this fact. For example, I believe today that it should have been compulsory for all country directors dealing with countries neighboring Nigeria (Benin, Cameroon, and Niger) to meet with their counterpart in charge of Nigeria, only to be aware of what was going on there and understand the possible implications for their responsibilities. Is it the case today?

The importance of Nigeria relates as well to the fundamental need to take a regional approach to development in West Africa. There should be no doubt that expecting progress strictly on an individual country basis is an illusion. Markets are too small. Population dynamics and geographic and socioeconomic conditions are such that no one country can expect to move forward alone. The Bank and other organizations are correctly acknowledging this new reality, but I have a sense that much more could be done to promote regional integration. In particular, the political dimension of regional integration could be worked on much more aggressively. I am pleased to note that the Bank seems to have made considerable efforts on this front in very recent years, but at the time, such efforts were still somewhat limited. The truth is that, in those days, the Bank was clearly reducing its financial commitments in the absence of an acceptable macroeconomic framework. Moreover, there was such a fierce antagonism to the way the French-speaking countries were mismanaging their affairs and such a fixation on the need for currency adjustment that very little attention went to any other issue, such as regionalization, institutional development, or the building of social capital.

This job was a unique managerial experience, particularly as I was so closely involved in the CFA franc devaluation. At that time, perhaps because of my previous association with France in my European Office position, I was perceived as having access to people who counted in Paris and in the Bank. Likewise, it did not take too long to establish good and trusting relationships with African leaders in the countries for which I was country director. I enormously enjoyed this assignment, particularly my dealing with my African counterparts. We were not short of having very intelligent, competent, and dedicated partners in the countries, both English and French speaking. I believe the relationships with African leaders at the time were very constructive and productive, largely based on openness, trust, and transparency in what the Bank was trying to do and why.

Some General Lessons

Throughout the period, I found a profound and, to my mind, unacceptable difference in the Bank's treatment of French- and English-speaking countries. For instance, over a period of several years, Ghana seemingly could do no wrong. As the darling of the international donor community, it could attract administrative and lending resources out of proportion to neighboring French-speaking countries such as Côte d'Ivoire. By any account, the francophone countries may have given the appearance of more disorganization, less seriousness, or less commitment to their own development. And yet I wonder whether a good part of this difference in treatment was not due to the bias of some managers in the Bank. At that time, the vice president, who could not speak French, was never fully able to disguise his mistrust, if not his contempt, of the French. This hostility was more than excusable, given his correct assessment that it was entirely because of France that the necessary devaluation had not taken place earlier, but it translated into a less-than-supportive position with regard to the French-speaking African leaders. How many times did I hear him vent his frustration—sometimes his anger—at these counterparts for their "cowardice" in not going forward in spite of the French opposition?

The whole CFA franc episode confirmed to me, again and again, the importance of being politically and diplomatically well attuned in our line of business. It is by no means sufficient to be technically right or correct. It was clearly urgent not only to convince others, but also to understand their positions, whether in Paris or in the African capitals. To some extent, however, the Bank showed arrogance, stubbornness, and impatience in making its case. To understand the internal politics of the French, the complexity of their relationships with the Africans, and the weight of history and culture required a genuine, collective effort by the Bank—something perhaps beyond its capacities then. Likewise, the Bank did not use well all the opportunities it could have seized to mobilize third parties and other partners capable of exercising strong and effective influence over the key decisionmakers, particularly the media and academics. In retrospect, the Bank could have done much better in explaining and convincing the professionals in universities and think tanks, editorialists and columnists in major papers, and others (including professionals in the private sector) in France about the benefits to be derived from the currency adjustment. I discovered long ago that it is not a bad strategy to have your own battles being fought by others on your behalf.

In fact, precisely the way we dealt with the press at the time of the operation contributed to a good measure of its success. The key was constant contact, with much technical information being passed on by the Bank and immediate corrections of misstatements by politicians. An example was the Bank's providing factual and quantified information to *Le Monde,* which printed a strong and very effective rebuttal of a major negative statement by President Mitterrand not long after the devaluation. Notwithstanding the comments made here, I must state my admiration and appreciation for the commitment that the Bank was showing on behalf of Africa at the time. There is no doubt that Kim Jaycox, as vice president, was an inspired, forceful leader, whose personal commitment to, or rather passion for, Africa was never in doubt, and the commitment of his immediate management team and the entire staff working on the region was equally admirable. The insufficient and disappointing achievements in Africa cannot be attributed to a lack of effort and dedication on the part of these people.

By the time I left the West Africa Region, I was reasonably optimistic that it had benefited immensely from the CFA franc devaluation. Countries such as Benin, Burkina Faso, Cameroon, and Côte d'Ivoire were reported to be doing rather well. I had a sense that the strategic agenda had been pretty well defined, with a mix of short- and medium-term structural adjustments that were expected to yield considerable benefits. I thought that there was a significant change in the leadership of many African countries, with politicians and government authorities much more ready to exercise their responsibilities in an efficient and responsible way. I thought that the international community never had a better chance of lining up together in support of the efforts demanded from the countries. The CASs made good sense, and it was reasonably clear that what needed to be done was just a matter of getting on with the job. Little did I know or could I anticipate the two or three critical things that apparently occurred after my departure and that made it impossible to deliver on what was expected at the time: (a) the terrible situation in Côte d'Ivoire, which was essentially the result of political mismanagement and had an impact on so many other countries in the region; (b) the unwillingness or inability of most countries to move on the essential next step of structural reforms; and (c) the general disaffection toward Africa in many quarters, not least within the donor community.

In retrospect, therefore, it seems to me that the Bank and other donors were remiss in not insisting much more at the time and much earlier on the issue of governance. We should have been much more proactive in supporting legislative and judicial powers and reinforcing by all possible means the democratic processes being put in place in so many countries. For instance, it is significant that the project that we were then promoting to bolster the legislative branch in Ghana—at the request of and with the strongest support from Ghana's executive branch—was stopped by the Bank's legal counsel on the grounds that the Bank should not get involved in such a blatantly political arena. And yet, as I found out in Ghana—and subsequently in Benin and many other countries—it means a great deal when parliamentarians do not even understand how to read a budget proposal submitted by the executive branch. What can be expected from judges who have no understanding of fundamental economic concepts when they pass judgments on very complicated issues of financial sector restructuring?

I also believe that the Bank followed the correct strategy with respect to Nigeria by stopping all new operations there while General Sani Abacha was in charge. Having had the dubious privilege of being one of the very few outsiders whom Abacha would see (he would see no senior manager from the IMF, the Bank, or any other international organization), I thought at one point that it could be worth pursuing a discussion with him. Abacha needed the Bank more than the Bank needed him, because he had the perennial, intractable problem of Nigeria's debt—especially with the Paris and the London clubs—and he needed the Bretton Woods institutions to present a credible case to both. I failed completely to convince him to start doing something serious to put his country back on a reasonable path, but I have no regret about trying. I believe strongly that it is always better to maintain a dialogue with whoever is in charge, because sooner or later the relationship with the Bank will normalize and the Bank will need all the knowledge that it can accumulate. And maintaining the dialogue is by no means synonymous to condoning the actions of an incompetent or crooked leader. In the case of Nigeria during that period, the Bank continued to disburse on existing projects—which was a wonderful basis from which to maintain both technical knowledge and a modicum of dialogue with technical agencies in the country—but no new commitments or disbursements were made.

Another lesson from that period is that the Bank should not trumpet so-called success stories prematurely, as was the case with Ghana. When I became country director in 1994, Ghana was doing less than well, after having been heralded as the wonder country of Africa for several years. I do not question that things had been working reasonably well for some time and certainly better than in many other African countries. But the situation in Ghana was distinctly not as good as had been claimed, and even if it had been, there was the risk that it would not stay good. The Bank should avoid the embarrassment of having to explain why things have not turned out as well as expected. We should remember the embarrassment of producing the optimistic "Asian miracle" document not long before the Asian crisis. I would feel much better if the Bank were to stick to simple realities: the country may be making all sorts of worthwhile efforts, the situation may be encouraging, and it may look like things are improving, but there is still a long way to go. In fact, our efforts should never stop—nothing is certain forever—so we should always continue our collective efforts. Why does the Bank have to consistently look for the role model in a Bolivia, Ghana, or Uganda?

The Latin American Period (1996–2002)

My assignment as country director for Mexico in the Latin America and Caribbean Region started in somewhat unusual circumstances. In 1996, I was rather happy and comfortable in the West Africa Region, and it required a number of circumstances—not least the 1996 internal reorganization completed by the new Bank President, James Wolfensohn—to give me the incentive and justification to accept the offer to take the job in the Latin America and Caribbean Region. It was a particularly attractive and tempting offer because Mexico was by then the most important borrower of International Bank for Reconstruction and Development funds. The Mexico position was a very prestigious and recognized one, and an added attraction was that I would be the first country director position located in the field in Mexico City. I knew virtually nothing about the new position and not much about Mexico, which was barely coming out of a major crisis (1994–95), and I had no idea as to what the Bank posture with respect to Mexico should be in terms of program, dialogue, technical team, analytical work, and so forth. I did speak Spanish.

During the six years that followed, even with the addition of Colombia and the República Bolivariana de Venezuela to my portfolio, Mexico's major macroeconomic and financial crisis represented the dominant challenge in my work and that of the Bank. This unprecedented blow to the Mexican economy, resulting in a fall in gross domestic product (GDP) of 7 percent in 1995, created a major trauma in the country, politically, socially, and economically. For me, it had certain features in common with the crisis that I had witnessed in Africa, in terms of the increases in poverty; the social shock; the inability of institutions to cope; the despair, resentment, and anger from people affected; and the usual tricks from the well-protected, privileged few who had the power and ability to ensure that taxpayers and the least privileged bore the costs, while the profits of privatization—when profits were feasible—went to benefit the very few.

I witnessed the valiant efforts and determination of the administration of Ernesto Zedillo to respond to the crisis and put the country back on an even keel. This remarkable effort once again confirmed that macroeconomic stability is the sine qua non condition for sustained development and the ability to reduce poverty on a lasting basis. A combination of measures aimed at establishing and maintaining a sound macroeconomic framework joined with a number of measures meant to address directly the problems of the poor, with the creation of well-designed and -targeted programs of poverty reduction (for example, the Progresa program). Many of those complementary strategies were directly originated and managed by President Zedillo and his office, giving a strong demonstration that a strategy conceived and supported at the highest level in the country has every chance of being implemented successfully. In spite of strong political opposition in Congress as of 1997–98, the administration never stopped trying to move forward the reform agenda. That effort confirmed my strongly held belief that a time of crisis and serious difficulties in a country is the appropriate and opportune time to push forward reform aggressively. The incentives are there to move forcefully, as they are not when things are going too easily and there is no political willingness to address the really tough issues and challenges.

I also witnessed the ability of the government and the country to withstand strong pressures from external shocks, thanks to correct macroeconomic and, particularly, fiscal management that creates the capacity to respond flexibly and rapidly to these shocks. This case was particularly evident in 1998, when strong pressures arose from the Asian, then the Russian, and then the Latin American crises. Mexico—largely thanks to its monetary policy (of flexible exchange rate), its trade policy (with the North American Free Trade Agreement), and its strict fiscal policy (successive drastic fiscal adjustments)—was able to navigate through a very disturbed period, unlike so many of its Latin American partners that were very negatively affected.

This period (1996–2000) was also very interesting to observe and participate in, from the standpoint of sequencing policy actions following the crisis of 1994–95. The three-step challenge for the Mexicans was to put the country back on a solid macroeconomic stand by (a) stopping the slide; (b) getting out of the trough and stabilizing; and (c) starting on a new path of sustainable growth. I believe that the Mexicans did this very well, under the outstanding economic leadership of President Zedillo, Minister of Finance Guillermo Ortiz, and Central Bank Governor Miguel Mancera. The changes in 1998 did not modify this basic strategy. To me, the process appeared extremely well managed, even though it took some effort to convince people that solving the problems of the financial sector—with the contribution of US$1.5 billion from the World Bank and the de facto bailing out of incompetent, if not crooked, bankers—was of the utmost urgency; and that the emergency packages to be put in place, unfortunately, had to take precedence over longer-term developmental concerns. I believe that the World Bank did its part in this sequencing process fairly effectively. In retrospect, of course, it is clear to me that there was a heavy cost attached to the emergency packages: (a) the US$100 billion cost of cleaning up the financial sector was fiscalized, meaning that it has to be supported by the taxpayer, to the tune of 1.5 percent of GDP annually over a 10-year period, and (b) there was the inevitable postponement of much-needed investment, particularly in infrastructure.

Perhaps the toughest lesson from my initial period in Mexico concerned the difficult relationship between the Bank and the Mexican government and the difficult situation within the Bank as a result of the 1996–97 reorganization. The Mexican government expected that the Bank would deliver on promises made immediately after the 1995 crisis and demanded US$2 billion annually for three years from the Bank. Arriving in Mexico, I found nothing close to those figures in the pipeline of projects. I was, therefore, caught between the Mexicans, who expected much, and the Bank senior managers, who also expected that we would disburse promptly. Some people in the Bank were even ready to bend over backward to accommodate the Mexican request as fast and as flexibly as possible.

One obvious path for Bank intervention was to move aggressively in support of financial sector reform. The Bank technical analysis, however, demonstrated conclusively that the reforms proposed by the Mexican government were falling very short of what was needed to put the system back on an even keel and that some of our counterparts in government were less than candid in sharing the necessary information with us. As a result, we recognized—to the great chagrin of several people in the Bank—that there was not enough substance for us to go forward with the amounts expected by the Mexicans. History has proved the country management correct. Our perception and position were unfortunately confirmed by what became the

Fobaproa scandal, and the Bank can consider itself pleased that its name was not associated with it. But the decision did create an extremely tense and uncomfortable situation for me, lasting several months. At one point, the Mexicans were asking for my
removal, as they thought I was obstructing their plans.

Another difficult, but useful, lesson of that period was the nature and extent of the
relationship that the Mexican government (the Ministry of Finance in particular)
expected to have with the Bank. When I was asked to take the job and be based in Mexico City, I was told that among my terms of reference would be the idea of extending
the reach of the Bank beyond the Mexican federal government to civil society, decentralized agencies (especially at the state level), the private sector, and academia. This idea
made good sense to me in Mexico as it had in Paris. Soon after my arrival, however, the
minister of finance told me in no uncertain terms that he considered my job to be
exclusively focused on two areas: "Speed up procurement and increase disbursement!"
he essentially told me. "And none of this business of talking to NGOs. We in the government are the truly elected representatives of the Mexican society, so there is no need
for the Bank to go and talk to those civil society troublemakers who are only politically
motivated, influenced by international political NGOs, and represent nobody but themselves." That conversation did not make for a very easy start for me. With time, the Bank
was able to reconstruct an entire lending program that was based on sound analytical
work, and the relationship improved steadily as the Bank started to deliver. My initial 18
months had been tense and difficult, but the following four-and-a-half years were
extraordinary in the nature, quality, and—I hope—productivity of the relationship.

The encounter helped me see that, from an institutional standpoint, in a country
such as Mexico the most important challenge for the Bank is to determine its exact
role and position. A middle-income member of the OECD and a very sophisticated
partner that is very advanced in many respects, Mexico is a country where the Bank's
financial and intellectual contributions are at a very different level from those made in
poorer or less endowed countries. The annual Bank contribution to Mexico in terms
of commitments may be of the order of US$1.0 billion to US$2.0 billion, or less than
0.5 percent of GDP. During my entire tenure, the situation regarding Mexico was the
subject of intense debate and controversy between the Bank and Mexico and within
the Bank. Some people in the Bank were of the opinion that Mexico should be grad-
uating from the Bank in view of its level of development, income, and access to international markets and technical knowledge. Many others believed that the levels of
poverty and inequality prevalent in Mexico and the very demands from Mexican
authorities still justified a strong financial presence by the Bank—even more so in the
area of technical assistance and knowledge transfer. I strongly subscribed to the latter
view, especially given the circumstances at the time, with the tremendous impact the
crisis had had on poverty in the country.[6] The question of the Bank's role in Mexico
may be much more open today, because Mexico has been rather successful in putting
its economy on a much more balanced and stable footing.

Perhaps one of the most exciting moments of this Latin American period—and,
indeed, of my career in the Bank—was the preparation, production, and dissemination of the Mexico Policy Notes (Giugale, Lafourcade, and Nguyen 2001). This set

of 30 sectoral and thematic notes was prepared by the Bank over the eight-month period preceding the presidential elections of July 2000, with the view of providing a complete assessment on Mexican economic development and with the prospect of presenting it to the new administration. This immensely useful and successful undertaking culminated in a two-day seminar in October 2000, shortly before President Vicente Fox took office, which allowed the Bank to present to and discuss its analysis and recommendations with both the outgoing team and the transition team at the highest levels. Several months later, the Policy Notes also served as the basis for a one-day meeting between Mexican President Fox and his entire economic cabinet and Bank President Wolfensohn and his management team.

The Policy Notes proved extremely useful in several ways: (a) they represented the full accumulation of the Bank's knowledge on Mexico at the time; (b) they were well structured, with a short description of the main issues, basic analysis, and brief and concrete recommendations in the various sectors and themes presented; and (c) they were couched in terms of sets of recommendations, options, and suggestions, which were open to debate and discussion, not as a blueprint for a Bank program. The Policy Notes did find their way into a very large number of government strategy documents, including the National Development Plan.

The addition of Colombia and the República Bolivariana de Venezuela to my portfolio created an enormous new challenge. Colombia was afflicted by war and conflict on one side and drug and corruption on the other, with predictable, resulting suffering and poverty for vast segments of the Colombian population—including perhaps as many as 2 million displaced people in a country of 40 million. With the FARC (Fuerzas Armadas Revolucionarios de Colombia) rebels drawing close to US$1 billion a year from drug trafficking alone, Colombia's external partners face major problems in providing support for the government's valiant efforts to maintain the appropriate measures and climate of economic development conducive to poverty reduction and sustainable development.

Colombia, in 2000, had several features similar to those of Mexico in 1996. The country was barely emerging from the major economic crisis of 1998–99. Growth had been negative for the first time in modern Colombian history. The fiscal situation was extremely serious and very fragile, with great challenges on the debt side—an area where Colombia had always shown outstanding behavior and impeccable competence in the past. Several much-needed reforms were stalled, and the peace process was not moving forward: there were serious social and political challenges to government actions. And yet, the Colombian government was totally transparent with the Bank, seeking Bank support in any way possible and readily listening to Bank advice with remarkable openness and candor.

A preelection exercise similar to the Mexican one was later launched in Colombia, in preparation for the presidential elections of April 2002, with equal success. The Bank prepared a new set of Colombia Policy Notes (Giugale, Lafourcade, and Luff 2002), which were discussed with the new administration during the transition period and eventually were highly instrumental in shaping the new government's development strategy and fundamental programs.

I quickly sensed that Colombia was not entirely responsible for all the problems it had to face. Certainly the situation of instability and violence is an unfortunate trademark of the country, one that it has carried for many years. But the drug problem and the recent violence are relatively new. The drug problem has been imported fairly recently, partly as a result of the success of the coca eradication campaigns in Bolivia. And the violence has lost all but its original strong political and ideological content, to the extent that the warring parties now (from left to right) seem motivated today more by drug money and violence for their own sake than by ideology. It also seems more and more plausible that violence is the product of a very small minority with minimal popular support—perhaps fewer than 50,000 armed people in the conflicting parties, besides government forces, and with probably no more than 3 to 4 percent of popular support—not exactly a full-fledged civil war. In any case, I have been immensely impressed by the quality, dedication, and courage of the Colombian authorities at the highest levels in two successive administrations. They do not get enough credit for trying their very best, in the face of extraordinarily complicated challenges, to keep their country afloat at such high personal risk to themselves and their families. They deserve every possible support.

The case of the República Bolivariana de Venezuela was unusual because of the extreme difficulty of finding appropriate ways and means to provide support to a government whose stated and laudable poverty reduction objectives are in total contradiction with the actual measures pursued to achieve them. The challenge clearly was to find ways of establishing a constructive and credible dialogue with the authorities.

Another challenge for the Bank was the reorganization of the Latin America and Caribbean Region in 2000, which joined Colombia and the República Bolivariana de Venezuela to the Mexico unit. Once again, I had to confront the issue of merging two different programs and structures. Predictably and unfortunately, the result of the addition of about two-thirds to the existing large and heavy Mexico work program came with much less than proportional added resources. The result put an extraordinary tax on the staff and management of the new unit in terms of responsibilities, work schedule, and travel—not an easy task to manage.

Within the Bank broadly, the major institutional challenge of the entire period was the Bank-wide reorganization that started in 1997–97 and introduced simultaneously the dual features of (a) the new matrix management system and (b) decentralization with the posting of country directors in the field. Much has already been written and said about this new way of doing business, and probably much more will be coming in the assessment of this important institutional change. As for me, I am a strong advocate of the decentralization process and, as I discuss later, I am somewhat more ambiguous about the presumed merits and benefits of the matrix management system.

One major novelty in the way the Bank conducted its business that affected me directly was the process—in stark contrast to the previous managerial situation in Africa—of decentralization of the country director and the Country Management Unit in Mexico. In a nutshell, I found the decentralization a monumental plus for managing the Mexico program (and subsequently the Colombia and República Bolivariana de Venezuela programs). There is no doubt in my mind that the change brought enormous advantages in most respects. First was the permanent connection to the real problems and concerns of the country, with direct communication with the authorities of the country. Being in the country, one is much more sensitized and sensitive to its realities by reading the papers, watching television, meeting people, and going places, to the extent that there is much more opportunity for empathy. Second, from a substantive point of view, there is the opportunity to be right on top of the issues in some detail—for example, allowing the country director to be in much more contact with Bank mission staff in the field. Third is the ability to act much more promptly and effectively and respond to the country's (in particular, the government's) needs and requests. I believe that, in my six years in Mexico, I came to a fairly good, deep, and broad understanding of the country, its challenges, and its realities.

Finally, being in the thick of things, I believe, creates more credibility in dealing with both the country and the Bank, especially the Bank staff in Washington, D.C. I feel strongly that there is no drawback to going native. Yes, there is every reason why I would become sympathetic to the country and be somewhat biased in its favor. This attachment, after all, is what the Bank business is all about. But I see no reason to suspect that I could have been biased, not objective, or not firm with the authorities when I needed to be. Conversely, in my previous position in the West Africa Region, I often felt that I was somewhat far removed from the field, in spite of my very frequent visits. The fact that the country director comes from Washington, D.C., inevitably brings some level of artificiality to the relationship with the local authorities and in-country Bank staff members. There is often a bit of a circus or road-show element to such trips when the locals organize the event, with its accompaniment of such staged events as visits to projects and receptions. In Mexico, I had the feeling of being much more part of the scenery, available to people for a phone call, a visit, a lunch.

The Mexicans are very demanding, very smart, often very good or outstanding professionals, and totally independent, and they will never yield to obvious pressures from anyone from outside. They have a very clear notion of what the Bank should be for them, knowing that they are an important shareholder of the institution and an important borrower, which does create a different set and tone of relationships with the Bank. The name of the game for them is added value; they expect it and will stop at nothing to make their case that it is their right to get it.

From a management perspective, I felt that the previous system of directorship in Africa was much more comprehensive, enabling me to manage things more effectively in terms of adjustment to the strategy, resource allocation, and supervision of people. In Mexico after the reorganization, I found that the costs of transaction were excessively high and time consuming. However, I very much liked the reality of having my management team with me in Mexico City, and I am a strong advocate of the sector leader system. In truth, I consider that I had an absolutely first-class team of sector leaders with me in the field, one without which I could not have managed. The possibility of interacting with them on a permanent basis in the field and much more extensively than would have been the case in Washington, D.C., made a huge difference, both in terms of formulating strategy and implementing programs, but also in terms of connecting with the members of the entire team working on Mexico.

Another big difference between the African and Latin American operations is the nature and extent of partnership with others. In broad terms, in the Africa Region, the Bank is called to work permanently with a myriad of partners in development besides the countries' authorities. The roster includes other multilateral institutions (mainly the IMF, the European Commission, the United Nations Development Programme, the African Development Bank, and others such as International Fund for Agricultural Development); bilateral agencies (British, French, German, Nordic, and U.S.); and a large number of national and international NGOs. By contrast, in countries such as Mexico, the Bank has very few partners—principally the IMF and the Inter-American Development Bank (IDB)—or competitors. There are virtually no bilateral agencies, and the United Nations system has only few and sparse operations. The resulting relationship means that the government tends to use the Bank as much as a consulting firm or a technical assistance partner as a financial institution, an arrangement that tends to simplify the Bank's role and activities, in contrast with the role of being one among many partners (sometimes a leader, sometimes a follower) in Africa to adjust to the complicated necessity of coordination of aid and consistency of policies and procedures. The Mexico case is worth understanding and learning from. It shows the Mexican authorities to be extremely smart and skillful in dealing with the two main players, the Bank and the IDB, sometimes putting them in competition (to hear different views on the same subject, such as banking or governance) and sometimes using them in full support of each other (for example, in the financing of water projects).

Broad Lessons

The previous specific comments and observations about my experience in Europe, Africa, and Latin America over the 10-year period are meant to be as objective as possible and can, by and large, be fairly critical. In offering an overall assessment of the period, and in spite of the specific shortcomings noted, I strongly believe that the Bank has done remarkably well under the circumstances. I believe that the Bank contributed immensely to pushing the agenda, responding concretely and correctly to enormous challenges in the countries and regions where we worked under difficult, challenging, and changing circumstances. The Bank has been critical of itself, it has tried to find solutions, it attempted to learn from its own mistakes, and it has engaged forcefully and honestly with its partners by enlarging the scope of its activities and its relationships with them.

The Bank did make mistakes. I certainly did, and it is clear that we should apologize for such mistakes and correct them as soon as feasible. But in my view, the track record is extraordinarily positive, and the right question to be asked is what would or might have happened without the Bank? I am proud of and pleased with what has happened throughout this period, and my only purpose here is to draw some positive and negative lessons from an incredibly rich set of experiences.

Development Paradigms

Perhaps the most important lesson is how the paradigms on development and development assistance have changed over the years. It is worth remembering that, broadly speaking, the Bank has gone through several successive approaches to its development assistance role. In this search, the Bank has by no means been alone or isolated. Still, it has always exercised unquestionable leadership and has acted as an initiator or instigator of new approaches to redefine paradigms.

In a very brief and simplified, if not simplistic, summary, the 1950s and 1960s can be characterized as the decades when the engineers were in charge. The famous trickle-down approach expected infrastructure development to bring about economic growth and development that would eventually percolate down to all sectors. The focus was essentially on *what* and *how*, with heavy emphasis on trying to meet the financial requirements of the countries, particularly their foreign exchange needs.

The 1970s saw a fundamental change, which was largely brought on by the famous McNamara speech of 1973 in Nairobi in which the president of the Bank truly focused attention on *who* should benefit from the development efforts. This fundamental shift in the way of operating the Bank brought an emphasis on the poor and much more attention to the rural areas and rural development. The shift was based on the observation that the vast majority of the poor in all developing countries was located in rural areas.[7] Thereafter, in the 1970s, the focus clearly moved primarily toward the micropicture, with heavy emphasis on identifying the true beneficiaries (the famous *target groups*) of the development process—hence the programs of rural development, urban development, and basic needs and the first focus on social programs and projects such as education, health, and nutrition.[8]

From the point of view of performance and results, however, the 1970s did not end very well: the energy crisis was in full force, and the debt crisis started building up. The first assessments of the poverty reduction programs and projects were not encouraging and pointed to two major flaws in the strategy: (a) the insufficient attention paid to the macroeconomic conditions under which the programs were being implemented and (b) the exaggerated optimism, not to say serious misjudgment, concerning the institutional capacities of the countries to manage the programs without external support. Programs that had received strong donor support and showed positive or encouraging results tended to fold and fail shortly once the outside donors left.

It is worth noting that, by disengaging in many cases so quickly from this poverty reduction strategy, the Bank did little more than throw out the baby with the bath water. Indeed, many positive lessons could have been drawn, in particular, in terms of beneficiary participation, consultation, community development, grassroots technical approaches, technical support to farmers, association and social capital building, and NGO participation. The Bank, however, moved very rapidly to an almost exclusive focus on macroeconomics. Seeing correctly that progress depended on creating and maintaining the appropriate macroeconomic framework, the Bank devoted the 1980s to such efforts.

The focus was no doubt correct. All countries evidently needed to adjust to new circumstances, to put their fiscal and financial houses in order, to rethink and revisit the exact role of the state, and to emphasize the role to be played by the private sector. This approach was right, but two problems emerged: (a) the incapability of the Bank (and other organizations) to present a credible version of the strategy so that all other partners could understand and accept it and (b) the often oversimplistic design of programs, which focused on the immediate and easy reforms (later to be called *first-generation reforms*) with an exclusively technical concentration without paying sufficient attention to the complexity of the political, social, sociological, human, and environmental dimensions of the proposal.

During this period, the very term *structural adjustment* came to symbolize the Bank's and the IMF's evil nature as the new colonialists, instruments of the world's capital and international corporations bent on imposing their conditionality on poor and defenseless populations. It probably would have been possible to explain much more convincingly that structural adjustment was no more and no less than suggesting to countries that they needed to manage their affairs in a reasonable and prudent way, like good responsible parents: spend no more than what you earn, put your finances in order, define clearly your priorities, borrow sensibly, and be fair and equitable with your children.[9]

After moving through trickle-down, infrastructure-powered development strategies to an emphasis on reducing poverty—especially in rural areas—and then to the structural adjustment focus on sound macroeconomics, the Bank began much more openly and effectively in the 1990s to introduce new concepts that were not exclusively technical into the paradigm and the processes of development assistance. This change did not come by itself. It was largely triggered by what happened with and after the fall of the Berlin Wall and the end of the Cold War: the quickening pace of democratization throughout the world, with its accompaniment of civil society participation, pressures from NGOs, and emergence of new legislative and judicial powers. I believe that the Bank responded well and fairly rapidly to the new challenges, broadening the agenda and building on the errors of the past and the lessons of experience. However, it became a little lost in all these new dimensions and had some difficulty in prioritizing, in differentiating from country to country, and in adjusting its response and its methods to widely different circumstances throughout the world.

A Bank Disease?

A continuing, grave problem throughout the various strategic shifts the Bank has made during my service has been its propensity to continue to search for—and sometimes claim that it has found—the ultimate answers to development. This pattern reflects the surprising belief that there may be a ready-made, relatively simple, permanent, and definitive response to a specific problem of development that can be applied universally and the belief that, if it worked well here, it will work well there. In Africa, the approach was first and foremost to stabilize the economy (often, if not always, sponsored and triggered by the IMF); embark on structural adjustment reforms; and deal immediately with all sides of the adjustment that were needed, giving little attention to the possibility of sequencing the adjustment measures. Thus, all programs needed to have their combination of fiscal adjustment, reduction of the role of the state, privatization, and focus on competitiveness and exports. Seldom were there real attempts at differentiating among countries and examining the different speed or the various degrees at which the countries were expected to adjust. It was as if only one pattern, one blueprint, or one correct path existed (see box 8.1 for an example).

The blueprint method applied to the Bank's proposed remedies and recommendations for Latin America just as it did in Africa. Essentially, the approaches, remedies, and instruments were all the same, so much so that, within the Bank, the procedural aspects were also the same, whether we dealt with middle-income countries or low-

BOX 8.1

Another Illustration: The Training and Visits System of Agricultural Extension

An interesting case in point of the Bank's rush to promote one blueprint is the famous and infamous training and visits (T&V) system of agricultural extension. The T&V system was developed initially in India, in the early to mid 1970s, as a rather well-structured, somewhat rigid organizational system of technical assistance to farmers who operated in the irrigated one-crop production method. This system had a very elaborate managerial structure and referral mechanisms that enabled farmers to be in constant and effective contact with professional services. The system was able to respond promptly to their specific problems at the field level, with a good referral system to research services. There is no doubt that the T&V system of agricultural extension provided good answers to the real problems of many farmers in India's specific circumstances. The T&V system was then seen by the Bank—and especially by the highest levels of management (including all successive presidents)—as the key to agricultural development. It became a sort of gospel that the system had to be introduced forcefully everywhere.

After being introduced in the Indian subcontinent and selected parts of Asia, the system was aggressively promoted in Africa. Careers in the Bank could be made and unmade on the basis of whether one was supportive of or reticent about promoting the system. It does not take rocket science to demonstrate that the system was not as wonderful and waterproof as its sycophants painted it, and it was not as bad and ineffective as its detractors claimed. There is, of course, no doubt that the T&V system worked reasonably well in certain parts of India, with monoculture of grains in irrigated conditions. It is less clear that it was so successful in very different circumstances, with multiple-crop and livestock farming systems in dryland conditions in parts of Africa. And yet, because of the stubbornness and heavy-handed way of some Bank staff members (not least the originator of the system), it was force fed to some countries that had neither the capacity nor the clout or political will to engage in a battle with the Bank, especially in view of the large amounts of lending money attached to T&V projects. It is no surprise that the T&V system was never accepted or applied much in Latin America, where countries such as Argentina, Brazil, or Mexico would never accept an approach promoted by the Bank that was presented in such a rigid, arrogant, dogmatic, and heavy-handed way. Given that the T&V system did have many very favorable and positive aspects, it is somewhat regrettable that it has now joined a number of other practices in the cemetery of the so-called definitive answers to development problems.

income ones. Admittedly, this pattern has clearly changed in the recent past, with the introduction of the Heavily Indebted Poor Countries (HIPC) initiative, Poverty Reduction Strategy Papers (PRSPs), and other institutional characterizations of countries and new types of conditionality. And yet the question still remains: is the Bank sufficiently flexible to propose and offer solutions that might be much more differentiated among countries and that may imply a very different path and speed of implementation of the various measures?

As a case in point, I am convinced that the concept of the individual project, the discrete intervention at a given point in time, is all but obsolete in sophisticated countries such as Mexico and Colombia, although certainly not in most countries in Africa. In Mexico and Colombia, what is important is to be able to influence the strategy and policies of the sector. What counts then is to be able to help shape the programs with the relevant sets of norms, standards, indicators, monitoring and evaluation criteria, institutional arrangements, training, and capacity building. The final technical detail of what and how the project will operate is less crucial; it is something that the local capacities are usually able to do. I admit that it is sometimes necessary to keep a close link with reality at the field level, where much can be learned to shape the sectoral policies. In Africa, in most cases, it is still absolutely essential to remain extremely closely connected to the field and help build the institutional capabilities throughout the entire sector, all the way to the very microelement at the grassroots level.

In the case of Mexico and other middle-income countries, it is worth asking whether the necessary financing for the country should not be totally disconnected from individual projects and instead be taken in the form of global, or at least sectoral, financing programs. This argument is further validated by the fact that Bank and other external financing in Mexico is not additional to the recipient executing agency. It is incorporated earlier into the overall budget before this budget is allocated to the sectoral agencies, with no additionality to them and, therefore, with little incentive other than intellectual input to work with the Bank.

The Complexity of the Agenda

Without doubt the agenda has become much more multifaceted and knotty than it was 10 or 15 years ago, when the Bank was essentially dealing with first-generation policy issues and focusing on the fundamentals: monetary policies, fiscal policies, balance of payments, immediate poverty reduction, and export promotion. All those issues were almost exclusively in the realm of the executive branch of governments. Only a few, barely hatched initiatives involved dealing with civil society, often on the grounds that the governments in place had little or insufficient democratic justification and that legitimacy could grow from seeking to expand the dialogue beyond the privileged few to society at large. Moreover, either the legislative and judicial branches did not really exist (as in most cases) or they were basically and often openly dependencies of the executive (as in Cameroon, Ghana, Nigeria, Togo, and elsewhere in Africa at the time). Where these branches existed, they were not equipped, organized, or even allowed to exercise a role counterbalancing or stimulating government initiatives.[10]

Over time, however, new issues and challenges kept adding to the already fairly heavy Bank agenda: environment, gender, indigenous populations, social protection, governance, and anticorruption. As extremely relevant and legitimate concerns for the development prospects of the countries, they all became points of tremendous interest and attention for the Bank. This extension, while perfectly legitimate, clearly brought an increase in the work agenda that was not matched by an increase in the financial and human resources necessary to take care of such expansion. Always adding on, never subtracting, raised the risk that the Bank would lose track of priorities in the process. With so many things on the agenda, everything became a priority.

Are Priorities the Correct Ones?

Considering my work on African matters, I wonder whether we were involved in so many things and at the same time so much focused on the macroeconomic side that we may have lost track of some of the most fundamentals aspects of our role and responsibilities. In addition to agriculture, I am now convinced that we should have focused much more on infrastructure in Africa and Latin America, instead of believing wrongly that the private sector would take charge. It certainly would not when the macroeconomic conditions were so bad, but it still did not when such conditions started improving, as they did in Mexico. And the reason is so obvious that it is curious that the institution did not recognize it much earlier: the private sector does not and cannot move everywhere (for example, building roads in the middle of nowhere in Oaxaca, one of the poorest states in Mexico). The public sector still has a role to play, and much more needs to be done to identify the appropriate public-private partnerships that would make it possible to attain the necessary levels of investment in infrastructure. I am aware that the Bank has very recently moved in that direction, but I wonder why it has taken such a long time to recognize this necessity.

Because of the focus on macroeconomics, it appears that the Bank may have lost part of its earlier, great comparative advantage with regard to the *micro*. It is indeed troubling that the number of specialists in fields as fundamental as agriculture and rural development has been decreasing so drastically over the years. Normal attrition has certainly played a part, but there is no doubt that the Bank has not been able to retain or replace some of the former high-caliber technical experts who gave it much greater credibility in many areas, if only in its ability to talk to counterparts in the countries. In my recent days in the Latin America and Caribbean Region, I found true, experienced agriculturalists and agricultural economists very scarce indeed. I understand that the number of experienced professionals in this area throughout the Bank is today a fraction of what it used to be some years ago.

Growth, Poverty Reduction, and Inequality

From any angle, it is clear that poverty reduction and growth are intimately related, and it is probably not very relevant to claim which comes first—the typical chicken and egg situation—when there can be no doubt that the two must come together. It is unfortunately also clear that in many (most?) cases growth is a factor of inequality. Although I believe that it is now reasonably clear what can be done to rescue people from the most abject forms of poverty, it is much less clear what can be done to reduce inequalities. I would argue that, beyond the extreme cases, poverty is a relative concept. It exists where many people are poor relative to other people. Take the United States, where I believe that the poverty level is defined around US$10,000, a huge sum by the standards of developing countries. It can also be convincingly argued with many concrete examples that growth does bring inequality and that, in the longer term, growth may be contributing to the creation of *relative* poverty. If that assessment is correct, in the longer term such a situation carries a set of serious potential problems of social disruption, political problems, and eventually economic troubles that can put in question the original validity of the virtuous circle of growth leading to poverty reduction.

It seems to me that this is precisely what may be happening in Latin America. I would, therefore, argue that the Bank, among others, has been very negligent in the treatment of this problem. Much has been done successfully in the area of identifying strategies and policies of poverty reduction that are also growth friendly. Unfortunately, I believe that today there are few very convincing, growth-friendly, poverty and inequality reducing strategies and policies. Such a shortcoming can be deadly when designing development strategies at the country level.

Employment and Employment Creation

Experience in Africa and in Latin America shows conclusively that the main and correct preoccupation of any serious government is to create employment and opportunities for the masses. Employment is a necessary condition for poverty reduction and, to a large extent, for reducing inequality as well. From a politician's standpoint, and especially from the government's point of view, this issue is of paramount importance. The unemployed quickly turn to creating problems: urban disturbances, political opposition, and social problems of drugs and violence.

When he became president of Mexico in 2000, Vicente Fox imprudently promised to create 1 million jobs a year, the exact amount of new people entering the job market annually. During his first year in office, 300,000 jobs were created. What became of the other 700,000 people entering the labor force that year? Many probably stayed where they were (for example, in rural areas), often in poverty, but many others found their way as clandestine workers to the United States or ended up as marginals in large, Mexican urban centers. Most are unlikely to be very strong supporters of the present government and will not hesitate to join the opposition or to start vocal, social dissent increasingly forcefully. The same holds true in several other countries in Latin America—witness the recent situation in Bolivia. I believe that the Bank has been less than successful in addressing this issue, particularly in Latin America, with concrete policy recommendations and practical measures.

My point is that the textbook approaches, dogmatic answers, unique thought (*la pensée unique*), ideological framework, and all those ideas that the Bank is geared to use at one point or another cannot give the required answers. I have too often heard the argument that, if we set the macroframework right, and things will change. Or if we give the right incentives, the private sector will do the job. Or if we set the governance issue right, the change will happen. We can do any combination of the above, and invariably we come short. No, the private sector will not build that road in poor Oaxaca. No, the right price policy framework will not create the nonagricultural job alone. No, full liberalization and privatization will not create new jobs or prevent the former public monopoly from ending up as a private monopoly. No, the trimming of government institutions does not automatically translate into full efficiency of the remaining cadre. And in the end, no, there is not one cookie-cutter approach or ultimate remedy that can solve all the problems at the same time in all countries.

The Rural Poor

From my experience both in Africa and in Latin America, helping the rural poor is an area where the Bank has failed massively. In the late 1960s and early 1970s, essentially by taking advantage of and promoting the Green Revolution (which was basically the introduction of better and resistant varieties of grains), India and a few other countries improved their situations dramatically, but their example never caught on so well elsewhere. And in Africa, in particular, the record is dismal. I cannot but think that in Africa the Bank has played the role of sorcerer's apprentice. Are we so certain that the remedies we recommended are so much better than the ills they were designed to replace? Has privatization produced so many more benefits? One typical case is that of the *filiere*, the line of production of selected crops—usually such industrial crops as cocoa, coffee, tea, sugar, and cotton. With the dismantling of the filiere, are we sure that the results are so much better than previously? I am told that the abolition of so many parastatals in Africa and the dismantling of others in so many presumably independent, efficient, competitive smaller units have resulted, in many cases, in the resurgence of equally or even more inefficient and corrupt systems than the ones they were meant to replace.[11]

In agriculture in general, both in Africa and in Latin America, I do not believe that we have our act together. In many countries and for a long time, the major problems of agriculture were those of productivity and competitiveness, and it became essential to introduce the proper macroeconomic framework and adequate incentives. In many cases, we did that fairly successfully, only to realize that (a) the measures concerned exclusively commercial or export crops and excluded large numbers of small subsistence farmers, and (b) even when it became appropriate, the macroeconomic framework was not sufficient to solve the problems.

In Mexico, the trade and liberalization policies put in place a number of years ago, at the instigation of the Bank and with applause from the Bank and the IMF, have clearly been beneficial to those who were already equipped to take advantage of the changes—commercial farmers with access to infrastructure, credit, and know-how. The same policies badly, if not fatally, hurt those who were and are less well equipped—subsistence maize farmers who will be wiped out when the North American Free Trade Agreement takes full effect. I fear that we have been much too simplistic—and perhaps too dogmatic—in our claim that liberalization policies would do the trick. They have not.

Of course, the previous systems were entirely wrong, promoting all sorts of inefficiencies, waste, and corruption. I am convinced that full, eventual implementation of these new policies is the main hope for progress, efficiency, and transparency. But the new systems put in place have not been sufficiently discriminating or adapted to specific local circumstances at specific points in time. Is it complete anathema to suggest that some amount of protection in specific conditions, some degree of subsidization in very particular circumstances, or some special treatment to respond to temporary situations could be justified once in a while?

Instead of playing the ostrich game and pretending that certain things do not happen, we should acknowledge that all agricultures of the industrial world have been and will continue to be protected under one form or another, however shameful and unfair that may be. I believe that it is the responsibility of the Bank and others to (a) denounce those abuses as the Bank increasingly does, but (b) more importantly, advise the countries on how they can and should react to this situation, perhaps with the recommendation of second- or third-best solutions that have the chance of helping over the medium and longer term, instead of offering perfect theoretical solutions that do not work.

The Form of Operating

A World Bank for all? An interesting challenge for the Bank, which I have experienced over and over again in my different managerial positions and especially in dealings with the outside world, is the reality of the multiple facets of the Bank and what it means to people and institutions. Indeed, the Bank means different things to different people at different times. This should come as no surprise. There are so many stakeholders in the game: the shareholders, which are both industrial and developing countries; the borrowers and the nonborrowers among Part II countries; and the donors among Part I and Part II countries. Among the borrowers are the executive, legislative, and judicial branches; the private sector in Part I and in Part II countries; and the civil societies in Part I and Part II countries. And within each group is a variety of advocacy, political, and special interest groups. All in all, these stakeholders represent a myriad of people and institutions, all with their own views as to what the Bank is, what it should be, what it should do, and what they expect from it.

For some, the Bank is an instrument of transfer of financial resources, no more. For others, it may be an agent of change. For others, it is instead an agent for maintaining stability and the status quo. For still others, it is a source and agent of the transfer of knowledge. To some, it may be a combination of or a part of all these descriptions. There are obvious and predictable contradictions among these definitions and among so many partners with very different views and expectations. Moreover, positions may change over time and may be contradictory within the same group. For instance, several advocacy groups that want the Bank to be much more forceful in exercising conditionality on governments to push their own agenda can, at the same time, be very critical of the Bank for exercising what they perceive as excessive conditionality on the same countries in another area. In my view, the minimum that the Bank can do in this respect is to be totally open and transparent, to point out these obvious inconsistencies and contradictions, and to be much more straightforward in its communication and information style. For example, I find it surprising that so few people are aware of the Bank's recent and valuable criticism of the unacceptable and negative effects of agricultural protectionism in industrial countries.

The past six to eight years have clearly seen a considerable change in this respect, largely attributable to the role played so effectively by Jim Wolfensohn. There should be no question that he has been able, as no one has before, to establish the Bank's credibility simultaneously in many forums. He got a seat at the table of the rich countries, the Group of Eight in particular, while maintaining—in fact strengthening—the Bank's reputation among poor countries as their true champion. And he managed to do so while establishing and promoting relationships with a wide variety of other partners and constituencies besides government officials, such as NGOs, academics, the media, the private sector, and religious groups. This is quite a remarkable achievement, one that did not occur overnight but required sustained effort, of which not everyone inside and outside the Bank is fully aware.

Internal Management

This enormous and successful effort by the Bank's president with respect to the outside unfortunately has not been matched inside the Bank. I contend that the internal management of the Bank over the past 10 years has been less than stellar in its performance and not equal to the mandate, importance, and role of the institution. The starting point was the reorganization of 1987. The objectives of this reorganization were probably correct ones, meant essentially to promote greater decentralization of decisionmaking, for example, with the creation of the largely autonomous country departments with a high degree of responsibility and accountability. But the way this objective was carried out was totally counterproductive. Likewise, the worthy objective of letting go the 10 percent of staff members who were deemed not sufficiently productive led to the very strange approach in 1987 of firing everybody in the Bank so as to rehire 90 percent of the staff, with the expectation that the undesirable 10 percent would not be re-recruited. It would have been much more effective and less costly to lay off the people who were not up to par.

The reorganization of 1996–97 de facto tried to undo some of the negative aspects of the 1987 reorganization, essentially through the introduction of the matrix management system. In my view, the 1996–97 reorganization introduced new ambiguities and confusions and did not solve what needed to be solved. It even introduced a new dimension of excessively high transaction costs to the conduct of the Bank's internal business.

Priorities, Flexibility, and Selectivity

Perhaps the most important challenge that the Bank has consistently faced is its ability to face changing circumstances and uncertainty. The world is changing constantly and certainly not in a coherent and consistent way, with change varying over time and among regions and countries. The one thing that the Bank cannot afford to do in this context is to remain (a) rigid and unable to adapt and (b) dogmatic, undifferentiated, and monolithic. On occasion, the Bank has tended to operate more reactively than anticipatorily, thus losing response time. I believe environment, governance, or gender issues are cases in which the Bank took a long time to react to pressures mounting elsewhere (from NGOs in particular). In other cases, the Bank has indeed tried to anticipate or be a leader, as with debt reduction (through the HIPC initiative) and anticorruption. By and large, however, the Bank has tended to be rather rigid, risk averse, and driven by a strategy and budget system that has tended to be insensitive to the volatility of the situations it has had to face. That tendency leads it to try to fix objectives and goals through, for example, CASs and other strategy and policy documents that leave little room for adaptation and, being cast in concrete, admit little possibility of swift and efficient adjustments when circumstances dictate.[12]

In this respect, one area of particular concern internally in the Bank is that of allocation and management of resources. I believe that the budget system in the Bank is not adequate. It is cumbersome, inflexible, complicated, hard to understand and manage, and incomprehensible to the vast majority of staff members. By definition, our work means that we never know for sure what will happen in the countries, with the combination of domestic and external shocks (economic, social, political, and environmental) to which the countries are constantly subject.

The business of the Bank is to try to anticipate as much as possible, but with realism. It is utterly impossible, however, to anticipate the next catastrophe or the next political or economic crisis, and it is, therefore, an illusion to expect that all procedures and instruments put in place by the Bank can cover all risks. And yet the Bank behaves precisely as if it could anticipate everything. The budgets are prepared on a yearly basis in such a way that there is no incentive—and no possibility—to make the most simple, straightforward adjustments to try to respond to changing circumstances. The costs of transaction have become prohibitively high; every single manager becomes aggressively protective of the unit's budget, leaving no room for reallocation when circumstances may dictate.

Instead, the Bank should seek a much more flexible operating system that is able to adjust to altered realities. This advice applies as much for human and budgetary resources management as for strategy formulation and planning and for programming of Bank activities. What should count more is the way in which transactions and adjustments need to be made, and the procedures and protocols of making adjustments and reallocations at minimal transaction costs, under a well-established code of conduct among the various negotiating parties within the Bank, with a high premium on cooperation, speed, and simplicity. My experience is that the Bank spends huge amounts of effort, time, and money to establish a budget for the year, which, immediately after it is agreed on, is submitted to all sorts of pressures for adjustment without the proper procedures to guide these necessary adjustments. As soon as a program is agreed with some countries, one can be sure that something will happen that will make the program unworkable by next Monday or next month. Just think of programming in places such as the Nigeria of Abacha, the Venezuela of Hugo Chavez, or the Zaire of Mobutu.

Another area that has consistently been the subject of much debate over the last 10 years (within management and the Board of Executive Directors among others) is that of selectivity. There is a legitimate concern on this point, because the Bank cannot afford to be spread too thin. The Bank should focus its efforts and resources as effectively as possible but should also be clear that, to be selective, it needs to know what to select from. And there is the hard part. In many instances, the Bank or the countries are just not equipped with sufficient knowledge to enable them to select correctly what should be the priorities among the vast number of areas that deserve attention.[13] Hence, I will argue that there are two fundamental prerequisites to being selective: (a) knowing what to select from, which of course implies that you have a good knowledge of the entire population (in the statistical sense), and (b) ensuring that what you select is also what the country wishes to select.

I have a strong sense that the Bank does not leave enough responsibility and accountability to its partners. We always tend to go for the first-best solution. This is correct, in the sense that we have an obligation to give our partners our very best technical advice. But we should be a little bit more modest, or practical, or smarter in recognizing that there is not only a technical answer to a problem. Other elements always come into the picture, whether they are social or political. Therefore, from the borrower's point of view, there is seldom the one-and-only answer. Most people at the highest level (presidents, ministers, and politicians) look for options and not so much for the definitive answer, which in many cases is just unworkable. We must, therefore, concentrate our efforts much more toward offering options and different possible solutions and leave the final decision to the country.[14]

Institutional Memory

Perhaps one of the most frustrating parts of working in the Bank for as long as I have is the strong feeling that we are constantly reinventing the wheel. High staff turnover—not so much in the Bank staff in general, as there is apparently little attrition, but rather in Bank senior management—and insufficient institutional and procedural mechanisms mean that the Bank forgets what it has done earlier, why things worked, and when they did not work. Essentially, the Bank must learn to work with its internal, dualistic approaches that are nothing less than normal and legitimate and with the perennial dichotomies of country versus project work (that is, strategy and macroeconomic approaches versus sectoral programs and project-specific approaches), investment versus adjustment, and corporate versus country-specific objectives and priorities. These dichotomies are the inevitable—in fact, necessary—

tensions that need to be acknowledged and require appropriate management and arbitration mechanisms. The issue is one of balance, and the pendulum tends to swing one way or the other.[15]

Communication

Harking back to my experience in the European Office, I strongly believe that the Bank is not doing the right job in the matter of communication. During the entire span of my activities in Africa and in Latin America, I believe that the Bank was totally inadequate in its dealing with the outside world. In these days of communication, networking, the Internet, and the like, it is inadmissible that the general knowledge and understanding of major development issues in the world are still so incomplete, distorted, and often wrong. It is the most frustrating thing for people as dedicated as the Bank staff members and many of the people in the countries to find out that the real story of what is truly happening is not being put forward in an accurate, massive, and comprehensive way.

How is it that schoolchildren in most industrial countries of the world care more about the status of animals, trees, and the environment than they do about other children of the world? How is it possible that people spend more on their pets than they do on helping other people? How is it that people do not get truly offended at the degree of inconsistency, if not outright contradiction, in the official positions of their governments in both developing and industrial countries (for example, the agricultural subsidy issue in industrial countries)? How is it that people can swallow some of the nonsense put out by some anti- or alterglobalization activists without having access to or caring about the realities?

Or at the very least, how is it that there is not more of a constructive debate on issues of development? Admittedly Jim Wolfensohn is doing wonders in this area, but his work is much too limited, and he certainly cannot do it alone. I just wonder if it may not be necessary to imagine a truly massive education campaign, to start with primary and secondary schools, where children could be presented and explained the real issues and challenges of development. This is food for thought.

Politics

Finally, in my years in the Bank, I have found time and again that Bank staff members in general, and many managers in particular, are critically lacking in political sensitivity, knowledge, and experience. How many times has the Bank missed opportunities because of an insufficient understanding of the local political issues? Many people tend to confuse being politically sensitive with the risk of politicization or political interference. They are very different matters. To be effective in the technical, economic, and social areas of competence of the Bank, one needs to know and be aware of the political forces at play. Yet I find that many people in the Bank are not only ignorant—and, therefore, run the risk of being played with by smart, skillful, politically motivated local officials—but are also not even interested or sensitive.

The necessary sensitivity comes from (a) knowing the country and (b) learning. I find it utterly unbelievable that many people in the Bank do not know the countries with which they work. I found people working on Mexico for several years who had never spent a weekend in the country, arriving on Monday and leaving on Friday; who had never gone to the field or visited an archeological site; or who had never read the local papers, watched the local television, or read a book by any Mexican author. What sort of empathy with the country does this demonstrate? I will admit that these people may be exceptions, but there are a few too many of them.

Conclusion

Overall, there is no doubt in my mind that, in spite of the many observations presented in this paper, the Bank has done remarkably well over the years. The 1990s, perhaps more than any of the previous decades, has been a period of momentous changes in the world and in the development agenda to which the Bank has responded well. It is also only fair to say that many of the problems and issues listed here have been or are in the process of being addressed or corrected. The progress made in the past few years is a testimony of the ability of the Bank to adapt itself to such changing circumstances. It is the confirmation that such adaptation can be done, and one of the key ingredients is continuity and stability in management. It is no surprise that the past few years of Wolfensohn's leadership, after close to 10 years of persistent efforts, are finally paying off in terms of the ability of the Bank to contribute more effectively to the worthy cause of development. I am particularly impressed with the renewed drive toward two essential goals, which indeed were always inherently part of the institution's mandate: (a) fighting poverty and (b) showing conclusive results. The recent drive toward the latter goal is particularly worth noting.

My last comment is that, as has become a leitmotiv of the Bank's senior management, the best asset of the institution is its people. I never cease to be amazed at the capacity, professionalism, and dedication of the Bank staff. My recommendation, thus, is that everything possible be done to unleash the full potential of staff members and managers. Let them loose, let them do what they know best, trust them, and help them. Do not restrain them or impose unnecessary burdens. Cut short the bureaucratic and administrative controls and hurdles, and create and maintain a non-threatening environment that is conducive to taking risks and being innovative.

Notes

1. This lack of knowledge had been particularly evident at the time of the Annual Meetings in Berlin in 1988, which were marked by extremely vocal opposition to the Bank and the International Monetary Fund from a wide spectrum of constituencies (particularly NGOs) around the debt issue.

2. The recent initiative by Jim Wolfensohn to engage in a dialogue with youngsters of the world (through youth associations and meetings such as the one that took place in September 2003 in Paris) is extremely laudable. These youngsters will be the future leaders of their respective countries in 15 to 20 years. Establishing a constructive relationship with them now

is bound to pay high dividends later on, in terms of their understanding of development and what institutions like the Bank are all about.

3. My predecessor in the Bank had been dismissed in a rather expeditious way, which had led many to think that the French had asked for his removal, as he may have appeared to be excessively visible and vocal, especially in the African countries, in his advocacy in favor of the devaluation of the CFA franc. I have never seen or heard conclusive evidence supporting this theory.

4. Remember that this effort took place at the time of cohabitation between leftist President François Mitterrand and center-rightist Prime Minister Edouard Balladur, with the need for convincing, coordinating, and managing institutions as diverse as the presidency, the Prime Minister's Office, the Ministry of Finance, the Ministry of Foreign Affairs, the Ministry of Cooperation, the Official Cooperation Agency (the then Caisse Française de Developpement), and the Ministry of Defense (which was mobilized because of fears of civil disorder following the monetary operation), among others.

5. As an illustration of this point, it is interesting to note that Michael Bruno, then the chief economist of the Bank, disqualified himself from making comments or recommendations on the subject, as he readily acknowledged that there was no precedent in the literature that could provide guidance to what was being attempted—simultaneous devaluation in 14 countries—an interesting comment from someone who was justifiably known for his remarkable handling of the devaluation of Israeli currency some years earlier.

6. The impact of the crisis on the poor was extraordinarily high. Consider the following figures: In 1984, the ratio of population in poverty was 60 percent. Ten years later, after a long period of economic stability and good poverty-targeted programs (for example, Solidaridad) with billions of dollars spent, it fell to 50 percent. In 1995, right after the crisis, it was back at 60 percent. After six years of good economic management and new poverty reduction programs (such as Progresa and Oportunidades), it is now down to 45 percent. This is a powerful argument to explain the need to maintain a sound and stable macroeconomic framework.

7. It is worth remembering that the Bank issued five policy papers on education, health, rural development, agricultural credit, and land reform in 1974, which were truly benchmarks in the Bank strategy and were later issued in 1975 as a book prefaced by Robert McNamara (World Bank 1975). The title of the book was *The Assault on World Poverty*.

8. There was also the first recognition that financial constraints of governments made it inevitable that external donors and financial institutions (including the Bank) would get into the financing of local expenditures and recurrent costs, whereas previously the Bank and other organizations were strictly in the financing of foreign exchange requirements and investment costs.

9. How revealing and interesting that there was the exact repeat of the same problem more than 10 years later with the treatment of the (in)famous Washington Consensus, which, after all, is nothing but plain common sense about sensible macroeconomic management and has now succeeded in being the equivalent of a four-letter word in many quarters.

10. This characterization was as valid in several Latin American countries as it was in Africa. Think of Mexico, where the PRI (Partido Revolucionario Institucional) ruled the country uninterruptedly for 71 years. When the Bank reached an agreement with the Ministry of Finance on behalf of the executive branch, there was no questioning the final word from the executive. Parliament and the judiciary had no reason or any real means of objecting to the decisions made by the executive. All that was expected, usually, was rubber-stamping by the legislative branch and silence from the judiciary branch.

11. That reminds me of the very pertinent remark of a former Bank colleague working on what was then Zaire. When someone had observed that the government (that is, Nzanga

Joseph Mobutu) was apparently behaving unusually well and was introducing reforms in some public management area in response to the Bank's insistent requests, my colleague remarked, "Don't be mistaken. Mobutu is already stealing the equivalent somewhere else, but we don't know yet where and how."

12. There are all sorts of exceptions to this general statement, of course, such as in the cases where the Bank can demonstrate incredible flexibility and effectiveness in responding to unforeseen circumstances (for example, earthquake rehabilitation in Colombia in 1999) or in new situations (for example, the CFA franc devaluation).

13. I have the unfortunate recollection of a Bank-prepared strategy for agricultural development in India, which was perfectly selective and so well focused on four areas that the then minister of agriculture gave me his unambiguous reaction: "Mr. Lafourcade, these may be wonderful objectives for the Bank, but they do not reflect our own priorities."

14. I remember the very effective way in which we often dealt with Prime Minister Kablan Duncan of Côte d'Ivoire after the CFA franc devaluation of 1994. The conditions on some adjustment operations were presented in the form of a menu of major and minor conditions and agreements, the implementation (sequencing and timing) of which was entirely left to the government, with disbursements adjusted to the speed and nature of this sequencing.

15. As I have already mentioned, one can just look at the wide swings in approaches and paradigms from the 1960s to the 1970s, 1980s, and 1990s.

Christiaan Poortman

*Former Country Director for the Balkan States
(1997–2002)*

Christiaan Poortman says his interest in development was "inherited." Inspired by his father, a physician who practiced in developing countries, Chrik was drawn not only to improving health in the developing world, but also to the process of development more generally. After completing a master's degree in development economics in his native country, the Netherlands, in 1971 Chrik joined the United Nations Office of Technical Cooperation as a macroeconomist in the Ministry of Finance and Planning in Swaziland. This position started the first of his many associations with Africa during the course of his career.

After gaining four years of valuable field experience, Chrik decided it was time for a change. As the World Bank shifted its emphasis from project lending to poverty reduction and rural development under the leadership of President Robert McNamara, Chrik felt the Bank "had more to say" on development and joined as a Young Professional in 1976. He spent the early years of his Bank career as an economist in the East Asia and Pacific Region, much of it working on the Philippines. He cites the Philippines of this period as a cautionary tale of debt and financial collapse: "It was a country poised to become the next Asian tiger, but we discovered it was defying gravity," and its poor macroeconomic management led to decline. "The lesson was to focus first on the fundamentals," he says. It was also a painful lesson about the interaction of economics and politics, something that would become an increasingly important factor in Chrik's work at the Bank.

Chrik returned to work on Africa in 1983, serving as senior economist first for West Africa, then Eastern and Southern Africa, positions he held until 1987. Then the Bank recognized Chrik's managerial potential by promoting him to division chief of the Industry and Energy Operations Division for West and Central Africa and again, in 1990, to resident representative in Zimbabwe in 1990.

Chrik joined the Eastern Europe and Central Asia Region of the Bank in 1994, at a time of tremendous change in the region. The challenge deepened in 1997, when Chrik became country director for Bosnia and Herzegovina and managed the Bank's crucial involvement in postwar reconstruction of the Balkan states. Chrik's challenge only deepened in subsequent years as leadership of the Bank's programs in Albania, Kosovo, the former Yugoslav Republic of Macedonia, and Serbia and Montenegro was added to his responsibilities.

Leaving the Balkan states in early 2003, Chrik enjoyed a brief respite as director of operations for the Africa Region, but he was soon back in the fire when he became vice president for the Middle East and North Africa Region in mid 2003. "My affinity for Africa made it difficult to leave the region so soon, but my current job is as challenging and rewarding as any other position I've held," he says.

Chrik's lengthy experience in Africa and the Balkan states makes him no stranger to the elements of conflict and rapid change that he faces in his current position as vice president for the Middle East and North Africa Region. "My job now is as much about politics as economics. What I learned elsewhere in my career is tremendously useful in navigating the current challenges." Chrik says that his time in the field around the world has been his most satisfying experience as a development practitioner.

9 Leadership, Learning, and Luck L33
Reflections on the Balkan States

Christiaan Poortman

(Bosnia, Herzegovina)

The Dual Challenge of the Balkan States

WHILE TOURING POSTWAR BOSNIA AND HERZEGOVINA EARLY IN MY TENURE AS country director, I came across many war-ravaged towns, where the major employer had been a single, socially owned enterprise. Having endured years of savage conflict, the residents were not only unemployed but also, in many cases, without adequate housing or access to public services. To them, the most effective means to ease their troubles was clear: just get us back to work at our former jobs, and we will be able to provide for ourselves.

Of course, we in the development community knew that the solution was not so simple. The statist economy that supported their families no longer existed. If we provided financing to restart their public enterprises, we would awaken a monster, but if we did not find a sustainable way to generate employment, we risked reigniting the tensions that fueled the war.

The dilemma of these small towns underscored the unique dual challenge for the World Bank and our clients in the Balkan states of facing not one transition, but two: from war to peace and from a planned economy to a market economy. For the country to succeed, both transitions had to be successful.

The task was enormous. Bosnia and Herzegovina had been devastated by war. Even though I did not arrive until 1997, after much progress had already been made in reconstruction, I felt immediately that the country was on its knees. The war had not only left many dead, but also destroyed entire communities, displacing and impoverishing many more people than it killed. The peace accords merely put an end to the fighting, but old resentments lingered.

In Bosnia and Herzegovina, the Bank was called on to help repair the damage, assist the vulnerable, restart growth, and establish the governance and market institutions necessary for sustained development. Later, we were called to similar tasks in Kosovo, then Serbia and Montenegro (previously known as the Federal Republic of

Yugoslavia). All of those tasks had to occur in rapid sequence, under the specter of a resumption of conflict. We faced a huge challenge.

I could summarize my experience as country director in the Balkan states as the permanent education of an economist. My training in economics revealed its limitations when the solutions most often available were not second best, but fifth or sixth best. I had to help navigate the Bank through a maze of political and ethnic tensions within those countries and through the differing priorities of the donor community from without, all while trying to maintain the Bank's apolitical orientation.

Three key themes marked my time in the Balkan states: leadership, learning, and luck. True to its original mandate, the Bank played a *leadership* role in postconflict reconstruction and performed admirably well. The thornier task of assisting and guiding economic transition, however, required constant *learning* from experience to sustain progress in an ever-changing environment. We were most successful where we applied our learning as a guide. And with so many tasks to manage and so many variables in play, *luck* also played a major part in the way things turned out. This chapter will examine the Bank's role in the Balkan states—specifically, my experience in light of these themes of leadership, learning, and luck.

Leadership: The World Bank in Bosnia and Herzegovina

Prologue: The War and the Dayton Accords, 1992–95

Bosnia and Herzegovina is a multiethnic state in which none of its three principal constituent ethnic groups—Bosniaks (Bosnian Muslims), Croats, and Serbs—holds a majority. The territory was part of the Socialist Federal Republic of Yugoslavia until 1992, when a referendum on independence passed and led to Bosnia and Herzegovina's international recognition as an independent state. Bosniaks and Croats supported independence, but Serbs largely boycotted the vote in opposition. Local Serb militias and the Yugoslav National Army challenged the new state's independence and, by the end of 1992, controlled almost two-thirds of its territory. Bosniak and Bosnian-Croat groups began fighting each other soon after, and though they later allied against rebel Serb forces, their civil war underscored the ethnic divisions in the country.

The war lasted until the end of 1995, a devastating three and one-half years during which as many as 250,000 people were killed and more than 2 million out of a prewar population of 4.3 million fled the country or were internally displaced. The physical damage was nearly as staggering: more than two-thirds of homes were damaged, with one-fifth totally destroyed; 70 percent of school buildings were destroyed, damaged, or requisitioned for other uses; and 30 to 40 percent of hospitals were destroyed, with 30 percent of health care professionals lost to death or emigration. Little wonder, then, that infant mortality nearly doubled from 1991 to 1995, from 7.4 per 1,000 live births to 14.0.

Peace accords signed at the end of 1995 in Dayton, Ohio, ended armed hostilities and set the political framework for Bosnia and Herzegovina. Under the Dayton Accords, Bosnia and Herzegovina was to be governed by a central state government and two constituent entities: the Federation of Bosnia and Herzegovina (hereafter Federation) and Republika Srpska (hereafter RS). The Federation corresponds to the Bosnian and Croat majority areas, whereas RS is the Serb-majority area. Each entity covers about half of the country's territory. The Dayton Accords also established the Office of the High Representative, an international body charged with overseeing implementation of the accords.

Under the constitution adopted in the Dayton Accords, the state government took responsibility for only a limited number of functions, among them foreign policy, foreign trade, customs and immigration policy, and monetary policy. Almost all other functions were devolved to the entities, including authority over separate armies and police forces, fiscal revenues, banking supervision, reconstruction projects, judicial systems, and social services. Denied any independent revenue sources, the state government was made dependent on fiscal transfers from the entities.

Thus, the Dayton Accords were a political agreement to solve an ethnic and military conflict. The significant autonomy that the accords left to the entities—and the weak central state government that resulted—was the only viable way to assure peace. The terms of the Dayton Accords were necessary to end the fighting, but the constraints they imposed on economic policy hampered efforts to craft and implement a strong development strategy, especially after reconstruction was largely complete. The vast autonomy granted to each entity forced us to duplicate many of our efforts. The Dayton Accords were not the source of institutional weakness in Bosnia and Herzegovina, but the effect of the accords was to hamper the development of institutions that were already weak.

Reconstruction: 1995–97

The first task for the Bank in Bosnia and Herzegovina was to assist in reconstruction efforts. The needs were enormous: gross domestic product (GDP) per capita had fallen from US$1,900 in 1990 to US$500 in 1995, and approximately 80 percent of the population was dependent on food aid by the end of the war. Postconflict reconstruction is often considered a relatively straightforward task of assessing needs, raising the necessary funds, and setting about to rebuild, but this perspective underrates the high stakes involved. For a population vulnerable to the resurgence of hostilities, as was threatened in Bosnia and Herzegovina, reconstruction means nothing less than securing the peace. It is a necessary but insufficient condition for subsequent economic development, requiring strong leadership, decisive action, and nearly immediate results.

The World Bank proved very successful in this reconstruction effort in Bosnia and Herzegovina, to the great credit of my predecessors. Before I arrived in 1997, the Bank had taken the lead in a massive effort of coordination among about 60 multilateral and bilateral donors, generating pledges of US$5.1 billion.

The Bank oversaw a flurry of successfully implemented emergency projects in 1996 and 1997 to repair damaged infrastructure and utilities, clear mines, provide employment, and demobilize combatants, among other urgent priorities. It was, in many ways, a return to the Bank's roots in post–World War II reconstruction, and there was much talk of Marshall Plans and learning from the past.

Reconstruction was not without its difficulties. Although the needs of a population emerging from such a terrible conflict are plainly visible and demand urgent attention, such immediate interventions frequently require circumventing the country's institutional limitations, generating tradeoffs between efficient reconstruction and institutional capacity building. A key element of the reconstruction strategy, for instance, was the establishment of Project Management Units (PMUs), which helped to overcome institutional weakness by teaming international aid officials with local counterparts in project implementation. Though the PMUs were highly successful in early reconstruction efforts, they could quickly outlive their usefulness. With the Bank in command of so many resources for reconstruction, we risked becoming a Big Brother in Bosnia and Herzegovina, exacerbating the postwar political vacuum and hindering the country's long-term development. Taking care to ensure country ownership was a delicate task, made infinitely more complex by the ethnic tensions threatening to pull apart the fledgling nation. We did not fully learn the importance of ownership until later in my time in the Balkan states.

The institutional challenges of reconstruction were only the beginning. Not long after I arrived, I learned how politics would also intrude on broader efforts at poverty reduction. Although the Federation had suffered more damage in the war, RS had lower incomes and more trouble restarting economic activity, in part because of wartime sanctions. Though major sanctions were lifted for RS after the Dayton Accords, they were soon reimposed because of RS's failure to live up to its Dayton commitments and because many donors continued to tie their aid to political conditions. Numerous RS municipalities, especially in the entity's eastern region, were blacklisted by certain donors or by the Office of the High Representative during this critical period of reconstruction for failing certain conditions, such as handing over accused war criminals thought to be harbored in their communities. Such blacklisting prevented us from reaching a number of RS communities.

As these economic sanctions on RS continued well after the war, its residents fell further and further behind, frustrating our desire to promote evenhandedness in postwar development. The economic inequality between RS and the Federation, and later between blacklisted and nonblacklisted municipalities within RS, was a threat to stability. Although I have no sympathy for the accused war criminals that motivated these sanctions, I feel that the donor community did not fully consider the potentially adverse impacts of its policies. Poverty in eastern RS risked generating fertile soil for political extremism and war-related hatred. The affected communities were frightening places to visit, teeming with radicalized citizens who were hostile to outsiders. When I traveled to eastern RS and encountered angry residents trying to stop or stone my car and that of other foreigners, I could not but think that political conditionality was a very blunt policy tool.

Political conditionality may have been necessary to promote justice in the aftermath of war, but its detrimental economic consequences are beyond dispute. Political conditionality hampered efforts to implement development in an equitable manner throughout Bosnia and Herzegovina, thus adding another layer of constraint to the institutional weaknesses caused by poverty, war, and the Dayton Accords.

Promoting Development under Political Constraints: 1997–2000

When I arrived in Bosnia and Herzegovina in 1997, reconstruction was well under way, and although the devastation of war was still apparent, I knew that my chief task would be to help the country shift its economy from planned to market, placing it on a path of sustained growth. My prior experience working in Bank operations in transition countries bolstered my confidence that I understood the set of reforms Bosnia and Herzegovina would need to stimulate growth.

Indeed, the Bank approach to transition countries at the time was somewhat orthodox: growth required dismantling much of the state apparatus and placing it in private hands, imposing prudent macroeconomic management, and opening the borders to trade and investment. In contrast to the heavy state involvement in enterprise in transition countries, privatization was seen as the primary engine of growth. There was only nascent recognition of the importance of institutions, as experience in the former Soviet Union and elsewhere demonstrated that markets cannot function well if not supported by the rule of law. In the period before development economists had assimilated the lessons of transition and the East Asian crisis, this type of market orthodoxy reigned.

From my perspective as an economist, I expected to be successful if I could apply the Bank's general approach to transition in its broad outlines, with some adjustments to suit the postconflict reality of Bosnia and Herzegovina. I had no idea, however, of the political morass into which I was stepping. Many decisions that I made during my time as country director were so tinged with politics as to limit the freedom to help design economic policy. Moreover, even when such constraints did not exist, it turned out that we were not always right on the economics.

Postwar Institutional Weakness

Postwar Bosnia and Herzegovina was largely an institutional vacuum. Each ethnic group used a different currency in its majority regions: Bosniaks used the Bosnian dinar, the country's only domestic currency; Croats, the Croatian kuna; and Serbs, the Yugoslav dinar. Fiscal policy—already highly decentralized under prewar Yugoslav rule—splintered further when fighting broke out between Bosniaks and Bosnian-Croats. The Dayton Accords magnified the difficulty of developing a coherent fiscal management system.

We at the Bank knew that fully overcoming ethnic divisions and the political terms of the Dayton Accords was beyond our capacity, but we felt that we could nonetheless help unite Bosnia and Herzegovina as an economic entity. With our comparative advantage in providing financial support linked to policy advice, the Bank's role was to lead in forging a single economic space out of these inchoate elements.

Among the major tasks at the outset were the establishment of a central bank and a common currency, a state budget, a uniform tariff and customs policy, and a framework for debt restructuring and management.Yet many of these immediate and necessary steps that would benefit all citizens of Bosnia and Herzegovina were subject to dispute. Lingering tensions and discontent with the outcome of war led many parties to attempt political blocking tactics to prevent passage of measures perceived to be more beneficial to their rivals than to themselves. This obstacle caused progress to occur in fits and starts; questions of sequencing often became secondary to questions of political feasibility.

The specter of war colored everything. The Dayton Accords were so carefully calibrated to prevent reemergence of hostility as to become almost sacrosanct, despite the institutional and economic weaknesses the accords enshrined. When we would say, "Well, Dayton says this, but for economic purposes we think it should be interpreted this way," the immediate reaction was often, "What are you trying to do? Are you trying to redefine Dayton?" People like me, who were not versed in politics, were getting drawn into these political debates; therefore, figuring out the political hangups threatened to take precedence over providing sound economic management.

One example was the issue of debt service. The Dayton Accords made the central government dependent on fiscal transfers from the entities, making the former vulnerable to bickering between the latter over the share and timing of their respective debt-service payments. For the Bank and for Bosnia and Herzegovina's other creditors, the economics of debt service were simple: timely payments from the central government would help demonstrate prudent fiscal management. But politics inevitably intruded: the entities were at odds over what proportion of the debt each owed, given that much of it was incurred under a previously unified Socialist Federal Republic of Yugoslavia or to finance wartime activities.Yet debt-service payments could not be met in full without the cooperation of both entities. Our role at the Bank was the difficult one of ensuring joint responsibility for the debt, while at the same time being careful not to take sides in the underlying political dispute.

Our general approach to politics in Bosnia and Herzegovina followed a similar script. Although acutely aware of the political maelstrom, we saw our role as that of an honest broker, promoting economic rationality as a win–win alternative to political divisiveness. Convincing all parties of the economic costs of their preferred political course of action sometimes helped to remove the political sting from cooperation between former combatants.

But we were not always successful in the political arena, especially when development issues were peripheral to lingering wartime tensions. At the local level, political difficulties were often the most acute. Municipal elections did not occur for several years after the Dayton Accords because of quarrels over rules of registration, which were complicated by the major demographic shifts caused by the war. When elections did occur, the results could be shocking. I recall a visit to Drvar, a city in northern Bosnia and Herzegovina that was part of the Federation. It had been a Bosnian-Serb majority area until the Serbs fled during the war. After the war, Bosnian-Croats settled in the city, making it 95 percent majority Croat. The city's displaced Serbs, who were allowed to vote in absentia in the municipal election, managed to elect a Serb mayor. The resident Croats were outraged. I met with the new mayor after he had arrived, under armed guard, to a municipal headquarters that was defiantly flying a Croatian flag (an illegal act). As the mayor sat in the corner of the conference room, away from the windows, the meeting took on a surreal tone: how could we possibly discuss practical matters of the city's recovery when the mayor's first concern was to avoid his own assassination?

Meeting with the newly elected mayor of Drvar was itself perceived by the town's residents as a political act, independent of the political motivations ascribed to our development strategy. Indeed, often the most seemingly mundane actions became politically charged in the delicate ethnic balance that was postwar Bosnia and Herzegovina. We could not pretend to be apolitical. I recall receiving an invitation to attend a victory celebration following an election in RS, and my initial reaction was that our presence would be a positive way to show our support for the democratic process in RS. I was not yet aware that the Office of the High Representative was frantically trying to contact representatives of the international community to urge them not to attend, as it had learned that a notorious Serb official associated with wartime atrocities (now under detention at The Hague) would be present. Fortunately, I was informed of the official's presence before committing to attend and stayed away, avoiding embarrassment and erosion of the Federation's trust in the Bank. Other members of the international community who attended the rally were not so lucky.

Private Sector Development and Privatization

Because our economic program for Bosnia and Herzegovina centered on transition from a planned economy to a market economy with private property as its foundation, private sector development was integral to our strategy. The broad term can encompass many dimensions; in transition countries it requires establishing a legal framework for property rights and contract enforcement, reducing the regulatory environment for private firms, and ensuring an enabling environment for small and medium enterprises (SMEs), as well as privatization of socially owned enterprises. Yet the overriding emphasis at the Bank among these priorities was on privatization. We adhered to this trend in Bosnia and Herzegovina to the detriment of other efforts to develop the private sector that might have had greater success.

The Bank's privatization agenda for Bosnia and Herzegovina was tremendously ambitious even before I arrived; an early country study recommended that authorities make a list of public enterprises that were *not* to be privatized, with the understanding that all others would be sold (World Bank, European Commission, and European Bank for Reconstruction and Development 1996, p. 55). We envisioned a rapid program, with economically viable enterprises reconstituting themselves under private ownership and others generating revenues through sales of salvageable assets. We succeeded in garnering government support, despite reservations about the speed at which we hoped to proceed.

The state government's objectives, however, went beyond privatization as a means of revenue generation and asset transfer from the public sector to the private sector. The state government faced a large number of outstanding claims in the aftermath of war, both from individuals (in the form of unpaid wages and pensions, claims for damage and other war-related losses, and claims on frozen foreign currency accounts) and from socially owned institutions (bad bank loans, government arrears to enterprises, and so forth). With output severely diminished, debt service high, and the ability to mobilize revenue low, settling such claims was beyond the government's fiscal capacity. But reneging on the claims would carry great political cost.

The solution worked out by the government, which we supported, was to exchange outstanding claims for privatization vouchers, which claimants could use to purchase shares of socially owned enterprises. We felt this scheme was a clever way to mitigate the social and political costs of outstanding claims on the state without harming its fiscal position, and the plan would also give citizens an increased stake in successful privatization.

As it turned out, we were overly ambitious in our hope that privatization would serve these multiple functions. As experiences in other transition countries and elsewhere have amply demonstrated, ensuring a successful outcome to the seemingly straightforward task of privatization is challenging enough without attempting to bring social objectives into the equation. In Bosnia and Herzegovina, the participation of claimants prevented the sale of many public enterprises to strategic investors with the capacity to transform the firms into viable private entities.

Given the remaining ethnic rivalries, particularly in the Federation, privatization became an intensely political process. Persisting with voucher privatization led to unnecessary delays in the program as battles were fought over which claims were valid and which group deserved property rights. The result was that many of the largest enterprises remained in public hands years beyond their intended sale date, and in the meantime, a failure to impose hard budget constraints allowed them to continue to be a drain on the state.

Another unfortunate consequence of our overemphasis on privatization was that it distracted from other efforts to promote private sector development. Early Bank assessments of the postwar situation recognized that privatization would be insufficient to meet the employment needs of the population and that providing an enabling environment for private enterprise, particularly for SMEs, would be crucial. Yet with the intense focus on getting privatization right, we neglected the needs of smaller firms, and we overestimated the adequacy of the institutional environment to support their functioning. Our first Country Assistance Strategy (CAS), released in 1997, overlooked SMEs almost entirely. We did make progress through financing microcredit programs and in privatizing smaller public enterprises in the first years, but it was far too little.

Our experience in private sector development was a success in one respect, however: it is an excellent example of the on-the-job *learning* that we later applied to improve our performance. As the frustrations of privatization became clear, both in Bosnia and Herzegovina and elsewhere, we increasingly turned our focus to other aspects of private sector development. Our second CAS for Bosnia and Herzegovina, released in 2000, explicitly incorporated support for SMEs, through both extension services and an enabling institutional environment, as a crucial element of employment generation and poverty reduction. In fiscal year 2002, we approved a business environment adjustment credit to improve the institutional environment for firm entry, operation, and exit. It was our first project to focus exclusively on improving the environment for private sector development, and its disbursement at a time of declining International Development Association (IDA) allocations for Bosnia and Herzegovina shows that we were incorporating the lessons learned in previous years. We continued to apply our learning as our mandate reached beyond Bosnia and Herzegovina and into Kosovo and Serbia and Montenegro.

Learning: The World Bank in Kosovo

Postconflict Kosovo presented a challenge similar in many ways to that of Bosnia and Herzegovina: both faced the dual transition from war to peace and from plan to market. Unlike in Bosnia and Herzegovina, however, the World Bank did not occupy a leadership role in Kosovo, because the United Nations (UN), with strong involvement by the European Union (EU), assumed leadership of Kosovo following the conflict in 1999. But even in our less prominent role, the experience we had gained dealing with a similar situation in Bosnia and Herzegovina helped to guide our approach to postwar Kosovo.

Kosovo, populated by a large majority (nearly 90 percent) of ethnic Albanians and a minority of Serbs, was an autonomous province of the Yugoslav republic of Serbia until 1989, when Serbian President Slobodan Milosevic stripped Kosovo of its autonomy. Serbian disinvestment in Kosovo in the ensuing years led to severe economic contraction, with GDP falling 50 percent by 1995. Ethnic Albanians in Kosovo rose up against Serbia, demanding independence. Milosevic moved to quash the rebellion, and in 1999 the North Atlantic Treaty Organization intervened, resulting in a 78-day conflict. The massive numbers of Kosovar Albanians who fled during the conflict returned to a Kosovo that was not an independent country, but instead a protectorate of the United Nations. A UN Security Council resolution affirmed the Federal Republic of Yugoslavia's sovereignty over Kosovo but granted substantial autonomy to the province. Lacking sovereign status, Kosovo could not be a World Bank member and, consequently, had to rely on special trust fund arrangements for Bank support in the initial period, rather than on IDA or International Bank for Reconstruction and Development resources, a status that limited the Bank's potential involvement.

The conflict in Kosovo ended at a time when we in the development community were internalizing the lessons of a decade of transition, and I, in particular, had received a crash course in the difficulties of transition in a postconflict environment in the preceding years. When the UN and the EU called on the Bank to play a role in Kosovo's reconstruction, our first step was literally to sit around a table and ask ourselves, "What have we learned so far?"

The Bank's team in Kosovo was largely the same group as in Bosnia and Herzegovina, making our learning process robust: it was a team with both technical and cultural expertise in the region, as well as an esprit de corps for the challenges ahead.

We learned from Bosnia and Herzegovina that we could have an immediate effect
on the pace of recovery, which strengthened our commitment. The continuity of
our team, as well as a similar level of continuity and commitment from the donor
community, was essential to our efforts in Kosovo.

Wiser from our work in Bosnia and Herzegovina, we approached our task in
Kosovo with much greater appreciation of the political constraints involved. Fortunately, the type of donor political conditionality that we faced in Bosnia and Herzegovina was largely absent, but still we knew that we had to be mindful of the strong,
underlying ethnic tensions. Additionally, we had to tangle with the heavy nostalgia
of Kosovar Albanians for the pre-1989 period, an era in which they enjoyed greater
political autonomy, but also in which the state played the dominant role in every
aspect of economic life. After a decade of unemployment and deterioration of living
standards, many Kosovars thought that the recipe for recovery was reactivation of
state-controlled industry. The challenge of establishing a strong property-rights
regime was further complicated by the uncertain political status of Kosovo, which
led many Serbs to claim that public enterprises and other assets were rightly the
property of Serbia. This argument created major hurdles to privatization, which were
difficult to overcome, at least in the short term.

As a result of our experience in Bosnia and Herzegovina, we placed an early and
specific emphasis on promoting SMEs. In this regard, we went beyond merely
attempting to help establish an adequate institutional framework for firms, to providing SMEs access to credit to a greater degree than we had in Bosnia and Herzegovina. We did so with caution, stipulating that any credit be based on sound credit
analysis and with the understanding that Bank support was a transitional measure.
Our approach to private sector development in Kosovo reflected how much we had
learned from Bosnia and Herzegovina.

Putting It All Together: The World Bank
in Serbia and Montenegro

After these tumultuous years in Bosnia and Herzegovina and Kosovo, I could only
smile when the Bank had me assume the additional role of country director for Serbia and Montenegro in 2000. Just when I thought my job could not get any more
challenging, along came another Balkan state facing economic and social transition
in a postconflict setting.

Serbia and Montenegro was a major test case for us, our important chance to
implement in a leadership role what we had learned elsewhere. As the only two
remaining republics of Yugoslavia, Serbia and Montenegro (previously known as
the Federal Republic of Yugoslavia) had faced a decade of intermittent conflict,
international sanctions, and political neglect under Slobodan Milosevic. Milosevic,
leader of Serbia since 1987, became president of both Serbia and Montenegro in
1997. His ambitions to forge the Balkan states into a Greater Serbia, his authoritarian methods, and his economic mismanagement, plus the increasing international isolation of Serbia and Montenegro, led to severe economic contraction in

Serbia (a decline in per capita income of 60 percent from 1990 to 2000) and to a lesser extent in Montenegro.

Milosevic was toppled in a bloodless, democratic coup at the end of 2000 that spread hope across the region. He soon ended up on trial for war crimes in The Hague. Serbia and Montenegro was another case of the Balkan states' dual transition from war to peace and from a planned economy to a market economy, but this time, reconstruction had much more to do with *software*—the neglected institutions of governance—than with *hardware*—buildings and infrastructure. The World Bank again played a leadership role in the donor community, but the hope inspired by the regime change led us to focus more emphatically this time on placing early leadership in the country's own hands.

As in Kosovo, our first task as a country team for Serbia and Montenegro was to gather together and reflect on what we had learned in the past. Our approach, refined in the course of our efforts in Bosnia and Herzegovina and in Kosovo, serves as a useful framework for postconflict environments in general. First, it involves carrying out a needs assessment, cataloging both existing needs *and* capacities, and consulting with government and donors on how to meet the former and work with the latter.

Second, any postconflict recovery strategy should focus on delivering quick results, not only to meet immediate needs, but also to generate trust and confidence in the reconstruction process and alleviate the potential for further conflict. In addition to reconstruction of infrastructure, priority needs in this phase include education and other public services, such as health, electricity, and water. Our approach also made greater and greater use of local initiative projects, engaging communities in their own social development. These projects are often small in scale with little direct effect on incomes, but they are essential to capacity building and restoring the social fabric in conflict-scarred communities.

Finally, a successful reconstruction framework must ensure that the peace dividend is widely shared, an essential step to securing the peace. In Bosnia and Herzegovina, this step meant dealing evenhandedly with RS; in Kosovo, it meant ensuring that the Serb minority was not shut out of development. Here again, local initiative projects are an important element of sharing the peace dividend and reconnecting marginalized groups with society.

In Serbia and Montenegro, we followed this approach and worked hard to ensure intense donor collaboration, aware of how important it was to our programs elsewhere in the Balkan states. The fact that the government of Serbia and Montenegro was rapidly taking charge of its future, as well as increasing emphasis within the World Bank on client ownership, made us redouble efforts to build the country's capacity.

The topic of privatization versus private sector development emerged once again, and here we decided to stay the course that we had charted in Kosovo, putting our emphasis on creating a supportive business climate, on promoting SMEs, and on the speed and transparency of privatization. After some initial agonizing, the government decided to go full speed ahead with privatization, liquidating four state banks in one swoop—an important step because merely marginal changes would not make over an inefficient and bankrupt financial sector—and setting a framework for the sale of socially owned enterprises. The government put in place a remarkably transparent process, in which each week about 30 public enterprises were to be publicly auctioned. In these auctions, the sales are televised, and bidders hold up their paddles as though they are at an art auction. Ideas to increase the transparency of privatization that we had only dreamed of were coming to fruition, and I felt that my time in the Balkan states was coming full circle.

The Importance of Luck

Many times, we as development practitioners think that our actions lead without any distortion to outcomes; we ascribe success or failure to whether we and our clients got policies right or wrong. This view may be useful in maintaining our sense of responsibility and commitment to results, but it disregards the many other factors beyond our control that contribute to success or failure. In Bosnia and Herzegovina and other postconflict environments, the peace dividend of recovery can obscure the true effect of many of our initial actions. With the country growing at 80 percent and 32 percent on a per capita basis in 1996 and 1997, respectively,[1] it was easy to confuse policy effects with the natural recovery of growth in a postwar environment.

Moreover, by drawing straight lines between policies (or institutions, for that matter) and outcomes, we can impede our ability to think critically and act flexibly when circumstances change in the future. Policies we think are right at one point in time or space may be inappropriate in other situations. Our approach can veer into dogma if we do not account for the role of luck. In Bosnia and Herzegovina, we had to take extra care to separate the distinct tasks of reconstruction on the one hand and recovery of sustained growth on the other to ensure that our strategy was on target.

Luck—in the form of favorable developments largely beyond our control—certainly played a role. There was bad luck in the form of donor political conditionality, as discussed earlier, but there was good luck as well. Bosnia and Herzegovina enjoyed a consistently stable macroeconomic environment throughout reconstruction, to the great credit of the government and our colleagues at the International Monetary Fund. Although in a sense it is difficult to speak of macrostability in a country unable to generate much output, the risk that price liberalization and the influx of foreign aid would lead to excessive inflation and current account imbalances was real but did not become a serious problem. I have already mentioned the importance of the continuity of our World Bank country team in promoting our learning and effectiveness as time went on. Though one could argue that it was a result of design and not luck, our team's continuity was sufficiently rare in the Bank, and the circumstances of our work were sufficiently adverse, that I feel tremendously fortunate to have worked for so long with such high-caliber colleagues, both in Washington, D.C., and in our field offices in the Balkan states. Our counterparts among other organizations in the development community enjoyed similar continuity, generating a virtuous circle of cooperation.

Another major element of luck in the Balkan states was the exceptional quality of the authorizing environment for development. The Balkan states held the attention of the world in the 1990s, leading the international community to push in unison for its development and to stay the course. Donor collaboration was remarkable, spearheaded by the EU, which recognized that the reconstruction of the Balkan states in Europe's backyard required its urgent and forceful attention. The favorable economic environment in the Organisation for Economic Co-operation and Development during this period also made disbursement of foreign aid to the Balkan states less politically problematic. Other postconflict countries have not been so lucky.

Drawing the Lessons

Several lessons emerged from my experience in the Balkan states. Although I think that they are of general interest, they are particularly applicable to postconflict and transition countries like those for which I was country director.

- *In a postconflict environment, act quickly to deliver immediate results.* Societies emerging from armed conflict are in a vulnerable position, with combatants still bitter and major sectors of the population in need of assistance. To secure the peace, it is vital to begin work quickly on reconstruction and social assistance efforts that will yield immediate results.

- *Understand the political constraints.* Pay attention to the politics as well as to the economics. First-best options are rarely available, and second-best options are often unavailable, too. Understanding the political constraints on the policy environment aids in forming policy and in managing client relationships. It is rarely, if ever, possible to be apolitical, so be aware of the political effects of decisions.

- *Strive for country ownership.* In the drive to promote rapid reconstruction and recovery, do not neglect the long-term benefits of country ownership and capacity building. In addition to capacity building at the national level, promote local initiatives to reengage communities with their societies, because small-scale activities can generate larger societal benefits.

- *Be evenhanded.* The cleavages in postconflict societies are wide, and perceptions of uneven development can make them wider, even in the presence of recovery. Actively seek to bring marginalized groups into the process of recovery.

- *Manage public relations well.* A positive image of your efforts yields benefits in any circumstances, but especially so in a postconflict environment. Broadcast your successes and counter your critics with a positive message. Inspiring the faith and confidence of a conflict-torn populace can mean the difference between fostering a virtuous or vicious circle of change.

- *Approach private sector development holistically.* Private sector development is multidimensional. Transition countries with little recent experience in entrepreneurship cannot be expected to develop a vibrant private sector without a push on many fronts. Privatization is not a magic bullet. Pay attention to the business climate for small firms as well.

- *Learn from your experience.* Reflect often on the lessons that accumulate from your experience, and strive to apply this learning to future situations. Be flexible, as new knowledge and new circumstances require new approaches.
- *Be aware of the role of luck.* Unforeseen circumstances can and will alter the course of events. Recognize those factors and adjust your perceptions accordingly.

Conflict in the Balkan states during the 1990s left the region a shell of its former self, and decades of economic mismanagement left it a mere fraction of what it could have been. Horrible atrocities were committed, and the human devastation practically defies description. Yet out of tragedy arises opportunity, and the Balkan states had the extraordinary opportunity in the 1990s to move from war to peace and from stagnation to growth.

From my perspective, it was a wild ride, one that often led to frustration when I saw ethnic and political feuds prevent progress. Yet there were also many uplifting moments of hope.

The most inspirational moment for me, as for many others familiar with the Balkan states, is the reconstruction of the Mostar Bridge. The bridge, built in 1566, connected the Bosniak and Bosnian-Croat halves of Mostar, a town in Bosnia and Herzegovina southwest of Sarajevo. It was an architectural marvel and a beautiful symbol of the country's diversity, but its destruction in 1993 at the height of war was equally symbolic of the country's troubles. As country director, I dreamed of seeing the bridge rebuilt and made something of a personal cause to see it through.

Although we knew that finding a wealthy sponsor for the project among donor countries would be relatively easy, we felt that the project needed the commitment of all of Bosnia and Herzegovina's major ethnic groups, as well as of the international community. Getting started was difficult, as the familiar ethnic tensions stood in the way, but eventually the project came together, with the political and financial support of Bosniaks, Bosnian-Croats, and Bosnian-Serbs; IDA funds from the World Bank; and funds from a host of other international organizations, including the United Nations Educational, Scientific, and Cultural Organization and various bilateral organizations and foundations. This extraordinary coalition of the committed was emblematic of the collaboration that has spurred Bosnia and Herzegovina's postwar recovery.

The rebuilt bridge, which was inaugurated with much fanfare in 2004, is a painstaking replica of the original, and it once again connects areas of Mostar that were formerly at odds. To me, it is a powerful symbol not only of the country's history and recovery, but also of the catalytic role that we in the World Bank can play in promoting development. The task of reconstruction is not a simple matter of bricks and mortar but of the reconstruction of fractured societies as well. As Bosnia and Herzegovina's prime minister, Haris Silajdzic, remarked to me, "We can do many good projects together, but this is the one for which we will be remembered."

Note

1. Statistics are from the World Development Indicators database.

Ajay Chhibber

Former Country Director for Turkey (1997–2003)

To hear Ajay Chhibber tell it, his career in economic development was decided by a coin toss. As a young man growing up in India, he and a close friend left boarding school together to attend the University of Delhi, where both were slated to study physics. For some reason, they felt that one should study something different. "We said that whoever lost should study economics. Unfortunately for me, I lost the toss!" Ajay went on to earn a degree in economics, distinguishing himself as a field hockey and tennis player.

After teaching economics in 1976 at the University of Delhi's St. Stephens College, he joined a team preparing India's sixth Five-Year Plan. "I learned that India's economic future would not be following the old Soviet-style *gosplan* approach," he smiles wryly. After earning a Ph.D. in economics at Stanford University, Ajay joined the World Bank as a Young Professional in 1983. Over the past 20 years, Ajay's career trajectory has alternated between research and operations, as he has contributed to major publications and collaborated on numerous country programs. He worked as a country economist for the Arab Republic of Egypt, headed the Indonesia and Pacific Division, was part of the team that prepared the *World Development Report* (WDR) in 1986, and then directed the WDR team in 1997.

A seminal feature of *World Development Report 1997: The State in a Changing World* (World Bank 1997) was the attention it devoted to the notion of corruption—the first Bank publication to systematically tackle the previously shunned "C word." Ajay explains that the political will to address corruption, previously lacking because of the Bank's reluctance to get involved in politics, came in 1996. The WDR team took up the challenge, and anticorruption efforts have been an integral part of the Bank's work on governance ever since.

Following publication of *World Development Report 1997*, Ajay became country director for Turkey, arriving at a point when new Bank commitments were at a decade low. Then the devastating August 1999 earthquake hit, killing 17,000 people. International donors pledged US$3 billion, one-third of which the Bank provided. The Bank's disaster management program, which met immediate relief needs, as well as worked to facilitate insurance policies for future

Portions of this profile appeared in *Bank's World Today,* May 1, 2003.

disasters, won the Bank President's Award for Excellence. Ajay also witnessed Turkey's financial crisis of 2001 and helped Turkey's economic team put together a successful recovery program.

Ajay left Turkey in 2003 to become director of the Operations Evaluation Department, his current position. Governance and institution-building concerns remain central to his vision of the Bank's role. "The more we can help countries build institutions, the better they will be," he says. "This is a long-run process, and we must persevere. Of course, crisis often offers an opportunity to trigger the start of a reform process. In addition, we need to redouble our efforts in middle-income countries to reduce our costs and remain competitive, and we need to find better ways to help build capacity in low-income countries."

10 Turkey's Tumult

Lessons from Crisis and Institutional Reform

Ajay Chhibber

AFTER GROWING RAPIDLY IN THE 1980s, TURKEY WENT THROUGH A TUMULTUOUS and volatile period in the 1990s, culminating in a massive financial crisis in 2001. During this period, the country experienced a major earthquake as well as economic crises. Despite the enormous pressures created by these events, Turkey maintained social harmony and with a well-designed economic program is recovering from that volatile period. As the World Bank's country director for Turkey from mid 1997 through mid 2003, I have drawn four lessons from my close involvement with Turkish policymaking and development strategy; these lessons were further informed by my thinking during the preparation of the *World Development Report 1997: The State in a Changing World* (World Bank 1997), which was completed just before I left for Turkey.

- *Lesson 1: Crisis only provides an opportunity to start reforms and generate recovery.* A successful recovery effort, like Turkey's 2001 program, must focus not only on correcting macroeconomic imbalances, but also—for growth—on key structural and institutional reforms to signal credibility.

- *Lesson 2: To maintain sustained and stable growth and to manage volatility, a country needs strong institutional capability, but this effort takes longer.* Other pulls and pressures must be present to create consensus for sustaining the reform process and to overcome reform fatigue. In Turkey's case, the prospect of European Union (EU) accession provides this pull.

- *Lesson 3: Less politicized and more rule-based institutions must be put in place.* The underlying causes of crises are an ineffective state and the lack of effective checks and balances in the system. This was the case in Turkey, where the reform program strengthened some existing institutions, such as the central bank, and created new ones in banking, energy, and telecommunications to regulate the market more effectively.

- *Lesson 4: Improving the state's effectiveness also requires a healthy civil society and greater decentralization.* Without those elements, the reforms are perceived as top-down, and other imbalances emerge quickly—especially lack of focus on inequality, corruption, and the environment. Turkey and other emerging markets must allow greater opportunities for civil society and decentralization to sustain the pressure for reform and encourage transparency.

A more internal lesson relates to the Bank. The World Bank's program in Turkey kept the Bank relevant by focusing on helping achieve stable growth and social protection. Especially in a middle-income country such as Turkey, where financial flows from the Bank form a small proportion of overall inflows into the country, work needs to focus on a few carefully selected areas to help develop the institutional capacity to achieve sustained growth and provide social protection—with good analytical work and financial support, which will produce maximum leverage. Excessive and simplistic focus on poverty in middle-income countries risks making the Bank less relevant and less effective.

Introduction

Little did I know when I went to work in Turkey in 1997, following a year of demanding work on *World Development Report 1997: The State in a Changing World* (World Bank 1997), how intensely involved we would become in Turkey's challenges, starting with the historic basic education reform of 1997, the Marmara earthquake in 1999, and the reform and crisis recovery programs of 1999 and 2001. Two vignettes illustrate the Bank's activities.

The first began on August 17, 1999, when Turkey was hit by a massive earthquake that left more than 17,000 people dead and more than 100,000 homeless. The Bank mobilized quickly to support Turkey with reconstruction. Two days later, I was back in Turkey with our team to help the Turkish authorities organize support. Some 16 months later—under one of the fastest responses in the world—the first permanent houses for earthquake-affected families financed by the World Bank were ready for distribution in the town of Duzce. We received a call from Turkey's housing minister to accompany him to distribute the keys to the families. But we went with some trepidation. The Bank's team had recommended 80-square-meter houses, which the Turkish authorities considered too small for Turkish families. Turkey agreed to the smaller houses reluctantly, but it also built 120-square-meter houses through its Public Works Ministry adjacent to the Bank-financed houses. We worried that the families chosen to occupy the smaller houses would criticize us. To our surprise, as we entered the site we were mobbed by families asking to move into the smaller Bank-financed houses, and as we looked at the buildings, it was obvious why. Bank-financed houses were clearly better built and could withstand 8.0 on the Richter scale because of good design and proper international tendering. As a mother with three children explained, "I and my children can sleep soundly again under this roof." Subsequently, Turkey decided to revamp its tendering procedures to bring them in line with international standards, ensuring better-quality public-financed construction. Safeguards, sensibly applied, matter, and helping countries change their own safeguard procedures matters even more.

The second vignette occurred in 1998, when a team of banking experts arrived in Turkey. After diagnosing the lack of effective supervision and the weak banking law, the experts advised the Turkish government to establish an independent banking regulatory authority styled on those of Canada and the United Kingdom. After initially rejecting the idea, the then Turkish economic team produced a proposal for a Turkish version of a regulatory authority, but with the economy minister chairing its board. Our team obviously opposed this counterproposal. After deliberations for more than a year, a board was finally established in mid 2000, some 18 months after the Bank team's first proposal, but the board was packed with political appointees. After the 2001 crisis, political resistance broke down, and Turkey's new economy minister, with parliamentary approval, established a new board, with more technocrats and a new chairman. The new team carried out large-scale surgery on the crisis-ridden banking system. It was a trial by fire for the regulatory authority, but the team made quick, nonpoliticized decisions and helped Turkey's recovery. Policy change is an uncertain process that requires huge patience and persistence. The initial work in setting up the authority—however imperfect—helped lay the groundwork so that the authority was ready to move quickly once the crisis came. Turkey would have found it difficult to deal with such a large banking crisis without an independent regulator.

The Bank team worked all through this period very closely with our Turkish counterparts and provided rich advice on a wide range of issues, from education, earthquake reconstruction, highway safety, and social assistance to banking reform, energy and telecommunication liberalization, and public sector reform. Our teams also worked closely with many international partners, academic and civil society organizations, and the private sector, as well as government counterparts. During this difficult period for Turkey, we were praised and thanked for our support, but we were also often blamed for the advice we gave and for the pain that came with the crisis. The town of Izmit named a boulevard after one of our former colleagues who had worked tirelessly on the earthquake reconstruction. But we received a good dose of criticism as well. Through it all, our teams continued to provide the best professional analysis and advice we had to offer.

In this chapter I draw four broad lessons, but first I offer a recapitulation of the country's history over the past two decades to provide a context for those lessons and for our involvement in support of Turkey.

Brief Economic History of the Last Two Decades

By the late 1970s, the import-substitution, state-led development model that a large number of developing countries had followed for almost three decades had collapsed. Many countries, including Turkey, switched gears in the 1980s and began to integrate with the world economy. They refocused their development strategy to rely on the private sector as the main engine of growth. But in many countries, including Turkey, the pendulum swung too far. The private sector began to be seen as the solution to all problems plaguing the public sector. It was believed that whatever the public sector could do, the private sector could do it better. These issues were high on the agenda in industrial and developing countries alike.

Even the mixed economies of the industrial world, in response to the perceived failures of government intervention, opted for a decided shift in favor of market mechanisms. International financial institutions, including the World Bank and the International Monetary Fund (IMF), not only followed this trend, but also helped propagate it in much of the developing world. Many felt that the logical endpoint of all these reforms was a minimalist state—one that would do no harm but also could not do much good.

Turkey followed those shifts in ideology, but without reducing the size of the state. The shifts led to weaker state institutions but a larger state. Like other middle-income countries, Turkey opened up to the world economy dramatically in the 1980s, after almost three decades of autarchic, import-substitution development strategies. Turkey integrated rapidly, the economy grew, and the private sector flourished (figure 10.1). Although this brought enormous benefits, Turkey did not use this period to build the basis of a competitive, well-regulated private economy. Instead, rapid political turnover and weak institutions combined to create the conditions for crisis. Populist policies and rampant corruption flourished, and the taxpayer paid for the state's largesse and its weaknesses.

Once the initial burst of productivity growth from trade liberalization slowed, Turkey began to look inward for resources to maintain growth. The economy was fueled by huge increases in fiscal spending, financed by domestic borrowing. The

FIGURE 10.1

Turkey Integrated Rapidly in the Past Two Decades: Trade to Gross Domestic Product Rose by More Than 50 Percentage Points

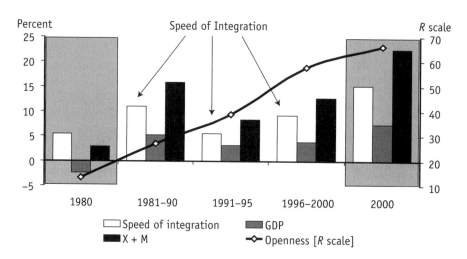

Note: Openness means the share in GDP of exports plus imports of goods and nonfactor services. *Speed of integration* means trade growth less GDP growth.
Source: World Bank data and Emergency Prevention and Preparedness Group calculations.

opening of the capital account in 1989 helped the inflow of the short-term portfolio capital needed to finance the fiscal deficit. Spending that pulled Turkey through a minicrisis was followed by several years of rapid growth, financed by public spending. But with the onset of the East Asian and Russian crises, emerging markets such as Turkey found that access to the international capital markets had become prohibitive, and growth fell once again (figure 10.2). The 1990s were characterized by extreme volatility, with sharp swings in output and other relative prices. Turkey could be characterized as the country with the highest levels of volatility in the world (figure 10.3). During the 1990s, growth fell, inflation accelerated (figure 10.4), and income disparities widened. From its position as a frontrunner among countries aspiring to EU membership, Turkey fell behind several newly independent East European countries. A huge economic crisis in 2001 and the country's desire not to fall further behind in the push for EU accession helped bring about important political and economic reforms. Together with a more stable government installed in 2002, after a decade of weak coalitions, the reforms carried out since the crisis helped Turkey recover and improve its prospects for the coming decade. But the costs of delayed reforms and weak efforts at institution building have been high—a huge debt burden and high unemployment—and the room for error, especially with growing uncertainties in the region, remains very thin.

I came to Turkey in mid 1997, fresh from having led the work on the *World Development Report 1997: The State in a Changing World* (World Bank 1997). That report tried to correct the extreme view of a minimalist state. It argued that this view was at odds with the evidence of the world's development success stories—the development of today's industrial economies in the 19th century and the postwar growth seen in East Asia. Far from supporting a minimalist approach to the state, those expe-

FIGURE 10.2

A Sequence of Crises during the 1990s

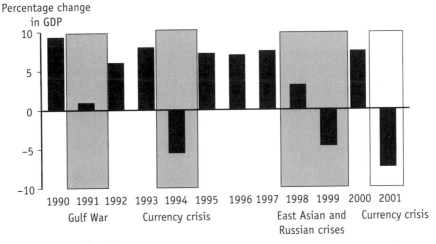

Source: World Bank (2003).

FIGURE 10.3

Turkey: An Outlier among Comparators in Volatility of Real Effective Exchange Rate and Gross Domestic Product Growth, 1990–2000

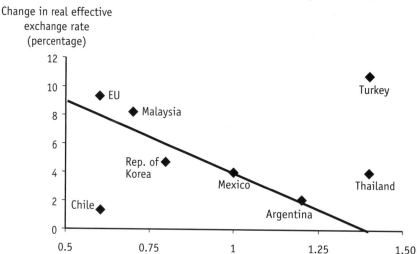

Source: World Bank (2003).

FIGURE 10.4

Growth and Inflation Rates in the 1980s and 1990s

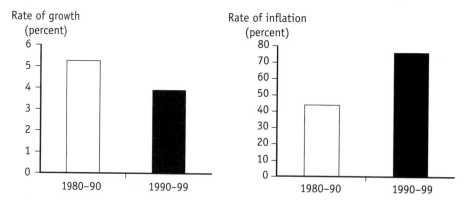

Source: World Bank (2002c).

riences showed that development requires an effective state, one that plays a catalytic and facilitating, but regulatory, role, encouraging and complementing the activities of private businesses and individuals, but also ensuring that development takes place in a system with predictable rules of law to underpin market transactions. At the same time, to be effective the state must play by the rules itself, acting reliably and predictably and controlling corruption. Effective institutions would provide the predictability needed for the private sector to grow, but would also provide, if properly designed, the checks and balances needed to restrain arbitrary and corrupt behavior. It was obvious that Turkey badly needed to recalibrate its development strategy; otherwise, the country was headed for a costly crisis.

But disentangling Turkey from its free-spending, roller-coaster growth model was not going to be easy. Vested interests were likely to oppose reforms. In Turkey's case, the nexus that had developed among politicians, business groups, and bankers (with banks often being owned by business groups) was too lucrative and difficult to break. The state had been captured by private interests. Rapid political turnover created greater opportunities for corruption. Each new government allowed a different section of Turkey's elite to have a seat at the table and benefit its political base. Even among many—though not all—of Turkey's able economists and policymakers who were in a position to champion reform, there was a strong sense that Turkey was somehow different. Turkey appeared to have broken all the rules of economics, having grown rapidly despite high and very variable inflation. It presented a challenge to domestic and international experts who had been predicting a crisis for some time. The country did have a minicrisis in 1994, but robust growth in 1995, 1996, and 1997 had wiped out any memory of that unfortunate year. The rapid recovery from the chaos of 1994 and the country's continuing growth in the face of high inflation were attributed to Turkey's uniqueness and special characteristics—a phrase one often hears, certainly not only in Turkey. We were reminded of those special attributes every time we raised the argument that Turkey could not defy the odds and that reform was badly needed.

Given the size of the macroeconomic imbalances that had developed by the mid to late 1990s, it was obvious that a crisis would eventually come, but it was difficult to predict when. We knew that deep distributional conflicts and constraints embedded in state institutions are at the heart of many countries' failure to reform, but they are not immutable. Ultimately, change comes when the incentives to throw out the old development strategy and old institutional arrangements become stronger than the incentives to keep them. An economic crisis, an external threat, or the arrival of a new government with fewer vested interests in the old system may provide the impetus for reform. Neighbors can also be powerful motivators for change—in Turkey's case, the beckoning EU.

The World Bank helped Turkey in the first half of the 1980s when it began to liberalize its economy and integrate with the world. But until the late 1990s, Bank advice to build better regulatory and budgetary systems went largely ignored, as Turkey's access to private capital helped finance the profligate and populist policies of that decade. Bank financial support to Turkey quite logically began to decline. The World Bank continued to produce and provide technical and analytical work on a range of policy issues, but Turkey's receptivity to these messages was low. By the mid 1990s, the relations between Turkey and the Bank needed some rehabilitation. This opportunity came in 1999, unfortunately through an unexpected crisis triggered by the Marmara earthquake. The Bank stepped in to assist Turkey's recovery from that disaster in a very significant way.

By the late 1990s, as access to international markets on easy terms began to dry up, Turkey increasingly turned to the international financial institutions for support. An economic reform program was introduced in the late 1990s, with large IMF financing supported by the World Bank. The Bank played a crucial role in helping design key structural and institutional reforms to improve the effectiveness of the public sector; introduce new procurement and debt management rules; clean up the state banking sector; institutionalize regulatory systems in banking, energy, and telecommunications; assist in agricultural sector reform; and better target transfer and subsidy systems to help the poor and those affected by the crisis. The Bank's current program builds on those reforms and is increasingly focused on helping Turkey achieve the necessary conditions for EU accession.

Crisis, Reforms, and Recovery

Could the financial crisis of 2001 have been avoided? This question was often asked as Turkey lurched through a series of close calls in the 1990s but managed to get through the East Asian and Russian crises. In a 1999 article in *Emerging Turkey*, I wrote:

> Turkey has defied all odds. Experts have predicted a crisis in Turkey for a long time, yet while other countries whose prospects were brighter have slipped into severe economic difficulties, Turkey has grown with remarkable resilience. However, looking at 1999 and beyond there are worrying signs. Turkey must obviously focus on the macro-programme for 1999 and beyond, but it must also address serious issues regarding the quality of institutions that govern the private sector, its privatization programme, and the financial sector. (Chhibber 1999, p. 58)

There were three reasons for Turkey's ability to avoid a crisis for so long: (a) the resilience and entrepreneurship of Turkish business and its lack of dependence on borrowed funds to finance new investment; (b) the flexibility of its labor markets, which meant that labor acted as a shock absorber as demand fell; and (c) its exchange rate management. Of those three aspects, Turkey was not unique on the first two—many middle-income developing countries could claim those features. But on the third—exchange rate management—Turkey was quite different. To quote again from my 1999 piece:

> Turkey's exchange rate management provides a lesson to other countries [that] are on the ropes. Turkey has defied the normal emerging market trend in this respect. It has not followed many other countries into a fixed exchange rate regime and, despite high deficits and high inflation, has managed to keep a fairly competitive exchange rate. Turkey is different from many countries that have gone into crisis in the past year or so such as Indonesia, Thailand, and [the Republic of] Korea, which had an informal, pegged exchange rate or pre-

announced crawl to the dollar, or countries such as Russia, which have a fixed exchange rate with a band. In this respect Turkey is different even from Brazil and Argentina, whose currencies have been under pressure recently. (Chhibber 1999, p. 58)

Some 12 months later, Turkey adopted an exchange rate–based disinflation program. The peg lasted for about 14 months, culminating in a massive collapse in February 2001 and one of Turkey's worst recessions since the World War II. IMF held the view that there are "few instances in which a successful disinflation from triple-digit inflation has taken place without the use of an exchange rate anchor—possibly a crawling peg" (Fischer 2001, p. 18).[1]

Although some slowdown in policy implementation in 2000 and other institutional weaknesses and corruption contributed to the crisis (see Chhibber and Linn 2001), many analysts, looking back, have argued that IMF must take the blame for the poor advice that led to the acceleration and the size of the crisis.[2] They argue that the slow convergence of the rate of inflation with the rate of depreciation led to overvaluation, which in turn exacerbated the current account deficit. Short-term capital (hot money) flowed in to finance the deficit. With a currency board–like arrangement, no sterilization of these inflows was possible. With the monetary base increasing, real interest rates fell sharply, fueling consumption and further exacerbating the current account imbalances. As real interest rates fell, banking sector profits that were heavily dependent on profits from treasury bills declined sharply, and banking sector weaknesses were exposed. The weakest banks collapsed, triggering a systemic banking crisis. But as subsequent events have shown, Turkey has been able to successfully disinflate without an exchange rate anchor and through extremely tight fiscal policy. With a fragile banking system, growing macroeconomic imbalances, and a huge debt, Turkey would eventually have run out of options—and into a crisis.

What lesson can we learn from this painful episode? Country fit is important, even for advice on basic macroeconomic policy, let alone on complex institutional issues. Turkey had managed to avoid crisis by maintaining competitiveness with a floating exchange rate. This aspect of its economic policy worked well and should have been preserved as other variables were used to bring down inflation. Some have argued that a better designed peg, combined with an upfront, one-step devaluation, could have worked. But as is shown later, the inherent structural rigidities introduced by the inconsistency between sound public finances and a profitable banking sector would always have created problems. A crisis was inevitable—but a less costly one was probably possible without the peg. The IMF has subsequently helped Turkey design and finance a successful recovery program in the happier period discussed next.

How a Quick Recovery from the Crisis Was Achieved

Once the crisis came, our main concern was twofold: (a) how to ensure that the program that would emerge from the crisis would lead to a rapid recovery; and (b) how to ensure that the recovery would be sustained. Fortunately, Kemal Dervis, a former

colleague at the Bank and a distinguished economist who understood the importance of structural and institutional reforms, took the post of economy minister. His
arrival ensured that Turkey's response to the 2001 crisis would be different from previous stabilization episodes. The program designed by Turkey's economy team
focused on major fiscal adjustment and financial sector restructuring, which were
successful elements of a quick recovery, very similar to those predicted in a paper by
Brahmbhatt, Burnside, and Demirguc-Kunt (2001):

> Economic downturns have lasted 2–3 quarters, with output falling 8–9 per-
> cent. With recovery, previous peak output has been regained in a median 4–6
> quarters from the trough. We expect Turkey's experience to be similar to the
> median path, given the relatively limited role of bank credit to the private sec-
> tor, less severe than the deeper and more extended recessions in Indonesia and
> Thailand. This judgment assumes quick and decisive progress on fiscal adjust-
> ment and financial restructuring. (p. 3)

In hindsight, this quick assessment by researchers at the Bank of the lessons Turkey
could learn from others was quite prescient. Much credit must go to IMF, not only
for providing support to help design a stabilization program with key structural and
institutional reforms, but also for providing the large upfront financing that helped
establish credibility.

In designing a program that had a real chance to succeed, we were all conscious
that Turkey could learn some useful lessons from countries that had gone through
similar crises in the last decade, especially Argentina and Mexico in 1994; Indonesia,
the Republic of Korea, and Thailand in 1997; and Brazil in 1999. Of that group,
Brazil and Korea were able to generate the quickest turnaround, with output falling
for only two quarters and recovering to precrisis levels within four quarters. If Turkey
could emulate those countries, recovery would be swift. The decline in output in the
countries in crisis in the 1990s had ranged from –2 percent in Brazil to almost –20
percent in Indonesia. Together with Thailand, the latter had also seen a very slow
recovery and had not yet recovered—some four years after the crisis—to precrisis
levels. Would Turkey's recovery be more like the quick recoveries seen in Brazil and
Korea, or would it be more drawn out, as in Thailand and Indonesia?

The answers to this question, we knew, depended on a few key factors:

- Rapidly cleaning up the banking sector

- Implementing a strong fiscal program that would keep inflation under control
  while the real exchange rate adjustment held to ensure rapid growth in exports
  and tourism

- Restoring confidence through decisive structural measures that would signal
  deeper commitment and bring down real interest rates

- Assuming credibility through resolute institutional reforms with respect to the
  regulatory environment

- Strengthening social assistance to help people adversely affected by the crisis, especially women and children

It was not enough simply to clean up the banking sector and put effective regulation in place. Those actions were necessary but, over the long run, insufficient conditions for a healthy banking sector. Serious restructuring and consolidation were needed as well. The normal explanation for the banking crisis is that confidence waned, liquidity dried up, and interest rates duly skyrocketed. That sudden spike is said to have led to a mismatch between liabilities and assets, leading to a crisis. The reality is not so simple. During the 1990s, interest rates spiked in several instances, but only twice—in 1993–94 and 2000–01—did those spikes trigger a banking crisis. During both periods, real interest rates had fallen sharply and turned negative, and the banking sector had been making losses for several quarters before the crisis. Hence, the banking sector's underlying structural problems, not the sudden spike in interest rates alone, contributed to the crisis.

Fundamentally, Turkey had too many banks. By 1999, the number had grown to 81, from fewer than 20 banks in the early 1980s. The ratio of banking assets had grown from 26.7 percent in 1980, to 38.6 percent in 1990, to 71.3 percent by 1999. At the same time, the banks had shifted their financing activity from lending to securities investments. Over time, concentration in the banking sector had declined.[3] An international comparison showed that the Turkish banks had relatively higher net interest margins, close to average overhead costs, and a relatively low concentration index. Entry of new banks had not dented profitability, as nominal and real profits of the sector were on the rise. Because the system's continuation depended on its producing windfall profits from high-interest treasury bills, and because a major drop in interest rates made a crisis inevitable, any stabilization program designed to bring down real interest rates very rapidly would put pressures on the banking system.

The system's structure was incompatible with the needs of Turkey's real economy and with stable public finances. When interest rates fell sharply in both 1993 and 2000, the real economy grew very rapidly, and Turkey's public finances benefited immensely. The banking sector, however, came under enormous pressure and snapped at its weakest points. The structure of the banking sector and the distorted manner in which it had evolved were incompatible with the needs of a stable economic system. As it looked forward, Turkey needed a deeper financial system—but fewer banks. Consolidation and structural changes were important elements of the progress in banking reform, but more remains to be done.

One important issue was how to absorb the enormous losses of the banking crisis (figure 10.5). Some argued that, though quick action was needed, it would entail large upfront costs. Experience elsewhere had shown that, whenever there is a systemic crisis, a large proportion of the losses are taken over by the government, regardless of whether the losses occurred in private sector or public sector banks. In Turkey's case, with 100 percent insurance on deposits irrespective of size, covering the depositors was a public responsibility.[4] More controversial was the coverage extended to creditors in 2001 to contain panic and make tough actions against problem banks possible. Had the credit guarantee not been extended, there might well have been a wider panic in the system and even greater losses—but this is one counterfactual we will never want to test again. The contrast between the experience of Korea, which had a clear and comprehensive plan for banking sector reform and restructuring and upfront guarantees for all liabilities, and of Indonesia, which did not, and the subsequent problems in carrying out banking reforms in Indonesia were instructive to Turkey's economic team (figure 10.6).[5]

With a comprehensive program, the economy recovered strongly in 2002, broadly achieving macroeconomic targets. The country's gross national product (GNP) grew by almost 8 percent in 2002 and by about 5 percent in 2003. The *v*-shaped recovery à la Brazil and Korea was achieved in Turkey, and the slow recovery that we have seen in Indonesia and, to some extent, in Thailand was avoided. A large part of the credit goes to (a) the design of the recovery program, which included a tough fiscal program combined with quick actions in the banking sector and key structural measures that signaled a new determination on Turkey's part to tackle difficult issues, and (b) the abilities of Turkey's economy minister in signaling credibility despite working in a fractious coalition government that clearly lacked consensus on all aspects of the program. Depoliticizing important elements of the program made it possible to implement a sufficient mass of core decisions needed for the program to succeed. A significant achievement was also a permanent drop in the rate of inflation. IMF and the World Bank supported Turkey both financially and technically during this critical period of recovery—with IMF gross financial support of about US$25 billion, supplemented by about US$7 billion from the Bank (including earthquake-related assistance).

FIGURE 10.5
Banking Sector Profit and Loss

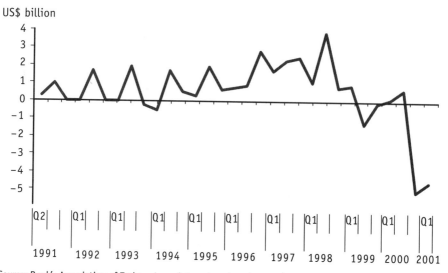

Source: Bank's Association of Turkey, *Annual Report,* various issues.

FIGURE 10.6
Fiscal Costs of Banking Crises since 1990

Percentage of GDP

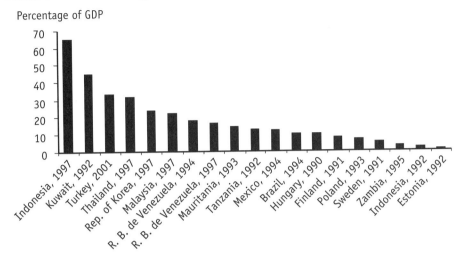

Source: World Bank (2003).

Forging a Balance between the State and the Market

Although, as noted previously, Turkey correctly moved away from a state-led model of development, it did not reposition the state to effectively provide the key institutional features of a modern capitalist state, such as regulation and social safety nets. As a result, a freewheeling capitalist system emerged in the 1980s that privatized the profits but socialized the losses and increased private returns with no individual risk. The reforms of the 1980s, designed to correct government failure, had swung too far in weakening state institutions without replacing them with new effective alternatives, thus making it necessary to correct the new market failures that had emerged.

The clearest examples of that problem were in the banking system and in the energy sector. In the banking sector, as discussed above, regulation capture prevailed. The treasury (on-site supervision) and central bank (off-site supervision) both reported to the economy minister (a politician) and shared the supervision of a corrupted banking system that was riddled with cronyism. With no effective oversight when problems surfaced, they were hidden from disclosure. The banking law—in terms of prudential regulations on loan loss provisioning, connected lending practices, and foreign exchange exposures—was not even close to standards set under the EU directives and the Basel Accord. The deposit insurance agency was under the central bank, and the rules governing when to intervene in banks were unclear. There was no legal framework for creditor rights, bankruptcy, and debt workouts. State banks were distributed to various ministers as political patronage among coalition partners. This system ended up costing the Turkish taxpayer close to 33 percent of GNP to clean up.

Our advice to Turkey well before the 2001 crisis was threefold:

1. Establish an independent regulator.

2. Reissue a new banking law to meet EU and Basle standards.

3. Privatize or close the state banks.

The first two objectives were largely achieved, although it took several attempts before they were effectively put in place. The last objective has not yet been achieved—only one of four state banks (Emlak Bank) was closed. The first attempt at an independent regulator failed because the board was loaded with political appointees. A new board was established, and a very able and courageous head, Engin Akcakoca, took over. The regulatory authority then played a major role in intervening in problem banks and establishing clear rules for intervention and cleanup. More than 20 private banks were eventually closed. The new banking law went through a similar process—it took several amendments to get it close to EU and Basle standards, and unresolved issues remain. An important step down the line is reform of the deposit insurance system, which helped stave off the panic in the 1994 crisis but also created incentives for more risky behavior afterward. Reform, including a limited form of deposit insurance, is needed to bring the system closer to EU levels.

It took almost three years to complete the banking reforms and several minicrises (in 1999 and 2000) and a large crisis (2001) to get the political system to agree to the reforms—the major lesson: *banking reform is possible only when motivated by crisis.* Several people have asked why the banking reform could not have preceded the stabilization program. The answer is that the politicians, bankers, and business community were so deeply involved in benefiting from a distorted banking system that only a crisis could force banking reform. The state banks were used for political patronage and were distributed among political parties.[6] Most of the private banks were owned and used by business groups, often in close partnership with the politicians. Only a crisis could create the conditions for strengthening the state institutions necessary to subject the market to effectively regulated development.

Another lesson from political economy is that one has to persist. Sometimes the initial steps are insufficient, but they help build the base for deeper reforms that are needed or can be pushed during crisis.

The energy sector was another area of imbalance between the state and the market. In an effort to bring the private sector into the electricity market, Turkey had relied on government guarantees, because the legal and regulatory framework did not provide private investors with safeguards that their investments would get adequate returns. But without an independent regulator or competitive bidding, the contracts had become hugely expensive, in some cases costing as much as US$0.15 to US$0.18 per kilowatt-hour. Moreover, the state was taking all the market risk associated with the build-operate-transfer and the related build-operate-own models used to attract private financing.

Those models were unviable because Turkey would be unable to pass on such high costs to the consumer and would be forced to absorb the contingent liabilities into the budget. On the basis of contracts signed by 2000, we estimated that the cumulative contingent liabilities to the Turkish treasury exceeded US$8 billion (figure 10.7).

FIGURE 10.7
Indicative Contingent Liabilities in Power Sector (US$ Million)

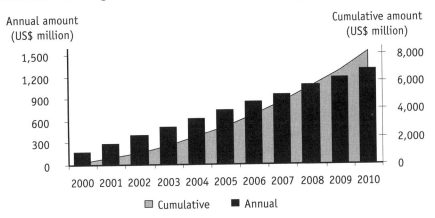

Source: World Bank (2000b).

If Turkey was not careful, energy could become a critical problem for its economic growth (figure 10.8). As part of a global trend, Turkey had turned increasingly
to the private sector to meet its future energy needs. With the crisis and fiscal pressure, Turkey was eventually forced to undertake reforms and to abandon this costly
model. Similar problems had arisen in Pakistan and Indonesia, where costly take-
and-pay contracts were subsequently renegotiated.

FIGURE 10.8
Electricity Prices for Industry

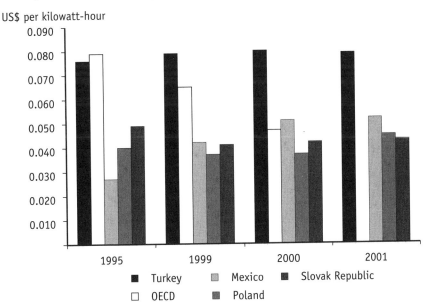

Source: World Bank (2002c).

Our advice was that Turkey must move from the single-buyer model, in which a public distribution company takes on guaranteed and expensive take-or-pay contracts, to a system in which multiple buyers and sellers operate under a well-defined market and regulatory structure. Turkey eventually did adopt this model, and an energy regulator, the Energy Market Regulatory Authority, has gradually established itself in the system.[7] Turkey will be forced to pay off the costs of a decade of expensive contracts. Its energy costs are already among the highest in Europe and are affecting its competitiveness. The lesson—a costly one—is that the market needs strong and effective state institutions working in balance with each other for effective development to take place. Without them, the market does not work efficiently.

Strengthening Civil Society

As Turkey works to improve the effectiveness of the state and strengthen institutions—in banking, energy, and other sectors—it must also begin to address the imbalance that arises from a weak civil society. Without the pressure for change that comes from a well-organized civil society, the reforms remain more top-down and less sustainable once the initial pressure dissipates. Without organized civic institutions, there is no mechanism for channeling citizen demands into a relentless pressure on the system for change. Some difficult reforms need precisely such constant pressure.

One small civil society project that the Bank supported and had huge success with on a very small scale is outlined in box 10.1. Turkey needs more bold and courageous civil society groups to keep the pressure on the system to be transparent and continue the reforms. Such movements keep policymakers aware of citizen interests and provide, in addition to the prospects of EU entry, another avenue for sustaining good programs and reforms more broadly.

With the benefit of hindsight, perhaps the Bank should have placed more emphasis on the role of civil society. Three examples that illustrate this point—one from our work on anticorruption, a second from social assistance, and a third from agriculture and natural resource management—demonstrate why a strong civil society is needed for equitable development.

Example 1: Corruption

Anticorruption was an area where sustaining action and interest calls for a more developed civil society. One way to check corruption was to correct the imbalance between the state and the market by strengthening state institutions to make policy, regulate the market, and reduce economic rents. The introduction of independent regulators in banking and energy and new legislation with much clearer rules and less discretion served this end. State tenders were another source of organized corruption. The initial bids in the tenders were kept low, but after initial contracts had been awarded, cost escalations were regularly approved and paid. Because of kickbacks to politicians, many projects ended up with higher costs than would have been the case in most industrial countries. A new system of state tendering was introduced with more transparent bid-

BOX 10.1
The Children of Hope Project

The Children of Hope was a project started by a former child of the streets, Yusuf Kulca, to help the street children of Istanbul. Kulca understood the problems and psychology of street children. He went on to study education and pedagogy. He realized that the efforts of the municipality were not enough to help the children. He established a laundry in Istanbul in 2000 with Bank support to provide shelter and rehabilitation for street children. Without Kulca's care, understanding, and leadership, the project would have failed. He built a bond between himself and the street children that was instrumental in its success.

Kulca now gives advice to other cities in Turkey on how to set up similar facilities to take care of their street children. Not only has he provided hope and a great service, but also his example demonstrates that civil society initiatives are badly needed in Turkey. The state cannot provide those unique services, either because of financial constraints or because many such projects require a level of dedication and empathy that state institutions are unlikely ever to be able to provide. We were proud to support this type of initiative.

ding procedures and with winning bids made public. Those three areas—banking, energy, and state tenders—provided the bulk of financial flows in the system and areas where massive corruption had been identified. The actions were taken after the 2001 crisis to stop grand corruption. They were visible but top-down actions.

But corruption had also infiltrated the more day-to-day aspects of society, such as customs and basic services. For a more comprehensive attack on corruption, changing the rules was necessary but not sufficient. Turkey benefited from the activism of a growing movement of citizens disgusted with the cumulative impact of corruption and populism that had led to Turkey's poor performance in the 1990s and culminated in the financial crisis from which everyone suffered. Turkey's new president, Ahmet Necdet Sezer, was known for his rectitude and was also a strong supporter of this movement. The World Bank began to support the work of the movement through a Turkish think tank called TESEV (Turkiye Ekonomik ve Sosyal Etudler Vakfi).[8] Despite strong opposition from some members of the government, TESEV Board Chairman Can Paker and Director Ozdem Sanberk began a series of well-publicized surveys on corruption, which we supported financially and publicly. The group's initial surveys made a huge splash and created a greater sense of public awareness of actions against corruption. In the 2002 elections, all political parties tainted by corruption failed to enter parliament. That outcome cannot be traced only to the corruption surveys—but they helped publicize the importance of corruption and the effectiveness of institutions (see figures 10.9 and 10.10).

Example 2: Social Assistance

For some time, the Bank and others had argued that a program for social assistance needed to be revamped and expanded. One of the best ways to help poor families is

FIGURE 10.9

What Is the Most Important Problem That Should Be Resolved in Turkey?

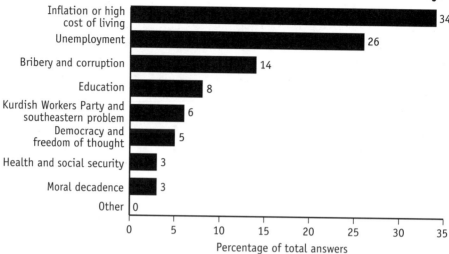

Source: TESEV (2001).

FIGURE 10.10

Trust in Institutions

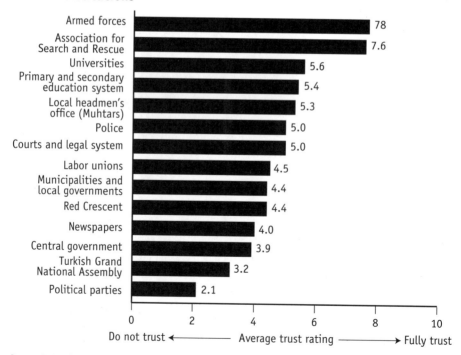

Source: TESEV (2001).

through support for their children to ensure school attendance and health care. If children in Turkey dropped out of school or their health care were neglected, as happens in many crisis-affected countries, the financial crisis would have intergenerational effects on Turkey's human capital and long-term development. If poor families were unable to cope with the crisis, they would pull their children—especially girls—from schools and would neglect their health care. Social assistance to prevent the potential long-term costs was, therefore, vital. Conditional cash transfers had been tried in other countries and had been very successful.

Initially, there was strong resistance to those suggestions. The bureaucracy opposed them because of the costs, and some officials felt such assistance would indicate that Turkey was a poor country. Educators were against it because it was seen to be interfering in Turkey's very rigid and centralized education system. It was not the Turkish way: people did not like charity. Turkey had a small, government-financed social assistance program (less than 0.5 percent of GNP), but Turkish citizens relied on and took pride in strong family and kinship networks to provide informal social assistance. Those strong bonds and generosity were a great strength of Turkish society, but they were not enough for a modern, rapidly urbanizing society. Once the program was unveiled, long lines of parents formed to receive the small handouts, and there was huge demand for the assistance. In rural areas, the program relied heavily on the teachers to provide the funds and to select the families. The program was a success; school enrollment slowed but did not decline, despite the crisis. But in hindsight, more should have been done to convince Turkey to bring civil society, such as parents' associations and other civic organizations, into the equation. Without this type of surveillance and active participation, the viability of the program will always be questioned.

Example 3: Agriculture and Natural Resource Management

One of the most successful projects supported by the Bank was the Eastern Anatolia Watershed Project. It involved helping farmers in Eastern Anatolia reclaim and rehabilitate farmland that had been rendered unproductive because of soil erosion. The project had a slow start in 4 provinces, but it gradually picked up momentum and was extended to 11 provinces in its first phase. The project involved close coordination at the local level among three ministries—agriculture, forestry, and local government—that did not typically coordinate well.

The key to the project's success was intense grassroots farmer involvement in various aspects of the project, thus building strong local ownership. The first phase helped more than 600,000 farmers double their incomes, and the project has become internationally famous, drawing teams from many countries to Turkey to try and emulate its success. But the project has been subject to political indifference because it lacks any forceful civil society involvement. The second phase of the project—to expand it beyond the 11 provinces—has been delayed. The benefit of hindsight shows that the project lacks a civil society champion and institutionalized structures that would ensure that funding is not subject to political influence. Despite the high rates of economic return, the project beneficiaries are spread out and are not organized politically.

Positioning the World Bank in a Middle-Income Country

One of the big challenges the Bank faces in a middle-income country such as Turkey is how to be relevant and effective. The financial resources that the World Bank provides to a typical middle-income country are large for the Bank, but they are quite small in relation to the market and quite small in relation to what is needed at a time of crisis, when compared with the resources provided by IMF and even some bilateral organizations. The World Bank committed more than US$7 billion between fiscal year 1998 and fiscal year 2003—a substantial increase from previous lending to Turkey. But that amount was small relative to the resources Turkey borrowed from private markets—more than US$100 billion every year. It was also a small amount compared with the almost US$25 billion that IMF committed from the end of 1999 to 2003. If the resources the World Bank provides are small, it is vital to determine how best to use them for the country's benefit and how best to leverage them to support the type of policies and institutional strengthening that will benefit the country.

The Bank's primary objective is poverty eradication. But a simplistic approach to poverty has created a growing perception that the Bank is relevant only for poor countries and not for the middle-income countries. The Bank's relevance in middle-income countries has been eroded, partly for reasons beyond its control, such as the availability of large private capital flows, but partly because of internal factors and poor positioning of the Bank's enormous strengths, such as its expertise in establishing the modern institutions for effective market development and growth. Yet those strengths are not always fully exploited or advertised. Because the absolute number of people living on less than US$1 per day is low—just over 2 percent of the population in Turkey in 2001 at the peak of the crisis—people ask whether the Bank should not be reallocating resources to other parts of the world where there are more poor people to assist. Staff members working on middle-income countries at the World Bank are faced with a continuous need to justify their work: in the country, to be relevant, and in the Bank, to justify the program.

Our teams faced those issues in Turkey. In assessing how to be more relevant, we chose to focus our knowledge and capability on delivering very high-quality analytical work and policy advice, especially on structural and institutional reform to achieve stable growth and pay attention to social protection. With an average income per capita of US$3,000, Turkey is a typical middle-income country. But in large parts of Turkey, average incomes are similar to those of a low-income country. Many of Turkey's eastern provinces, where some 15 percent of its people live, have an annual income per capita ranging from US$500 to US$1,000. Moreover, the proportion of the population at less than one-half the median income is around 15 percent, and the proportion of people below a local basic needs basket is as high as 35 to 40 percent. Not only is economic vulnerability more broadly defined high, but so is inequality (figure 10.11). More rapid and sustained growth is likely to be Turkey's best solution

FIGURE 10.11
Inequality in Turkey and Comparator Countries

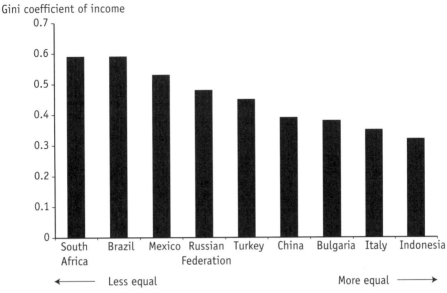

Gini coefficient of income

Source: World Bank (2002c).

for lowering the identified vulnerabilities and modernizing the institutions needed for delivery of social protection.

We made four other strategic decisions that made the Bank a key interlocutor for Turkey:

1. Scaling up by concentrating resources strategically in a few interventions that made a significant effect—rather than scattering thinly across a wide range of issues—and by using programmatic lending

2. Linking interventions to knowledge

3. Partnering effectively—for example, with IMF on crisis-related reforms, with the EU (increasingly) on longer-term reforms, and with the European Investment Bank and the United Nations (especially the United Nations Development Programme and United Nations Children's Fund) on disaster response and social issues

4. Focusing on institutional strengthening so that Turkey would not need our assistance in the future

The Bank program was scaled up by moving from small projects to larger sectoral and programmatic approaches. The average International Bank for Reconstruction and Development loan size increased from US$95 million in fiscal years 1994–97 to US$440 million in fiscal years 1998–2002 (figure 10.12). As a result, the Bank could offer Turkey meaningful support in the areas selected. Also, our support could be used more strategically for policy change and institutional improvements with the

FIGURE 10.12

Scaling Up: Average IBRD Loan Size to Turkey, 1994–2002

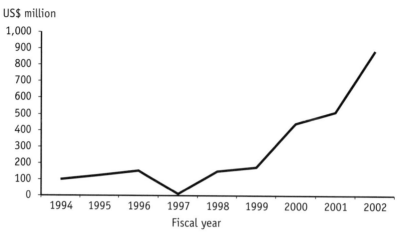

Source: World Bank data.

use of programmatic policy lending. The Bank became a significant adviser to the government in several key areas—energy, telecommunications, agriculture, and education—but chose not to lend for health care and transportation because of insufficient ownership of necessary reforms in those areas.

A second strategic decision was to link knowledge to lending (figure 10.13). Financial or technical support was preceded by careful analysis that was shared with the relevant policymakers and disseminated widely. Even when we provided quick support for Turkey's reconstruction on an emergency basis after the 1999 earthquakes, we carried out a quick assessment of the impact of the disaster, which helped very significantly in shaping the subsequent response.

A third strategic element of the Bank's work in Turkey was working with partners to leverage our effect and support to Turkey. Turkey had no consultative group framework in which to arrange donor coordination. Therefore, the partnerships were created more strategically and individually. The Bank worked in close partnership with the European Investment Bank and the United Nations on the earthquake disaster response, with IMF on the financial crisis response, and—increasingly—with the EU on Turkey's longer-term institutional agenda. The last relationship began to intensify in 2003 as the prospects of EU entry became much more real.

The fourth aspect was helping build institutions that would enable Turkey to help itself in the future. The focus in almost all Bank interventions was not just financing for infrastructure or some service, but also support for institutional capacity building that would ensure that Turkey would not need our support in future. We did not always succeed, but our goals were clear. For example, for reconstruction after the Marmara earthquake, the Bank provided Turkey more than US$1 billion in four roughly equal portions: one-fourth for immediate cash relief for families living in tents; one-fourth for construction of new housing; one-fourth for reconstruction of other infrastructure, such as power lines, roads, schools, and hospitals; and one-fourth

FIGURE 10.13
Linking Knowledge to Lending

Country Economic Memorandum, Turkey: Structural Reforms for Sustainable Growth (World Bank 2000b)	Economic reform loan—Agriculture Reform Implementation Project—Energy policy dialogue Privatization Social Support Project
Public Expenditure and Institutional Reviews	Programmatic loans
Marmara earthquake assessment	Emergency earthquake recovery loan— Marmara Emergency Earthquake Reconstruction Project
Corporate sector: assessment of the impact of the crisis	Contributions to public debate on "Istanbul Approach" Corporate Rehabilitation Project (under preparation)

for a new earthquake insurance system and for the establishment of institutional capacity at the central and local levels to cope with future earthquakes. The insurance scheme came into being, and housing and other reconstruction was a big success, but the institutional capacity to cope with future emergencies remains weak. The intention not just to focus on financing but to ensure that institutional capacity was strengthened was always a key element of the assistance program.

Lessons and Conclusions

As I stated at the opening of this chapter, I draw four key lessons from this tumultuous period of engagement with Turkey and from the backdrop of my work on *World Development Report 1997: The State in a Changing World* (World Bank 1997).

- *Lesson 1: Crisis only provides an opportunity to start reforms and generate recovery.* A successful recovery effort, like Turkey's 2001 program, must focus not only on correcting macroeconomic imbalances, but also—for growth—on key structural and institutional reforms to signal credibility. Turkey's 2001 crisis came after a decade of growing macroeconomic imbalances and inadequate structural and institutional reforms. This painful crisis, foreseen for some time, had been delayed by some deft financial management and a competitive exchange rate policy. Once the crisis came, it was important to emphasize to the Turkish authorities that stabilization alone was not enough. Turkey had emerged quickly from a similar crisis in 1994 through a heavy dose of stabilization, followed quickly by a rapid recovery that was led by strong fiscal stimulus and financed by heavy recourse to domestic debt. In 1999, Turkey put together another reform package, which included some key structural elements, although serious banking reform was excluded. But by 2000, because of the combination of a quick recovery and a feeling among key policymakers that lack of consensus on structural reforms was hurting credibility, the structural elements of the program were not seriously implemented. However, with a major crisis in 2001, Turkey's new economy minister—helped by a strong team—put together a program that included a strong package of structural and institutional reforms.

- *Lesson 2: To maintain sustained and stable growth and to manage volatility, a country needs strong institutional capability, but this effort takes longer.* Other pulls and pressures must be present to create consensus for sustaining the reform process and to overcome reform fatigue. In Turkey's case, the prospect of EU accession provides this pull. With two years of recovery behind us, the structural reforms are slowing down again. The lesson that I draw from this experience, combined with Turkey's history, is that maintaining the momentum for reform that will lead to sustained development requires other pulls and pressures that go beyond the crisis. The prospects and the growing consensus for EU accession are likely to be a major impetus for continuation of structural reforms, as we have seen in southern Europe in the 1970s and early 1980s and over the past few years in Central and Eastern Europe and the Balkan states.

- *Lesson 3: Less politicized and more rule-based institutions must be put in place.* The underlying causes of crises are an ineffective state and the lack of effective checks and balances in the system. This was the case in Turkey, where the reform program strengthened some existing institutions, such as the central bank, and created new ones in banking, energy, and telecommunications to regulate the market more effectively. Turkey moved from a state-dominated, autarchic model of development in the 1960s and 1970s to a mixed model in the 1980s, weakening certain core state economic and regulatory institutions without establishing new regulatory systems to help regulate the market. At the same time, the size of the state was not reduced. Many of the reforms in Turkey, especially following the 2001 crisis but even earlier, were explicitly or implicitly designed with the perspective that the effectiveness of the state had to be improved through institutional strengthening. New regulatory systems for banking, energy, and telecommunications were established. New tendering systems and strengthened social assistance programs were introduced. Fiscal discipline and a new debt law to check borrowing were introduced.

- *Lesson 4: Improving the state's effectiveness also requires a healthy civil society and greater decentralization.* Without those elements, the reforms are perceived as top-down, and other imbalances emerge quickly—especially lack of focus on inequality, corruption, and the environment. Turkey and other emerging markets must allow greater opportunities for civil society and decentralization to sustain the pressure for reform and encourage transparency. Although much was accomplished with a well-designed recovery program in place, it became clear by 2003 that the reforms needed to go much deeper and were often perceived as somewhat top-down. What was missing was a more active role for civil society and decentralization. Without a strong push from below by civil society for reforms—the demand side, so to speak—the likelihood of the sus-

tainability of the program and certain important aspects of sustainability remain
unresolved. Turkey needs a more inclusive participatory development strategy
and greater decentralization to ensure that sufficient attention is placed on
issues like inequality, corruption, and the environment.

In addition to those four lessons on development policy, a more internal lesson
can also usefully be drawn from the World Bank's experience in Turkey, where the
program kept the Bank relevant by focusing on helping achieve stable growth with
attention to social protection. Especially in a middle-income country such as Turkey,
where financial flows from the Bank form a small proportion of overall inflows into
the country, it is necessary to focus on a few carefully selected areas to help develop
the institutional capacity to achieve sustained growth and provide social protection—with good analytical work and financial support, which will produce maximum leverage. A simplistic poverty-focused agenda makes the Bank appear
unrealistic and irrelevant to the needs of middle-income countries.

The effectiveness of the Bank's support to middle-income countries is currently
under some discussion. Questions have arisen for three basic reasons: (a) the Bank's
heavy focus—and some would say simplistic focus—on poverty alleviation has led
many middle-income countries to think that the Bank is no longer interested in the
issues that concern them, because they have a very small proportion of people below
the poverty line; (b) the financial flows from the Bank to middle-income countries
form a very small proportion of overall capital flows to these countries; and (c) lending
to middle-income countries has declined as market access has improved and the costs
of doing business with the Bank have increased. The solution to these issues of the relevance of the World Bank in middle-income countries is threefold: (a) refocus the
attention in the Bank on issues of growth, which are of relevance to both middle- and
low-income countries; (b) focus Bank assistance in middle-income countries strategically on a few relevant areas; and (c) reduce the cost of doing business with the Bank.

During my work on the *World Development Report 1997: The State in a Changing
World* (World Bank 1997), I came to believe very strongly in the importance of institutions. As Napoleon Bonaparte once said, "Men are powerless to secure the future;
institutions alone fix the destinies of nations." I continue to believe in the power of
good institutions to fix nations' destinies. But I also learned that people matter as
well. Through this tumultuous period in Turkey, one saw how people mattered.
Kemal Dervis, as a newly arrived economy minister, made a huge contribution to
Turkey's recovery by designing and implementing a very difficult program in a fractious coalition government. Yusuf Kulca made a huge difference to the street children
of Turkey with his selfless dedication (see box 10.1). Turkey will continue to produce
such leaders when it needs them. But as it moves forward, its institutional strength
and capacity will matter a great deal. If we were able to make a small contribution in
supporting Turkey's building and strengthening its institutional capability, we can say
we made a difference.

But the stakes are even higher. As a young, Muslim, secular democracy, Turkey
could be a role model for many other parts of the world. If Turkey succeeds, it would

blaze a path for many other countries to its east, especially in Central and South Asia. If Turkey fails, many extremist elements would argue that Turkey must return to Islamic fundamentalism. Turkey is not just another middle-income country. It is one with a path of secularism, democracy, and free-market ideas that sent much wider signals all over the world. Turkey is a beacon to many other countries. With greater political stability provided by the new Adalet ve Kalkinma (Justice and Development) Party government and its willingness and leadership on the issue of EU accession, Turkey is moving forward on a range of economic and social issues. I hope it stays firmly on that path.

Notes

1. Despite growing evidence that pegged exchange rates do not work and a realization that Turkey, in 1998, avoided the crisis that afflicted emerging markets with pegged rates, IMF advised Turkey into peg with a currency board–type arrangement (see Fischer 2001).

2. Similar advice was given to Argentina to use a pegged exchange rate for disinflation (see Kuczynski and Williamson 2003).

3. For a more detailed discussion, see Demirguc-Kunt and Levine (1999).

4. This insurance was introduced during the 1994 crisis to contain panic in the system.

5. For a detailed discussion on this issue, see IMF (2003).

6. I often joked with my counterparts that in most countries ministers are provided free housing, cars, travel, and other perks—but never given banks to play around with.

7. An independent regulator was also established for telecommunications.

8. In Turkey, TESEV was more active than Transparency International.

Inder Sud

Former Country Director for the Middle East (1995–2001)

With a degree in engineering from his home state of Punjab, India, and a doctorate in engineering economics (a combination of the two disciplines with focus on optimization models) from Stanford University, Inder Sud says of his interviews for a Young Professional position, "The traditional World Bank economists couldn't really understand what kind of person I was. I thought we could model the world." But his engineering-economics background accorded well with the technical analysis required in the Bank's emerging economic sector work programs, and Inder joined the Bank in 1971.

Inder's tasks during his first years at the Bank ranged across regions and sectors, with a particular focus on urban development, housing, water supply, and transport policy. He recalls a particularly rewarding early assignment in which, at Bank President Robert McNamara's request, he reviewed the prospects for developing countries' entrance in the global shipping industry and concluded that, despite its surface appeal as a lucrative industry, the economics of international shipping was dubious at the time and the developing countries would be better served to remain on the sideline. It was an early instance of Inder's developing philosophy to stand up for his position, regardless of controversy. "I've never been worried about walking on eggshells," he says.

In 1979, Inder became chief of infrastructure for East Asia and the Pacific, beginning a long association with the region. He describes the period as inspiring: "We had good countries, good people, and good projects. Things were happening." He attributes the region's success to its steadfast adherence to economic goals, its home-grown solutions, and its willingness to buck the latest intellectual trends. "We once advised [the Republic of] Korea not to develop an auto industry," Inder recalls. "It's a good thing they didn't listen!"

After more than a decade working on East Asia, Inder became director of cofinancing and financial advisory services, responsible for Bank cofinancing programs with official sources, as well as work on privatization, financing of private sector projects, and development of World Bank guarantees for private sector infrastructure projects. "I had been spoiled by East Asia, where governments were committed to economic reforms," he recalls, but Inder now had to contend with countries that showed less commitment and where success was more elusive. He emerged from the experience with a more sophisticated view of the elements of successful reform. "Reform is trial and error," he says, and though one can—and should—know its general direction and goals from the start, no formulas exist. Seeing how even the Bank's best-laid plans could falter in the absence of sufficient country ownership, he became increasingly convinced that conditionality was futile without client commitment to reform and political consensus to sustain it.

That philosophy served Inder well in his next position, as director of the Middle East Department from 1995 to 2001, responsible for country operations in the Arab Republic of Egypt and the Gulf states—Bahrain, Jordan, Kuwait, Lebanon, Oman, Qatar, Saudi Arabia, Syria, the United Arab Emirates, and the Republic of Yemen. "I tried the best I could to be supportive of the governments' own reform efforts rather than being in front of them," he says. "I don't believe you can succeed by pulling them against their will."

Ready for a change, Inder left the Bank in 2001 and now splits his time between teaching in the Elliot School of International Affairs at George Washington University; serving as managing director of Washington Associates International, an international development consultancy; and working on various nonprofit and philanthropic endeavors. "Every position I've had has brought different challenges," he says. "I've been very lucky." After more than three decades of observing the process of economic reform, Inder says, "Reform is not just mechanical; it's more art than science"—a significant conclusion for an engineer once determined to model the world.

11 Reflections on Development

Inder Sud

WHEN SHAHID HUSAIN, THEN THE VICE PRESIDENT OF HUMAN RESOURCES, PHONED to tell me of senior management's decision to appoint me the country director for the Middle East, I was puzzled. I had spent my career working in Asia. I also had worked a bit in Latin America. I had expressed a desire to work in the transition economies, mostly as a matter of intellectual intrigue and challenge. I knew nothing about the Middle East and had only heard of it as the "backwater" of the World Bank! Husain, as usual, was brief and crisp with his response: "You know development as well as anyone else. The issues are the same. Only the context is different. Besides, we need some fresh perspectives in the Middle East. As you have heard me say, 'Everything is learnable except for basic intelligence.' I am sure you will do just fine."

This brief telephone conversation in March 1995 sealed my fate for the next six years and started what turned out to be for me yet another wonderful stint in my World Bank career. I came to love the Middle East, making many friends in the region. I believe I did make a contribution to the Bank's work in the region. But I also finished my stint much more aware of the difficulties and challenges of implementing economic reforms in a country and of the severe limitations on what the Bank (and outsiders generally) can contribute to the process.

My Prior Views on Development

My thinking on development policy and practice had been conditioned by two key experiences: my work in the 1970s and 1980s in East Asia and the Bank's early work on privatization in the early 1990s, when I headed the department responsible for supporting operational advice on privatization and private financing of infrastructure. Both experiences had put me firmly on the side of policies that were to be tarnished—unnecessarily in my view—by the unfortunate choice of the term the *Washington Consensus*. In those years, I had seen firsthand countries in East Asia transform themselves from low-income to middle- and high-income economies within a short period (figure 11.1). The only cars on the streets when I first visited the Republic of Korea in 1980 as a division chief for urban development were the few official cars, including those assigned generously to the visiting World Bank missions!

Thailand was rapidly emerging in the 1980s as a major exporter and a place of investment for multinational corporations. Rapid growth was making our worries about "poor prospects for the Northeast" obsolete. Malaysia had successfully transformed itself from a commodity producer to a broad-based exporter of industrial goods. On my last visit to China in 1989, I wondered about the enormous change I had seen since my first visit in 1979, a change that has accelerated even more since. Although a lot has been written about the East Asian "miracle," I had the good fortune of being in the middle of it.

What had impressed me the most was the simplicity and pragmatism of the East Asian policymakers. They were perhaps not the deepest economic thinkers. Their ideas were simple and practical—keep your economic balances in check; educate your people; have good infrastructure (some of the best power companies and highway authorities, even in the 1970s, were in East Asia); and be open to the outside world, particularly foreign investment. It is not only what they did but also how they did it that intrigued me. They were single-minded and consistent. I vividly recall the slogan

FIGURE 11.1

East Asia's Growth Was Rapid between 1970 and 1995

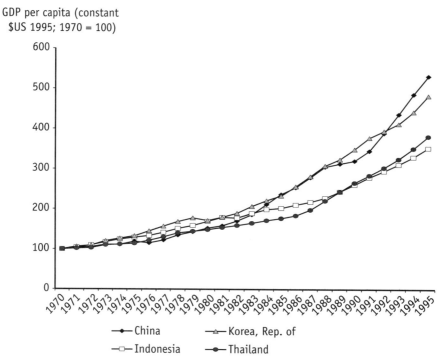

Source: World Development Indicators database.

on the luggage carts at the Seoul airport: "Export is our future." They tended to be pragmatic and not ideological. I remember well a meeting in China in the country's very early years of opening up. The ministry officials responsible for rural water supply left the visiting Bank mission that I was leading nonplussed with a long lecture on why it was so important for everyone to pay for the services they receive. We had gone to the meeting fully expecting to have to convince the communist Chinese about the importance of cost recovery! I could only remark, much to everyone's delayed laughter, "You are lucky you do not have a Socialist Party in China," a joke that reflected my frustration over several poorly performing water projects in India.

So the East Asian experience of the 1970s and 1980s had shaped much of my thinking on development policy. But there was one area where I had been a bit ambivalent. Although several East Asian countries (most notably Malaysia) had embarked on privatization programs of some sort or another, it was not the front end of their reform programs. This pattern arose in part because those countries did not have large state-owned enterprises (SOEs) operating in the commercial sector to start with and also because the SOEs in infrastructure and services were generally well run and, thus, did not present a compelling case for privatization on efficiency grounds. Indeed, in the 1980s, I had been a bit agnostic about privatization. In East Asia, I had been involved in promoting programs for SOE reforms and performance enhancement much more than privatization per se. However, I had also seen in my work in South Asia the tremendous inefficiencies of many SOEs. Most had been serious drains on the treasury. Most had been hijacked by politicians and civil servants for rent-seeking and patronage. I often wondered why South Asians, who in some respects had better human capital, could not have better power companies and highway authorities like those in East Asia.

I was tipped much more strongly toward privatization as an essential component of a reform program after my assignment as the director of cofinancing and financial advisory services in the early 1990s, when I saw firsthand the pervasive problems of SOEs throughout the world. Sadly, the problems of SOE inefficiency and waste were not confined to South Asia. Indeed, I concluded that the good performance of East Asian SOEs was an anomaly that I still cannot fully explain to this day. I came to believe much more strongly in privatization for a number of reasons: as an important instrument for achieving much-needed efficiency gains, as a way to make room in public expenditures for higher-priority needs, and as a positive signal to private investors.

Two other aspects of my East Asian experience had shaped my thinking about development. First, in contrast with most country directors of my time, who tended to come from the ranks of country operations and macroeconomics, I had come to the job with project and sector experiences in transportation, urban development, water supply and sanitation, energy, industry, and finance. My knowledge and experiences in macroeconomic policies were also derived from my sector experiences, first as division chief for industry, trade, and finance for a group of Association of Southeast Asian Nations countries and, subsequently, when I headed the department for privatization and private sector project finance. I was a true believer in the Bank's project work, particularly in projects' being a good vehicle for building institutions.

Project and sector lending was by far the dominant form of Bank lending in East Asia. Virtually every project that the Bank financed was a success. Some of the most successful public sector institutions, particularly in infrastructure, but also in the social sectors, openly acknowledged the positive role of the Bank in their establishment, development, and maturation. Our project staff members—power engineers, urban planners, sanitary engineers, education specialists—were highly respected by the clients. Even successful countries such as the Republic of Korea and Malaysia were reluctant to graduate from the Bank, wanting to continue to benefit from the advice of our sector specialists.

I had developed the view that institution building is done best through sustained project and sector lending, which allows Bank staff members to develop long-term relationships of mutual trust and thus be in a position to offer solid advice. Conversely, I was highly skeptical—and became more so after witnessing numerous failures—of technical assistance as a tool for institutional development and capacity building. This is not to say that our country economists were not respected. Quite to the contrary, several of them (many of whom today deservedly occupy senior positions in the Bank) had done superb economic work that the core ministries appreciated. But because the entire focus of our work was on projects and sectors, I believe it was the project staff that set the tone of the relationship.

Second, I had developed a very jaundiced view of the effectiveness of conditionality as a tool for reform. The East Asians were reforming their economies, not under the Damocles sword of International Monetary Fund (IMF)–World Bank conditionality, but because they believed in the changes. What was impressive was that, while they sought Bank advice liberally, they were the ones who decided what to implement. And when their views differed from Bank advice, it was not a cause for acrimony but rather an understanding among equal partners that there are not always right and wrong answers and, indeed, that there are many ways to skin a cat. Bank staff members also acted with suitable restraint. For one thing, it was hard to argue with success. But also, Bank staff members reciprocated the East Asians' respect for them by doing their best to accommodate the clients' concerns. Although I could never fulfill my desire to do a conditionality-free project, we did our best to keep conditionality to the minimum—normally consistent with what we knew the country would do anyway, and what we could sell to the higher-ups in the Bank! I believe it was Robert Wade who coined the term of Bank staff members as *mediators* between what they know is feasible on the ground and what they know the bureaucracy will demand. Our staff members in East Asia were mediators par excellence!

Despite that role, I also believe that Bank staff members were actually quite influential in helping East Asians formulate and implement development policy. This influence came not from conditionality designed to push them into action. Rather, it was sound advice put to good use by clients who had a clear view and control of their own development agenda. It was a true partnership between equals, with the countries in the driver's seat.

At the same time, when, on occasion, we did find that a client was being difficult, we did not hesitate to walk away, but without the disagreement's becoming an issue of discord. I worked for Gautam Kaji, one of the finest country directors at the time, if not of all times, who did not hesitate (a) to take Bank operations to zero (for example, Thailand in the mid 1980s) if there was not a meeting of the minds and (b) to resuscitate the relationship when we could see common ground. We were never satisfied with a low-level equilibrium in Bank-country relations. We felt that the relationship should go either up or down, but never stay at a level that causes nothing but frustration on both sides. We discovered that even difficult clients like clarity of thinking.

I put this philosophy into practice when I was responsible for supporting the Bank's work on privatization. We had an excellent team of highly experienced professionals who had extensive hands-on experience with the design and implementation of privatization programs. We had decided that we would be happy to provide our best advice to clients who are committed to privatization but who have questions only about details such as sequencing, method, or public awareness. We did our best to stay away from clients who we judged were seeking our help to pacify Bank conditionality through more studies on things such as the benefits of privatization. The approach served us well, with our staff members employed happily in several countries that had made genuine commitments to privatization.

So the most effective operational model, I believed, was not one dominated by conditionality. Rather, it was the Bank being supportive of a client who was clear about pursuing its own development agenda. There are plenty of terms floating around the Bank these days that attempt to describe this type of development: *country ownership*, *client in the driver's seat*, and *home-grown reforms*. But I have not been convinced that those terms are, in reality, practiced in most countries. I was determined to put it into practice when I became a country director.

The Middle East Era

The Middle East, I found, on taking over my position in March 1995, could not have been more different from East Asia. Most countries were facing economic crises of one form or another—stagnant economies that had not experienced much growth in per capita incomes for over a decade (figure 11.2), significant consumption subsidies that were increasingly unaffordable, and large and pervasive public sectors and inefficient civil service. Most countries had maintained fixed exchange rates over many years, with some even maintaining dual or multiple administered exchange rates. Most had yet to adjust to the secular decline in oil prices that affected them negatively through reduced oil revenue or worker remittances or both. In addition, Lebanon and the Republic of Yemen had experienced major civil wars from which they had yet to recover. On the positive side, most countries in the region (except the Republic of Yemen) had invested in education and health, which—along with food subsidies and civil service employment—had kept most of the population above the absolute poverty line. But those programs were not affordable in the new realities of constraints on public expenditures. In addition, the social expenditures faced major problems of efficiency and effectiveness. There was a clear need for economic policy reforms. Yet, commitment to reform was at best half-hearted or—more usually—nonexistent.

FIGURE 11.2

The Middle East's Growth Decelerated after 1985

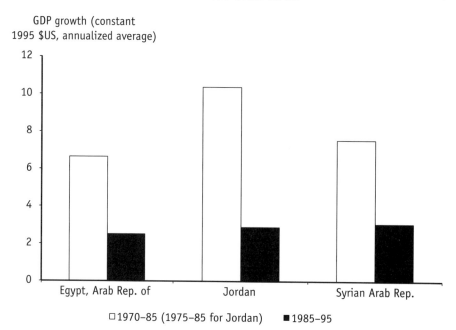

GDP growth (constant
1995 $US, annualized average)

☐ 1970–85 (1975–85 for Jordan)   ■ 1985–95

Source: World Development Indicators database.

Relations with the Bank were strained in most countries, except Jordan. The Bank was blamed by the public in most countries (and continues to be so today) for causing economic hardship and misery. This attitude was surprising given the fact that no country had really undertaken much serious structural reform. In large part, the public did not distinguish between the Bank and IMF, the latter having supported stabilization programs in the Arab Republic of Egypt and Jordan, in both of which riots greeted government attempts to eliminate the bread subsidy. This problem of Bank image, unfortunately, continues even today and is one of the factors that has led me to think about a totally different approach to Bank lending: away from structural adjustment lending with ex ante conditionality to budget support based on ex post performance—but more on this later.

The demand for project lending was modest for different reasons in different countries—reluctance to borrow expensive International Bank for Reconstruction and Development (IBRD) funds (Egypt), more interest in balance of payments support (Jordan), recent civil war (the Republic of Yemen), and nonaccrual status (the Syrian Arab Republic). Lebanon was on the Bank's watch list because of concerns about its economic stability.

This context illustrates why the Middle East had the reputation as the Bank's backwater. Coming enthusiastically to my job, I was determined to change the status quo. Within the overall environment discussed earlier, the individual country circumstances, of course, varied. So our approach to bringing about change in each country was also different. In the following sections, I will first review the experience in each country during my tenure as country director. From those summaries, I will draw some lessons about development generally and policy reform specifically.

Country Experiences

My department handled Bank work in five eligible developing countries—Egypt, Jordan, Lebanon, Syria, and the Republic of Yemen—and the six oil-exporting Gulf Cooperation Council (GCC) countries, where we provided reimbursable technical assistance. The developing countries varied from very low-income (Republic of Yemen) to middle-income (Lebanon) and in between. Each needed reform to get out of economic stagnation and to create more jobs for growing populations. Lebanon and the Republic of Yemen had the additional burden of postwar recovery. Each undertook reforms in varying fashion and with a varying degree of commitment and success. Each offers a unique ex post perspective that I discuss below. The GCC countries—Bahrain, Kuwait, Oman, Qatar, Saudi Arabia, and the United Arab Emirates—also undertook reforms, in some cases with Bank advice. However, their experiences are rather unique reflections of their position as capital-surplus countries, and the Bank's role was quite limited. I do not, therefore, discuss them in this chapter.

Egypt: The Pretend Reformer

Egypt is the acknowledged leader in the Arab world. It is the largest country (in terms of population) and the largest developing economy in the region (excluding the GCC countries). But its importance also derives from its history and politics. It has been a close ally of the United States since it made peace with Israel in 1979, ties that give it considerable clout in the region and with the donors. So a natural thing for me to do when taking over as director was to visit Egypt. This plan, however, turned out to be not so simple and revealed some important issues between Egypt and the Bank.

The first response from Egypt to my expressed desire for a visit resulted in the usual polite response that I was most welcome to visit but that the "timing was not convenient for the government." I did not think much of that response and went on to visit other countries first. But when, in the next four months, we still had not found a mutually convenient time, I became concerned. Fortunately, Khalid Ikram, an old Egypt hand who was highly regarded by the Egyptians and who became country director for Egypt when the Bank reorganized the Middle East Department, had taken over at about the same time as the Bank's resident representative in Cairo. In due course, Ikram was to discover that the Egyptians' reluctance to receive me was based on the apprehension that, as had apparently been done by some others before me, yet another Bank manager would lecture them yet again about their reform program.

Thanks to Ikram's personal relations at the highest levels of the government, I conveyed to the Egyptian officials my message: I wanted to come simply to see what was working and what was not, and I had no agenda to pursue. I also assured them that I did not plan any press statements that would embarrass them.

The visit was thus arranged for late summer of 1995. I was received most warmly. The Egyptians are gracious hosts. They have a long history and an ancient culture (of course, an understatement!). The government officials had taken me at my word and used the visit as an opportunity to educate me from their perspective on their development priorities and relations with the Bank. On my part, I was determined to be true to my word and be a listener.

The Egyptians had two gripes. First, they detested the Bank's pushing them on economic reforms, believing that what they had done was quite adequate. Second, they expressed unease with the Bank's pushing lending on them when they had ready access to significant bilateral grants. They acknowledged the Bank's intellectual contributions and hoped that we could find ways to help them technically.

The complaint about the Bank's being too pushy on economic reforms is an interesting story that offers some pertinent lessons. By virtue of having signed the peace treaty with Israel and its subsequent pro–United States stance during the first Gulf War, Egypt had won very significant support from the United States and other Group of Seven (G-7) members. That support included a virtual write-off of its large debt to the G-7. However, as a condition of this debt write-off, the G-7 had imposed the customary requirement: having an agreed IMF program in place, with successive tranches of debt relief being linked to continued compliance. The main elements of the program were the customary IMF fiscal and monetary targets. The principal conditionality on structural reforms was defined targets for privatization of SOEs. Unlike programs in most other countries, the IMF program was not accompanied by a Bank structural adjustment program, because the Egyptians presumably did not need more money. Rather, the Bank had agreed to be the monitor for the privatization program. The program included nothing (or not much, as I recall) on regulatory reforms or exchange rate policies—the former, I suppose, because of the difficulty of defining a meaningful program absent a willing client in an inherently difficult area (discussed more later), and the latter because IMF was perhaps unable to carry the day with the Egyptians and had obfuscated the issue through the usual phrases such as "improving competitiveness through productivity improvements."

My briefings had advised me that the Egyptians were not committed to economic policy reforms, and my discussions in Cairo certainly confirmed that view. It was clear that they saw the IMF agreement purely as a way to get their debt write-off through and as nothing more. IMF was in an untenable position. Even though in theory it had the ability to obstruct or delay the debt write-off, in practice IMF understood that some members of the G-7 were not beyond pressuring it to take an understanding view of Egypt. But IMF had to go through at least the semblance of some monitoring to satisfy its board of directors. It was truly caught between a rock and a hard place.

The Bank's monitoring role puzzled me. Our staff members had been clear that the Egyptians were unlikely to implement agreements on privatization, for which the United States had provided an enormous amount of technical assistance that had resulted in nothing more than massive studies by highly paid foreign consultants that lined the shelves of the privatization ministry. Moreover, the Bank had virtually no leverage (although I have little faith in Bank leverage as a way to influence government behavior), given that Egypt did not want or need Bank lending. Under those circumstances, the only value added by the Bank was the nuisance value of making pronouncements from time to time about the "slow pace of privatization" and of throwing sand in the well-oiled Egyptian machine that was nicely and surely headed toward debt write-off.

I was also very skeptical of the argument that, by staying involved, we could add value to Egyptian thinking. The Egyptian officials individually were as qualified and competent as any of us. They surely did not need the Bank staff to teach them about the concept of economic reforms. What were clearly inhibiting a serious reform effort were political considerations—some well founded and perhaps others simply a fear of the unknown. We had little to offer the Egyptians on this score. My Asian experience had taught me that our advice is good when the client knows what it wants and uses the excellent Bank staff for cross-country experiences that can refine the approach and ensure smooth implementation. Absent the political will, we could never turn a country into a reformer by sheer force of our technical advice.

Soon after my return, I convinced my bosses that we were spinning our wheels in Egypt on economic policy reforms. We decided (to the chagrin of IMF) to withdraw from monitoring privatization. It was not that I did not believe in privatization. Quite to the contrary, I was, and continue to be, a strong proponent. But I also had a strong belief that unless the policymakers at the highest levels believed in the private sector, any external pressure to force the issue was virtually assured of failure. In Egypt, as it turned out, IMF eventually declared the country in compliance. The debt write-off was completed, and the privatization program continued to founder. On the positive side, I earned some good and lasting personal friendships with the Egyptians.

The Egyptian economy was (and to some extent continues to be today) mired in serious structural problems—regulatory impediments, a state-owned financial sector with administered interest rates, an overvalued exchange rate, and a poor quality of civil service. What it needed was not just a push on privatization (which had become the focus of dialogue on policy reforms between the Bank and Egypt), but also a comprehensive package of reforms that over time could transform the economy into a more efficient private sector and an export-led economy that created sufficient jobs to absorb the still growing, young labor force. However, such a reform could succeed only if the Egyptians themselves came to the conclusion—as the Indians did in the early 1990s—that continued slow growth is untenable. With the good fortune of having abundant grant flows from bilateral donors, Egypt was in a good position to defer reforms for political reasons. It was surprising that donors did not see the contradiction of pushing reforms with one hand while with the other hand pouring in large sums of aid that allowed the Egyptians to delay reforms. The Egyptian case is an illustration of how aid can sometimes not only not do good but also cause harm.

The second complaint about the Bank's pushing lending had an equally bizarre story. Egypt's per capita income meant that it was still eligible for International Development Association (IDA) funds. But some in the Bank questioned this status, given that Egypt was receiving large amounts in grants from bilateral donors and because of its creditworthiness for borrowing IBRD funds. Egypt, on its part, had no interest in IBRD borrowing because of its access to large amounts of soft bilateral funds. It found IBRD loans too expensive, anyway. So it preferred to borrow only IDA funds (although many in Egypt found even the IDA terms too onerous). The compromise reached permitted the Bank to continue to give Egypt some IDA funds (about US$150 million per year), provided that there was a 50:50 blend between IDA and IBRD funds in Egypt's overall program. Egypt had accepted this compromise, but in practice it found reasons either not to go forward with the IBRD projects at all or, for blend projects, to cancel the Bank-loan portion during project implementation. In some cases, Bank staff members had worked hard to develop a project for IBRD lending only to be told by the Egyptian officials, at a very late stage, that the Egyptians had changed their minds about the project or that a bilateral donor had decided to fund the project as a grant. That situation caused a lot of consternation in the Bank and inevitably caused friction with the Egyptian authorities. Those problems underlay the Egyptian complaint about the Bank's pushing lending.

I could not find any merit in the Bank's position. Forcing an IBRD loan on Egypt just so we could justify IDA lending to the Bank's Board of Executive Directors made no sense. Egypt's access to other, more favorable external sources made borrowing from the Bank unnecessary. I was able again to convince my bosses that we should go with a small IDA-only program, focusing on a few sectors where we had positive experience (such as agriculture) and on the social sectors. (The Egyptian Social Fund, which we funded, has become one of the most successful social funds in the world.) Again, the Egyptians were grateful for the decision. But it did not satisfy the internal needs of the Bank—Bank staff members were unhappy with having less work, and Bank management was unhappy about the modest program for a country as large and important as Egypt. It illustrated how lending can sometimes become a perverse motive in the Bank (and, I am sure, among other donors as well).

Jordan: The Willing Reformer

Jordan was the only country in the region to have embarked on an economic reform program—one supported by both IMF and the World Bank. Relations between Jordan and the Bank were excellent. The reform had been considered a success (as measured by renewed growth). Yet in Jordan, too, the Bank and IMF were very unpopular among the population for having imposed hardships on the people—a situation that never changed during my six-year tenure and that I believe continues today. I will explore possible reasons for it later in the chapter.

Jordan's reform efforts started in 1989, forced by a financial crisis. Not having adjusted to the decline in oil prices, which reduced its worker remittances and aid flows, in the early 1980s, Jordan had borrowed heavily with the hope that the crisis would be temporary. By 1989, the situation had become critical. Per capita gross domestic product (GDP) growth had been negative for several years, both because of a slowdown in growth and because of continued rapid population increase. Per capita consumption had declined by about 30 percent since 1985, and the fiscal deficit had grown to 12 to 15 percent of GDP in 1987–89. The debt–to–gross national product ratio for civilian debt stood at 100 percent and considerably higher when the substantial military debt Jordan had contracted in the 1980s was included. Reserves had dwindled to two weeks of imports. Jordan was unable to meet its debt-service obligations.

IMF responded with the classic stabilization program, with a major fiscal adjustment at its heart. The Bank provided additional support through an industry and trade policy adjustment loan, with tariff reforms as the main ingredient. IMF and Bank support was instrumental in turning things around, helped also by the construction boom that ensued as several hundred thousand Jordanian workers were forced to return to Jordan from the Gulf countries after the first Gulf War (Kuwait and Saudi Arabia considered Jordan to have been on the wrong side) and invested their savings in housing. The agreement with IMF allowed Jordan to reach the first of several agreements to follow with the Paris club on debt reduction and rescheduling. The economy was recovering in the early 1990s, with growth reaching double digits in 1992.

Interestingly, reforms were not much discussed in the years immediately after the initial stabilization. Perhaps the initial growth spurt had made the policymakers complacent. IMF had, of course, converted its standby program to an extended fund facility and had been closely monitoring fiscal and monetary policy. But there is no evidence that much was being done on the much-needed, longer-term structural reforms. The Bank provided two sector adjustment loans in late 1993 and 1994, for energy and agriculture. The two loans were developed quickly to respond to a deteriorating reserve situation; Jordan faced an unanticipated problem of redemption of Jordanian dinars held by the Palestinians in the West Bank and Gaza following the first Oslo Accord. Both of the loans had reasonable sector objectives. But when I arrived in 1995, both faced major problems of delays in compliance with conditionality (and, hence, tranche release). I had to waive some conditions that, while useful, were not based on a realistic assessment of implementation capacity or feasibility. Most important, looking back, one has to wonder why the Bank (and the government of Jordan) chose to start the structural reforms with these two sectors when neither was critical to renewed growth. Preoccupation with reserve buildup (through Bank adjustment loans and IMF facilities) appears to have been the main motive instead.

Nevertheless, the concept of economic reforms had been well entrenched in the Jordanian thinking. When I arrived in 1995, our staff was about to appraise the next trade policy adjustment loan. The Country Assistance Strategy envisaged Bank support largely in the form of adjustment lending to support the government's reform program. A secondary goal that often seemed in the following three years like a primary one was to use adjustment loans from the Bank along with bilateral cofinancing to continue to build up reserves that still remained in the uncomfortable zone of under three months' worth of imports. Further tariff reforms (mostly reduction and rationalization) and support for export institutions were planned to be the principal focus of this second trade adjustment loan. However, during the internal review of the loan, my operations adviser, an old and seasoned Jordan hand highly regarded by the Jordanians, suggested a very interesting alternative approach to the operation.

A few months earlier, my lead economist had arranged a visit to Jordan by Her‐
nan Buchi, previously minister of finance of Chile, to share with the Jordanians the
Chilean experience with economic reforms. Buchi, who made quite an impression
on the Jordanians, pointed out the following key lessons from the Chilean experi‐
ence: (a) it was important to consider the reform not in a piecemeal fashion but as a
comprehensive package that everyone buys into; (b) the broad package should rep‐
resent the long‐term vision and goals; and (c) actions should be sequenced and taken
opportunistically, depending on the circumstances at any given time and the politi‐
cal space available. Buchi was quite critical of the standard tranche conditionality of
the international financial institutions, saying that it tended to narrow the room for
action and that, in any event, it was utterly unrealistic to have an advance blueprint
for actions for structural reforms in an inherently uncertain environment. The pro‐
posed trade policy loan fitted none of Buchi's directions. Fortunately, we had an
excellent team working on the loan that, to its credit, saw the merit of an approach
different from what it had gone quite far with. My discussions with our key inter‐
locutor, the minister of planning, indicated her strong support for the revised
approach. Within three months, our team had converted the trade policy loan to the
first of a series of economic reform and development loans or (ERDL‐I) that were
to change qualitatively the nature of the discussion about reforms in Jordan.

ERDL‐I set out a three‐ to five‐year vision for reform in four key areas that we
(the Bank and government) believed should underpin growth in Jordan: trade, pri‐
vate investment, privatization, and the financial sector. The government took what‐
ever actions were feasible in each of the areas, going further where its thinking was
the most advanced and taking only initial preparatory steps where it was not quite
ready. We converted the loan into a single‐tranche operation, with the entire loan
disbursed on the basis of prior actions. The government also identified tentative
actions it would take in the second and third years but without tying itself to them
as hard conditions. The second and third ERDLs followed in the next two years,
building on the same concept. I particularly pushed for single‐tranche operations, in
part to take to heart Buchi's admonition about the folly of tranched loans. But I also
thought that this approach could be one way to get around the criticisms of the
Bank's dictating reforms to the government, because the loan was made on the basis
of the government's own prior action and no further conditions were required. I was
grateful to see that both the regional chief economist and the vice president imme‐
diately saw merit in the approach and subsequently helped us shepherd the concept
through the Operations Committee and the Executive Board.

Using a series of single‐tranche reform loans worked reasonably well, providing a
much more predictable source of financing to the government. (The minister of
finance often complained, in part based on the protracted tranche release problems
we had faced for the previous two sector adjustment loans, that Bank financing was
unpredictable and that he could not plan his budget as a result. He very much liked
the predictability of IMF financing.) The reformers in the government felt that the
practice strengthened their hand in pushing reforms. (The government was less than
united on the subject, given continued public criticisms and negative reactions from

the reconstituted parliament, which was much more independent than the rubber-stamp parliaments of the past.) The economy grew at about 3.5 percent per year in 1995–2001—much less than the 6 percent target everyone felt was necessary to create adequate jobs, but nevertheless comparable to average growth in the Middle East and North Africa and in Europe and Central Asia, and better than that in Latin America (figure 11.3). Of course, it was nowhere close to the high growth Asia experienced in the period. This performance is certainly not remarkable, but it was not too shabby, particularly when considered in the context of an unsettled region.

Yet, in retrospect, several shortcomings also existed. The Jordanian people continued to be highly critical of the reform program and of the Bank and IMF as the purveyors of hardship. We continued to agonize about the reasons for this disconnect between what we (the government and the Bank and IMF) were seeing and what the people perceived to be the case. Particularly with the benefit of hindsight, I can think of at least the following reasons: (a) the growth, while respectable, was still not high enough to create sufficient jobs for the new labor force entrants; (b) unemployment, as a result, continued at 15 percent or more; and (c) the reforms were carried out largely by the technocrats, with the political leadership remaining above the fray and doing little to own or sell the rationale for reforms to the people. The sub-

FIGURE 11.3

Jordan Performed Well Relative to Most Developing Regions in the Late 1990s

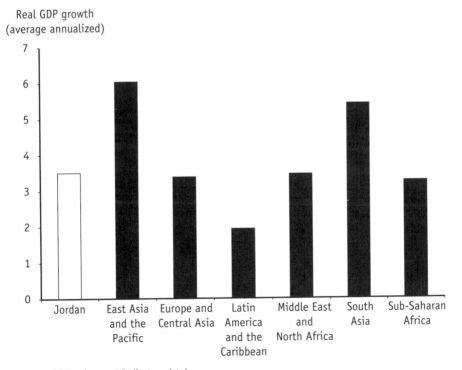

Source: World Development Indicators database.

tlety of our approach of single-tranche loans with no conditionality escaped most Jordanians who, not without justification, assumed that the Bank had had a hand in determining the prior actions.

Often wondering what more Jordan could have done to achieve higher growth, I have drawn three conclusions. First, to the extent Jordan aspired (and still aspires) to an export-led economy (as in Mauritius and Chile), it is difficult to reconcile the fixed exchange rate policy that it has followed with the IMF's blessing. The rationale for the policy of exchange rate–based macroeconomic stability is understandable, given the difficulty Jordan has had maintaining fiscal discipline. But this gain has come at the expense of keeping the cost of labor high and thus retarding labor-intensive exports. Basic tenets of economics tell us that to promote exports and create jobs, the cost of tradables vis-à-vis nontradables and labor vis-à-vis capital should decline. Giving up exchange rate flexibility takes away an important policy instrument.

Theory aside, the most compelling argument I find against fixed exchange rates is that not one country in the world has maintained export dynamism at fixed exchange rates. The source of trade friction, I recall, between the Republic of Korea and the United States in the 1980s used to be the U.S. allegation that Korea maintained the won artificially low. The same issue has arisen in recent years vis-à-vis China.

Second, in our discussions, businesspeople often used to report about the lethargy and lack of responsiveness of the Jordanian civil service when timely decisions were needed. It is difficult to quantify this aspect, but it certainly played a role in the attitude of investors. Businesspeople often cited the very slow and halting progress on privatization in 1995–99 as illustrative of Jordanian ambivalence toward the private sector.

Third, I believe that both of the previous issues are linked to the lack of visible high-level leadership mentioned earlier. Besides the technocrats, I do not recall any of the leaders—the prime minister or the king—talking about reforms openly and frankly. There was nowhere close to the selling of reforms I had seen in China when Deng Xiaoping was often seen on television explaining why all Chinese "cannot eat from the same bowl." Since ascending the throne in 1999, King Abdullah II has taken a much stronger interest in, and leadership on, economic issues; this involvement bodes well for the Jordanian future. I would rank his "Jordan First" initiative of the past two or three years as among the best examples of motivating people toward high goals. Leadership matters.

With adjustment lending occupying most of our operational dialogue and resources during the period, there was not much room for project lending. We did finance a few projects that performed satisfactorily. But I had increasingly become skeptical of their value given their increasing claim on staff resources to meet growing Bank fiduciary requirements and the limited effect we could have with so few possible projects. In the latter part of my tenure, I tried to persuade the Jordanians and the country team in the Bank to move our entire lending to budget support while using the Bank's excellent sector skills for analytical support for the government. The idea generated a lot of resistance from the Bank's sector staff, and I did not persevere in the limited time available. Reflecting further since leaving the Bank, I am even more convinced that this approach must be the future if the Bank is to stay relevant, particularly in middle-income countries. I also feel that such an approach would avoid the outstanding problems of negative public perceptions of adjustment loans.

The Republic of Yemen: The Constrained Reformer

In 1995, the Republic of Yemen was not on anybody's map. It had not yet been linked to terror. Osama bin Laden was an obscure figure, with only tenuous links to the country. Outsiders only knew the Republic of Yemen as a peculiar country with rather fascinating tribal traditions. The Bank had had an active lending program in the previous People's Democratic Republic of Yemen and Arab Republic of Yemen, but Bank projects had suffered badly in the early 1990s, first from the consequences of unifying two diametrically opposed economic systems and later from the ensuing civil war. When I arrived in 1995, there was a lot of pessimism about the Republic of Yemen in the Bank. The combined economy was highly distorted. It looked as if it had joined the poor economic policies of the communist People's Democratic Republic of Yemen with the poor governance of the Arab Republic of Yemen. Most development projects supported by the Bank and other donors had come to a standstill. New Bank lending had naturally come to a halt. Our country operations staff had little faith in the government of the Republic of Yemen—in its capacity and in its commitment to development. Interestingly, our sector staff felt differently, asserting that the Republic of Yemen was not different from any other low-income country. They pointed out that there were, indeed, some very good people in the government (as evidenced by the well-performing portfolio in the People's Democratic Republic of Yemen in the past) and argued that it was only a matter of helping them with the difficult position before we would see improvements.

Experience in the following five years was to prove our sector staff right. When I left in 2001, the Republic of Yemen had implemented an economic reform program. Bank lending had grown to about US$200 million per year from virtually nil five years before. Portfolio performance had gone from highly unsatisfactory to satisfactory. The Yemenis, indeed, deserve a great deal of credit for this turnaround. But so does the Bank staff, which persevered under difficult circumstances.

The economic reform program in the Republic of Yemen had to be kept simple and held to only those critical actions that could be taken within the limited capacity of the government. The issues of first order were to reduce the fiscal deficit by (a) eliminating the multiple, administered exchange rate and creating a single, market-driven exchange rate and (b) simplifying and collecting trade taxes. Both actions brought immediate results. The exchange rate stabilized at 125 rials per U.S. dollar (official rates were 12 and 50 rials), somewhat lower than the prevailing black-market rate. Tax collections improved largely because of the greater simplicity and higher valuation of imports at market exchange rate. Financial support from IMF and the Bank allowed the government not to have to cut its already inadequate (but quite inefficient) development expenditures. The IMF program allowed the Republic of Yemen to receive substantial debt write-off at the Paris Club. A small IDA credit helped the country buy back most of its outstanding commercial debt at a deep discount.

Growth rose immediately to 6 percent in 1996 and to 8 percent in 1997. In the following years, the Republic of Yemen also removed the highly distortionary and wasteful flour subsidies. Not surprisingly, farmers began to grow wheat, a crop they had abandoned. Unfortunately, domestic khat production also increased, in part because the previous strict controls in the South broke down as democracy of a sort in the new Republic of Yemen brought the tribes back to positions of power and in part because importation from neighboring countries became more expensive. Throughout my tenure (and I suspect since then, too), we struggled with trying to find solutions to the khat problem through a number of studies. But alas, no solutions emerged. It remains a very difficult and possibly intractable problem in the Republic of Yemen for some time to come.

The issue the Republic of Yemen faces is what to do next. It needs all the other elements of reform—shedding the public enterprises that have been a drain on the economy, having a competitive banking sector, and inviting greater private investment. But all those factors require a much stronger institutional capacity than the country currently possesses. Its civil service is highly inefficient and loaded with lots of ghost employees and people who owe their allegiances to their tribes instead of to the government. There is also a lack of adequate numbers of qualified people. Private sector people told me that corruption was very high. Although we tried the usual civil service reform programs, my honest view is that the chances of those making a meaningful difference are small. I personally saw them as providing a basis for giving the Republic of Yemen some budget support, because there were limits to the numbers of projects we could support within the constraints of Bank administrative resources and the limited capacity of the country.

So the Republic of Yemen is a country with the political will and leadership for reform (President Ali Abdallah Salah was one of the few Arab leaders who talked about the necessity of economic reforms), but it lacks the capacity. Donors unfortunately cannot fill the capacity gap through technical assistance. The poor record of technical assistance is well documented in Operations Evaluation Department studies. I had seen its wastefulness firsthand in many countries, including the Republic of Yemen. It will take a long time for the country's institutions to become more competent. Over time much will be learned by doing. There are few shortcuts. Moreover, as in many other oil exporters, the will for reform in the Republic of Yemen tends to stall when oil prices are high, as they are now. Again, Yemenis themselves have to decide (as did the Malaysians in the late 1980s) whether they want to continue to live off oil or whether they must reform and diversify for a future when oil may not provide a sufficient cushion.

Before leaving the Republic of Yemen, I will make a brief aside on project lending. As I noted earlier, the successful reforms (largely stabilization actions) allowed us to substantially increase our project lending. We opened a resident mission and posted a number of sector staff members in Sana'a. We were also able to recruit some excellent Republic of Yemen staff members—all former civil servants who performed admirably with improved pay. Portfolio performance improved dramatically. Some of our projects were exemplary—the Social Fund, the Public Works Project, the Flood

Control Project, the Tihama Agriculture Projects, just to name a few. But I still question whether our projects were not simply isolated islands of good practice with little effect on improving overall governance in the country. They also created some perverse incentives for government staff members working on them; these civil servants never wanted to see a project end or always wanted a successor project so as not to lose the better pay provided by the project.

Similar perverse incentives affected Bank staff members as well. Despite my strong attempt to have a sharper focus in Bank operations around a limited set of issues, I was under constant pressure from sector staff members to get into additional areas that corresponded to their areas of interest and expertise. Resisting such pressures, which I tried my best to do, was not easy. It was difficult to convince Bank staff members that just because a problem is important is not reason enough for the Bank to get involved. I have concluded that project lending cannot continue to be the underpinning of development 60 years after this mode first originated in thinking about development assistance. However, I am not sanguine about change because of the abovementioned incentive system for project lending both in the Bank and in the country.

Lessons in Development

As the foregoing experiences illustrate, my journey through the Middle East was far from being in the backwater about which I had been warned. We tried different things. We improved lending. Some countries even undertook reforms. One country—Lebanon—marched to its own tune in managing the economy, often in contradiction to Bank advice (see box 11.1). Did we succeed? It is difficult to say. In a narrow sense of the Bank—judging by the lending outcomes, good policy dialogue, and satisfactory outcomes of the country strategies as assessed by the Operations Evaluation Department—we probably were quite successful. But stepping back and taking a dispassionate look at continuing poor economic performance in most countries, as illustrated by the recent *Arab Human Development Report* (United Nations Development Programme 2003), one would have to be much less sanguine. Despite the best of intentions, most countries in the Middle East are yet to emerge from the low-growth trap and far from the much-needed 6+ percent growth that can have a noticeable effect on job creation (see figure 11.4). The somewhat better growth in Egypt and the Republic of Yemen is driven respectively by periodic spurts in oil prices and continued generous aid flows rather than by a basic restructuring of the economy. This apparent contradiction between the Bank's definition of success and the reality on the ground figures in my reflections on lessons in development.

A Renewed Emphasis on Growth Should Be Given Priority

One clear lesson stands out from the development experience of the past 60 years: countries that have grown and grown consistently have done much better than countries that have not. They have improved the incomes of all their citizens and

FIGURE 11.4

The Growth of the Middle East Has Been Uneven in the Late 1990s

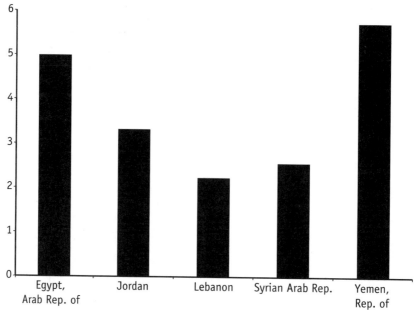

Real GDP growth
(average annualized)

Source: World Development Indicators database.

been successful as well in improving their social indicators. To me, the case is compelling. Yes, growth has not solved all the problems of society that idealists would like to see: income distribution may indeed worsen (although the evidence on this is not compelling); it may cause environmental degradation (but one does see improvements when incomes go beyond a certain level—witness Bangkok); and, yes, it may not immediately bring about Amartya Sen's "development is freedom" dream or the World Bank's vision of "empowerment" of the poor. But even on those counts, I believe that growing incomes do bring progress. It is just that we are unable to model such societal transformations. Growth underlies the happy story of East Asia. A lack of growth explains the continuing dissatisfaction in the Middle East.

If the case for growth is so compelling, as I believe it is, then why has it not received the single-minded attention of development institutions such as the World Bank? One has seen few Country Assistance Strategies that thoroughly discuss why a country has not grown and what it (or the Bank) may have been doing wrong. My speculation is that the failure of many countries to achieve sustained growth has led development practitioners to doubt the value of growth rather than to redouble their efforts. As I discuss below, growth is not an assured outcome, despite the best of intentions; the world of the 1990s was—and that of the 21st century is—much tougher than the world of the 1970s and 1980s, when the East Asian economies

BOX 11.1
Lebanon: The Mystery Economy

Lebanon stands out as a country quite apart from others in the Middle East—and elsewhere, for that matter. Whereas the rest of the Middle East needs a more dynamic and functional private sector, Lebanon needs a proper public sector. There are no national account data available; these data are derived from the financial sector flows. There has not been a census for many years, and there are no prospects of one happening in the near future because of the fear that it will most certainly upset current assumptions of ethnic balance. Lebanon has been running huge fiscal deficits for the past 15 years and somehow is able to sustain them. The exchange rate had been—and continues to be to this day—pegged to the U.S. dollar. Yet Lebanon has made an impressive recovery from a devastating civil war. Things do not quite add up.

My initial briefing on Lebanon talked about an impending collapse of the economy. Its external debt had reached some 120 percent of GDP and was growing. It had been running a primary deficit for the past 2 to 3 years. The government had continued to maintain an expansive fiscal stance to meet the massive needs for physical reconstruction. It was placing its bets on the postreconstruction economy to bail it out. It showed no inclination to accept IMF and Bank recommendations for structural reforms that would bring the much-needed fiscal correction.

The macroeconomic situation in Lebanon continued to deteriorate over the five years that I was there, and it has deteriorated even further since then. The debt-to-GDP ratio now is about 200 percent. A few measures have been taken to augment revenues and reduce expenditures, but both IMF and the Bank considered them insufficient. The alarms of an imminent collapse in the Bank (and IMF) have been ringing louder and louder. Yet Lebanon continues to manage and, by some standards, even to thrive. Growth, though not adequate, is still positive. Lebanon has consistently declined all offers from the Bank for adjustment loans.

There are various plausible explanations offered for this mystery of Lebanon's ability to defy the dire predictions. Perhaps the economy is a lot larger than that captured by the derived national accounts. Perhaps the private economy is much more dynamic than we think. Or perhaps the government's approach to growing out of the problems is the right strategy. All I can say is that so far none of the dire predictions of collapse has materialized fully 10 years after they were first made. It makes me wonder if perhaps our crystal ball is not as good as we think. Lebanon so far has shown that domestically owned policies are more durable than the ones imposed from the outside. It is hard to argue against success. I was, and continue to be, mystified about Lebanon.

flourished. I suspect policymakers will need to work harder and to persevere to put their economies on a high-growth trajectory. The idea is not to question the value of growth but to achieve it first, and then to worry about how to make it broad based. Ultimately, I am convinced that robust economic growth will also bring about the social transformation of poor countries that we all seek.

There Is No Alternative to Outward-Oriented Growth Policies

My East Asian experience had convinced me of the wisdom of (a) developing out-ward-oriented economic policies that emphasize macroeconomic stability; (b) focus-ing on export competitiveness; (c) attracting foreign direct investment not only for achieving a higher level of investment, but also—more significantly—for transferring technical and managerial know-how and for developing exports; and (d) encourag-ing a greater private sector role in the economy. The East Asians followed those poli-cies years before John Williamson coined the term *the Washington Consensus*. Some of the Middle Eastern countries have tried to implement them but with much more limited success. But in each case, as I have indicated earlier, the reasons had more to do with the partial nature of reforms, a lack of domestic leadership, or the capacity constraints in the government to sustain the reforms. Nothing that I saw in the Mid-dle East would make me question my initial faith.

Much has been written in the past 15 years about the limitations of the Washing-ton Consensus. Some have simply questioned the whole rationale of external-oriented policies. Others have lamented its "incomplete nature," arguing for a "post-Washington Consensus." Still others have written about the lack of a human face. All of those criticisms are based on examples of one sort or another where the researchers did not find progress despite adherence to Washington Consensus poli-cies. In my view, those criticisms are off the mark.

As T. N. Srinivasan pointed out in one of his lectures at the Bank a few years ago, economic reform is not a mere science. It is not a recipe that one carefully measures and adds to the cooking pot, covers and lets simmer, and—voila!—economic growth emerges. The art of reform is just as important. One has to adapt to local conditions and also constantly adjust to changing circumstances, internal or external. East Asians never viewed their reforms as being on autopilot. Policymakers would need to be agile—much more so than in the 1980s when there were still only a handful of countries chasing the global pie—to manage economic policy. Indeed, as discussed earlier, sustained domestic leadership is critical.

Some have also attempted to portray the East Asian policies as being somehow different from the Washington Consensus. I disagree. The East Asians did everything that Williamson later captured in his summary term. They kept strong fiscal disci-pline, held their external debts at prudent levels, followed a mostly flexible exchange rate policy, and promoted direct foreign investment and private investment. Some have pointed to one policy or another that differed in emphasis in one or another country—for example, the heavier role of government in the Republic of Korea in industrial promotion than the Washington Consensus is presumed to advocate. In my debates on the subject, I have often told the protagonists that they should forget about the policies of the Washington Consensus, borrow whatever unique ideas they think the East Asians had, and put forward what they think should be the policy for their country. This advice often results in lofty statements about "public-private part-nership," "careful privatization," and so on. But never have I seen a clear alternative put forward. I am convinced that except for the lesson about the hazard of opening up the capital account too quickly absent a strong financial sector, the East Asian experience confirms all the underlying tenets of the Washington Consensus.

It does not follow, however, that every country that follows external-oriented reforms is destined to become another Asian tiger. As indicated earlier, there is much more to reform than simply following the right policies; domestic leadership and consensus also matter. Moreover, there are countries that face constraints of geography (as Jeffery Sachs has written), weak institutions (like those of the Republic of Yemen), small size, or perhaps even factors that we do not fully understand (for example, in Bolivia). Unfortunately, there are no alternative-development paradigms available for such countries, as some seem to suggest. They are still better off following macroeconomic policies of fiscal prudence and external openness, hoping that in time they may be in a position to reap greater benefits from globalization.

Focus on a Few Critical Sectors: Education, Power, and Roads

The debate about macroeconomic policies often overlooks the fact that the successful reformers also emphasized critical sectoral investments. Of course, whether growth allowed countries to make sectoral investments or whether the sectoral investments themselves caused growth remains an interesting empirical question. My own view is that it is probably a bit of both. But within the sectoral programs, I believe countries can benefit from a sharper focus on a few critical sectors that appear to me to have the greatest effect on growth: education, roads, and electricity. I would recommend to any policymaker to make sure that the institutions in those sectors work well.

In education, the requirement is a high-class department or ministry of education, because the government should have the preeminent role (direct provision at the basic level and an enabling role and targeted financial support for higher education).

For roads, I am in favor of a commercialized highway authority that has its own earmarked source of funds.

For electricity, I feel that we went a bit overboard in our thinking about privatization with the result that much-needed investments were delayed. Interestingly, the initial wave of privatization in electricity focused on generation; resource constraint in the public sector was considered to be the biggest motivation for inviting the private sector. I believe that the key motivation should instead look to attracting private management in the distribution sector, where many of the inefficiencies lie. Again, East Asians were the first ones to have strong publicly owned utilities run on commercial lines; many of those utilities have since even been privatized. The Bank was a partner of those utilities and contributed to their development. There is room to revisit the privatization enthusiasm of the 1990s for most low- and middle-income countries.

Governance Matters, but Creating It Is Doubtful

Much recent discussion has suggested that an adequate focus on governance has somehow been the missing element of policy reform. Some studies have tried to show a correlation between governance and growth. I have never been too convinced by those studies, most of all because I believe that the ratings on governance are themselves influenced by a country's track record of economic performance. Nevertheless, from my own experience, I believe that countries that have better governance (meaning a better public sector) are likely to do better. Having said this, I am not so sure that governance can be created, particularly by outside actors such as aid donors. I tend to believe that the process of improving governance is a long one that is influenced by a variety of social and cultural factors that we do not quite comprehend. It is not something that can be fixed through external advice and technical assistance. Even more than in the case of economic reforms, the process must be a domestic one led by domestic leaders.

We do know that higher-income countries tend to have a higher level of governance than lower-income countries. Countries that have grown also seem to have improved their governance. (I recall the debates in the late 1970s when Bank staff members used to complain about "weak institutions" in Thailand!) Although the issue of cause and effect exists, I come down on the side of those who believe that income growth contributes to improvement in governance rather than the other way around.

Lessons for the Bank

Refocus on Growth as the Central Agenda of Country Strategies

Few in the Bank will disagree with the proposition to refocus on growth. Yet, I have been surprised how lightly the Country Assistance Strategies deal with underlying factors that inhibit a country's growth. To the extent that there is a discussion of the subject, it tends to remain at the economic policy level (the science) with little analysis of country-specific political, leadership, cultural, and geographical factors that are equally important. When a country has not been growing, alarm bells should sound and a commitment should be made to find the most critical inhibiting factors. Bank support should then focus like a laser beam on those critical factors.

Reward Winners, Help Losers with Limited Public Goods

The history of the Bank has been to try to influence the behavior of governments that otherwise would not have followed the right policies. Indeed, lending to successful countries was seen as something to be avoided. This bias was based on the assumption of the 1980s (incorrect as it turned out) that Bank capital is scarce and thus must be devoted to helping countries that are not doing well. I remember vividly when a requirement was added in the Bank appraisal documents to justify the "rationale for Bank involvement," a tradition that interestingly continues today when the effort is precisely the opposite!

I believe that Bank lending should be only for countries that have demonstrated a good track record of performance. I would suggest linking lending to a single indicator: the track record of growth. I would argue that if a country has been growing steadily, it must have the right combination of economic policy, governance, and institutions that will enable it to make good use of Bank lending. Conversely, there must be some elements missing that we do not fully understand when a country continues to stagnate despite what appear to be good policies and governance. I would argue for a true outcome-based assessment of development worthiness for Bank lending.

Unfortunately, a large number of countries, most in Africa, would not pass the development-worthiness test. The reasons may be varied—poor policies, poor governance, internal conflict, or just plain bad luck. What should one do about such countries? My view is that such countries deserve help with humanitarian assistance in the form of IDA grants focused on a handful of public goods such as basic education and maternal and child health. It is difficult to argue for IDA loans for general development for such countries in the hope that the future will be better than the past. Alas, the record of the past several decades on this score is not very comforting.

Terminate Adjustment Lending

We have all learned that good policies are far more important than financing and are even critical to aid effectiveness. Yet, as indicated earlier, I do not believe that reforms can be brought about through external pressures and agents. I am convinced that domestic leadership and ownership are critical for the success of economic reforms and much more important than getting each item of reform precisely right. I would even argue that domestic ownership must mean that countries implement not first-best but second-, third-, or fourth-best policies. Only the country policymakers themselves are in the best position to judge what is feasible at any given time, as Hernan Buchi of Chile told us. I find Bank adjustment lending inherently contradictory to the notion of country ownership. We all know that Bank history and culture heavily based on conditionality assume that we must persuade, cajole, or even bribe a country to get it to reform. True reformers need none of these incentives.

Some in the Bank have argued that structural adjustment lending is a good way to support the reformers in a country. I do not find this view compelling given my general views on domestic leadership that owns the reform program, a point about which I was reminded by a senior Syrian official (see box 11.2). If a minister of finance needs the Bank to protect him or her against the president or his or her cabinet colleagues or a recalcitrant parliament, this situation should be seen as a warning sign that the necessary leadership does not yet exist in the country to sell the reforms or that the reform program has a high likelihood of being reversed. Having domestic leaders in front and talking to their people should, in my view, be a primary indication of domestic ownership.

In recent research done by one of my students, we analyzed the experience of Bank structural adjustment lending between 1980 and 2000. We reviewed the performance of countries that had made use of Bank structural adjustment loans. Data showed that 20 of the 38 African countries in that category between 1980 and 2000 experienced a decline in per capita incomes. Only five relatively small countries (Botswana, Lesotho, Mauritius, the Seychelles, and Swaziland) showed a per capita

BOX 11.2
The Syrian Arab Republic: The Impossible Dream

After the Arab Republic of Egypt, the Syrian Arab Republic is the next biggest developing economy (excluding GCC countries) in the Middle East. Its economy is highly distorted, resembling in many respects the socialist economies. It has not been in any crisis, having kept a lid on public expenditures and borrowing. But like most other countries in the region, Syria suffers from a crisis of slow growth and inadequate job creation. The population has been restless, but it has been kept under control in the tight grip of the Baath Party. The need for reform has long been recognized, and indeed the government has taken a few small steps from time to time (for example, allowing entry by foreign banks and unifying the exchange rate). But the government has not been prepared to undertake reform in a comprehensive manner. Some observers have suggested that reforms are hindered because of the continuing political problems with the Israelis. I do not quite fathom the link.

We tried our best to convince the Syrians to move with the reforms. Syria had been in arrears to the Bank to the tune of about US$550 million accumulated since 1988. It had the ability but not the will to clear the arrears. As a part of our attempt to bring Syria around, we made a deal on arrears whereby Bank management agreed (and the Board of Executive Directors approved) the proposal to let Syria clear its principal arrears first and clear the interest arrears over three years. This plan kept the Syrian arrears from growing (since, contrary to the normal financial practice, the Bank did not charge interest on interest arrears). The deal was a bit unconventional and was opposed vehemently by the Bank's finance staff. But Jim Wolfensohn personally endorsed the plan because he saw the benefit of a normal relationship between the Bank and Syria as greater than the theoretical chance of recovering the small additional amount of interest on interest. It showed Bank decisionmaking at its best—not a normal practice in that a lack of consensus is more likely to hold up such decisions.

The Syrians were grateful for the Bank's gesture. The arrears clearance deal did earn us considerable goodwill (vis-à-vis our predecessors, whom the Syrians blamed for not being understanding). But we never did succeed in engaging the Syrians further on economic reforms, and there was no resumption of Bank lending or any meaningful economic and sector work. The situation continues to this day.

During my last visit to Syria, I had a very friendly meeting with a high-level, official decisionmaker. Because the visit was my swan song, he chose to be quite open with me. He explained to me that the Syrians well understood what needs to be done but could not act until the political leadership judged the time to be right. He went on to say that he welcomed the Bank's help and particularly appreciated all I had done for them (he was being kind to an outgoing director). But then he remarked, quite perceptively, that the Syrian government would be hesitant to invite the Bank into the reform process because that would mean a loss of ownership. I was impressed with his perspective. He definitely left me something interesting to chew on as I made the transition from development practitioner to development thinker.

income growth of more than 2 percent per year. In Latin America, Chile is the only major country to have experienced a per capita income growth rate of more than 2 percent, with most of the other 19 recipients of structural adjustment lending—including Argentina, Brazil, and Mexico—experiencing only modest growth. In Eastern Europe, Latvia is the only country among those receiving structural adjustment loans to have experienced more than 2 percent growth in per capita income.

The results look even worse when one examines the data from the largest and most consistent users of structural adjustment lending. Since 1980, there have been 12 countries, including 6 in Africa and 3 in Latin America, that received more than 10 structural adjustment loans or credits from the World Bank. In Africa, five of the six largest users of such assistance (Côte d'Ivoire, Ghana, Senegal, Togo, and Zambia) experienced a decline in per capita incomes. Only Malawi showed a modest increase of less than 1 percent. In Latin America, of the three biggest recipients, incomes declined in Jamaica and stagnated in Argentina. Only Mexico experienced a modest growth. In East Asia, the Philippines, which was the slowest-growing economy in the entire region, was the only country to receive more than 10 adjustment loans. Turkey was the best performer among the large borrowers, with growth of just under 2 percent.

It is also interesting to note that many successful countries—Botswana, Chile, China, India, the Republic of Korea, Thailand—have avoided or made sparing use of Bank adjustment lending. What made those countries forgo this supposedly easy money? The answer, in my view, lies in their realizing the inherent contradiction between domestic ownership and getting an external agent such as the Bank involved in the process.

Provide Budget Support Instead of Project Lending

Although I came to my job with a strong project and sectoral bias, I have concluded that the time has come for the Bank to phase out project lending for all IBRD countries and replace it with budget support for a number of reasons. First, as we have learned, the old notion that individual projects would somehow become beacons for development has not quite materialized. So-called good projects have often not translated into economic growth. Indeed, there is some evidence that individual donor projects may actually detract from a government's overall development effort. Bank projects (and those of other donors), even when performing well, tend to be isolated islands of good development practice. It would be a much better use of Bank resources to focus on the country's overall development program.

Second, as is well known around the Bank, its project loans have been so thoroughly loaded with a variety of requirements that more and more countries are simply voting, or threatening to vote, with their feet. A Bank that is left with only the most desperate borrowers, while appealing in terms of taking it back to its true raison d'être, is likely to leave an intellectually depleted institution. I find it difficult to see how the Bank will simplify or streamline its various requirements to make its project loans more palatable for the more successful clients. Most of those requirements have been bundled under the label (mislabel in my view) of "fiduciary requirements," making the simplification task politically impossible.

Third, the heavy requirements of Bank projects (labeled first-world conditions by
Sebastian Mallaby in his recent book *The World's Banker*) have taxed the already limited institutional capacity of governments and thus detract from their own development efforts. I have been shocked at the growing role played by expensive consultants
in most Bank (and donor) projects. Rather than building institutions in developing
countries, donor projects may actually be depleting the governments' reserves of
experience and expertise.

I propose that the Bank replace its project lending with annual budget support to
its clients. The support will be based on a businesslike, annual, transparent review of
the government's development efforts, and the level of Bank financing will be linked
to the degree of assessed development worthiness. The past record of growth should
play a very significant role in this assessment. But one can also think of a select list of
additional considerations, such as the focus on poverty in public expenditures or
gender equality in public expenditures. I have often been surprised how little Bank
staff members know about a country's annual budget, which is probably the single
most important indication of development intentions. Budget support would require
Bank staff members to focus much more on annual budgets than they do now.

An exclusive focus on budget support will free very considerable Bank staff
resources to be diverted to helping the government with hands-on technical assistance in sectors, much as they used to do in the 1970s and 1980s. A large number of
highly skilled Bank sector staff members are today preoccupied for most of their time
(I would hazard a guess of 80 percent) in managing the bureaucratic and fiduciary
requirements of projects. The governments are likely to find them much more valuable in a technical assistance and advisory role. On their part, Bank staff members
may find this work more rewarding.

I want to reiterate that budget support is not yet another incarnation of structural
adjustment lending. In contrast with the ex ante conditionality of adjustment lending, it would be an ex post award based on demonstrated performance, not on promises of performance, and free of any conditions.

Project support should be limited to IDA projects that are designed to support
basic public goods in countries that are not deemed sufficiently development worthy for IBRD budget support. Thus, IDA lending will be based not on income but
on development worthiness. If it is decided that IDA lending should continue to be
made available, as now, on the basis of income, I would propose that it, too, be in the
form of budget support for development-worthy, low-income countries.

The only other exception for project lending may be for large and lumpy infrastructure projects that are so complex and unique that Bank technical expertise
could help. However, such projects are likely to be few in number.

Concluding Remarks

We have been in the development business for some 60 years now. Much has happened in this period. Some countries have moved on from the status of developing

to industrial. Others are currently going through major changes. Far too many, unfortunately, are still too poor and falling behind.

It is troublesome that, despite the wealth of experience, we are far from an agreed consensus on development. To be sure, the increasing complexity of development has made the achievement of a consensus even more difficult. But I do believe that there is much to learn from those who have been successful. I have tried to do so on the basis of my own experiences. What matters is not to believe in *the* orthodoxy. What is more important is for policymakers to have a set of beliefs that they pursue for their countries vigorously and consistently.

My 30 years in the Bank was a highly rewarding experience. I was fortunate to be in the Bank when we pioneered new approaches to development, whether in work on urban poverty during the 1970s, on structural adjustment during the 1980s, on the debt crisis during the 1980s, or on the Washington Consensus during the 1990s. The Bank has a unique collection of highly motivated and experienced development professionals that is unmatched by any other multilateral institution. It has the most in-depth knowledge of development business from around the globe. But it must recognize that the world around it has changed, and it must adapt accordingly.

James W. Adams

Country Director for Tanzania and Uganda (1995–2002)

When James Adams joined the World Bank after completing a master's of public affairs at Princeton University 30 years ago, he says, "I didn't know what I was getting myself into." He jokes that his previous job—as a zookeeper at the Utica Zoo in his native New York—"has given me many insights in terms of surviving and prospering in the Bank."

Originally planning on a stay of only a few years, Jim found his early work as a loan officer in the East Africa region so rewarding that he decided to make a career of it. Jim particularly enjoyed the chance to contribute to the Bank's strategic direction for the region and gained a reputation for his ability to blend analytical capacity with a pragmatic approach to operations.

Jim joined the East Asia Region for a five-year period in 1980, where his work focused largely on Indonesia. He then returned to the Africa Region as the Bank's resident representative in Nairobi, Kenya. Jim relished the chance to base his work in the field, taking advantage of the opportunity to forge strong relationships in government. "Field jobs are the best in the Bank," he says.

Returning to Washington, D.C., in 1990, Jim first put his extensive operations experience and management skills to use as chief of the Human Development Division for the Southern Cone countries of the Latin America region, and then in 1993 as director of the Operations Policy Department. Two years later, he began his most challenging, and ultimately most rewarding, job in the Bank, as country director for Tanzania and Uganda.

Initially based in Washington, D.C., Jim moved to Dar es Salaam, Tanzania, in 1999. As country director, he put to good use his knowledge of East African history and politics and the wide-ranging relationships he had fostered among government officials. Although working with two governments simultaneously "was a very real challenge, we made real progress" in both countries. The experience led Jim to grow even more attached to the region. "I felt terri-

---

Portions of this profile first appeared in "Adams Family Values," *tOPiCS* (internal OPCS newsletter), October 2002.

bly responsible for everything that happened in Tanzania and Uganda," he says. Family concerns led him to return to Washington in 2002, "but otherwise I'd still be in Dar es Salaam, enjoying the sun."

When Jim returned, President James Wolfensohn appointed him vice president of Operations Policy and Country Services (OPCS), a job analogous to Jim's previous position as director of operations policy. Although the responsibilities of the positions are similar, he returned to a changed institutional environment. "The Bank is more supportive now, more open to reform and change," he says. Under Jim's direction, OPCS is playing its part in this change, notably through its work in simplifying Bank procedures.

From his perspective of working in East Africa during four different decades, Jim says the key development lessons from the region are fairly simple. "I'm a big believer in the economic fundamentals," he says, "and there must be leadership from the government; it can't come from us."

12 The Right Approach to the Right Policies

Reflections on Tanzania

James W. Adams

WHEN I BECAME COUNTRY DIRECTOR FOR TANZANIA IN 1995, BRIAN VAN ARKADIE, a long-time consultant on Africa (and sometime resident), told me that the country was a success story. I was taken aback: though I was more optimistic about Tanzania than anyone in the Bank, it was at the time seen as an economically unstable country on the verge of macroeconomic crisis, vilified by the international donor community for corruption and mismanagement. Van Arkadie explained that when the current macroeconomic imbalances were righted, the country's progress in sustaining structural reform and its underlying technical capacity would allow it to flourish. No one believed him at the time, but over the span of the past decade he has been proven absolutely correct.

Tremendous change has taken place since the mid 1990s in Tanzania, where from 1995 to 2002 I served as country director (including the period 1999–2002, when I was based in the World Bank field office in Dar es Salaam). During that time, Tanzania transformed itself from a country headed for crisis into one with a stable and growing economy and in charge of its own development. Although I also served as country director of another successful African country—Uganda—during that period, I will focus on Tanzania here, because while it is less well known, its progress is equally compelling.

The numbers reflect clearly Tanzania's success: from 1.1 percent average annualized growth and about 30 percent annual inflation in 1991–94, Tanzania grew 4.6 percent on an average annualized basis from 1995 to 2002 and reduced annual inflation to below 5 percent by the end of the period.[1] Poverty rose 11 percent between 1991 and 1994 but declined by 28 percent from 1994 to 2002 (Muganda 2004). Moreover, those improvements were sustained in spite of a series of external shocks, including El Niño, the Congo conflict, and the Asian financial crisis. In this chapter, I will describe the three key elements of this turnaround, as seen from my perspective as country director: (a) country ownership of the economic program, (b) capacity building in the public sector, and (c) strengthened economic policy fundamentals. In short, Tanzania succeeded, and continues to be successful, because it took the right approach to the right policies.

The Right Approach: Country Ownership

Tanzania has long shown an independent streak. Under President Julius Nyerere, the country's first president, Tanzania pursued a program of "African socialism." After a period of active donor support for Tanzania's program in the 1970s (including from the Bank), the country's relations with the International Monetary Fund (IMF) and the Bank broke down in 1980 over the issue of how to address the economic crisis the country was facing.[2] The breakup of the East African Community, a series of economic reversals, and the war with Uganda in the late 1970s presented a daunting economic challenge, but the government rejected IMF and Bank advice on the key elements needed for a credible program of reform. The economic collapse that followed was not effectively addressed over the remainder of Nyerere's administration.

Under President Ali Hassan Mwinyi, Nyerere's successor, the country developed a home-grown economic recovery program in 1986. That program was initially very successful and mobilized significant resources from both bilateral donors and the international financial institutions (IFIs). Supported by the economic reform, significant economic progress was made over Mwinyi's first five-year term. In the early 1990s, however, Tanzania's economic stability and its relationship with international donors began to break down again. By 1994, economic growth had slowed to less than 2 percent, inflation climbed above 30 percent, and perceptions of government mismanagement and corruption peaked. A misguided fiscal reform laden with tax giveaways reduced tax receipts and increased evasion, leaving the government short of revenue. The Mwinyi administration responded by asking for increased support from the international donor community, but at the same time it blamed donors for being unfaithful and excessively demanding. This criticism infuriated the donors, who saw the request for more support following the botched fiscal reform as a substitute for a legitimate government tax effort.

With Tanzania the target of much international criticism, government-donor relations reached an impasse: donors made it clear that additional resources would not be forthcoming in the absence of a credible government reform program. In that environment, Denmark, traditionally a strong aid supporter of Tanzania, brokered a deal to appoint an independent team of five experts to examine the country's aid relationships and offer recommendations for their improvement. Gerry Helleiner, a University of Toronto economist with long ties to Tanzania and a reputation as an honest critic of both the government and the IFIs, chaired the team; it also included two Tanzanians who were unaffiliated with the government.

The team delivered its report (Helleiner and others 1995) in June 1995, shortly before I came on board as country director; in fact, this "Helleiner Report" was one of the first things on my desk as country director. The report included a tough indictment of the Tanzanian government, arguing that its failure to deliver macroeconomic stability through credible reform was the country's main problem, not the perceived heavy hand of the IFIs. But the team had also been directed to report on the issue of Tanzanian government ownership in the aid relationship and issued an equally forceful indictment of donor failure to trust the government with development policy and implementation. The report noted that, though the donors and IFIs talked about promoting country ownership, they were not living up to their rhetoric. It gave a number of examples of donor "misbehavior," including a specific reference to an incident in which World Bank behavior undermined Tanzanian ownership. The Helleiner Report was thus a significant milestone in that it highlighted *dual* responsibilities in the aid relationship, rather than just those of government. As the report forcefully concluded, both sides needed substantial changes in their operational cultures if real progress was to be sustained.

The report might have had little effect, however, if Benjamin Mkapa had not been elected to succeed Mwinyi as president at the end of 1995. Mkapa, well known in foreign policy circles, was largely an unknown on economic matters, yet he proved to be an extremely effective steward of Tanzania's economic program. He made clear from the start of his tenure that he wanted to repair relations with donors and maintain a robust macroeconomic program with the IMF and World Bank in order to underpin a stable regime and long-term growth. But he also made clear that Tanzania was to be in the driver's seat and used the Helleiner Report to underpin his approach to the donors. President Mkapa's commitment to a stable economic program, with donor support as critical but Tanzania firmly in control, established the basis for sustained improvements in Tanzania's aid relationships and economic performance.

An important outgrowth of the Helleiner Report was its reinforcement of donors' efforts to harmonize their support to Tanzania. Spurred by the report's recommendations, donors moved the consultative group meetings to Dar es Salaam, allowing them to become more in touch with the country's priorities. At the same time, the Bank's efforts to center our economic policy and social sector work in the field (which I will describe in more detail in the next section) facilitated greater donor coordination on macroeconomic and sector issues. Monthly meetings among donors were marked by honest, productive discussions that underscored the urgency of making the changes in donor behavior outlined by the Helleiner Report. Improved donor harmonization led to the broad acceptance of joint analytical work, which bolstered broader efforts to promote Tanzanian ownership. Indeed, over time Tanzania became an international leader in advancing donor harmonization, highlighted by an invitation to President Mkapa to deliver the keynote address at the High-Level Forum on Harmonization in Rome in February 2003.

Gerry Helleiner returned to Tanzania and issued a progress report in 1997 to assess both parties' progress in the intervening years; he made a more comprehensive evaluation in 1999. In both cases, he found impressive progress with respect to the government-donor relationship (Helleiner 1999). Tanzania had begun exercising significant leadership in macroeconomic management, budget control systems, and other policy areas. Donors had improved their attitudes toward the relationship and had involved the government more in selection of personnel for technical assistance tasks. However, the evaluations also acknowledged that much remained to be achieved, particularly in aligning technical assistance with demand from the government and in more actively using Tanzanian capacity. In each area of concern, Helleiner made concrete suggestions about ways the situation could be improved. By balancing his criticisms of both donor and government performance, Helleiner ensured that the reports were seen as objective and useful by both sides.

A key long-term element of the 1999 assessment was the recommendation to institutionalize the process of independent monitoring of the aid relationship, with specific performance criteria for both parties. In addition to the familiar criteria for government performance, donors agreed to be evaluated on the timeliness of their disbursements of aid and information, plus the extent to which aid is untied with respect to country of procurement, among other areas. Thus, the Independent Monitoring Group was established in 2000, serving to institutionalize ownership and accountability in the Tanzanian aid relationship; it remains the only such body of its kind today.

Another milestone occurred when President Mkapa attended a partnership conference with donors in Stockholm in 1999. At the meeting, he highlighted the progress his government had achieved after taking ownership of its economic program in 1995. This personal endorsement of ownership from the Tanzanian leadership was both a testament to the success that had been achieved and a stimulus for further progress.

Thus, a confluence of factors contributed to Tanzania's taking successful ownership of its development program. The Helleiner Report and President Mkapa's leadership initiated the process, and the donor community responded favorably to increased government commitment. Ironically, with so many things going poorly in the country-donor relationship in 1995, donors were unusually willing to experiment and take risks with new approaches, and they rewarded signs of progress and ownership by fulfilling their commitment to provide adequate resources (as growth accelerated in the late 1990s, aid per capita increased). On the Tanzanian side, a highly competent core group of government technocrats at last had the authorization and political capital to pursue sound policies. That they did so with strong results increased the donors' confidence in ownership transfer, and a virtuous circle ensued.

I am not naive enough to think that the playing field has been fully leveled or that Tanzania now exercises complete ownership over its development program. Yet during my tenure as country director, the Tanzanian government gained a voice—and the space to raise it—that did not exist before. It is a shame that this chain of events is all too uncommon in Africa and other developing regions, a theme I will return to later.

The Right Approach: Capacity Building

Closely related to the role of country ownership in Tanzania's success was the capacity of government to conduct economic analysis, formulate sound policies, and implement those policies well. Ownership and capacity are necessary complements: without capacity, ownership will result in failed policies, failed implementation, or both, and donors will move quickly to reassert control; but without ownership, capacity is left underused.

As previously noted, in mid 1995, when I became country director for Tanzania, there was little faith in the government's capacity to deliver a credible economic reform program. Despite the poor record of the second term of the Mwinyi government, I believed at that time that more capacity existed in Tanzania than was commonly realized. A number of points supported that belief. First, when I initially worked on Tanzania in the 1970s, international advisers were central to formulating Tanzanian economic policy, and it was precisely those policies that led to the economic collapse referred to above (Helleiner 2000).[3] When I returned in the mid 1990s, I recognized that, despite the problems that remained, Tanzania's economic policies had improved dramatically from the 1970s under the clear leadership of Tanzanian professionals—where others saw problems, I saw opportunities. Essentially, I felt the challenge was how to tap into the significant domestic capacity that existed, as well as how to increase it further.

Second, Tanzania's experience in the 1980s had fostered the growth of a solid core of technical specialists committed to reform. A series of policy seminars held by the University of Dar es Salaam since the 1980s (after the break with the IMF and Bank) had regularly brought together leading economists and policymakers from across the political spectrum to engage in analysis and debate on key issues. The seminars became so popular that even the prime minister began attending. At a time when there was much rancor in Tanzania toward the international community, the sessions helped define economic policy issues, not through the prism of the country versus the IFIs but in terms of how to design and implement the policies necessary for Tanzania to succeed in today's world. The group of talented and committed reformers that emerged was instrumental in developing Tanzania's home-grown programs in the late 1980s, and these reformers would later be key players when given the opportunity under President Mkapa's leadership. Third, immediately after his election, President Mkapa reached out to a number of talented Tanzanian staff members at the IMF and the Bank and asked them to return to Dar es Salaam to work with him on improving the economic policy framework.

In the Bank, we also sought to use and build this capacity by taking innovative approaches to analytic work. Hiring a Tanzanian, Benno Ndulu, as lead economist (and basing him in Dar es Salaam) in 1998 was a major catalyst in aligning our work with that of government. Ndulu was a well-respected figure in the country, with many ties to the policymaking and university communities. He was given full responsibility to lead the Bank's economic program from Dar es Salaam. He identified Tanzanian researchers with whom we conducted our country economic work and helped strengthen their skills, allowing us to benefit from their country expertise; working with Ndulu became a sought-after position for Tanzanians.

A good example of how Ndulu helped transform our work was the changed approach to public expenditure reviews (PERs). Each year the Bank produced a PER to analyze the government budget and to suggest ways to make public spending more efficient; the process was historically conducted entirely by Bank staff members and external consultants, with minimal input from the country (the first PERs during my tenure as country director faithfully followed this traditional model). When Ndulu came on board, he led a sustained effort to reorient the PER as an exercise conducted jointly with Tanzanians, focusing on building their capacity to improve the budget-making process. That approach was also promoted by Allister Moon, a Bank economist with previous PER experience in Uganda. Moon constantly emphasized that the key product of the PER was not the report that we produced but its contribution to the process of strengthening budget-making capacity.

In parallel to that effort, we brought other donors into the PER process. The donors were committed to promoting ownership and had an important influence in the budget process through their projects and programs. Their response was overwhelmingly positive. Donors put a large amount of funding into the effort, ensuring that resources were not a constraint. They also agreed to hire the best international experts available (rather than merely those from their respective countries, as had typically been the case in the past under bilateral programs), as well as to hire talented Tanzanians and engage them fully in the process. This new model for PERs was tremendously successful: not only did it build Tanzanian capacity, but it also created internal political pressure to improve the government's budget process as the Tanzanian participants became committed to the reforms that they were engaged in developing.

Over time this form of joint country-Bank-donor work became a model for analytic work generally. One good example emerged in the agricultural sector, where strong donor support led to hiring the Washington-based International Food Policy Research Institute to take the lead on an agricultural report. The donors provided significant funding for that effort, thereby ensuring adequate resources to fund both international researchers and a range of Tanzanian experts. The work reconciled contradictory data on the country's agricultural sector, developed a broad strategy for future work, and commenced an ongoing collaboration between donors and local researchers on agriculture issues.

With such opportunities to demonstrate and build its capacity, Tanzania's confidence in taking the lead on analytic work increased rapidly. The Tanzania Poverty Reduction Strategy Paper (PRSP), which was completed in 2000 and set out the country's economic strategy for the coming years, was developed entirely by the government (United Republic of Tanzania 2000a). Interestingly, the IFIs initially expressed concern about the technical quality of this document, touching off an internal debate about whether technical excellence must precede ownership or vice versa. We ultimately decided that promoting country ownership was the best way to promote technical excellence in the long run: thus, Tanzania's PRSP was a reflection of both the country's emerging capacity and the IFIs' willingness to provide Tanzania the space to exercise ownership. Concurrently, the Country Assistance Strategy (World Bank 2000c) was conducted in parallel with the government's work to develop a Tanzania Assistance Strategy (TAS) (United Republic of Tanzania 2000b). The TAS set out the country's development priorities, and it involved broad consultations with civil society throughout the country. Indeed, the Helleiner group's follow-up evaluations of the aid relationship specifically commended the Bank for making strides in working with the government, particularly through strengthening the Bank's capacity in Dar es Salaam.

A project-based example of how Tanzania used the complementarity between ownership and capacity to its benefit occurred in 1997, when storms caused by the El Niño effect destroyed the major rail line. The government first approached a foreign contractor that was financed under an ongoing International Development Association (IDA) railway project to conduct the repairs. This team, realizing the country was in a vulnerable position, tried to overcharge the government for the needed work. Rather than pay the inflated price, the government said that it would perform the repairs by force account (in which the public sector manages the project directly rather than contracting it out). In most circumstances, the Bank would advise against this method: force account work is seldom efficient or timely. But this time the task manager decided to take the risk, given his faith in the government's ability to perform. And indeed the government did the job well, completing it for about one-third the cost quoted by the foreign team. To us, it was a powerful message of what the merger of ownership and capacity can accomplish. Tanzania consistently took advantage of such opportunities to perform.

I feel the Bank was successful in tapping Tanzanian capacity because of systematic thinking about how to involve Tanzanians across the entire work program. As we improved our ability to engage Tanzanians in the production of quality analytical work, our challenge increasingly became—and indeed remains—how to leverage strong analytical work to influence and drive policymaking. I believe we are still just scratching the surface of Tanzanian capacity right now. The success of privatized firms (which I discuss in more depth in the next section), in which the overwhelming majority of staff is Tanzanian, offers further proof that domestic capacity flourishes under the right conditions. This latent capacity is certainly not unique in Africa to Tanzania, and our challenge in the Bank is how to help bring it to the fore.

The Right Policies: Economic Fundamentals Based on the Washington Consensus

Thus far, I have told the story of Tanzania's success as though the policies that the country adopted mattered little, which is certainly not the case. Indeed, the policies mattered greatly and had significant effect. Tanzania adopted policy reforms at a pace and in forms suited to its preferences, but largely consistent with the key messages of the Washington Consensus. Although many countries have, primarily in response to international pressure, followed the same guidelines, Tanzania did so largely on its own, with the ownership and capacity already described central to sustaining broad-based political support for reform.

Although supporting the Washington Consensus has fallen out of fashion these days, I believe that is because its critics have succeeded in defining the consensus as something that it was not intended to be. If one reads the original formulation of the Washington Consensus as described by John Williamson (1990), it is a set of 10 economic policies widely regarded as desirable by major Washington-based institutions (principally the U.S. Treasury Department, World Bank, and IMF). Williamson never claimed that the list was exhaustive or sufficient to lead to growth and development, only that it constituted points of agreement on basic economic policies. Yet in the years since, it has been held up as a sort of gospel of development, which in my view was never its author's intent.[4]

As a self-contained, universally applicable prescription for development, the Washington Consensus is easy to criticize. But as a basis for a fundamentally sound macroeconomic environment and investment climate—true to its original intention—I believe the key role of the policies involved remains valid and relevant. Certainly for Tanzania, this has been the case. As incoming president, Mkapa galvanized both the government and the donor community around a sound economic reform program with macroeconomic stability at its center. Although I will not go into great detail about the policy elements that led to this remarkable turnaround, I will highlight some key contributing areas of the Washington Consensus to illustrate the scope of Tanzania's reform program.[5]

Fiscal Management

Immediately after President Mkapa's election in 1996, Tanzania kept expenditure in check by adopting a strict cash budget system, which permitted spending only up to the equivalent of estimated revenue, plus grants, in any given month. However, as time passed, policy changes improved performance, and institutional development led to the emergence of a subtler and far more effective fiscal system. In parallel with the emphasis on controlling expenditure, the country established and strengthened a separate revenue authority (the Tanzanian Revenue Authority) and reformed the incentives for tax collection. In addition, Tanzania introduced a value added tax to broaden the tax base, eliminated many distortions in the tax system, and strengthened the judicial system to reduce evasion and minimize revenue leakage. Those measures led the fiscal deficit, excluding grants, to decline from 7.5 percent of gross domestic product (GDP) in 1993 to 2.8 percent in 1996. Although there was one subsequent fiscal crisis in 1999, the government quickly clamped down on expenditure, perhaps too hard, reflecting its determined commitment to macroeconomic stability. The work on the annual PERs provided important inputs into all those efforts. Over time, work on strengthening the budget process and on capacity development resulted in a less rigid and far more effective budget system.

International support also played an important role in improving Tanzania's macroeconomic environment. Benno Ndulu, as lead economist, maintained an excellent relationship with the IMF resident representative in Dar es Salaam, thus facilitating a productive partnership between the Bank, IMF, and the donors regarding macroeconomic issues. IMF's consistent endorsement of Tanzania's macroeconomic program led donors to provide increased budget support to Tanzania, the initial focus of which was on debt relief (in the days before the Heavily Indebted Poor Countries, or HIPC, initiative), and when HIPC brought formal debt relief to

Tanzania in 2000, the released resources were converted into support for a program focused on poverty reduction.

Monetary and Exchange Rate Policy

Along with prudent fiscal management, strict control of growth in the money supply held inflation in check and allowed reserves to increase more than fourfold between 1995 and 2002. Tanzania had a history of overvalued exchange rates that eroded its international competitiveness, but President Mkapa sustained the firm commitment to market-driven exchange rates that had been initiated during the Mwinyi period. That enhanced competitiveness played an important role in allowing nontraditional exports to increase more than threefold between 1993 and 2002.

Privatization

Tanzania aggressively privatized state-owned enterprises, but only after initial successes provided the political space to do so. Among the first privatized companies was the national brewery, Tanzania Breweries Limited (TBL), which was transformed quickly from a drain on the public budget to a profit-making company that contributed 1 percent of GDP to government revenue. TBL's success in generating revenue and increasing productivity and employee wages (not to mention the availability of beer!) paved the way for the broader effort of privatization, as many stakeholders increasingly saw the benefits of transferring state enterprises to the private sector. Sometimes privatizations have unintended benefits: one of the interesting discoveries of the new owners of TBL was that they owned an old brewery that had been disassembled and was in storage in a warehouse in the Czech Republic. After rehabilitating the main brewery in Dar es Salaam, TBL brought this equipment to Tanzania and established a second plant in Mwanza.

Privatization of the ports and telecommunications companies—industries whose privatization held clear benefits to consumers—followed. The telecommunications sector now boasts a robust cellular system; a privatized landline system; and an overall environment of greater competition, efficiency, and quality with lower prices than previously. Privatization of the ports has allowed for rapid expansion of capacity and increased productivity, has led to fewer supply bottlenecks, and has made Tanzania a more attractive destination for regional commerce.

But in my view the privatization effort with the most significant effect was in the banking sector. The country's state-owned and largest commercial bank, the National Bank of Commerce (NBC), had a long record of providing poor banking services and had many nonperforming loans on its books, which continuously drained public resources. Although Tanzania allowed private banks to enter the sector in the early 1990s with some success, a large IDA credit to privatize NBC had made only limited progress by the time it was fully disbursed in the mid 1990s. When we subsequently decided to continue to provide support for privatization of NBC with a small technical assistance credit, there was considerable (and reasonable) skepticism on the part of the World Bank executive directors, given the failures of the previous financial sector credit to facilitate progress. The process also faced opposition from Tanzanian civil society: many powerful interests had benefited significantly from NBC loans that were never fully repaid. Retired president Nyerere was also opposed—he did not believe that private bankers could adequately address Tanzania's needs.

We overcame this impasse by giving the government broad discretion regarding the pace and form of banking privatization. After reviewing a number of possible options for privatization, the government decided to split NBC into a commercial bank and a microfinance institution before selling the commercial bank assets to the private sector. Although the process took much longer than the Bank had projected, it was ultimately successful. In retrospect, exercising patience—including being prepared to explain to both the Bank and the IMF board the reasons for delays from our original, overly optimistic timetable—and promoting Tanzanian ownership of the process were key elements in the success. Banking privatization has had a dramatic effect on the functioning of the economic system, replacing a fiscal drain with a profit-making private firm and helping channel credit more efficiently to private productive uses.

Investment Climate

Procedures for establishing a business were simplified, and the legal framework for foreign direct investment was strengthened, including protection against expropriation and legislation of additional investor rights. Land titling procedures were reformed to reduce application processing time for both urban and village lands. Trade was also liberalized progressively; the average most-favored-nation tariff fell from 22 to 14 percent between 1998 and 2001. President Mkapa meets every two years with chief executive officers of global companies interested in investing in Tanzania; he also holds regular meetings with the domestic business community to discuss constraints to business, including government performance.

Governance

Tanzania's civil service reform has slowly emerged as one of the strongest reform programs in the country. I emphasize *slowly* because this reform was another case in which the Tanzanians went at their own pace. There was an early retrenchment effort, but it took more time for the combination of strong domestic leadership and the financial support of the Bank and other donors to emerge and facilitate government implementation of a program that has had an enormously positive effect on the quality of the civil service. Among its other accomplishments, Tanzania's civil service reform established a performance enhancement system, and it reformed and streamlined the pay structure for those who remained in service.

Progress on reducing corruption has been more mixed. When elected in 1995, President Mkapa commissioned a panel led by a former prime minister, Justice Joseph Warioba, to report on corruption in the country. The frank and comprehensive "Warioba Report" focused on the full range of the country's governance problems (United Republic of Tanzania 1996). However, follow-up to the report was inconsistent, and corruption remained a significant constraint on reform. Because of the growing concern that donor frustration with limited progress in this area would undermine the strong government-donor relationship on other issues, the Tanzanian government established a dialogue on improving governance with the recently retired president of Finland, Martti Ahtisaari, who had served as Finland's ambassador to Tanzania in the 1970s. Ahtisaari was willing to ensure that a more balanced assessment of both progress on corruption and remaining issues be put in place: much like Professor Helleiner's work, this approach ensured a more objective assessment of progress and allowed for a more open dialogue with President Mkapa.

A key message that emerged from Ahtisaari's work was that donor concerns tended to focus too narrowly on the issue of corruption, often without giving due regard to other governance issues. This restricted view clearly exasperated the government, which believed it was making good-faith efforts to reform. In response to this message, the donors developed a matrix of Tanzania's overall governance situation, in which corruption played an important part, but which helped establish a more balanced view of areas of concern and progress. On the Bank side, we also learned firsthand of the difficulty of the governance challenge, as many of our own analytic instruments proved of limited value. A major exception was the service delivery survey, which provided direct and useful feedback to public service providers, helping them tailor their agendas to consumer needs.

Social Spending

Following the early gains in reducing the fiscal deficit, the Mkapa government prioritized social sector spending in the late 1990s, increasing efforts in education, health, water, agriculture, and HIV/AIDS, among other areas. Fiscal space created by international debt relief also allowed for increased spending targeted at poverty reduction. Strong analytic work directed at putting in place a stronger program for primary education together with subsequent international financing for the program helped Tanzania recoup the progress that it had made in the 1970s but had lost in the interim because of fiscal constraints. Fiscal deficits rose moderately as a result of increased social spending, but this trend had the full support of the Bank and IMF. Moreover, as growth continued to accelerate, poverty declined.

Although this list of policy reforms is incomplete, it offers a clear sense of Tanzania's focus on getting the fundamentals right. To be sure, its economic reform program was not perfect—progress on AIDS has been limited; infrastructure improvements, notably in transport, were underemphasized by both the government and the Bank; and we had a number of disagreements on specific issues. But Tanzania's steadfast adherence to a sound and credible economic program emphasizing macroeconomic fundamentals and growth undoubtedly contributed to the country's overall progress and to the increasing willingness of the donors to increase both their aid programs and the space for decisionmaking by the government.

Although Tanzania certainly did not consciously set out to mimic the policy tenets of the Washington Consensus, the country's successful program did address most of them (see box 12.1), and the results were undeniably positive. Indeed, I often point to the example of Tanzania whenever I hear economists say that we know little about what causes growth: this assertion may be true for predicting business cycles in advanced economies, but for developing countries with stagnant growth and deficient policies, most of the policy directions are clear. I often fear that undue criticism of the Washington Consensus, even by well-intentioned and well-informed economists, provides cover for developing countries to stray from the macroeconomic fundamentals essential for growth.

BOX 12.1

Tanzania and the Washington Consensus

Tanzania's economic reforms under President Benjamin Mkapa and during my time as country director are remarkably similar to the recommendations of the Washington Consensus. A point-by-point comparison of John Williamson's original list of the 10 Washington Consensus policies with those Tanzania pursued is set out here:

Washington Consensus	*Tanzania*
1. *Fiscal prudence:* "Budget deficits . . . . small enough to be financed without recourse to the inflation tax."	1. Substantial fiscal reform and deficit reduction were pursued, though deficits were increased in the late 1990s to allow for greater social spending.
2. *Public expenditure priorities:* "Redirecting [public] expenditure from politically sensitive areas . . . . [that] receive more resources than their economic return can *justify* . . . . toward neglected fields with high economic returns and the potential to improve income distribution, such as primary health and education, and infrastructure."	2. Fiscal waste and inefficiency were reduced in favor of prioritizing social spending; debt relief was used to increase the poverty reduction program.
3. *Tax reform:* " . . . . [to broaden] the tax base and cut . . . . marginal tax rates."	3. A value added tax was adopted to broaden the tax base; strengthening of the Tanzanian Revenue Authority was a key institutional objective.
4. *Financial liberalization:* " . . . . [with] an ultimate objective . . . . of market-determined interest rates."	4. Financial opening was cautious, but banking privatization led to market-determined interest rates.

BOX 12.1
(CONTINUED)

5. *Exchange rate policy:* "A unified . . . . exchange rate . . . . at a level sufficiently competitive to induce a rapid growth in non-traditional exports."

5. A free-floating exchange rate was adopted; nontraditional exports increased more than threefold between 1993 and 2002.

6. *Trade liberalization:* "Quantitative trade restrictions should be rapidly replaced by tariffs, and these should be progressively reduced until a uniform low rate of 10 [to 20] percent is achieved."

6. Continuous trade liberalization took place: the average most-favored-nation tariff decreased from 22 to 14 percent between 1998 and 2001.

7. *Foreign direct investment:* "Barriers impeding the entry of foreign [direct investment] should be abolished."

7. Transparency of the legal framework for foreign direct investment was enhanced by protections against expropriation and other investor rights.

8. *Privatization:* " . . . . of state-owned enterprises."

8. Aggressive privatization was pursued, with about two-thirds of state enterprises sold under Mkapa.

9. *Deregulation:* "[Abolition of] regulations that impede the entry of new firms or restrict competition."

9. Procedures for establishing a business were simplified; administrative controls were reduced across the board.

10. *Property rights:* "The legal system should provide secure property rights without excessive costs, and make these available to the informal sector."

10. Procedures for land titling were simplified.

Source: Williamson (2005).

Conclusions

Tanzania is an impressive story of progress in a continent for which success stories have been too few. Many factors—including the leadership of President Mkapa, the strengthening of the country-donor relationship beginning with the Helleiner Report, the increased capacity of the government, and the government's commitment to sound economic fundamentals—contributed to this record. So many things fell into place, in fact, that it may seem as though Tanzania relied on a "perfect storm" of positive events to succeed, and therefore its achievement is unlikely to be replicated elsewhere. However, I would argue that, although many things did go well in Tanzania, the basic elements of its success—country ownership, capacity building, and sound economic fundamentals—are readily transferable to other country contexts. I would, in fact, argue that they are central to sustained progress on the continent.

Let me highlight three lessons for the World Bank arising from my time as country director for Tanzania: the importance of trusting the client, the importance of good relationships, and the importance of economic fundamentals.

The Importance of Trusting the Client

Transferring ownership to the country is often difficult for us in the Bank because we are unwilling to trust the client enough to allow the client to commit mistakes. Yet true ownership means that we must allow the client to make difficult decisions, even when we think the client may err. This strategy does not mean that we remain silent—we are still free to disagree and should ensure that our views are known—but it does mean that we must be supportive of the client's willingness to take risks and experiment, and pick fights only over the major decisions that affect the country's strategic vision, not the minor ones. Building capacity becomes essential to this trust because it generates the skills and confidence necessary for the client to successfully exercise ownership. Trust is also a two-way street, and in this respect the accountability enforced on the donor community through the Helleiner process and the Independent Monitoring Group led the Tanzanians to trust donors as well. I would argue that this approach to ownership is the exact opposite of conditionality, which imposes a rigid, one-way relationship. In my experience in Tanzania, trusting the client and allowing the client to make mistakes created space in which the policy process became nearly as important as the substance, making problems more manageable and over time facilitating significant improvements in policymaking.

The Importance of Good Relationships

I have already described at length how improvements in the Tanzanian government's relationship with us—and with the wider donor community—led to positive results. Also important in these successful relationships was our excellent rapport with the IMF staff members, with whom we worked closely. Although we had plenty of disagreements with IMF in Tanzania, we made sure to reconcile our differences enough to provide the country with a consistent message. Too often the Bank allows a good cop–bad cop dynamic to evolve with IMF, in which we play the benevolent development agency to IMF's stern disciplinarian. Such behavior serves only to complicate the picture for an aid-dependent client that cannot possibly prosper in an environment where it is confronted with having to choose between Bank and IMF views: you choose the Bank, you lose IMF accreditation of your macroeconomic program; you choose IMF, you lose Bank resources. Our relationship with IMF, then, was an important part of the overall soundness of the aid relationship in producing positive results in Tanzania.

Working more broadly with the donor community on harmonization was also a strength of the program in Tanzania. The government provided a supportive environment for this harmonization—confident that the process would not result in a pattern of leaving en masse by the donor community. But donors across the spectrum also engaged willingly to undertake joint analytic work, to finance sector programs developed by the government (often with one lead donor), to contribute to the financing of the Independent Monitoring Group, and so forth.

Finally, the Tanzanian government developed increased capacity to engage in consultation with civil society. In view of its long-time status as a one-party state, Tanzania did not have a very rich tradition of engagement with civil society. However, during President Mkapa's tenure, nongovernmental organizations were invited to participate in the PER process, they were invited as observers to the consultative group meetings, and—for the first time—they became directly engaged in sector-wide programs. All those efforts reflected well the increased confidence of the government both in itself and in Tanzanian capacity. Although no one would argue that Tanzania today has the strongest civil society in East Africa, the case can be made that the Mkapa presidency witnesses the key initial opening of dialogue in this area.

The Importance of Economic Fundamentals

Tanzania's success with a set of Washington Consensus–inspired policies reflects, in my view, the tremendous importance of getting the economic fundamentals—fiscal discipline, low inflation, and market-driven exchange rates—right in any successful economic program. Without macroeconomic stability, investment and growth are compromised, and the economy becomes vulnerable to crisis. Beginning with the fundamentals is essential, and emphasizing them in Tanzania was a key part of our productive relationship with IMF. The Washington Consensus, though not all-inclusive, provides very useful benchmarks for a successful economic program.

Tanzania combined the right policies with an innovative approach to the aid relationship and strong ownership of its policy. Let us hope that other developing countries in Africa can follow its model—and with equally successful results.

Notes

1. Information from the World Development Indicators online database.

2. University of Toronto professor Gerry Helleiner recalls that Nyerere once welcomed a visiting IMF mission by saying, "You know, gentlemen, I asked for money, not advice!" Helleiner says, "A more succinct statement of the problem of conditionality has probably never been made" (Helleiner 2000).

3. Helleiner recalls "Nyerere's famous public outburst (in 1981): 'Who elected the IMF to be the Finance Ministry for every country in the world?' (or words to that effect)" (Helleiner 2000, p. 4).

4. One reflection of this misconstruction was the explicit inclusion of the key policies of the Washington Consensus in the World Bank operational policy on adjustment lending (OP 8.60). I am pleased to note these prescriptive references were all removed in the Bank's recent review of that policy.

5. The source material for the policy reforms described in this section is Muganda (2004).

Myrna Alexander

Former Country Director for Argentina (1997–2002)

Myrna Alexander concedes sheepishly that her career in economic development sprung from less-than-noble aspirations. Hailing from a small town in Alberta, Canada, "I had a desperate need to get out and see the world," she says. When World Bank recruiters came to the campus of the Massachusetts Institute of Technology as she was completing her degree in finance and international business, she says, "I had no idea what the Bank was, but these people were going to pay me to travel!" She jumped at the chance to explore the world and joined the Bank as a Young Professional in 1975.

Myrna began her Bank career performing financial analysis of private sector investment in the Africa Region. She recalls of her first mission, to Sierra Leone, "I barely knew where it was. I got off the plane thinking, 'This is exotic.'" But if she was a self-described "naive and innocent" young analyst, her work allowed for a smooth transition to the development field, giving her the opportunity to apply her skills in financial analysis to practical issues of private sector development in Africa.

Myrna then spent most of 1979 as personal assistant to Senior Vice President Peter Cargill, a position that offered her a chance to closely observe strategic decisionmaking at the top. "It was fascinating watching [Bank President Robert] McNamara" and his colleagues at work, she recalls. Myrna took a brief hiatus from the Bank in 1980 to return to Canada but came back to the Bank and the Africa Region in 1984. "I planned on coming back to the Bank for a couple of years, which became 17!" she laughs.

Immersed again in the challenges of African development as a manager in the region's Public Sector Management unit, Myrna came to realize that regional progress would be stalled without the effective provision of basic public services like roads, electricity, and education. "You have to get the basics right," she says. She winces when thinking about the violence that has afflicted the region in the past decades, noting that many of her counterparts in government have become its victims.

In 1990, Myrna became resident representative in Argentina. She describes the transition from Washington, D.C., to the field as "sharp." She recalls that in the hyperinflationary environment in which she arrived, "I had to go to the bank and stuff a big purse full of bills" in order to pay her staff's payroll. As time went on, however, inflation came under control, and Myrna won the trust of her colleagues in government.

Although she left Argentina in 1993 to return to Washington and work for the Latin America Region and later as director of Operational Policy, her experience in that country greatly facilitated her return in 1997 as director for Argentina, Chile, Paraguay, and Uruguay. With extensive knowledge of the country context and the Bank's history there, and with established relationships throughout government, "Coming back to Argentina as country director was amazing." Her strong connection to the country made facing its crisis in 2001 all the more painful. "We were watching the crisis in slow motion," she says. "It was a horrible thing to see it unravel."

Although Argentina's crisis postponed her plans a bit, Myrna still managed to meet her goal of an early retirement in 2002. Residing now in Mexico, she continues to consult for the Bank on various matters. "Between seeing family and friends and professional work, I'm very happy." Reflecting on her Bank service, she marvels, "You can be really influential in these jobs. It's surprising how many times an individual or a small group can make a real difference working in the Bank."

13 A Practitioner's Perspective of the 1990s

The Case of Argentina

Myrna Alexander

ALTHOUGH MY STORY SPANS 22 YEARS WITH THE WORLD BANK, INCLUDING EXPERI-ences in Sub-Saharan Africa during the 1970s and 1980s and in the Bank's central policy function in the mid 1990s, this paper concentrates on my work in and with Argentina when that country went through massive changes in the 1990s. My focus is on Argentina's structural reforms, contrasting the heady times of the early 1990s with the unraveling in the late 1990s.

I have learned a lot from those experiences. I stress getting the basics right, taking a long-term view, and moving along step by step. My experiences demonstrate the importance of a country's legacy in shaping its development path and in political factors in determining outcomes. It is not all about good analysis. I have tried to convey the complexity and challenges of development, its risks as well as its opportunities. My story ends with optimism.

Country Context

It starts with knowing the country. Argentina should not be a developing country. Among the 10 wealthiest countries in the world in 1910, it has a resource base similar to that of Australia and Canada and was for many years similar to many Latin American countries on several fronts, notably education. So why was Argentina in the position it was in at the end of the 1980s?

For the purposes of this chapter, it is not necessary to answer that question fully. Much has been written about Argentina and its failure to prosper, despite its assets and accomplishments. It was always a country of great promise, but one that failed to deliver on those promises. Starting in the 1950s (and there were other crises before that), recurring episodes of macroeconomic instability produced attempts at stabilization programs in 1952, 1958–59, 1962–63, 1966–69, 1973–74, 1976–78,

1981–82, 1985–88, and 1988–89. In fact, Argentina received its first financial support from the International Monetary Fund (IMF) in 1958.

The main reasons for Argentina's failure to prosper are chronically poor policies and weak institutions, certainly as far back as the 1920s and the Great Depression. Argentina has endured oscillating economic policies for decades as those advocating liberal policies have struggled with economic nationalists. Historic tensions between the center and the provinces and between rural landowners and urban consumers have continued. Institutions such as parliament and the judiciary fail to mediate among special interests. A corollary is the self-interest pursued by politicians, officials, unions, and private businesses to gain from the public sector. Political structures and processes have continued in an outdated model with little accountability, creating fertile ground for corruption, rent-seeking, and clientelism. A history of strikes and protests led to political instability and military intervention. In addition, like many other Latin American countries, Argentina had unresolved issues of its legacy, including inequitable land distribution and slow universalization of education as compared with Canada and the United States. Many economic policies have historically penalized the rural sector, precisely the sector where Argentina's comparative advantage lies. Paying taxes is anathema.

Social capital in Argentina is weak. There has been little autonomous collective civic action, and what exists is mainly driven by clientelism.[1] The family unit is very important, and Argentines put their confidence in those in their immediate circles.[2] Public institutions garner low trust; collusion and corruption have inevitably contributed to a large gap between the population and its leaders. That said, policies through much of the 20th century have created a climate of dependence on the state, especially to create jobs. Undoubtedly, the repression under the last military rule, from 1976 to 1982, undermined solidarity within the population. Moreover, Argentines have suffered through many economic booms and busts: they know that when a period of prosperity ends, a price usually has to be paid. As a result, Argentines, averse to taking long-term risks, keep their savings in U.S. dollars abroad.

The Early 1990s: The Starting Conditions

Those were the conditions that I encountered when I was assigned in 1989 as the World Bank's first resident representative in Argentina. When riots broke out and supermarkets were looted in mid 1989, I sensed that Argentine society had realized that the bottom had been reached. Because the state was effectively bankrupt, living off it was no longer a viable option. Everyone would have to get to work. I recall the president of the central bank saying that one of his goals was to make sure that no one could earn enough to live on by speculating with only US$50,000 in the exchange rate markets.

There was an initial optimism and high energy. In the early 1990s, Argentina was at the fore in redefining the boundary between the state and the private sector. This was a brave policy platform that broke with the past and redefined the rules of the game. I lived through those changes, leaving the country in 1993. By then, the initial phase of the economic reforms was largely complete.

I have memories of what it was like to live with hyperinflation and its aftermath. Here are some examples. I would go to the local bank with a large briefcase in which to stuff local bills (australes, with the largest, the 5,000 one, worth US$5) for payroll and other expenses. I had to explain to the World Bank's Financial Department that we paid for everything—including the purchase of a car—in cash, as no one would take checks. Public servants in the ministries waited in long lines to receive their wages in envelopes filled with cash every two weeks. The ministry of economy paid all of its other expenses by checks written by hand, as there was no automated system.

I was lucky to get public services, even though their quality was poor and their costs high. Many of the poor got none. My apartment had two telephone lines, since it was not certain that either would work. The building had its own electricity generator and water tank in case of cuts. The rich drank bottled water because water from the tap, albeit treated, was brown. In the office, there were days when we could not get a telephone dial tone. We had to pay more than US$3,000 to acquire a new telephone line, only to have it sabotaged regularly so that we would have to pay someone to repair it. When going to the airport at night or during rain, we took extra precautions, as the roads had deep potholes and there were no streetlights.

Inflation kept the people preoccupied with managing household budgets and finances. Argentines were well versed in economics, tracking what was going on with an abundance of economic data and analysis in the daily newspapers. Pedestrians on Florida Street kept their eyes fixed on the digital screens that showed second by second the value of the local currency relative to the U.S. dollar. People spent hours standing in lines to withdraw cash for the next two or three days' expenses or to reinvest in short-term deposits to keep up with inflation. The system of prices broke down to the point that items for sale carried no set price. I would order an item first, not knowing the final price, and be told the cost only when the item was finished.

The Initial Effects

Stabilization efforts during 1990 worked. Inflation peaked at 3,100 percent in 1989, fell from 95 percent in March 1990 to 35 percent in August 1990, and then subsided to 10 percent per month by the end of the year. After the convertibility plan was introduced in April 1991, fixing the exchange rate at 1 peso to one U.S. dollar, inflation dropped to 10 percent for the year, the lowest rate in 25 years. In some ways, the convertibility plan institutionalized what already existed: Argentina had a highly dollarized economy, with the U.S. dollar the preferred store of value and the benchmark for setting prices. Local currency had been relegated to use in petty transactions and for paying taxes. With price stability came a sense of normalcy: prices were marked in the shops, people began to go out at night again, and imported goods reappeared. Once Argentines could save knowing that their savings were backed by U.S. dollars, bank deposits rose. The banking system began to provide credit and clear checks. The agenda went well beyond stabilization and included structural reforms in the role of the state, health and education, provincial finances, banking, tax policy and administration, pensions, and trade liberalization.

Much has been written on Argentina's performance during the first few years of the 1990s. The economy boomed, with the gross domestic product (GDP) growing at an average of 7 percent per year, before the "Tequila" crisis hit in 1995. Along with rapid reactivation, productivity increased significantly, unemployment fell to about 6 percent, and poverty fell from 41 percent in 1990 to 22 percent in 1994. After fiscal deficits that averaged 10 percent of GDP in most of the 1980s, a budget surplus was achieved in 1993. Defense spending and subsidies to public enterprises were reduced, creating room for a significant rise in social spending, especially pensions. A Brady debt deal was agreed in 1993, normalizing relationships with private banks following the default declared in 1982. Foreign capital flowed into the country, and investment rebounded to more than 20 percent of GDP, almost twice the mid-crisis level. Technology also leaped forward; by the end of 1993, the ministry of economy had an average of one computer per employee. Public services began to work, thanks to investments in modernizing and repairing infrastructure. Privatization meant that those corporations that had formerly lived off inflated public sector contracts had to earn their profits competitively. The cost of equipping telephone lines fell from US$4,500 per line in the 1980s to US$1,500 per year once the contract with the same supplier was renegotiated with the private operators. Much of the cost savings were passed on to the consumers through lower tariffs.[3]

Subnational Governments

One feature of Argentina's economic program was its extension to the provinces. Argentina is a federal state, with provinces providing many basic services and having a relatively high degree of autonomy. There are 23 separate administrations plus the city of Buenos Aires. Very diverse, the provinces in the northeast and northwest have more in common with neighboring Bolivia and Paraguay than with the wealthier provinces in the center of the country, let alone the capital. Provincial administrations were an integral part of Argentina's problems, with fiscal laxity, high indebtedness, tax evasion, excessive public sector staffing, loss-making public enterprises, and poor quality of services affecting both levels of government to varying degrees. As a result, most reforms in Argentina have involved the provinces too.

The provinces were keen to work with the Bank on reforms and to secure financing for investments. I remember our first meeting with all the provincial ministers of finance in a smoke-filled room in the ministry of interior in early 1990. To our surprise, they asked the Bank for financial support for carrying out their own structural adjustment programs, like the program being designed at the federal level. We had to say no, because, at the time, the Bank's policies did not include adjustment lending for subnational governments, and we had to find other ways to work with the provinces. This initial contact flourished, and over the following years—at differing paces and with differing outcomes—we supported provincial efforts at public sector reforms, capacity building, investment in infrastructure, flood rehabilitation and protection, education, and health. By the late 1990s, about half of the Bank's portfolio, excluding support on special terms, was with the provinces.

The Bank's Contribution in the Early 1990s

The Bank was prepared to help Argentina in 1990. Much of the economic program pursued in the early 1990s had been analyzed in the course of earlier prior economic and sector studies. After having assisted in several failed attempts at creating stabilization in the mid to late 1980s, the Bank invested in building country knowledge on the key reforms that would be needed eventually and in building capacity in the social sectors, in public sector management, and in tax administration. When the time came to apply this country knowledge to operations, there were experts prepared to take the lead. As documented elsewhere, we were heavily involved in some of the main privatizations: water, electricity, gas, and railways.

The government trusted us. The Bank was seen as neutral and without its own agenda. The low level of social capital in Argentina resulted in a system whereby most officials relied on *hombres de confianza,* often family members (resulting in high levels of nepotism) as well as school chums and long-time associates. Those practices undermined meritocracy in the public sector. There were factions in the government, with special interests competing for political power and control of resources. Authorities who were constantly on their guard could let down that guard with the World Bank.

That confidence was demonstrated in many ways. One was the space created for Bank staff members to provide advice even when there may have been many skilled Argentines who could have done the same. It was also demonstrated in the open communication with our counterparts. I remember being cautioned that the telephones might be tapped. But I was told not to worry, whoever was doing the tapping was interested in who told the Bank some information, rather than what the Bank would do with the information. So we continued to share information, simply not mentioning the names of the sources.

Our dialogue was frank. After the failure of the earlier Bank support for economic reforms in the 1980s, there was caution and an expectation that Argentina would have to perform this time. Getting a grip on the deficit was at the top of the agenda. During a visit to Argentina in 1990, the Bank's senior vice president gave a public speech on the need for improvements to the tax collection system. Comparing the experience of the United States and Argentina, he said that the difference was not the willingness of one population to pay taxes as compared with the other but the effectiveness of the respective tax agencies in collecting those taxes. Initially, we made great advances in that area, thanks to a dedicated professional in the ministry of economy.

Besides our direct counterparts, there were other key players in this early stage. The reform process got support from surprising quarters. One was the leader of the white-collar union for the public sector. He did not oppose civil service reform and instead saw it as an opportunity to advance the interests of his constituency. He foresaw higher salaries and better working conditions for those in the public sector who had highly skilled jobs. He was largely correct. We also got support from private business. Seeing the central role of reforming the public sector, a coalition of private leaders raised funds to support the government's efforts. Those monies were used to create a pool of specialized consultants available to the government to put in place its reforms and to retrain civil servants, complementing funds from the World Bank.

The Pending Agenda

Many good things were started in the early 1990s but not fully realized by the end of the decade. Modernizing Argentina's public sector is one. While there had been considerable improvements in pensions, budget formulation, external auditing and internal control, administrative structures, and the role of the state, much remained for Argentina to do to achieve its goal of being a "normal" country, even a member of the Organisation for Economic Co-operation and Development (OECD). The unfinished business has to do with improving governance, disciplining public spending, and collecting taxes at both the federal and the provincial levels. The state, still a heavy and bureaucratic burden on the economy, needed to be more supportive of investment and job creation by simplifying taxes and taking other measures to reduce transaction costs. Many provinces are far from being able to provide the services that they have to under Argentina's federal system. In addition, there are still many unresolved structural issues—health insurance for the poor, reproductive health, education quality, environmental protection, and elimination of the backlog of infrastructure deficiencies at the provincial level. Importantly, Argentina had yet to find an overall path that effectively addressed poverty and job creation. In each of those areas, attempts at reform did not advance as fast and as far as they should have. Although the political costs of the reforms may have been high, the costs of inaction were also high, as the later years of the 1990s demonstrated.

Some reforms have proved very difficult. One was reforming the law of coparticipation or revenue sharing between the federal and provincial governments. No one in Argentina defended the system as it was, and many academics and policymakers agreed on the direction change should take. The Bank had been very active in studying the problem and promoting an internal debate on possible solutions. However, the process required 100 percent agreement by the provinces. It was considered a zero-sum game: total tax collections were considered fixed, so each province argued to increase or at least not decrease its share, and collectively the provinces argued to reduce the share of the federal government. For the federal government, there would, no doubt, have been high political costs to negotiating with the provinces in order to achieve unanimity. To this day, there is no political consensus on how to reform the system.

The failure to complete other reforms during the later part of the 1990s is harder to explain. An important example is tax administration. Argentina continues to have one of the highest rates of tax evasion in Latin America, collecting only about 30 percent of value added taxes, with overall evasion estimated at about 50 percent.[4] There were positive results in the early 1990s, as new systems came on line to track the largest contributors and to institute audits, supported by two World Bank–financed tax administration projects. A heavy investment was made in computerization, much of it financed in the second half of the 1990s with funding from the Inter-American Development Bank. However, those efforts got bogged down after a few years. The courts ruled against the aggressive measures taken to close evading firms, and there was resistance within the tax authority against taking strong legal measures to pursue evaders. Internal corruption was pervasive, and even when the government took action to dismiss and charge employees, the courts did not uphold the charges. The program of tax audits was cut back, and critical data were not shared with other agencies—let alone within the tax authority. Essential elements, such as creating a unique taxpayer file so that the authority would know in real time the status of taxes due and paid by a given taxpayer, have still not been implemented.

Social programs were not immune to political interference and self-interest. A major difficulty was confronted in the consolidation of beneficiary rolls across social programs at both the federal and the provincial levels. We had long argued for consolidation of programs, as there were too many with too much duplication. The next best option was to have a unique roll of beneficiaries or a facility for cross-checking names. But this alternative, too, has been resisted. A benign interpretation credits internal bureaucratic resistance, with each structure protecting its own program. A less benign one is that political interests were not served by having one database of beneficiaries or the ability to cross-check.[5]

The Importance of Fiscal Performance

Some of the pending reforms were critical for maintaining convertibility, whereas others were part of improving overall well-being and achieving Argentina's long-term development goals. The critical one has to do with fiscal performance. Although others may disagree, I am of the view that this area was the weakest link.[6]

The first set of reasons has to do with Argentina's debt dynamics. First, even if one could justify a fiscal deficit to cover the transitional costs of the pension reform enacted in 1993, on intertemporal grounds, that level of deficit—some 1 to 1.5 percent of GDP—would still result in a considerable accumulation of debt over time. Second, Argentina's economy remained relatively closed, despite considerable trade liberalization in the late 1980s and early 1990s, because of transport costs that gave Argentine producers natural protection and because of remaining international and domestic barriers to trade and commerce. That situation meant that the ratio of its debt service to exports was quite high. Third, Argentina had a number of outstanding and contingent liabilities not reflected in its usual fiscal accounts. The resolution of those liabilities during the 1990s by issuing debt obscured the overall fiscal situation and added to the total debt burden.

The second set of reasons has to do with political economy. Argentina was striving to be a first-world country, a member of OECD. Although Argentina had a fiscal deficit of about 2 percent of GDP, countries such as Chile had consistently produced fiscal surpluses for most of the 1990s. Others, such as Canada, had adopted stringent fiscal policies when their debt burden became an issue. Thus, the country's fiscal performance was an important signal, among other things, that Argentina should do likewise. Moreover, within Argentina, the stance that the federal government took exerted considerable moral suasion on the provinces: if the federal government was going to exhort the provinces to practice fiscal prudence, it had to practice prudence itself. This posture was particularly important in the late 1990s when the fiscal performance of the province of Buenos Aires, the largest province, deteriorated significantly. Moreover, resolution of the pending issues related to revising the law of federal-provincial revenue sharing rested on making sure that fiscal performance by all parties could be controlled. Establishing fiscal balances as a minimum criterion would have to have been part of that agreement.

Resolving tax evasion was critical. Tax evasion is the most pervasive form of corruption in Argentina, where only about 50 percent of total taxes are actually collected. Collection of value added tax was only around 30 percent. Rough estimates show that a reduction in tax evasion to the level set in Chile would be more than enough to eliminate the deficit and reduce taxes, a move badly needed to keep Argentina competitive, make taxes more equitable, and increase incentives to investment. Tax evasion gave politicians the pretext of addressing the fiscal deficit by increasing taxes—knowing that the raise was not likely to increase total revenues—thus getting the best of both worlds: the appearance of fiscal discipline with the knowledge that, because people were not likely to pay, there would be little political cost.

The third, very important reason has to do with prudence. The convertibility plan meant that someday Argentina might face an economic downturn in which its options for redressing the situation would be limited by the intrinsic nature of the convertibility plan. Thus, it was only prudent that the government exercise countercyclical measures. It needed a fiscal cushion and debt space to be able to do so.

The Lack of Political Will

The political economy is no doubt a key factor in explaining resistance to resolving the fiscal situation and addressing some of the pending structural issues. As noted above, the fiscal challenge was not so great—on average only 2 percent of GDP. But there must have been formidable challenges. The first one was likely ideological. Philosophically, the Peronist Party was supported by a mix of unions and center-right interests. Although the party was conservative in some respects, it needed to appeal to a wide base of supporters, who spanned the political spectrum. Indeed, the initial support from the right, notably the Unión Cristiana de Dirigentes de Empresa Party, helped President Carlos Menem advance on privatization, but that party lost political support once its platform had been basically absorbed by the Peronist Party. Thus, there was no strong wing of the Peronist Party advocating stronger fiscal performance. Moreover, the opposition parties—notably the Radical Party—were also not motivated to make fiscal performance an issue: they too benefited from the state's largesse and saw no political gain in taking this stance. Given Argentina's history on fiscal matters, it is quite understandable that the key policymakers thought that a 2 percent fiscal deficit was already a major achievement. Moreover, they were not receiving signals from the capital markets that they were out of line. The markets turned only much later.

The second locus of resistance probably has to do with corruption. It is likely that certain public programs that were susceptible to bribery and fraud were longstanding sources for business, union, and political leaders to collude in financing political campaigns, to compensate loyalists, and to accumulate wealth. One can clearly identify the tax administration; union-run health insurance schemes; PAMI (Programa de Atención Médica Integral, a program providing health insurance for the elderly); and funding of public universities as sources for under-the-table monies and graft. There are no doubt more. During the course of implementation of Bank-supported programs in these areas, we were confronted with resistance to changes that would have helped considerably to resolve Argentina's fiscal problems. Most notable of these areas was the collection of taxes, as will be discussed in further detail. Pension administration was another case.

Some claim that the decreased zeal, after 1993, to undertake deeper structural reforms in those areas was by design. It is notable that most of the major reforms were complete by 1993: privatization of the major public utilities, administrative reform, strengthening of the central bank and banking supervision, tax modifications, decentralization to the provinces, and pension reform. The contention is that the Menem administration allowed the international financial community to be involved in only those core economic functions vital to stabilization and recovery within the public sector, keeping other functions off limits.

To its credit, the government reacted quickly to the Tequila crisis in 1995 and acted forcefully to curb the fiscal damage and to restructure the banking system. But the general consensus is that, for several reasons, political will and the zeal to reform faltered toward the end of the 1990s. One explanation is that President Menem saw his main mandate as resolving the macroeconomic crisis. By 1993, when this goal was by and large achieved, further reforms were not imperative, leaving the system of patronage intact. Another interpretation is that in 1994 (that is, before the 1995 elections), President Menem had reached an agreement with the Radical Party (which had influence in certain agencies) to continue to share power in return for political support in Congress for constitutional reforms allowing President Menem to run for a second term. This agreement perpetuated the existing system. A third interpretation is that there are parts of the public sector that were, in fact, not controlled by the administration at all but independent fiefdoms run by local "mafias."

A fourth explanation is that, by 1996, after the dangers of the Tequila crisis were over, President Menem had lost the ability to manage the deepening factions within the Peronist Party, because it became likely that he could not run for a third term. This loss of power is probably best demonstrated in the defeat in Congress of the draft bill to reform Argentina's outdated labor regulations: the bill put forward in 1996 by President Menem failed to receive the support of the 40-member wing of the Peronist Party from the province of Buenos Aires. The political role of the province of Buenos Aires—no doubt always important—became even more so. The province, home to an increasing number of poor, expanded its spending considerably from 1997 onward. This situation presented a complicated political scene for the central administration, considering that Provincial Governor Eduardo Duhalde could be a major contender in the 1999 election (as he was). Indeed, President Menem's strength was considerably weakened by the loss of control in the 1997 congressional elections. After so many years, adjustment fatigue may have taken over. Exhorting for reforms and responding to shocks takes a toll; each effort uses up available political capital and goodwill.

Argentina could not rest on its laurels, contrary to the popular characterization that the economy had been set on automatic pilot in the late 1990s. Regardless of the reason, it was apparent that the political will to carry out reforms at the federal level waned as the years passed, with only select provinces continuing to show any zeal. Given the rigidities of the convertibility plan, there was a serious risk that, if policies and institutions were held constant, the rate of growth would eventually slow as the benefits of past reforms were realized. Given the dynamics of the convertibility plan and changes in the international environment since its introduction, a continuous process of productivity improvements and cost reductions in the economy was imperative. More critical was the increasing disparity between the two goals of preserving stability and maintaining social cohesion. Even in the years of good economic performance in 1996 and 1997, unemployment and poverty were slow to improve, so that when the economy started to decline in late 1998, there was no social cushion.

The Risks and the Rewards

The convertibility plan is not for everyone. The conditions that made it a viable option in Argentina in 1991 were unique and had much to do with the country's legacy of failed attempts at stabilization and the high degree of dollarization within the domestic economy. The convertibility plan was rigid. It was intended to counter the lack of confidence in the durability of economic policies and to restore the faith in the banking system that had been lost with hyperinflation and the repeated, failed attempts at stabilization in the past. The risk that past policy mistakes or the poor implementation of good policies could be repeated in the future led to a strong desire to have macroeconomic stability locked in under the law, subject to very little discretion by political leaders. Authorities could not print money to resolve any fiscal problem, as they often had done in the past.

The idea was to force the authorities to rely on fiscal measures to the extent that markets were not willing to finance the public sector's deficits. This course exposed Argentina to the risks that the capital markets might not be open to the country for whatever reason and that, if the markets closed, the country might not have much time to react. It also exposed Argentina to the risk that global market perceptions could change, thereby adding to the country's risk premium and raising its cost of borrowing. All of those risks were realized during the late 1990s, starting with the Asia crisis in 1997 and followed by the currency devaluation by the Russian Federation in mid 1998.

The convertibility plan eliminated the use of exchange rate policy to adjust to shocks and changes in underlying competitiveness regardless of whether the changes were attributed to factors endogenous to Argentina. Thus, the plan opened Argentina to the risks, for example, that the U.S. dollar could change adversely to Argentina's interests (as it did in the late 1990s) or that Argentina's main trading partner, Brazil, would devalue its currency (as it did in early 1999), thus affecting Argentina's exports to that country. Moreover, it meant that all adjustments had to be made by the real sector, through employment, wages, and prices. To the extent that such adjustments, especially downward ones, could not be made easily or rapidly—because of internal factor market rigidities—the plan was at risk.

By and large, the convertibility plan worked as expected. On average, between 1993 and 1998, the economy grew substantially—close to 4 percent per year, including the effect of the Tequila crisis. The financial sector performed very well, particularly following the restructuring in the aftermath of the Tequila crisis, when the loss of deposits necessitated the consolidation of banking institutions and overall reinforcement of the system. Reserves were high, and the one-to-one backing of the local currency was respected. Productivity improved considerably throughout the 1990s, and exports grew rapidly and became more diversified until the shock of Brazil's devaluation in early 1999. Moreover, there was little evidence of major overevaluation of the peso until much later. Even then, the results of studies suggesting such overevaluation can be debated. Internal adjustments were being made, first by low inflation, then by deflation in the late 1990s. Wages began to fall, primarily in the informal sector. Argentina continued to have relatively low flexibility in its formal labor market so that much of the burden of the adjustments fell on employment creation.[7] Fiscal performance was good, but ultimately not good enough. In retrospect, it should have been better—particularly in the good years of 1996 and 1997. Notably, one study suggests that with relatively modest primary surpluses in the good years, Argentina's debt would likely not have been perceived as a problem in 2001.

The shocks experienced in Argentina in the late 1990s tested the convertibility plan. The least costly way to exit from convertibility would be when conditions were favorable, not in the midst of a crisis, a judgment that opens the issue of when Argentina could and should have exited and to what alternative. In the late 1990s, the government was keen on full dollarization, which also would have had problems, but other options were not clear, given the high level of dollarization within the economy. We also knew that the risks in staying with convertibility were high, but there were fears that the alternative—floating or managed exchange rates as had been used in the past—could be worse, as Argentina's previous 50 years had demonstrated. As a result, there was considerable internal consensus, reaffirmed during the 1999 elections and as part of the platform of the Fernando de La Rua administration, that Argentina needed to maintain convertibility.

It is not apparent that maintenance of macroeconomic stability under convertibility could produce a happy outcome. There may have been a point when society would not accept the consequence of the adjustment process—through wages, prices, and employment—implied under the convertibility plan. This territory was

unknown, and it is not clear that politicians and the public understood or acknowledged the full ramifications. During the 1999 presidential campaign, a future minister of economy and a contender for the presidency in 2001, Ricardo López Murphy,
proposed a 20 percent cut in public sector wages. His proposal was rejected out of
hand as political suicide.[8] Increasingly, Argentina faced a dilemma: to continue with
convertibility, including appeasing the vested interests in the dollar economy while
confronting the social costs, or to exit, a large and probably messy unknown.

Changing Social Parameters

Social issues that had not initially been critical became increasingly important. In the
early 1990s, robust growth and abundant employment opportunities facilitated the
internal adjustment. However, by 1994, there were signs that the social costs of the
transition to a more efficient economy could be high. The Bank's first poverty assessment in Argentina, using 1993 household data, showed that poverty was rising among
the urban and working population. It documented the shedding of labor in
Argentina's industrial sector. The effect was most noticeable among textile and other
import-substitution firms located in Greater Buenos Aires, where the bulk of the
country's small and medium-scale businesses were located. In addition, the volatility
of employee contracts increased as employment shifted to the informal sector and
from manufacturing to commerce and construction. At the same time, the wage premium for educated workers rose, reflecting technology change as well as supply
problems. Unfortunately, the Bank's poverty report was never authorized for release
by the government, inhibiting its internalization in the policy dialogue and sharing
with civil society.

The social situation was obscured by the Tequila crisis in 1995, which drove
unemployment to 18 percent and poverty to more than 30 percent in the following
year. It was hoped that this surge was only temporary and that employment would
rebound when the markets stabilized, with attendant effects on reducing poverty,
which was closely associated with employment in Argentina. To help in the transition, the government, with Bank support, implemented a number of new social protection programs, including the Trabajar Program, which was aimed at addressing
temporary employment problems. Even with renewed growth in 1996, employment
creation was not robust, and unemployment remained at 16 percent. Modifications
to temporary employment contracts, following the defeat of a draft bill to modern-
ize labor regulations in 1996, spurred employment for a time, with the joblessness
rate dropping to just over 12 percent in early 1999. But the economy was weakening, first because of the Asia crisis, then by the devaluations in Brazil and Russia.
Poverty had gradually risen back to more than 30 percent of the population by 1998
and, as 1999 came to an end, poverty and unemployment were clearly mounting. But
addressing those problems was put on hold until the outcome of the 1999 presidential elections.

Not all of the rise in poverty in Argentina can be attributed to economic performance, external shocks, or global trends in technology. In fact, there is no evi-

dence that trade liberalization contributed to poverty increases, and some policies, such as the elimination of export taxes on agriculture, contributed to improved equality across regions and stimulated growth outside of the central core of Buenos Aires. Importantly, there were other social phenomena. One was increased participation in the labor force, particularly noticeable among women but also among the elderly and youths (partly attributable to the secondary-worker effect). The most striking change in Argentina's poverty profile is the alarming increase in the number of children in poor families. Argentina is one of the few countries in Latin America in which family size among the poor increased during the 1990s. That growth can be attributed only to a failure to address reproductive health issues.

The Lack of Consensus on What to Do

That changing poverty profile clashed with popular conceptions in Argentina. When we released our updated poverty analysis in 1999–2000, the results alarmed policy-makers. The figures spurred much dispute in the press and denials among officials. In contrast to how the situation was popularly conceived—prosperous cities with poverty kept at the periphery—the major urban centers in fact bore the brunt of the labor dislocation. By the mid 1990s, Greater Buenos Aires had higher unemployment rates than the national average, and by the end of the 1990s, it had higher poverty rates. This problem no doubt contributed to a shift in political risks within the country. Argentina had long been considered one of the most equal societies in Latin America, with a large middle class centered in the Greater Buenos Aires area, which was now becoming impoverished.

Even during bad times, Argentines were accustomed to full employment. All through the 1980s, when the economy was in shambles, unemployment never went over 6 percent of the labor force because of overstaffing in both the public and the private sectors.[9] Not having a job meant lower status. Moreover, a job was defined as one with all the benefits, not a temporary or part-time job. This sentiment helped to defeat an effective program of temporary employment contracts in the private sector that was terminated in 1999 during the political campaign. Much of this discontent reflected nostalgia for the past: Argentina's middle class reached its zenith in the 1940s.

The confusion continued in the realm of what to do. In the past, quasi-full-employment policies had effectively negated the need for major safety nets for the unemployed. There also was an element of "machismo": politicians were keen to direct support to male heads of households, even when support might better have been directed to poor women with children. The confusion was compounded by fiscal conservatives, who considered social spending too high and who were reluctant to endorse social programs without more improvements in efficiency and targeting. Argentina was already spending well above the expenditure in other Latin American countries on social programs—mainly pensions—so there were genuine questions of the fiscal impacts. Participants in work-fare programs, such as Trabajar, complained that these jobs were not permanent—they were indeed intended to be temporary and not to address chronic problems—and liberal leaders in civil society were against targeting, as that stigmatized the participants.

As the economy worsened in the midst of the 1999 presidential campaign, there was no consensus on what to do. One option was to let wages adjust, as they had been, in order to stimulate employment but to compensate lower wages with intensified social programs. This course is what the Bank's chief economist advised when asked what to do during a meeting with the leading presidential candidates, and de facto it is what has happened. But social assistance has been relatively limited: it is not clear that increased inequality—implicit in providing minimal compensation for those with low wages—was acceptable for society at large. It was not clear that society would accept that it was better to have a low wage than not to work at all. Thus, despite its flaws, the main program supporting poor families as the economy slipped into recession was Trabajar, the public works program started under the Tequila crisis. Its successor, Jefes de Hogares (Heads of Households), began in 2002.

Confronting the Shocks of the Late 1990s

Could Argentina have avoided collapse if it had completed its reform agenda in time (particularly the missing fiscal dimensions), a condition necessary for maintaining the convertibility plan or exiting from it with a soft landing? Could it have done so if other events—namely, the Tequila crisis (1995), Asia crisis (1997), Russia devaluation (1998), and Brazil devaluation (1999)—had not intervened? Unfortunately, by 1999, President Menem was in his last year in office, with no chance of reelection. Moreover, political campaigning aggravated the situation, precluding effective action to counter the deterioration in the external environment and creating a climate of uncertainty.

The first few months of 2000 brought a reprieve and signs of an incipient economic recovery. Moreover, the many solid aspects of Argentina's economy, despite the ongoing recession, gave the new administration under President de La Rua an opportunity to address the external shocks that Argentina had suffered and to renew the reform agenda. Along with good intentions in early in 2000 and a considerable fiscal effort in both 1999 and 2000, there were also mistakes. The imposition of new taxes met resistance, and the corruption scandal associated with the passage of the labor reform bill provoked a political crisis, which led to the resignation of the vice president in October 2000.

There were signs of the executive's inability to handle the situation. Although Argentina had mobilized commitments of US$40 billion in external resources under the *blindaje* (the "shielding," as the IMF-approved bailout package was called), no action backed it, and the initial positive response by the markets soon dissipated. The resignation of the minister of economy in January 2001 was followed by the short-lived administration of his replacement and the appointment of a third minister in a matter of weeks. But when fiscal measures were finally put in place in mid 2001—the zero-deficit policy—they were seen as a last-ditch measure with slim chances of success. Eventually, the inability of the government to address the growing problems led to a withdrawal of bank deposits starting in July 2001, and a full-blown political crisis developed after the blocking of bank deposits at the beginning of December 2001. On December 20, 2001, President de La Rua resigned. Argentina declared default on its debts and ended convertibility in early 2002.

Underlying the crisis was the lack of credibility in Argentina's political institutions and leadership, whether under President Menem during his second term or President de La Rua in his two years in office. Congress failed both of them, in part because President Menem was a lame duck in his second term. Later the failure resulted from the composition of the governing Radical–Frente por un País Solidario coalition, which was designed to win the elections but not necessarily to lead.[10] The crisis also was linked to the inability of Congress and the executive to address the underlying fiscal problems. Most political leaders retained the hope that Argentina would grow out of its fiscal difficulties and that deeper reform of the public sector could be avoided. The lack of confidence in Argentina's leadership was pervasive.

The Bank's Contribution during the Late 1990s

After two years as senior operations adviser in the Latin America and Caribbean Region, where I joined the teams to help both Argentina and Mexico work their way through the Tequila crisis, and after two years as director of operations policy in Washington, D.C., where I worked with senior management and the Bank's Board on updating operational policies and processes, I was back working on Argentina in July 1997. My move was part of the Bank's program of decentralization of country directors to the field. In my case, I was also responsible for the Bank's programs in Chile and Uruguay, with Paraguay added later.

I was barely settled in Argentina when it became time to start preparing for a possible crisis. Even though Argentina was the fastest-growing country in the world in 1997, with GDP expanding by 8.4 percent, we were concerned by warning signs of the deteriorating external conditions and by their potential impact. The Bank's latest economic report, *Fiscal Dimensions of the Convertibility Plan*, raised flags about the sustainability of the fiscal path, highlighting continuing tax evasion, Argentina's rising debt burden, and the weight of extrabudgetary items (World Bank 1998). Moreover, despite rapid growth in 1997, unemployment and poverty continued to be relatively high. The last Country Assistance Strategy had shifted focus to the provinces and a renewal of infrastructure and social sector investments, leaving modernization of the public sector to the Inter-American Development Bank.

In March 1998, we began to prepare for the crisis, which materialized when Russia devalued its currency in August 1998. The Bank's chief economist just happened to be visiting Argentina, and I recall our discussions with officials in the central bank and the ministry of economy on what recourse Argentina would have. The response was that Argentina would defend convertibility and, if that did not work, dollarize. By September 1998, we had moved into high gear preparing support for Argentina. The Bank and IMF Annual Meetings that year became the setting for negotiations with the government.

Marked by considerable worry, this was a time of high uncertainty about the crisis spreading to emerging markets and about the ability of the global financial system to tolerate more shocks. There was also a concern about the capacity of the international financial institutions to help countries withstand widespread collapse, because IMF was in the process of replenishing its resources. High-level decisions had to be made as to where to put the Bank's resources and how much to allocate for each country, given the long line of countries requesting Bank support. Among others, Uruguay was not to receive support from the Bank.[11]

Argentina became one of the countries to receive support. New funding came from the Bank and the Inter-American Development Bank while the country renewed its agreement with the IMF. Large amounts were required to convince the markets that Argentina had the financial resources to honor its debts. In November 1998, the Bank approved a package of US$3 billion on special terms, in accordance with the Bank's new policy for helping countries facing short-term limitations in their access to international capital markets. The package, or special structural adjustment loan (SSAL), was aimed at shoring up Argentina's defenses, particularly in the banking sector; preparing for the social consequences of an economic shock; and keeping structural reforms on the radar screen while Argentina moved through both this difficult period and the presidential elections in 1999.

This was a brave attempt to ward off crisis. Initially, the program seemed to have worked, as Argentina regained access to international capital shortly thereafter. Moreover, confidence in the banking system remained high. Unlike the experience during the 1995 Tequila crisis, this time there was no massive withdrawal from Argentina's banking system until much later. Foreign capital continued to flow into Argentina, and the basic parameters of the economy, including the fiscal deficit, were manageable. However, the efforts under the SSAL were eventually overtaken by the events that culminated in the exit from the convertibility plan in January 2002. It was painful to watch the crisis unfold.

The Bank continued to try. We supervised the SSAL, gaining the adoption of almost all the reforms contained in the package, including those taken by the de La Rua administration. We continued to look for ways to engage and identified a number of provincial governments willing to address their structural problems. Our goal was to have a critical mass of provinces. Two large ones—Santa Fe and Córdoba—eventually received assistance, but our efforts to include the province of Buenos Aires did not result in an agreed program.

We worked on innovative social programs, building niches and experimenting with ways to address gaps and integrate social policy. There were further analyses of poverty in Argentina, a government-led public expenditure review, and benchmarking on fiduciary systems (procurement and financial management). We provided the new administration with a synthesis of our knowledge on a wide range of issues as well as the details of the Bank's operational program. Civil society was consulted on what our strategy should be in the country. As the crisis deepened in 2000 and 2001, we repeatedly offered our support and provided a list of policy reforms that we thought were needed. Our attention turned once again to modernization of the federal public sector, particularly those elements—such as tax administration—that had been lagging. Unfortunately, few measures materialized before the crisis hit at the end of 2001. We carried out various risk analyses and prepared a contingency plan for how we would respond if and when Argentina confronted another crisis.

But the seeds for Argentina continuing on a long-term path to development have been sown. I firmly believe that our contribution to development in Argentina will outlive the current crisis. The programs that we supported during the 1990s in health, education, social protection, gender, environment, renewable energy, infrastructure, flood protection, bank restructuring and supervision, tax administration, public sector management, anticorruption, judicial reform, public enterprises, and provincial reforms will endure. This message was the one that I left with staff when I retired in August 2002.

Lessons Learned

I left Argentina with renewed respect for what it meant to be a development practitioner. There is no question, as demonstrated in the case of Argentina, that development is a tough field. If that were not the case, then there would be many more success stories and fewer disappointments. Some lessons from my 22 years of experience follow.

Bridging Optimism and Realism

We have to expect a bumpy ride. Not everything works out as expected, and what happened in Argentina was ultimately not a surprise. As development practitioners, we have the unenviable role of having to be optimistic at the same time as we are realistic. We have to be optimistic to motivate ourselves and our colleagues, encourage our counterparts, and project this confidence to the press and general public. Yet we have to be realistic about the chances of success and seeing results, at least in the short run. In Argentina, we saw all the risks of the convertibility plan eventually realized by the end of the 1990s. But we were all convinced that the program under convertibility had a reasonable chance of success.

Taking a Long-Term View

Although we have to be realistic, we should not give up. Argentina has gone through many ups and downs during the past 100 years. I am sure that it will recover. More generally, it can take generations to see changes in the quality of life of the poor. Some of this interval is attributable simply to demographics. For example, the lag in changing the skills of the country's labor force may take several decades. Chile has done very well in improving the quality of its education system, the flow, but it was disappointed to learn that its overall labor force, the stock, had a low level of functional literacy compared with the labor force in OECD countries. This situation came about because many workers taught in the 1960s and

1970s did not advance beyond primary education. In response to this revelation, Chile embarked on a program to retain workers and offer opportunities for those already outside the system to return to complete their education. In Argentina, the changes made during the 1990s were likely only the start, considering the preceding 50 years of poor policy and weak institutions. Looking back at our expectations in the heady days of the early 1990s, we should have seen that considerable time would be needed.

Getting the Fundamentals Right and Covering the Basics

So much needs to be done. In the words of the Bank's Operations Evaluation Department, we need to do the right things and do them right. This is a double obligation. Certainly there is consensus on getting the macrofundamentals right, and I have seen how debilitating macroeconomic instability can be, whether in Argentina, Ghana, or Guinea. The Millennium Development Goals are also a good guide for development priorities. But we need consensus on core public services, focusing first on essential government functions and public goods. In the case of Argentina, we might not have conceded leadership so easily in efforts to improve tax administration. In Sub-Saharan Africa, development strategies might focus on the basic services of health, education, and transport, which have strong long-run implications for development outcomes. What would be different today if universal primary education had been the centerpiece of development in the 1960s, instead of large-scale physical infrastructure? I recall a conversation with Jim Adams, now vice president of operations policy and country services, in which he asked what would have happened if we had focused only on educating girls? Jim admitted that such an approach would not have been politically feasible. But this observation is worth thinking about, making sure that the basic areas are covered and are covered well.

Making Step-by-Step Improvements

I am reminded of the fable of the tortoise and the hare. Given the need for a long timeframe, it is probably too much to ask that development happen fast. Although some countries, such as Argentina, have taken bold steps quickly in crisis situations, theirs is not likely the most common route—nor may it be the right route for all aspects of development, because it creates the perverse need for a crisis to stimulate a response. Moreover, changes made may not be sustainable if they are not firmly rooted within society. Thus, it is more likely that sustainable development will entail a progression of step-by-step changes, or boot-strapping, with each step building on the last and advancing along a given path. This approach requires vision and foresight. Such an approach was the intention of two new instruments within the Bank, namely, the learning and innovation loan and the adaptable program loan. Both were created while I was director of operations policy to provide more flexibility in matching the Bank's lending instruments with the pace and nature of the development process. The development model pursued in Chile during the 1990s under the left-of-center coalition, the Concertación, is slow but sure. I recall a former minister of finance of Chile reflecting on his experience: he thought that it was better to stick with a given policy, even if it was not perfect, than to have rapid changes that the public could not absorb.

Going for Broke

Sometimes shocks are needed. A leader may have to be audacious to change expectations and break away from dependency on a certain path. Some situations are binary and call for all or nothing. Sometimes, as for Argentina in 1990, there is no time to wait. The country had failed so many times in the past that it could not afford to do so again. It adopted radical measures, notably convertibility to stabilize the exchange rate and privatization to alter the rules of the game. But such measures are not for everyone, and Argentina's choices reflect its unique circumstances. From the outset, it is clear that convertibility was high risk, but it seems that President Menem accurately gauged the pulse of the Argentine people and determined that rapid change was needed. Argentines can be impatient and seem to have a national trait of looking for the quick fix. Moreover, their human capacity is so well developed that change can be absorbed more readily. Yet because of the lack of urgency when economic performance was good, especially in 1996 and 1997, Argentina ran out of time to complete its reform agenda when hit by a series of external shocks. If I had the luxury of living life over again, knowing what I now know, I would have gone for broke on the law of revenue sharing and reduction in tax evasion.

Working with the Markets

It may be futile to try to beat the markets, but maybe we should not count on them too much. One can try to reduce imperfections or regulate, as Chile did for many years, making it harder for capital flows to exit quickly. But it takes an enormous effort to change market sentiment once the outlook has turned negative. Attempts by Argentina did not work. By and large, the Bank's instruments to attempt to change market perceptions have had only marginal and transitory effects. This is the case for the 1998 SSAL and its accompanying policy guarantee in 1999. The efforts by the international financial institutions in late 2000 under the *blindaje* were ultimately ineffective. The promise was that Argentina would get its house in order but, as time went by, economic policy fell in disarray, and credible actions were not forthcoming. The markets eventually lost faith and increasingly doubted the debts could be honored. By mid 2001, this skepticism turned into a self-fulfilling prophecy. This time, limiting our exposure, the Bank held back and provided only funds that had been committed previously. We may have expected too much from the markets. Under Argentina's convertibility plan, the markets were to act as a check on fiscal deficits, signaling if and when they thought that fiscal performance and debt levels were not compatible with the maintenance of the convertibility plan. Whether because of the general exuberance of the markets during the early 1990s or because of an underestimation of what level of fiscal performance was sustainable, the market continued to finance Argentina's deficit for a very long time.

Seeing the Importance of Politics

Politics is pervasive. It is an intrinsic part of development, especially under democratic systems. Moreover, the three dimensions of development—economic, social, and political—work in concert. When policy formulation no longer resides only in the executive branch of government, power and responsibilities are shared by the executive, judiciary, and legislature. Increasingly, the process is participatory, and society's consent has to be sought. The biggest failure in the case of Argentina has been the inability of the three powers to work together, with the weakest link perhaps the political dimension. Unlike postdemocratic Chile, Argentina's political institutions failed to recognize the critical state of the country's situation. Although there were deep political differences, Chile's governing coalition found a way to work with the opposition, gaining backing for its socially progressive agenda. It also found a way to run an administration effectively, incorporating officials from the parties that made up the coalition. And it progressed in promoting the rule of law and ensuring access to the legal system, despite the judiciary's legacy from prior military rule. Argentina was not able to do the same. Like many countries in Latin America, Argentina has a long tradition of personalized power, which is centralized in the presidency. There is a history of political instability, weak mandates, political stalemates, electoral fraud, manipulation, and violence. Reform of Argentina's political institutions was one of the issues that had been on the agenda of the de La Rua administration, only to be waylaid by the crisis. It continues to be badly needed.

Having a Common Language

Words count. Much of what has happened in development in the 1990s has been polarized by words, and as development practitioners, we are faced every day with explaining what we do and why we do it—often to anxious populations. Unfortunately, the 1990s seems to have been a decade in which the vocabulary used by development practitioners differed considerably from that used by opponents to change and to global trends. A notable example is the term the *Washington Consensus*. To me, that term is shorthand for the range of measures undertaken in Latin America and elsewhere. To others, it connotes dominance by the Washington-based international financial institutions and adoption of a neoliberal, capitalistic ideology. *Structural adjustment* became synonymous with layoffs and budget cuts even though it also meant reducing tax evasion, increasing budget allocations for social programs, and eliminating subsidies to the rich. As practitioners, we can overcome these problems by being frank and direct. I recall addressing a group of university students in Argentina in the early 1990s. One asked why the World Bank promoted the elimination of free tuition at public universities. I responded that 70 percent of university students had attended private secondary schools, indicating that most families could certainly afford to pay. I added that, if there were public monies available for education, I would rather see that money benefit children who lived on the streets and had no chance to attend school, let alone a university. The students applauded. There is now a public program of scholarships to help keep poor children in schools, and public universities have the right to charge fees, even if only a few do.

Remembering That Luck Plays a Role

The convertibility plan in Argentina had a strong chance of working. It provided macrostability for the longest period since the 1950s and the platform for many ultimately positive and lasting changes. But the risks were high, maybe too high, given the many unknowns, random events, and variables that ultimately came into play. It is clear that Argentina's convertibility plan was right to control inflation in 1991, but it may not have been right for Argentina given what happened during the intervening period. What would have been the outcome if the U.S. dollar traded at $1.25 per euro as it did in 2001, as compared with $0.80 per euro in 1998, or if Brazil had not devalued its currency in early 1999? What would have happened if 40 Peronists representing the province of Buenos Aires in Congress had voted for the reform of labor laws in 1996? Going back in time, what would have happened if the United States had included Argentina as one of the countries able to sell grains and other foodstuffs to Europe under the Marshall Plan in 1948? Argentina could now be in the same position as Canada and Australia, two countries that benefited greatly from being able to sell their products in postwar Europe. No one knows.

Moreover, it is hard to determine in retrospect what was right or wrong. What is considered good practice one day can be reversed the next, because economics and development are not pure sciences but social sciences. This is the case of capital controls, which were earlier considered poor policy but now are recommended. Would Argentina's outcome have been different if our knowledge about such things as capital controls or how to manage a banking system in a dollarized economy were better than it was in 1991? More generally, a country's development path is made up of its historical legacy combined with how it reacts at critical points. Undoubtedly, there have been many decisive moments in Argentina's history that have shaped what it is today. As development practitioners, we cannot predict those moments or control their outcomes. The most that we can do is facilitate understanding; bring experiences to bear; and, while hoping for the best, help the country to be ready for whatever happens, including negative outcomes.

Notes

1. The movement known as Mothers of the Mayo Square, protesting the disappearance of children during the last military rule, is the big exception to the rule. The more recent experience of the neighborhood protests by the middle class over the blocking of bank accounts at the end of 2001 is likely to have been spontaneous, but even then there were attempts to subsume this movement into the established political parties.

2. Argentina rates particularly low on the dimension of trust within society, much lower than member countries of the Organisation for Economic Co-operation and Development and developing countries such as China and Costa Rica. See World Bank (2002a).

3. Privatization in Argentina resulted in lower tariffs for many privatized services, notably, electricity, telephones, and water. Services were expanded, reaching new clients—mainly the less well-off, who had not received services in the past. In addition, consumers enjoyed improved quality of services and did not have to invest in alternative services as in the past. Among the additional benefits appear to be improved health indicators in those areas with privatized water services. See Walton and others (2004).

4. One explanation for this situation is that countries achieve a political economy equilibrium with respect to the size and nature of their fiscal system and stay there until they are shocked into a new equilibrium. See Walton and others (2004).

5. A local survey on tax evasion indicated that the cross-checking of different data sources was the biggest fear of tax evaders. A Bank-financed project, called the Social and Fiscal Identification System, was approved in 1999 with the express purpose of cross-checking public databases to identify duplication and fraud.

6. See the views of Michael Mussa, senior fellow, former IMF chief economist (Mussa 2002).

7. After the draft bill to reform Argentina's labor regulations was defeated in Congress, President Menem attempted to put the same reform into effect by executive order. However, the courts declared this attempt unconstitutional. The next best alternative to stimulate job creation was to lower nonwage labor charges, especially for social security. The government embarked on that course even though the loss in revenue needed to be offset by cuts in public spending.

8. Professor Arnold C. Harberger, in his work, "The View from the Trenches," describes the risks that big depreciations will translate into big deflations and will impose huge costs (Harberger 2000). He acknowledges that Argentina may have been a special case for using a fixed exchange rate, in light of its 20-year battle with inflation, and the fact that the people (up to that point) had borne the costs of persistent deflationary pressures, feeling that this was the price that they would have to pay for stability. Harberger contends that, to be successful, fiscal performance should have been better at the outset.

9. The extent of overstaffing in public enterprises during the period up to 1990 was extraordinary, judging from the fact that after privatization, employment in key public enterprises fell from 300,000 in 1988 to about 50,000 by 1994.

10. World Bank (1999) analyzed the general weakness of coalition governments in pursuing reforms.

11. It turned out that Uruguay was relatively unaffected by the events in 1997–99 and was able to tap the international capital markets throughout this period. However, when the crisis in Argentina worsened in 2001–02, Uruguay was affected. The international financial institutions provided considerable support to Uruguay in 2002 and 2003 to help contain the damage to its banking system and to restore confidence. As of 2004, that program is holding, and the country is recovering from a sharp downturn.

Jayasankar Shivakumar

*Former Country Director for
Thailand (1997–2001)*

Jayasankar Shivakumar ("Shiva") has spent all 44 years of his working life in public service, but he never planned it that way. After earning a master's degree in physics in India, he somewhat reluctantly took the Indian Adminstrative Service exam, prodded by his family of career civil servants. When Shiva finished in the top 15 among the tens of thousands who took the exam, he made the difficult decision to leave science and enter public service. "I never looked back," he says, and he has since spent a career in development evenly divided between service in South Asia, Africa, and East Asia.

Working in the Indian civil service "opened up whole new worlds of relationships to me," Shiva recalls. Whereas his previous success had been built on scientific acumen, his posts in the Indian government—where he served as administrative head of one of the largest districts in the country and as special assistant to two finance ministers in the 1970s—led him to develop a new set of skills, focused on problem solving, management, and leadership. "I learned that the most important thing is to apply common sense," he says, advice that is equally valid in people management and policymaking.

Shiva left India in 1977 to earn a master's degree in public administration at Harvard University. Rather than return to his home country at a politically tumultuous time, Shiva decided to shift gears and join the World Bank. He describes the choice as the best for his family as well as for himself. A rising star in Indian government, he knew that joining the Bank offered him a chance to shed the stresses of growing power and prestige. "I was very comfortable becoming unimportant," he says in his naturally self-effacing manner.

At the Bank, Shiva has exercised and further refined his management skills, serving in a variety of posts across many sectors. He began with a 14-year stint in the Eastern Africa Region, managing agricultural operations and later serving as program coordinator in the Office of the Vice President. He shifted to the East Asia and Pacific Region in 1992, serving first as the region's chief of human development and then of infrastructure. His managerial aptitude was recognized in 1997 with an appointment to country director of Thailand, shortly after the devaluation of the baht precipitated the East Asian crisis. Shiva left Thailand in 2001 and now serves as a senior adviser in the East Asia Region, where his manage-

rial talent has once again been tapped to advise on the Nam Theun 2 Project in Lao People's Democratic Republic (PDR), one of the most complex and controversial dam projects in
the world.

Of the lessons learned from his long and varied experience in development, Shiva says,
"There are no ready-made solutions. You must keep inventing." Technical analysis should illu-
minate challenges and suggest potential alternatives, rather than impose a straitjacket on
policy, he feels. Even one's "experience is a handicap if applied blindly." Despite the enormity
of development challenges around the world, he says confidently, "You need to see the glass
as half full. The client knows the way out." The challenge for the Bank "is to articulate it."

Shiva concedes that his lack of formal training in economics "makes me a strange animal in
the Bank." But he sees this difference as an asset rather than a hindrance to his effectiveness
as a development practitioner, allowing him to apply his flexible approach to problem solving
to the variety of regions and sectors in which he has worked. He remains relentlessly upbeat
about his work and his prospects. "Right through my career, I have not had a dull day."

14 Bank Engagement in a Country

A Practitioner's View

Jayasankar Shivakumar

THIS CHAPTER IS NOT A RIGOROUS STUDY OF ISSUES AT HAND BUT RATHER A COLlection of impressions and opinions drawn from the experience of a practitioner. I have prepared it with the object of stimulating debate on the subject of Bank engagement in a country. It offers ways to improve the Bank's mode of country engagement, while keeping mindful of the changes that the world has witnessed since the 1990s.

It begins with personal reflections on the problems faced in Thailand during the economic crisis of the late 1990s and examines how Bank operations in the country evolved, leading to the emergence of the Country Development Partnership (CDP). Conclusions are drawn from those experiences. Some personal reflections are also provided on certain past Bank activities in which a different form of engagement could have produced better outcomes, alternatives that, at that time, the environment did not support. The chapter then makes the case for mainstreaming the CDP as a mode of Bank engagement. The chapter concludes with suggestions regarding certain reforms needed in the Bank's organizational structure to support that shift.

The Thailand Experience

The Bank's reorganization of 1997, like all reorganizations that preceded it, was a trying time for its managers, particularly those who belonged to the marshmallow-middle. In the words of a colleague, "It is a time when job satisfaction is reduced to the satisfaction of having a job." I was, therefore, much relieved when the regional vice president informed me that I was likely to be offered the position of country director of Vietnam—a country I immensely admired. But the relief was only temporary: I was told a few days later that the deal was off and instead I would be offered Thailand, which had a reputation as a difficult country, where the role of the Bank was not particularly appreciated. In fact, a decision had been made a year before to close the resident mission in Thailand after the Bank's relevance had hit a new low. Sensing my disappointment, the regional vice president assured me that the challenge was to

315

strengthen Bank engagement in Thailand and said that, if I failed, it would not be held
against me. Lacking the luxury of other, less unattractive options, I reluctantly joined
as the Bank country director for Thailand on July 1, 1997, and reconciled myself to
having an unexciting job—rationalizing that a potential benefit could be the opportunity to develop other interests so absent in my life. But that was not to be.

All Hell Broke Loose

Just 24 hours after I formally took charge of the new job, the Thai baht was devalued, triggering a huge economic crisis. The country crisis soon spread to the region
with an impact that was global. The International Monetary Fund (IMF) arrived
with the usual fanfare. It brought with it policy packages, money, and influence in the
financial markets. All three were in demand, but the last was critical given that outside intervention was needed to overcome the international community's loss of
confidence in the domestic leadership in Thailand. Vultures from financial markets in
New York also began to descend on Bangkok, demanding drastic action by IMF
while searching for corpses with assets that would help them line their pockets. The
media, with television crews and cameras flashing, followed international teams
everywhere. The Bank suddenly became an important player. But the timing for this
newfound visibility could not have been worse.

The Government Leadership Was Inept

The government in charge in Thailand was widely known as inept. Shell-shocked and
demoralized, it had little grasp of the issues that led to the crisis and no clue as to how
to respond. The finance portfolio had changed hands often, and the reputation of the
Bank of Thailand, once the pride of the country, was now in the doldrums. No solid
and reliable analysis was available on which to plan strategies for handling the crisis.
The arrogance previously shown by government officials evaporated and gave way to
an open admission of helplessness. Demand for Bank assistance rose exponentially.

The Bank Was Caught Unprepared

The first phase of the Bank's involvement in the crisis was plagued by obstacles.
The Bank had done little economic work on Thailand before the crisis. The few
Bank economists who anticipated problems in Thailand were a discouraged lot,
scoffed at by their counterparts in the country and viewed as Cassandras by colleagues in the Bank. At the time, macroeconomists also felt undervalued by Bank
leadership, and the role of the Bank relative to that of IMF was unfortunately seen
by some who mattered as duplicative, not complementary. In that context, it is not
surprising that the Bank's annual economic work program in Thailand focused on
environmental issues, entailing opportunity costs in terms of the loss of grip over
macroeconomic and financial issues. Projects focused on the power and road sectors. The Bank's knowledge base on macroeconomic, financial, and corporate sec-

tor issues was abysmally weak, and those were precisely the sectors from which the crisis stemmed.

IMF Led the Reform Effort

IMF, too, came in raw. But, of course, that did not deter it from taking charge of the emergency room operations and demanding a whole range of specific reform measures—right or wrong—that would give comfort to financial markets. Given the nature of its role in a financial crisis, IMF does not enjoy the luxury of working in a timeframe that allows it to study issues in depth, appreciate nuances, and see implications that relate to a range of disciplines beyond macroeconomics and finance. Most importantly, it does not have to listen to the various stakeholders, particularly local ones, before pressuring the government to accept the IMF program, one that inevitably reflects a one-size-fits-all philosophy and is manufactured at headquarters before the mission is launched.

IMF's mission leaders are empowered to control mission members tightly, silence dissent wherever it emerges with an iron hand, and always deliver on time. However, to be fair to the IMF staff members, it must be appreciated that this behavior is partly driven by their mandate, and many of them, who are excellent, dedicated professionals, have little choice in the matter. Given this constraint faced by IMF, the Bank—as its most important partner with a long-term development view—has an obligation to complement IMF efforts and help strengthen its program just as the family doctor's influence on emergency room decisions could be in the interest of the patient. In Thailand, however, this collaboration did not happen.

The Bank Was Initially Ineffective

Bank staff members did join IMF missions, but no matter how gifted, they did not find it easy to be effective as a member of such missions. Three preconditions were missing. First, Bank staff members must have at hand a thorough grasp of country-level issues so that viable solutions can be worked out with IMF and the government. Second, Bank staff members must have existing relationships with government officials in order to offset the unusual level of power that IMF staff members exercise over a country at the time of crisis. Third, they must possess confidence that there will be unwavering support from the higher echelons of the Bank if conflicts arise within the mission. The Bank makes many of its decisions in the field at different levels of management. IMF decisions are made at high levels in Washington, D.C. Effective interventions by the Bank at Washington are vital.

Bank participants in the initial IMF missions had none of the necessary advantages at the time that the crisis erupted. The absence of Bank analytical work had a crippling effect on staff members' grasp of issues. Because of the impasse in Bank-country relations, communication with the client had to start from scratch in most cases, a complication compounded by the fact that, because the Bank had undergone major reorganization on July 1, 1997, a whole set of new staff members and managers was now involved. Financial Operations had become a new department manned by several new Bank staff members—some of whom were excellent professionals but had never worked abroad. Many of the Bank sector managers, though they had a strong background in their field, were new to the Bank and were quite lost in their new environment. The hierarchy within the Bank simply did not function with new managers, vacant positions, and confusion regarding matrix management.

This situation was compounded by a sense of loss of direction in development economics. The East Asia crisis shattered the Washington Consensus and with it the confidence that the World Bank and the IMF had all the answers. The managements of these institutions at Washington were unable to reverse this perception quickly enough. Matters were made worse by a running battle between the Bank chief economist, Joseph Stiglitz (whose views on issues were generally right on the mark but offered little operational guidance, instead spurring acrimonious but inopportune debate on brilliant new paradigms), and top managers at IMF (who were sometimes inseparable from U.S. Treasury officials).

Therefore, insofar as the initial IMF program was concerned, the quality and effect of the Bank's contribution left much to be desired. Bank economists and financial practitioners in the frontline, however, should not be blamed for a situation dictated by the extenuating circumstances.

The Bank Got Its Act Together

Fortunately, the managing director and the vice president got personally involved in the crisis at its early stage and gave the personal support needed for rapid response. They did not hesitate to bring the ineptitude of the government to the attention of the highest authority in the country and the Bank's Board of Executive Directors. Whether or not as a consequence of this candor, the government changed in Thailand, and a competent government with a highly regarded finance minister stepped in.

Meanwhile, an ad hoc Bank team did an admirable job of working closely with country counterparts in a control room atmosphere and prepared an International Development Association (IDA) financial technical assistance (TA) project. The operation broke historical records by taking less than two weeks from concept to Board approval. An economic TA followed soon thereafter. The two TA programs laid down a medium-term operational program and a framework for Bank involvement. Building an effective and balanced Bank team was, however, a real challenge given the managerial changes happening within the Bank. It took three to six months to bring together a first-rate team of economists and financial practitioners from the silos within the Bank. Fortunately, at the same time, the government also changed in Thailand. The stage was set, therefore, for a stronger Bank–country relationship.

Initially, Success Remained Elusive

For a variety of reasons, the economy did not respond positively to the initial IMF program, nor did it show signs of recovery for quite some time.[1] As a result, IMF was seen by many in Thailand as part of the problem, not the solution. Whenever I visited rural areas, villagers would refer to the crisis as the *IMF*—a new word, meaning calamity, added to the Thai language! I will mention just five areas in which the IMF program faced problems: the closure of finance companies without thinking through next steps, the reduction of the fiscal deficit at a time when spending should have been boosted, the neglect of corporate sector issues when those issues drove the crisis, the rather indiscriminate extension of guarantees to deposit holders, and the imposition of outside models in regard to reform of the legal framework for the financial sector. To its credit, IMF took swift measures to address those problems as they manifested themselves.

But three important factors handicapped efforts to find solutions. First, the reform program was, unfortunately, driven mainly by solutions imported from abroad—solutions that did not take into account the local situation, particularly social and cultural factors and Thai business practices. Second, the quality and effect of the program were diminished by its limited ownership, which was restricted to a narrow group of counterparts. Third, even within that narrow band, the silo characteristics of the Ministry of Finance and the Bank of Thailand fed an unwillingness to cooperate with each other. The Bank, with a strong team now in place, began to help overcome those handicaps thanks to the generosity of donors who provided trust funds. To its credit, IMF began listening to the Thai finance minister. The Bank moved into the second phase of its postcrisis involvement in Thailand, and constructive relationships between the government, IMF, and the Bank characterized this period.

The Bank Got Going with Adjustment Lending

The two TA projects mentioned earlier focused on the fundamental causes of the crisis, to the extent they—not just the symptoms—could be identified in the short time available. The programs were designed with the interests of Thailand in view, not the financial markets in New York. The establishment of such a program provided an overview of the crisis, set in motion work on solving problems, and built the relationships with country officials. But answers to many complex problems remained elusive and required more time for analysis and consultations. The Bank was under pressure to act. I recall the wise remarks of a Thai journalist who said that IMF makes wrong decisions on a timely basis and the Bank makes right decisions when it is too late.

The two TA projects went a long way toward providing foundations for the Bank's adjustment lending program and led to the approval within two years of four structural adjustment loans (SALs) involving US$2 billion. The adjustment loans supported a knowledge program that focused on finding answers to the complex problems that cried out for remedy. The three economic and financial adjustment loans covered critical issues such as the resolution of failed financial institutions, restructuring and recapitalization of the remaining financial institutions, enhanced supervision and regulation, corporate debt restructuring, limited deposit insurance, accounting and governance reform, development of the government bond market, and public debt management. The fourth adjustment loan was the US$400 million public sector reform loan. It was the first ever programmatic adjustment loan, a form of loan that has now become the main mode of adjustment lending in the Bank. It used the open-

JAYASANKAR SHIVAKUMAR

ing provided by constitutional reform and the fiscal crisis to push cross-cutting public sector reforms in public expenditure management, civil service reform, decentralization, and public accountability.

In addition, an innovative and successful investment project, the US$400 million Social Fund project, provided direct relief to the poor and the vulnerable through nongovernmental organization (NGO) networks tapping Thailand's exceptionally talented NGO leadership. An innovative guarantee operation, which reintroduced the Electricity Generating Authority of Thailand to the financial markets by enhancing a bond issue, was also implemented. All those valuable interventions would not have been possible without the remarkable contribution of the country's officials, led by the Thai finance minister himself, and the support of the prime minister and his other colleagues. In terms of lending, the Bank delivered more than the US$1.5 billion that was promised at the Tokyo Donor's Meeting on August 12, 1997, when the US$17.2 billion assistance plan for Thailand was finalized.

A Social Fund Project Made a Difference

The Social Fund project deserves special mention. The severe social dimensions of the crisis and their implications for the poor received little attention until the Bank highlighted them. This action legitimized the role of the Bank as an institution that cares about people.[2] Indeed, the project represented the best the Bank can do in a country. Bank staff members—backed by the Bank network and by consultants with global expertise, who were working with NGOs at the ground level, dealing with real people in villages, and hearing voices pleading for assistance—designed mechanisms to work in the local context. The great benefit gained from dealing with Social Fund projects is that they compel you to listen to stakeholders; solutions to design issues have to originate from them. Audit rules had to be simplified, supervision and results monitoring had to be devolved to NGOs, suitable works had to be identified by beneficiaries, and construction methods appropriate in the local context had to be adopted—all within a very short timeframe. The project was highly successful and helped to mitigate the impact of the crisis on tens of thousands of Thais. A large part of the credit for its success goes to NGO leaders in Thailand, who fully owned this operation, and the government, which provided encouragement.

An Unexpected Turn of Events Occurred

Returning to the adjustment program: before enough progress could be made, an unexpected turn of events occurred. Thailand's reserves position improved dramatically. The success of the program—initially drawn up by IMF but modified by strong leadership from the new government working with IMF and the Bank—became evident. What contributed most to this accomplishment was the turnabout in international perceptions of Thailand, thanks to the performance of the government and particularly the finance minister. With the improvements evident, and mindful of the external debt situation, Thailand rightly decided not to borrow any more funds from the Bank. The comprehensive reform program driven by lending was suddenly orphaned by the abrupt reduction of Thailand's borrowing needs. The clout of a lender was no longer available to the Bank. And the influence of the IMF waned as well. A third phase—as it turned out, a sustainable form of Bank-country engagement—was launched.

A New Relationship Was Needed in the Absence of Lending

The decline in Thailand's borrowing needs did not signal the end of its problems. Indeed, the issues faced in deepening the reform program and sustaining its momentum remained. Because the reforms required increased capacity for implementation and knowledge transfers, the government had to seek help through capacity-building support and technical assistance for strategic areas such as competitiveness, governance, social protection, and the environment. Therefore, a new mode of cooperation was needed to support the Thai government's reform agenda. That cooperation was essential to help the government convert its development goals into strategy, push the implementation of the Ninth Plan (framed in the context of a new constitution), and benefit fully from the productive partnerships that had already been established. This mode of cooperation had to allow the government to maintain leadership of the reform program while gaining access to global experience and expertise. Given Thailand's interest in knowledge sharing, the mode of cooperation also had to facilitate the dissemination of information on Thailand's reform program to international markets and transfer lessons learned in Thailand to the world outside.

The Country Development Partnership Was Born

Necessity is the mother of invention. The Country Development Partnership, drawing inspiration from the Comprehensive Development Framework (CDF) and learning lessons from the benefits of participation gained from the Thailand Social Fund project, was formulated by government in cooperation with the Bank and launched by Bank President James Wolfensohn. This instrument, not yet formally included in the Bank's array of instruments, has now firmly taken root in Thailand and currently underpins Thailand's Country Assistance Strategy, covering the key areas of economic competitiveness, social protection, poverty, and governance. The CDP is now the instrument that drives Bank involvement in comprehensive reforms in Thailand and positions the Bank to harvest the fruits of some years of experience with this instrument. Many of the Bank's existing instruments are compared to a hammer that makes every problem look like a nail. In sharp contrast, the CDP is extremely flexible and can be likened to a toolkit, containing many tools—not just a hammer—that can be used in different combinations.

The CDP Is a Country-Led Management Instrument

The CDP, to provide a summary description, is based on a framework anchored on four key interrelated principles pursued at the country level: a long-term vision and strategy, enhanced country ownership of development goals and actions, more strategic partnership among stakeholders, and accountability for development results. It is an approach that builds on the lessons of worldwide cooperation between external partners and developing countries. It begins with the creation of a development matrix, provided by the government, which highlights a country's medium-term development goals, as prioritized by the government, in partnership with civil society and the private sector and with support from the Bank and external donors. The matrix, which can build on an adjustment-lending framework, provides a suitable context for effectively determining the flow of development assistance from the Bank and other donors. Setting up the development matrix leads in turn to the establishment of a partnership matrix, which is prepared by the government or a lead partner invited by the government to assist with a specific CDP. It is founded on partnerships and promotes technical assistance and capacity building with a view to helping clients carry out their own development. Founded on key principles of the CDF, the CDP is a holistic approach to development that balances macroeconomic and structural, human and physical development needs.

The CDPs in Thailand Are Described

In the case of Thailand, CDPs support the objectives of Thailand's Ninth Economic and Social Development Plan. The CDP, through the development matrix, provides a suitable context for effectively linking the Bank's Country Assistance Strategy with other donors' development assistance. The CDP is not a legally binding agreement with external donors because it does not necessarily involve lending and performance conditions in the traditional sense. It is, therefore, a flexible instrument. The focus of donor involvement is through technical assistance and support for capacity building, with the government taking the lead on donor collaboration. Donors have the option of supporting the country's development and reform program by taking the initiative to support specific high-priority CDP exercises in line with their own comparative advantage and interests. The CDP provides an integrated framework for the government's reform strategy, as embodied in the Ninth Plan, for a particular area of development (for example, poverty or governance). The CDP sets forth a three-year plan for progress in a particular reform area, specifying objectives and a program of actions, and identifies the supporting technical assistance required.

Each CDP framework consists of three one-year modules; as the first year's module is being implemented, the preparation of the second will be taking place, a schedule in tandem with the government's budget cycle. Although the CDP does not involve borrowing, it could facilitate future borrowing—should any become necessary—because it maintains close engagement with external partners in a manner that enables resources to be accessed quickly in case of an unexpected setback in Thailand's macro position. In addition, the CDP objectives can be supported by borrowing in certain priority areas, and highlighting the borrowing need by analytical work and supporting it by the partnership, a feature that broadens support for the Bank's lending efforts.

The Bank decided to support Thailand by carrying out four high-priority CDPs: enhancing competitiveness, improving governance, strengthening social protection, and reducing poverty. It must be noted that, without decentralization of Bank operations to the field, it would not have been possible to engage in such direct collaboration with domestic partners—a critical component of this instrument. In part because of the mandate of the 1997 Constitution, the government is developing participatory processes that engage the private sector and civil society in a more meaningful way. To ensure that reforms take hold, these domestic partners help drive the national agenda and are involved actively in both policymaking and capacity building. Thus, a key feature of the new partnership is to facilitate the empowerment and participation of domestic partners. The CDP also helps break down compartments within government itself, strengthening cooperation among different parts and thereby overcoming a key obstacle to reform in the past. The CDP also serves as a useful mechanism for informing international markets on the country's progress in implementing its reform and development program effectively.

Our Experience So Far with CDPs in Thailand Is Described

Since the crisis, the engagement between Thailand and the World Bank has progressed from primarily a borrower-lender relationship toward a true development partnership in the three phases described above. Although financial support remains an important part of the partnership, especially from International Finance Corporation transactions, the Bank's role has evolved more toward facilitating knowledge sharing and providing policy advice on medium-term structural issues. Building on this evolving approach, the new Thailand–World Bank Group partnership, capably formulated by the present country director and his team, focuses on providing a comprehensive diagnostic overview that is mainly delivered through the Country Monitor series, the periodic development policy and other reviews, the CDPs (built around the national development agenda), and financial transfers associated with select transactions with the International Bank for Reconstruction and Development, the International Finance Corporation, and the Multilateral Investment Guarantee Agency.

The Bank, in collaboration with other development partners, is currently supporting four government-driven CDPs (social protection, financial and corporate competitiveness, poverty assessment, and monitoring and governance) through analysis and advice on development policy and strategy, capacity building, and provision of technical support. US$5 million in grant funds are being used to support the four CDPs.[3] Progress on the CDPs' development activities is generally on track and much has been achieved. Many components of the CDP on social protection and the CDP on financial and corporate competitiveness are expected to be completed in 2004, with full completion by the end of 2005. In the meantime, discussions are under way to develop two new CDPs on education and the environment. The Bank's analytic support on information, communications, and technology was evaluated in December 2003, and further assessment is being carried out to see whether this area should become a broader CDP on knowledge economy and management or should be combined with a related CDP.

The CDP Emerges as a Robust and Effective Bank Instrument

All indications so far show that the CDP is an instrument that has vigorously withstood the swings in Bank relationships with Thailand, which were caused, among other things, by a sharp fall in resource transfer requirements and the establishment of a new government with a totally different mindset. The government that successfully steered the country through its crisis through restoring confidence and initiating implementation of reforms was rejected by the electorate because the measures it formulated ran counter to the Thai way of doing things. They were seen as elitist and out of touch with the poor. A charismatic, imaginative, and dynamic prime minister was elected to office, with much less interest than his predecessor in completing the reforms that the Bank and IMF supported but with the ability to generate confidence that accelerated the recovery. Indeed, the new prime minister had a well-articulated reform program of his own with a strong Thai flavor, which was somewhat hostile to the previous government's program and distinctly less open to outside ideas. Even in that context, supported in Thailand by the Economic Monitor and other widely circulated Monitors, the CDPs have been successful in maintaining a level of Bank engagement and understanding of the Thai situation that would have otherwise been impossible in the absence of significant lending. Under the new prime minister, the self-confidence of the Thais has been restored, and recovery has been more rapid than expected. Thailand has resumed 5 to 6 percent annual growth, but because of the heterodox policies followed, the jury is out on the sustainability of that pace. Through all those changes, the original reform agenda has been kept active, and lessons from the new approach are being gathered, thanks to the CDPs.

The contribution of CDPs to knowledge development and to synergy between different government players previously working separately cannot be overstated. There now exists a stable platform from which the next wave of reforms can be launched when the government at the top is more receptive and, therefore, the time more opportune. On this foundation, the battle plan can be forged much more realistically if and when another crisis hits Thailand. The Thailand CDP, therefore, offers lessons that can be applied more widely, as a modality to strengthen engagement with clients and implement the CDF principles and as an instrument that positions the Bank to be more effective in both fair and foul economic conditions.

Conclusions Can Be Drawn from the Thailand Experience

At this stage, I would like to list some lessons from my Thailand experience.

- The CDF introduced in the late 1990s, though it failed to impress Bank staff at its start, has provided the foundations for a changed development paradigm that recognizes the sovereignty of governments and legitimizes the participation of a wide range of stakeholders. It thus positioned the Bank to continue to be relevant in the changing world of the 1990s and the 21st century.

- Implementing the CDF has been difficult, but the key to success is to reform the modalities of Bank engagement in a country rather than to focus excessively on specific analytical products, lending, or particular strategies.

- The 1990s saw remarkable changes in the world that opened the doors to many new ways for the Bank to engage with countries. Many of those opportunities have been exploited in different contexts, but a more comprehensive and structured approach to relevant Bank options has still to emerge. Basically, the Bank now has to engage with civil society, academics, and the private sector at the international, national, and local levels. Gone are the days when a dialogue with a small coterie of government officials can drive engagement.

- To be effective, therefore, the Bank must engage with a country in a manner that ensures continuity; underpins a working relationship with external donors, government officials, civil society, academia, and the private sector; provides a critical mass of Bank staff members with a good understanding of country issues; overcomes the silo mentality in governments and also within the Bank; and provides a two-way sharing of expertise between the country and the rest of the world. This form of engagement has to be strong enough to weather the ups and downs of country borrowing needs and changes in government mindsets and policies. The decentralization of the Bank opens up new opportunities for this enhanced form of engagement.

- This form of engagement can be highly productive when underpinned by Bank reports that are widely disseminated—such as the Development Policy Review and Monitors on the economy, environment, governance, poverty, and other critical themes. Those reports should be timely, be written in simple language, reflect candor, and be made available on the Web. The influence that such reports have on the various in-country and visiting stakeholders can be immense. Thanks to globalization, foreign stakeholders demand reliable information that can be absorbed quickly, and the Monitor publications are in high demand, particularly by the international financial community, whose lack of appreciation of national issues is often alarming. This form of engagement gains real substance from a series of CDPs, covering key themes and providing a mechanism for the kind of countrywide participation in policy and institutional reform development that emerged in the 1990s as a sine qua non for successful implementation.

- The importance of a lending relationship with a country cannot be underestimated. The clout it furnishes plus the on-the-ground implementation experience it provides is invaluable for the Bank. However, the Bank has to reconcile itself to periods of drought in lending operations and use reports and the CDP mainly as knowledge instruments to maintain active status in a country. Not to do so entails severe costs when lending resumes. It is shortsighted to link country administrative budgets too closely with the fluctuations of the lending program, particularly because CDPs do not require high levels of Bank budget support and the level can be adjusted up or down depending on the context.

- The Bank has an important responsibility to complement IMF when a country crisis arises by furnishing a broader stakeholder view and a longer-term development view. Currently, IMF programs are seriously handicapped by the lack of such perspective. The form of continuous engagement chosen by the Bank should support the objective of maintaining the Bank's influence at a level that allows it to be equally effective during crises and in normal times.

- The Bank should never again be caught napping when a sudden crisis develops in a country, as it was in Thailand. Given that reorganization is the way of life in the Bank, contingency arrangements should be made to establish ad hoc teams in the event of a crisis occurring during a reorganization. The arrangement should allow a regional vice president to yank suitable staff members from different parts of the Bank to form a team to deal with the crisis without having to obtain the prior consent of their managers. Of course, what constitutes a crisis has to be defined carefully since even vice presidents in the Bank tend to be creative.

- The Bank's internal organization and matrix management are not conducive to rapid response. They also do not serve well the objective of blending local and global knowledge to forge solutions to country development problems in the context of the CDF and the CDP. Besides, although professional tribalism within the Bank needs to be put down, the present organizational structure encourages it. Overcoming silos within the Bank to mobilize a multidisciplinary team to work on a thematic area (for example, information technology or private sector development) can be a nightmare for a country director, who is the closest to being the surrogate of the country within the Bank. New and emerging areas are particularly difficult to tackle because of the Bank's internal inertia and turf battles. In the 1990s, thematic tasks became more relevant than sector tasks, but regional units were mainly sectoral. The continuity of teams is a serious issue, one that Thai officials have not hesitated to highlight.

- The most important factor ensuring the success of a Bank operation is the quality of the team leader or task manager. Currently, quality is mixed, and good task managers are not empowered.

- From the political side, the credibility and standing of a prime minister and finance minister and the confidence they generate in the financial markets are more important than all the help IMF or the Bank can offer in the management of a crisis. In the 1990s, when capital began moving freely, this lesson emerged starkly. In a major crisis, the Bank cannot address this issue by taking shelter behind its nonpolitical mandate. The leadership shown by the managing director and vice president at that time in addressing this issue frontally in Thailand deserves applause.

- Finally, on a personal note, I now recognize that I had been totally wrong in my initial assessment of Thailand when I was offered the position of country director. It is a country for which I now have immense admiration—for its history, culture, artistic talent, natural endowments, and work ethic, but most of all for its wonderful, friendly people.

Reflections on Other Experiences

Sudan Irrigation Sector in the 1980s

I was involved with the irrigation sector in Sudan for 14 years, from 1978 to 1992. During that period, I undertook more than 40 missions to Sudan as a project officer and later as a manager. We were operating with well-staffed multidisciplinary teams and carried out several pieces of sector work, both formal and informal, and prepared and implemented several irrigation rehabilitation projects. In the early 1980s, we also initiated three policy-based agricultural rehabilitation projects, with quick-disbursing funds supporting policy and institutional reform, an approach then—before SALs were launched—considered innovative.

Of course, the policy agenda then was not as deep and broad as it can be today. Then, there was no consensus on the importance of markets. The private sector was still a dirty word. The government frowned on wide participation, and stakeholders other than government officials were seldom given recognition. Civil society was hardly organized—not to speak of the primitive state of communications before the information technology revolution. Nevertheless, we did address several issues frontally. These issues included (a) reversing decapitalization of the parastatal-run schemes (4 million acres under Nile irrigation) through IDA investments, (b) improving incentives for farmers (tenants) through reform of the joint account system that then governed both the sharing of the sale proceeds of cotton between the parastatal and the tenants and the recovery of the cost of services provided by the parastatals, (c) improving the efficiency of services provided to tenants by the parastatals, (d) increasing the efficiency of water delivery systems, and (e) designing better technical packages for farmers within their constraints.

That the schemes are still running is a tribute to the efforts the Bank undertook then. But the fact that the schemes are not sustainable and are draining the exchequer every year despite IDA investments shows that our efforts were not wisely designed. With the advantage of hindsight, it is now clear that we addressed only the symptoms, not the fundamental issues. The fundamental problems were inefficient tenancy systems that required dismantling; inappropriate division of responsibilities between the parastatals, the private sector, and the tenants in regard to services that required development of private sector alternatives; and inefficient water management that required much greater farmer participation. All those matters involved major social, governance, and political issues, on which progress was impossible without full exploration of the potential of the market, reform of institutions, participation of the private sector, and involvement in decisionmaking by the whole range of stakeholders. Furthermore, internal compulsions to lend, egged on by IMF's on-and-off pressures, as the country passed through good and bad periods in its relationships with IMF, skewed Bank involvement toward "I am the expert and I will decide" mode. One cannot help thinking that if only a CDP type of instrument had been available then, the failure of Bank initiatives in Sudan could have been prevented. But the world and the country were far from ready for this type of approach at that time.

Sugar Projects in Uganda, Sudan, and Mauritius

I worked on sugar projects in Sudan, Uganda, and Mauritius right through the 1980s. The Sudan Sugar project was a public sector one, unlike the Uganda project, which had an enterprising private partner. The Mauritius operation involved the entire sector, which was mainly in private hands, and was quite different from typical projects in that it dealt with a major dispute between government (dominated by Indians) and the private sugar factories (dominated by the French) on the sharing of rents generated by the European Economic Community sugar pricing regime for Mauritius. The Sudan and Uganda operations were straightforward, involving a limited number of stakeholders, well-understood technology, and management improvements that did not involve rocket science. It was, therefore, possible to handle them through the expert mode of engagement without special participation arrangements, and the results were satisfactory in both cases, though much better in the private sector case for reasons that are well known.

The Mauritius case was distinctly different. The range of stakeholders involved the entire population of this small country. The message that had to be delivered was that, if stakeholders did not hang together, they would hang separately. This message gained acceptance through a series of analytical exercises and workshops with the participation of stakeholders, orchestrated by competent TA staff based in the field. It led to consensus around the contentious issue of export duty rates as well as to a modernization program. Government had threatened to nationalize private sugar factories before the Bank entered the scene. As a result of Bank efforts, stakeholders joined hands and resolved issues relating to export duty and modernization. Although the Bank withdrew from active participation in the early 1990s, the healthy dialogue among partners, I believe, continues. This experience is a successful but little-recognized instance of empowering country players to handle their own affairs. The limitations of standard Bank instruments were overcome by the flexibility displayed in the field, and what resulted was an informal CDP mode of engagement that continued even after the Bank withdrew. This enlightened country was ready for this form of engagement even then.

East Asia AIDS Epidemic

I was involved with addressing the HIV/AIDS issue in East Asia during the early 1990s and again dealt with the matter as the chair of the UN Theme Group on HIV/AIDS in Thailand at the start of this century. In the early 1990s, we initiated dialogue with governments on HIV/AIDS, conducted analytical work, formed some partnerships with civil society, and implemented projects to address the problem. We even got a US$1 million grant approved by the Development Grant Facility of the Bank early during the epidemic to strengthen the analytical basis for support in the region, but it bombed because the Global Program on AIDS and the Joint United Nations Programme on AIDS (UNAIDS) hired a highly motivated medical doctor with his own agenda instead of a well-trained economist to manage the research agenda. Our own analytical work met with limited success, because many governments were still in a state of denial and donor efforts were not embedded in a national strategy. What we learned was that analytical work or individual projects take you nowhere unless there is broad participation of stakeholders and wide ownership of programs as well as a comprehensive national-level strategy and program in place.

HIV/AIDS is an area in which the issue of the form of Bank engagement rises to the surface. In Thailand, 10 years later, while there was no CDP-type instrument in place for HIV/AIDS, arrangements that foreshadowed the CDP did operate—not so in many East Asian countries. Unfortunately, the weakest link in the chain from the global level to the local level is the national level. UNAIDS and now the Global Fund have been able, through excellent advocacy, to raise the international profile of the epidemic and mobilize dollar resources. At the local level, communities and NGOs have responded wonderfully. It is at the national level that strategies are still weak, public resources still misapplied, and coherent policies and institutional objectives still missing. Here again, the CDP offers a great opportunity for the Bank to intervene and help countries get their houses in order, to strengthen strategies, and to streamline programs, but its potential has yet to be exploited, except perhaps in Africa, where HIV/AIDS has received greater attention than elsewhere in the Bank.

The Nam Theun II Project in Lao PDR

I began my association with the Nam Theun II project in Lao PDR in 1995. The project is expected to go to the Bank's Board of Executive Directors in 2005. There are reasons (besides me!) for this long period of elapsed time. Of course, there was the disruption caused by the East Asian crisis. But, we must also remember that Lao PDR is among the poorest countries in the world. It is a large, landlocked, mountainous country with poor infrastructure and a population of just 5 million people. It does not have the tax base to drive rapid development unless it taps revenues from natural resource exports, including hydropower. It badly needs more revenues. The size of its infrastructure needs is immense, and its human indicators are dismal. The primary benefit from the Nam Theun II project would be the incremental revenues (through royalties, taxes, and dividends) flowing to the government of the Lao PDR for several decades, starting in 2009. Such revenues, when accompanied by governance improvements and human capital development—and if used effectively—would help the country reduce poverty and boost economic growth. If successful, such a large project could also encourage multinational companies to invest in Lao PDR and enlarge the country's access to international financial markets.

The Nam Theun II project is probably the most challenging project currently in the Bank's lending program. It is highly controversial because of its environmental and social effects, the apportionment of its economic and financial benefits, and the weak governance in Lao PDR. Yet the benefits would far outweigh the risks, provided that the latter are properly managed and successfully mitigated. The issue in the ultimate analysis boils down to a consensus among several stakeholders involved—who include the poor local residents, even poorer directly affected persons, Lao citizens, consumers of power in Thailand, local and foreign investors, and several advocacy groups—that the benefits and losses are fairly apportioned and that the risks are equitably distributed with regard to stakeholders' capacity to control and bear such risks. Over the past decade, the processing of this project has led to unprecedented levels of analytical work and has surpassed historical levels of expert involvement in a dam project. Although consensus is growing, the project is still on the learning curve in regard to development of partnerships and stakeholder consultation. The Poverty Reduction Strategy Paper (PRSP) process has had a profound effect on the country. Still, one cannot but observe that the potential exists for a CDP-like engagement—before and particularly after the project is approved by the Bank—to fill institutional gaps that are a threat to constructive participation of stakeholders and the enforcement of government accountability.

Empowering People to Do Development

In complex operations that go beyond the scope of standard Bank instruments, the form of engagement becomes a moot issue. The Bank now has greater flexibility than ever before to work with multiple stakeholders in a process underpinned by knowledge and experience sharing and in a mode that promotes sustainability through consensus and participation. The Bank's history is filled with cases in which this mode of operation would have made the difference between success and failure. The Bank needs to learn from this experience and not shy away from new paradigms and new ways of engaging with governments.

Indeed, one of the key lessons learned about development over the past 50 years is that the only effective and sustainable development approach is to help people gain effective control and carry out their own development. Since the launch of the CDF by President Wolfensohn in January 1999, the Bank has taken a major step in this direction. This approach and that of partnership have begun to gain popularity in recent years as a result of the increased emphasis on participatory approaches to development and a broadening of the consultative process so as to engage more stakeholders in development discussions and welcome their inputs. One of the main factors contributing to the development of this approach is the increased willingness of governments to reach out to and engage with civil society, the private sector, and academics. Empowering people to "do" development should be the Bank's goal in the 21st century, and its mode of engagement should support this goal.

The Country Development Partnership
Management Principles Underpinning CDP

A management specialist[4] whom I consulted had little difficulty identifying well-documented, proven management principles that underpin the CDF and also the CDP:

- *Empowerment.* Employee involvement and empowerment are techniques for unleashing human potential in organizations. The central idea is to delegate power and decisionmaking to lower levels and, by using concepts such as shared visions of the future, to engage all employees so that people develop a sense of pride, self-respect, and responsibility. When applied to national development, empowering governments and stakeholders within a country can also lead to a shared vision of the future, active engagement in the implementation process, and collective responsibility for achieving results. This empowerment is precisely what the CDP does.

- *Cooperation.* Group behavior research suggests that cooperation in many situations promotes productivity. This finding seems to be particularly true when the task is complicated and requires coordination and sharing of information. Development, by definition, is a very complex set of challenges and tasks confronting all countries. It requires cooperation and coordination among stakeholders, which involves the sharing of information and common work toward a unified vision. Teamwork is a basic principle of the CDP.

- *Collective ownership.* There is an accumulation of evidence demonstrating that, when ownership is shared among group members, the energy and investment expended to achieve results increase greatly. This record suggests that it is particularly important for governments and stakeholders to own their country's development and reform program. The CDP fosters collective ownership.

- *Selective use of expertise.* Attempts by management to hire external experts to assist a company with tasks that can be as effectively carried out by staff members undermine employees and often lead to a lack of cooperation with experts, thus potentially compromising the results. In the case of development, the introduction of foreign technical advisers has frequently both undermined local capacity building and has frustrated the commitment of local experts. The CDP provides a framework for technical assistance and capacity building that strengthens the interface between foreign experts and their counterparts.

- *Internal versus external control.* Locus of control is the degree to which people believe that they are masters of their own fate. The overall evidence suggests that those who are internally controlled perform better on their jobs, search more actively for information before making a decision, are more motivated to achieve, and make a greater effort to control their environment. In development, if a government and its stakeholders have a greater sense of internal control, they are more likely to take the necessary actions to realize their own development goals and not become solely dependent on external assistance and guidance from donors. The CDP provides this internal control in determining development priorities.

- *Situationally driven development—one size does not fit all.* The success of all organizations depends on the extent to which they are in tune with, and build on, their unique characteristics or situation. This principle is also true of development. Experience shows no blueprints for development that can be applied across nations. Each country's development will need to be situationally driven in terms of its key development variables, among them macroeconomic situation, history, philosophy, political system, cultural diversity, social integration, and spirituality—including predominant religious heritage. The CDP allows those factors to play a role in the development process through wider participation and debate. Any attempt to impose a particular economic model or agenda of the one-size-fits-all variety is doomed to failure.

- *Development that builds on a country's unique features and characteristics.* Organizations prosper when they build on their unique features and characteristics and capitalize on their comparative advantages. Likewise with development, the comparative advantages of a country may lie in its culture, geography, major alliances, or—indeed—macroeconomic beliefs. Whatever these characteristics are, the road to development will need to build on them, not try to negate or circumvent them. The CDP supports this principle.

- *Global position and information technology.* Globalization and the role of information technology increasingly influence today's world organizations. Unless organizations adapt to these two overarching influences, they will fail. Countries, likewise, must be integrated into an increasingly globalized world through information technology development. The CDP facilitates access to global experience through partnership with global networks, including the Bank's internal networks. And a CDP for information technology can make a huge difference to the ability of a country to tap the potential benefits of such technology.

- *Diversity.* Organizations are increasingly forced to address diversity among their employees. Those that have successfully introduced diversity programs and helped to integrate employees have seen positive results. Countries, likewise, have to address the diversity issues confronting their people and find ways to integrate the interests of all stakeholders in society if they are to achieve their development goals. The CDP provides a forum for such diversity to express itself.

- *Monitoring and evaluation.* Monitoring and evaluation are key factors included in all successful change and development programs in organizations. The same is true in development. Countries need to have clearly stated benchmarks or milestones to measure progress in their development or reform programs. Those milestones are also valuable contexts to use when a country informs the international community of its success or progress in achieving its development or reform goals. The CDP is based on a strong and effective monitoring system.

Features of the CDP

Besides being grounded on strong management principles, the CDP has a number of attractive features:

- The CDP is primarily a management tool for the government to help manage its development and reform programs.

- It provides a medium-term focus on high-priority areas. The government identifies the priority areas in partnership with civil society, the private sector, and academics, with the support of the Bank and external donors.

- Those high-priority areas then become the subjects of specific CDPs that are studied and analyzed, resulting in the creation of a development matrix and a partnership matrix. The high-priority CDPs, taken together, provide a more integrated approach to a country's medium-term development goals and cover the essentials of a holistic development framework.

- The development matrix, which is provided by the government, sets out priority areas for development or reform, a detailed work program and schedule, suitable objectives and outcomes, and appropriate implementation benchmarks or milestones for monitoring and evaluation.

- The partnership matrix identifies a list of tasks, national inputs, and total financing needs from both government and external donors and is linked to a multi-year timetable. This partnership matrix is prepared by either a domestic or an international partner at the government's request, to provide technical support for the preparation of a specific CDP and assistance with the implementation and monitoring of the relevant reforms. The lead partner will also assist in the coordination and mobilization of technical assistance.

- The CDP thus provides a framework for donor involvement. Thanks to greater coordination among stakeholders and donors, everyone knows what others are doing. Government, stakeholders, and donors can then focus on those strategic priority areas that will have the greatest development effect. Donors can then help design projects that complement each other, within their areas of comparative advantage and interests, and thus avoid duplication.

- Although the CDP does not involve lending per se, it facilitates a quick response should the government decide to borrow, and it provides a platform for future lending in strategic areas.

- In addition, the CDP supports and provides incentives to attract external investment. Reform milestones, once reached, signal the international investment community that progress is being achieved in implementing reforms.

- The CDP holds the government accountable for meeting the reform milestones identified in the development matrix. Accountability and transparency are enhanced through the CDP's biennial evaluation meetings.

- The CDP provides an opportunity for all country stakeholders and donors to be involved in monitoring reform through attending the biennial evaluation meetings. Consultations and workshops can help form consensus on the best ways to attract and use development funds.

Scaling Up the CDP

Looking beyond Thailand, we see that the CDP is particularly suited to middle-income countries where borrowing requirements are shrinking but the need for capacity building and knowledge management remains. In the case of countries under adjustment, the CDP strengthens the analytical foundations of the program, strengthens the government's capacity, and builds partnerships in support of such lending. It also serves as a useful mechanism for informing international markets about a country's progress in implementing its reform and development program.

The CDP holds great promise in low-income countries as well. Although the PRSP process embodies CDF principles in IDA country operations and is meeting with striking success in several countries, the range of issues covered by a PRSP can sometimes make it collapse under its own weight. Its quality can be compromised by an inability to involve the wide range of expertise that needs to be drawn into the exercise. Building a PRSP on the back of four or five thematic CDPs could go a long way in improving the quality, range, and ownership of the PRSP. From the Bank's point of view, management of the PRSP process can be strengthened by inducing sector experts to lead CDPs and for the PRSP leader, basically an integrator, then to synthesize recommendations that are more substantive than those presently generated. Because it is too much to expect a PRSP task manager to be fully conversant with, let alone competent in, the wide range of issues covered, breaking the PRSP down into more manageable CDPs, therefore, makes sense.

Potential for CDPs in Current Operations: Two Recent Examples

Two examples from my own recent experience demonstrate the CDP's potential to increase the Bank's development effectiveness greatly. These cases are typical, and I believe that the conclusions drawn from them have wider application:

1. *Tamil Nadu Reform Program.* Over the past few years, I have been working with the Tamil Nadu Bank team. For me, this is a special privilege as it let me return to a state where I worked in the finance department 30 years ago—only to witness many of the current reforms dismantling policies that were launched during the period I was there. It brought to the fore two issues: (a) how the economic environment in which policies had to be formulated had completely changed, with the result that policies that made sense years ago look absurd today, and (b) how closed the policymaking process still was. Tamil Nadu has a number of very well-educated, bright people in its private sector, civil society, academic institutions, and civil service. Yet the number of such people who add value to the decisionmaking process relating to policy and institutional reforms is miniscule. I came away convinced that there had to a be a more open process for policy reform with partic-

ipation of all stakeholders and that the Bank can act as a catalyst to expand and deepen the policy reform process by fostering wider participation and inducing greater expertise from within the state, from within India, and indeed from the global arena in ways acceptable to government. What was needed was a CDP, and the time appeared right for such an initiative. A CDP supported by a string of SALs can deliver far greater benefit to the state than SALs supported by more traditional Bank country economic and sector work. The postelection defeat reversal of government policy in May 2004, which resulted in the Tamil Nadu SAL being withdrawn from the Board on the morning of its presentation, has lessons to offer. One of them is that a SAL should no longer drive policy reform through conditionality that exposes the Bank to political bashing. A government should be rewarded with SAL financial support if it moves forward on its own on the reform agenda through a CDP-like process that ensures broad consensus on reform measures through broad participation and public debate.

2. *Public Financial Management and Accountability Program.* I recently had the opportunity to study the Bank's Public Financial Management (PFM) program. The Bank is currently required by the Board to undertake a Public Expenditure Review, Country Procurement Assessment Report, and Country Financial Accounting Assessment in each borrowing country and to keep those reports up to date. The existence of separate instruments raises transactions costs for countries, but the more serious problem is that the inflexible requirement for three reports produced by three separate parts of the Bank does not foster an integrated approach to PFM diagnosis and reform. The new approach that is emerging is based on a single reform program, which is led by the government, within which all external support is coordinated. Under that approach, a single assessment, which is designed to meet the needs of all donors, is undertaken. The assessment process will be delinked from the reform process, though it will inform it. A programmatic approach is envisioned that will work with other agencies to provide coordinated technical and financial support to a government-led process that will analyze the issues and prepare and implement a prioritized program to improve PFM over a three- to five-year period. Standardized assessments of the financial management situation in all borrower countries will replace the mandatory requirement to undertake all three existing instruments. The standardized assessments will use common performance indicators to permit comparability between countries and over time, in order to assess the extent and nature of fiduciary risks. They are to be owned by donors, not by the government—although governments may be encouraged to undertake their own assessment. Although the assessment process can depend on traditional Bank instruments, I can think of no better form of engagement than the CDP to push the country-driven PFM reform process forward.

Mainstreaming the CDPs

My conclusion is that the time is perhaps right to mainstream the CDP as a key operational vehicle in both International Bank for Reconstruction and Development countries and IDA countries, with PRSPs remaining dominant in the latter but underpinned by CDPs. The CDF has provided the philosophical underpinnings for such a change. The CDP and the PRSP, among many other innovations, offer the possibility of pushing the agenda forward.

The example set by the present management team in Thailand—of converting the Country Assistance Strategy to a partnership instrument; building CDF principles into it; and using a blend of reports, CDPs, and selective lending products— deserves to be more widely replicated. It should lead the way to an enhanced form of Bank engagement in its member countries. This step, however, entails some implications for the way the Bank is organized and managed.

Implications for the Bank's Organizational Structure

The first challenge is to build further on decentralization. Day-to-day contacts between the CDP partners and Bank staff members are critical for the success of the CDP. The CDP cannot, therefore, be thought of except in the context of a decentralized Bank. The team leader on a CDP will have to be based in the field but have status and strong institutional links to the Bank network relating to the CDP. In fact, an ideal country director office would ensure that each of the four networks had a strong staff member position reporting jointly to the country director and the network.

The second challenge relates to the quality of task team leaders and development of a sufficiently large number of suitable staff members within the Bank. If one had to entrust a CDP to either an excellent manager or an excellent team leader, and the two were not available to work together, one would unhesitatingly choose the latter—so critical is the CDP team leader. The Bank staff member who leads the exercise for the Bank requires such special attributes as a sound development background, integrative skills reflecting the ability to work across sectors and disciplines, strong communication skills, an appreciation of country-level constraints, and a level of drive and resourcefulness needed to tap to the fullest both global knowledge and the expertise within the Bank.

Also, the personal qualities needed for successful engagement were perhaps best expressed in a successful CDP task manager's comments to me.[5] Engagement with countries, he explained, is not just a matter of instruments, terms and conditions, and design brilliance—the usual variables that are invoked to explain the success or lack thereof of successful dialogue and operational outcomes. Some of the top determinants of successful engagement are the following principles:

- *Manage the relationship smartly.* Start with trust in the bona fides of your partners and then adjust tactics as the situation unfolds. Suspicion and blind trust are enemies of meaningful engagement, no less than an attitude of condescension toward partners.

- *Recognize that communication style is critical.* Listen more than speak. Question more than announce. Learn more than teach. You may have the perfect solution well defined in your mind, but it will be of little use if clients do not dis-

cover the idea on their own through an iterative, balanced process of inquiry
and discovery.

- *Have a clear plan and outcome vision and introduce them opportunistically to give pace
  and direction to the engagement.* This effort is obviously in tension with the two
  points mentioned above, but it is dangerous to allow the engagement to lag. If
  the client is unable to manage critical decisions and moves, the Bank team must
  quickly provide the way forward.

- *Take on responsibility.* Share the burdens on an equitable basis with partners, and
  always follow through on what you agree to do as your part of the engagement. If you promise to send a consultant next month, demonstrate your commitment with a contract and an itinerary so that you are seen as consistently
  reliable.

- *Challenge the client to do the heavy lifting on the more political and sensitive policy segments of the engagement.* Never assume that the Bank is best placed to do this
  work.

- *Fortify your lead counterparts.* Give them every form of financial, technical, and
  partnership support that the Bank can provide and that they might want so that
  they know they are backed, not led.

The third, and perhaps more serious, challenge is to make teams work well. Currently,
task managers and team leaders draw their members from different units, and coordinating their inputs and planning missions can be a real challenge. Task managers have to deal
with the priorities the sector managers have for team members, which are often quite different. The silo problem is no less serious within the Bank than in governments. The lack
of real teamwork and proper mission planning because of the silo mentality prevents synergy from developing between sectors and disciplines and dilutes the quality of Bank
contributions. There is obviously a case for empowering team leaders and moving toward
self-standing dedicated teams being formed with a thematic or sectoral basis. The establishment of empowered self-standing teams would lower the demand for managerial layers of supervision and would also make for simpler management structures. And the
self-standing teams must include local staff members as full-fledged members.

The fourth challenge is how to improve synergy between locally and internationally
recruited staff members on the team. My view is that Bank management has sent the
wrong signals by de facto treating the two categories as fungible, thus managing their
expectations less than optimally. Because the roles are complementary in either static or
dynamic contexts, opportunities should exist for local staff members to become international staff members. In the static context, international staff members bring in international experience of their own and experience of the network within headquarters. Local
staff members provide expertise on what will or will not work in the country, how to
apply development lessons within a country, and how to deal with in-country processes.
The CDP will require that complementary role to be implemented on the ground.

The fifth challenge relates to knowledge management. Currently, field experiences are not harvested systematically. The CDP offers a rich crop of knowledge to

be harvested and marketed. Unfortunately, the organization of the Bank divides staff members into two groups: those in the center, who are supposed to have knowledge and are given the opportunity of building up their stock, and those in the regions and in the field, who need this knowledge and also generate knowledge on their own. The concept that accumulation and transfer is a two-way street along which each staff member has the flexibility to move in either direction needs to gain wider support from the Bank's organizational structure.

The next reorganization of the Bank may well be around the corner. If it is driven as a country-up process rather than a Board-down one, major distortions in the present arrangements can be addressed. Strengthening decentralization, reducing managerial overhead, empowering team leaders, breaking down silos, forming self-standing multidisciplinary teams that add real value at the country level, exploiting the synergy between local and international staff members, and removing the artificial distinction between those who generate knowledge and those who apply it should be the main outcomes of the next reorganization.

Notes

1. For a description of the reform effort in Thailand, I refer readers to *Back from the Brink: Thailand's Response to the 1997 Economic Crisis*, which I had the privilege of coauthoring with Ijaz Nabi as part of the World Bank's *Directions in Development* Series (Nabi and Shivakumar 2001).

2. The newspaper *Business Day* was perhaps overgenerous when it branded the Bank as the "voice of conscience" in one of its editorials ("Voice of Conscience" 1999).

3. The amount includes active trust finds approved to support all four CDPs.

4. A. Noel Jones, a former Bank staff member and now a consultant.

5. Christopher Chamberlin, who led the Bank's Thailand Social Fund team and the CDP on social protection, shared these thoughts with me.

References

Besley, Timothy, and Roberto Zagha, eds. 2005. *Development Challenges in the 1990s: Leading Policymakers Speak from Experience.* Washington, D.C.: World Bank.

Brahmbhatt, Milan, Craig Burnside, and Asli Demirguc-Kunt. 2001. "Lessons for Turkey from Recent Emerging Market Crisis." Washington, D.C., World Bank. Processed.

Burki, Shahid Javed. 1970. *A Study of Chinese Communes, 1965.* Cambridge, Mass.: Harvard University East Asian Research Center.

———. 1980. *Pakistan under Bhutto, 1971–77.* London: Macmillan.

———. 1991. *Pakistan: Fifty Years of Nationhood.* Boulder, Colo.: Westview Press.

———. 2000. *Changing Perceptions and Altered Reality: Emerging Economies in the 1990s.* Washington, D.C.: World Bank.

Carlyle, Thomas. 1840. *On Heroes, Hero-Worship, and the Heroic in History.* Reprinted 1993. Berkeley: University of California Press.

Chenery, Hollis, Montek S. Ahluwalia, C. L. G. Bell, John H. Duloy, and Richard Jolly. 1981. *Redistribution with Growth: Policies to Improve Income.* New York: Oxford University Press.

Chhibber, Ajay. 1999. "Is Turkey a Typical Emerging Market?" *Emerging Turkey 1999.* Hampshire, U.K.: Oxford Business Group.

Chhibber, Ajay, and Johannes Linn. 2001. "The True Cause of Turkey's Crisis." *Financial Times,* January 19, p. 15.

David de Ferranti, Michael Walton, Francisco H. G. Ferreira, and Guillermo E. Perry. 2004. *Inequality in Latin America: Breaking with History?* Washington, D.C.

Demirguc-Kunt, Asli, and Ross Levine. 1999. "Bank-Based and Market-Based Financial Systems: Cross-Country Comparisons." Policy Research Working Paper 2143. Washington, D.C., World Bank.

Fischer, Stanley. 2001. "Exchange Rate Regimes: Is the Bipolar View Correct?" American Economics Association Meetings Distinguished Lecture, New Orleans, La., January 6. http://www.imf.org/external/np/speeches/2001/010601a.pdf.

Geertz, Clifford. 1963. *Agricultural Involution, the Process of Ecological Change in Indonesia*. Berkeley, Calif.: University of California Press.

———. 1973. *The Interpretation of Cultures: Selected Essays*. New York: Basic Books.

George, Susan, and Fabrizio Sabelli. 1994. *Faith and Credit: The World Bank's Secular Empire*. Boulder, Colo.: Westview Press.

Giugale, Marcelo M., Olivier Lafourcade, and Connie Luff, eds. 2002. *Colombia: The Economic Foundation of Peace*. Washington, D.C.: World Bank.

Giugale, Marcelo M., Olivier Lafourcade, and Vinh H. Nguyen, eds. 2001. *Mexico: A Comprehensive Agenda for the New Era*. Washington, D.C.: World Bank.

Hausmann, Ricardo, and Dani Rodrik. 2003. "Economic Development as Self-Discovery." Harvard University Kennedy School of Government, Cambridge, Mass. http://ksghome.harvard.edu/~drodrik/selfdisc.pdf.

Harberger Arnold C. 2000. "The View from the Trenches." In Gerald M. Meier and Joseph E. Stiglitz, eds., *Frontiers of Development Economics: The Future in Perspective*. Washington, D.C.: World Bank.

Helleiner, Gerald K. 1999. *Changing Aid Relationships in Tanzania (December 1997 through March 1999)*. Dar es Salaam: United Republic of Tanzania.

———. 2000. "The Legacies of Julius Nyerere: An Economist's Reflections." Center for International Studies Working Paper 2000-3. University of Toronto.

Helleiner, Gerald K., Tony Killick, Nguyuru Lipumba, Benno J. Ndulu, and Knud Erik Svendsen. 1995. *Report of the Group of Independent Advisers on Development Cooperation Issues between Tanzania and Its Aid Donors*. Copenhagen: Royal Danish Ministry of Foreign Affairs.

Ianchovina, Elena, and Wil Martin. 2002. *Economic Impact of China's Accession to the WTO*. Washington, D.C.: World Bank.

IMF (International Monetary Fund). 2003. *IMF and Recent Capital Account Crises: Indonesia, Korea and Brazil*. Washington, D.C.: IMF Independent Evaluation Office.

Kuczynski, Pedro Pablo, and John Williamson. 2003. *After the Washington Consensus, Restarting Growth and Reform in Latin America*. Washington, D.C.: Institute for International Economics.

Lewis, W. Arthur. 1954. "Economic Development with Unlimited Supplies of Labor." *Manchester School of Economic and Social Studies* 22: 139–91.

"Luz no Privilégio" ("Shining Light on Privilege"). 2000. Unsigned editorial. *Jornal do Brasil*, October 4, p. A10.

Mallaby, Sebastian. 2004. *The World's Banker: A Story of Failed States, Financial Crises, and the Wealth and Poverty of Nations*. New York: Council on Foreign Relations Books, Penguin Press.

Martin, Wil, and Vlad Manole. 2003. *China's Emergence as the Workshop of the World*. World Bank: Washington, D.C.

Meier, Gerald M., and Dudley Seers, eds. 1984. *Pioneers in Development*. New York: Oxford University Press.

Muganda, Anna. 2004. "Tanzania's Economic Reforms (and Lessons Learned)." Case study for the World Bank Shanghai Conference on Scaling Up Poverty Reduction, Shanghai, China, May 25–27.

Mussa, Michael. 2002. *Argentina and the Fund: From Triumph to Tragedy*. Washington D.C.: Institute for International Economics.

Nabi, Ijaz, and Jayasankar Shivakumar. 2001. *Back from the Brink: Thailand's Response to the 1997 Economic Crisis*. Washington, D.C.: World Bank.

Papanek, Gustav F. 1969. *Pakistan's Development: Social Goals and Private Incentives*. Cambridge, Mass.: Harvard University Press.

Papanek, Gustav F., and Walter Falcon, eds. 1972. *Development Policy: The Pakistan Experience*. Cambridge, Mass.: Harvard University Press.

Streeten, Paul, and Shahid Javed Burki, eds. 1982. *First Things First: Meeting Basic Human Needs in the Developing Countries*. New York: Oxford University Press.

Summers, Lawrence H. 2005. "Development Lessons from the 1990s." In Roberto Zagha and Timothy Besley, eds., *Development Challenges in the 1990s: Leading Policymakers Speak from Experience*. Washington, D.C.: World Bank.

TESEV (Turkiye Ekonomik ve Sosyal Etudler Vakfi). 2001. *Diagnostic Household Survey, February 2001*. Ankara.

United Nations Development Programme. 2003. *Arab Human Development Report 2003: Building a Knowledge Society*. New York: United Nations.

United Republic of Tanzania. 1996. *Tume ya Rais ya Mfumo wa Chama Kimoja au Vyama Vingi vya Siasa Tanzania* [*The Report of the Presidential Commission of Inquiry against Corruption* ("The Warioba Report")]. Vols. 1 and 2. Dar es Salaam.

———. 2000a. *Poverty Reduction Strategy Paper*. Dar es Salaam. http://www.imf.org/external/NP/prsp/2000/tza/02/

———. 2000b. *Tanzania Assistance Strategy: A Medium-Term Framework for Promoting Local Ownership and Development Partnerships*. Dar es Salaam.

"Voice of Conscience Reminds Us of the Right Priorities." 1999. *Business Day*, January, p. 4.

Williamson, John. 1990. "What Washington Means by Policy Reform." In John Williamson, ed., *The Progress of Policy Reform in Latin America*. Policy Analyses in International Economics 28. Washington D.C.: Institute for International Economics. http://www.iie.com/publications/papers/williamson1102-2.htm.

———. 2000. "What Should the World Bank Think about the Washington Consensus?" *World Bank Research Observer* 15(2): 251–64.

———. 2005. "The Washington Consensus as Policy Prescription for Development." In Besley and Zagha 2005.

World Bank. 1975. *The Assault on World Poverty: Problems of Rural Development, Education, and Health*. Baltimore, Md.: Johns Hopkins University Press.

———. 1979. *World Development Report 1979.* Washington, D.C.

———. 1980. *World Development Report, 1980: Poverty and Human Development*. Washington, D.C.

———. 1981. *China: Socialist Economic Development*. Report 3391-CHA. Washington, D.C.

———. 1982. *Focus on Poverty*. Washington, D.C.

———. 1985a. *China: Long-Term Development Issues and Options*. Baltimore, Md.: Johns Hopkins University Press.

———. 1985b. *IDA in Retrospect: Twenty-Five Years of International Development Association*. Washington, D.C.

———. 1990. *World Development Report, 1990: Poverty*. New York: Oxford University Press.

———. 1993. *The East Asian Miracle: Economic Growth and Public Policy.* Washington, D.C.

———. 1994a. *Averting the Old Age Crisis: Policies to Protect the Old and Promote Growth*. Washington, D.C.

———. 1994b. *Brazil: An Agenda for Stabilization*. Report 13168-BR. Washington, D.C.

———. 1997. *World Development Report 1997: The State in a Changing World*. New York: Oxford University Press.

———. 1998. *Argentina: Fiscal Dimensions of the Convertibility Plan.* Vols. 1 and 2. Washington, D.C.

———. 1999. *World Development Report 1999/2000: Entering the 21st Century: The Changing Development Landscape.* Washington, D.C.

———. 2000a. *Brazil: Private Participation in the Water Sector: Case Studies, Lessons, and Future Options*. Report 19896-BR. Washington, D.C.

———. 2000b. *Country Economic Memorandum, Turkey: Structural Reforms for Sustained Growth.* Report 20657. Washington, D.C.

———. 2000c. *Tanzania Country Assistance Strategy.* Report 20426-TA. Washington, D.C.

———. 2001a. *Attacking Brazil's Poverty: A Poverty Report with a Focus on Urban Poverty Reduction Policies.* Report 20475-BR. Washington, D.C.

———. 2001b. *Rural Poverty Alleviation in Brazil: Towards an Integrated Strategy.* Report 21790-BR. Washington, D.C.

———. 2001c. *World Development Report, 2000/2001: Attacking Poverty.* Washington, D.C.

———. 2002a. *Argentina: Together We Stand, Divided We Fall: Levels and Determinants of Social Capital in Argentina.* Report 2481-AR. Washington, D.C.

———. 2002b. *Brazil: The New Growth Agenda.* Report 22950-BR. Washington, D.C.

———. 2002c. "Turkey: Greater Prosperity with Social Justice," *Policy Notes,* November 21.

———. 2003. *Country Economic Memorandum, Turkey: Towards Macroeconomic Stability and Sustained Growth.* Report 26301. Washington, D.C.

———. 2004. *Brazil Country Assistance Evaluation.* Washington, D.C.

———. 2005. *Economic Growth in the 1990s: Learning from a Decade of Reform.* Washington, D.C.

World Bank and Institute for Applied Economic Research (Instituto de Pesquisa Econômica Aplicada). 2003. *Brazil: Inequality and Economic Development,* Report 24487-BR. Washington, D.C.

World Bank, European Commission, and European Bank for Reconstruction and Development. 1996. *Bosnia and Herzegovina: Toward Economic Recovery.* Washington, D.C.

World Economic Forum. 1998. *Global Competitiveness Report 1998.* Geneva.

———. 2004. *Global Competitiveness Report 2004.* Geneva.

About the Editors

Indermit S. Gill is a sector manager in the Poverty Reduction and Economic Management (PREM) unit in the World Bank's East Asia and Pacific (EAP) Regional Office, and economic adviser to the EAP chief economist. Before his current assignment, he was the economic adviser to the PREM vice-president and head of network. During 1997–99, he worked as a senior country economist in the Brazil Country Management Unit. Upon his return to Washington, and between 2000–2002, he served as lead economist for human development in the Latin America and Caribbean regional office. He has a Ph.D. in Economics from the University of Chicago.

Todd Pugatch is a junior professional associate in the Poverty Reduction and Economic Management Network at the World Bank. Prior to joining the Bank he studied economics as a Morehead Scholar at the University of North Carolina at Chapel Hill, and as a Rotary Ambassadorial Scholar at the Universidad Nacional de Costa Rica. In 2005 he will begin a doctoral program in economics.

Index